In the Name of Allah, the Gracious, the Merciful

****

Study the Qur'aan in Qur'aanic light to understand Islam in its pristine simplicity, clarity, beauty, and purity

****

QUR'AANIC STUDIES – A Modern Tafsir

Manzil II

by

Mohammad Shafi

<u>**PREFACE**</u>

Below the Arabic text of every Verse of the Qur'aan in this book, its transliteration, followed by translation and Chapter Notes, if any, essentially based on the Qur'aan itself, is given. Please remember that the Arabic text is divine and, therefore, sacrosanct, but the transliteration, translation and the Notes are human and, therefore, subject to correction. Please also remember that the human-made Notes cannot, and do not, explain the divine Verses. They seek to explain the human translation only and/or to relate the Verse to present circumstances or to divine explanations given in other Verses of the Qur'aan.

I have adopted the transliteration method employed by the Muslim Students' Association (MSA) of the University of Southern California. And, in this regard, I may usefully quote from their site:

> "MSA-USC would like to thank muslimnet.net for making their transliteration of the Qur'an publicly available.

> 'We would like to emphasize that this [transliteration] text is not a substitute for the original Arabic Qur'an. It is only an attempt to help those who are trying to learn to read the Arabic text, since it is as close to the written text as possible.

> It is important to practice pronouncing the letters as directed in the transliteration table, especially the underlined letters, before starting to read. It will be helpful if an Arabic speaker can help you.

> This work is free for use to everyone as long as no changes that might distort it are done to it. We request from those who benefit from it to pray for us. We pray to Almighty Allah to help you learn to read the Holy Qur'an, and to do every good thing.'"

I present this humble work in the earnest hope that it will prompt my Readers to try and understand the divine Message in its original Arabic text. They should remember that no translation however meticulously done can ever equal the original Arabic text in its divine grandeur and pristine clarity.

One may wonder why this yet another addition to the existing plethora of Translations and Commentaries! The answer to this question lies in the beauty of the fact that the divine Message of the Qur'aan remains valid for all times and ages since its revelation until the Last Day. The Message therefore needs to be studied from time to time in the changing perspectives of the changing times. It would be wrong to confine this universal Message for mankind to the circumstances and situations of a period in the past. Unfortunately, however, most of the commentators so far have based their understanding of the Qur'aan in the strict perspective of the circumstances and situations prevailing at the time of its revelation way back in 7th century A.D. The Muslim mindset generally has thus got stagnated and therefore unable to cope with the changing situations of the changing times. This humble attempt of mine is to help Muslims generally to come out, Allah willing, of that crippling stagnation.

This Part (Manzil) of my Qur'aanic Studies relates to Chapters 5 to 9 of the Qur'aan.

Mohammad Shafi
Mumbai, INDIA,
17th December 2018.

Transliteration Table

Arabic	Translit.	Example	Arabic	Translit.	Example
ا + فتحة	a	about	ن	n	nurse
آ	a	cat	و	oo	pool
ع	AA	say "a" twice distinctly with an open mouth	أ	o	on
ب	b	box	ق	q	queen ("k" sound made in back of throat)
د	d	door	ر	r	rabbit (Rolled "r" sound, similar to Spanish "r")
ض	d	heavy "d" sound (Open jaw but keep lips slightly round i.e: duh)	ش	sh	ship
ي	ee	feet	س	s	sea
ف	f	fish	ص	s	heavy "s" sound (Open jaw but keep lips slightly round)
غ	gh	the sound you make when gurgling (Touch very back of tongue to very back of mouth)	ت	t	tan
ه	h	hat	ط	t	heavy "t" sound (Open jaw but keep lips slightly round)
ح	h	heavy "h" sound (Drop back of tongue to open back of throat, then force air out for "h")	ث	th	think
إ + كسرة	i	ink	ذ	th	the
ج	j	jar	ظ	th	"th" sound as in "the", but heavier (Open jaw but keep lips slightly round)
ك	k	kit	ضمة	u	put
خ	kh	gravely "h" sound (Touch back of tongue to roof of mouth and force air out)	و	w	water
ل	l	look	أ + ع	/	pronounce the letter before but cut it short by stopping suddenly
م	m	man	ي	y	yarn
Bold letters are silent i.e w: write			ز	z	zebra
			(-) is to make some words easier to read		

<u>CONTENTS</u>

**[Against the Qur'aanic Chapter No. in every line below are: the Chapter name &
no. of Verses in it in ()]**

Chapter 5: Al-Ma'idah (The Table Spread)

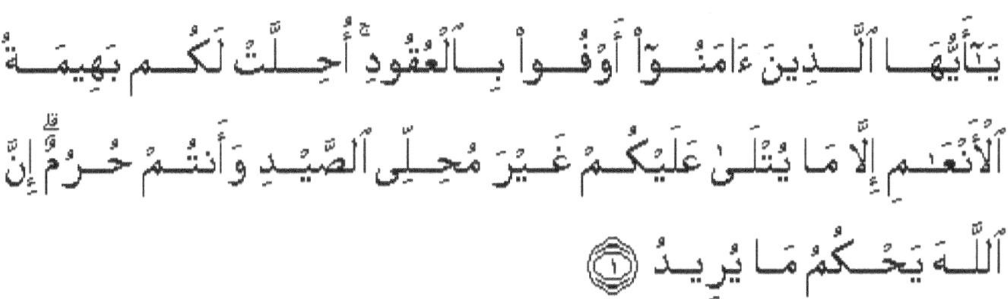

In the Name of Allah, the Gracious, the Merciful

1. Ya ayyuha allatheena amanoo awfoo bialAAuqoodi ohillat lakum baheematu al-anAAami illa ma yutla AAalaykum ghayra muhillee alssaydi waantum hurumun inna Allaha yahkumu ma yureedu

5:1. O you who believe! Fulfill the obligations. Permitted to you are the quadruped cattle except what is mentioned to you[1], provided the prohibition against hunting is not violated while you are in the state of *Ihram*[2]. Indeed, Allah orders what He pleases.

1. The prohibited things are mentioned below in Verse 5.3.

2. I.e. while performing rites of pilgrimage, during which hunting is prohibited.

يَٰٓأَيُّهَا ٱلَّذِينَ ءَامَنُوا۟ لَا تُحِلُّوا۟ شَعَٰٓئِرَ ٱللَّهِ وَلَا ٱلشَّهْرَ ٱلْحَرَامَ وَلَا ٱلْهَدْىَ

وَلَا ٱلْقَلَٰٓئِدَ وَلَآ ءَآمِّينَ ٱلْبَيْتَ ٱلْحَرَامَ يَبْتَغُونَ فَضْلًا مِّن رَّبِّهِمْ وَرِضْوَٰنًا

وَإِذَا حَلَلْتُمْ فَٱصْطَادُوا۟ وَلَا يَجْرِمَنَّكُمْ شَنَـَٔانُ قَوْمٍ أَن صَدُّوكُمْ

عَنِ ٱلْمَسْجِدِ ٱلْحَرَامِ أَن تَعْتَدُوا۟ وَتَعَاوَنُوا۟ عَلَى ٱلْبِرِّ وَٱلتَّقْوَىٰ وَلَا

تَعَاوَنُوا۟ عَلَى ٱلْإِثْمِ وَٱلْعُدْوَٰنِ وَٱتَّقُوا۟ ٱللَّهَ إِنَّ ٱللَّهَ شَدِيدُ ٱلْعِقَابِ ۝

2. Ya ayyuha allatheena amanoo la tuhilloo shaAAa-ira Allahi wala alshshahra alharama wala alhadya wala alqala-ida wala ammeena albayta alharama yabtaghoona fadlan min rabbihim waridwanan wa-itha halaltum faistadoo wala yajrimannakum shanaanu qawmin an saddookum AAani almasjidi alharami an taAAtadoo wataAAawanoo AAala albirri waalttaqwa wala taAAawanoo AAala al-ithmi waalAAudwani waittaqoo Allaha inna Allaha shadeedu alAAiqabi

---

5:2. O you who believe! Treat not irreverently the rites sanctified by Allah; nor the sacred month, nor the offerings, nor the garlands, and nor those going/coming to the Sacred House seeking the Favour and Pleasure of their Lord. And when you are free from the obligations of the pilgrimage, then hunt. And let not hatred of a people, because of their stopping you from going to the Sacred Place of Worship,[3] lead you to transgression. And co-operate with one another in goodness/righteousness and piety, and do not co-operate with one another in sin and transgression, and fear Allah. Indeed, Allah is severe in giving punishment.

---

3. The reference here is to an event that occurred before the fall of Makkah to the Muslim forces. The Prophet (peace be upon him), with some of his companions had come out from Medina for visiting the Kaabah, and the Makkans had then prevented the Prophet's party. But the divine statement here has a general import. It is applicable to all situations, wherein human tendency is for persons to commit transgression in dealings with those who had done some wrong to the former, earlier.

حُرِّمَتْ عَلَيْكُمُ ٱلْمَيْتَةُ وَٱلدَّمُ وَلَحْمُ ٱلْخِنزِيرِ وَمَآ أُهِلَّ لِغَيْرِ ٱللَّهِ بِهِۦ

وَٱلْمُنْخَنِقَةُ وَٱلْمَوْقُوذَةُ وَٱلْمُتَرَدِّيَةُ وَٱلنَّطِيحَةُ وَمَآ أَكَلَ ٱلسَّبُعُ إِلَّا مَا

ذَكَّيْتُمْ وَمَا ذُبِحَ عَلَى ٱلنُّصُبِ وَأَن تَسْتَقْسِمُوا۟ بِٱلْأَزْلَٰمِ ذَٰلِكُمْ فِسْقٌ

ٱلْيَوْمَ يَئِسَ ٱلَّذِينَ كَفَرُوا۟ مِن دِينِكُمْ فَلَا تَخْشَوْهُمْ وَٱخْشَوْنِ ٱلْيَوْمَ

أَكْمَلْتُ لَكُمْ دِينَكُمْ وَأَتْمَمْتُ عَلَيْكُمْ نِعْمَتِى وَرَضِيتُ لَكُمُ ٱلْإِسْلَٰمَ دِينًا

فَمَنِ ٱضْطُرَّ فِى مَخْمَصَةٍ غَيْرَ مُتَجَانِفٍ لِإِثْمٍ فَإِنَّ ٱللَّهَ غَفُورٌ رَّحِيمٌ ﴿٣﴾

3. Hurrimat AAalaykumu almaytatu waalddamu walahmu alkhinzeeri wama ohilla lighayri Allahi bihi waalmunkhaniqatu waalmawqoothatu waalmutaraddiyatu waalnnateehatu wama akala alssabuAAu illa ma thakkaytum wama thubiha AAala alnnusubi waan tastaqsimoo bial-azlami thalikum fisqun alyawma ya-isa allatheena kafaroo min deenikum fala takhshawhum waikhshawni alyawma akmaltu lakum deenakum waatmamtu AAalaykum niAAmatee waradeetu lakumu al-islama deenan famani idturra fee makhmasatin ghayra mutajanifin li-ithmin fa-inna Allaha ghafoorun raheemun

5:3. Forbidden to you are the carrion, and the blood, and the flesh of swine, and that which is consecrated to anyone other than Allah,[4] and the strangled and that beaten to death, and that killed by a fall and that killed by being smitten with the horn and eaten by beasts unless you slaughter it properly before its death, and that which is sacrificed over idols and that you try to know your future by means of arrows[5]. That is a transgression. – This day, those, who have suppressed the Truth, have despaired of your religion; so, fear them not, and fear Me. This day I have perfected for you your religion and completed My Favour upon you and approved for you Islam as religion. – [6] But if one is compelled by hunger, and has no intention to sin, then Allah is indeed Forgiving, Merciful.

4. The words so far in this Verse are like those in Verse 2:173. Please therefore go through the study notes thereunder.

5. This is an allusion to the practice among Arabs, at the time of revelation of the Qur'aan, to use blunted arrows as a means for knowing or divining their future. It was akin to the modern-day popular newspaper column: 'what the stars foretell'. Here, the stars are made use of for foretelling what the future holds for newspaper readers. There, the people had devised some method of using blunted arrows for the same purpose. The divine Verse here prohibits all such attempts at knowing one's future. The future is known only to Allah, and He has kept it hidden from His creatures. All attempts by the creatures to defeat Allah's purpose would of course be futile. Allah has called all such attempts as transgressions.

6. This part of the Verse, in parenthesis, is very important. It unmistakably denotes the completion of the divine Message of the Qur'aan. It denotes that no further divine instructions for mankind have come thereafter in the form of Qur'aanic revelations. But a question arises as to why this important piece of divine revelation is placed so inconspicuously, as it were, in the midst of another divine instruction,

obviously revealed earlier. The only explanation for this that occurs to my mind is that it is one of the divine ways to show that the Qur'aan has remained unpolluted. Man is unable to effect any changes therein surreptitiously. If Man were able to do that, he would have taken this important revelation out from its present inconspicuous position and placed it elsewhere. Allah knows best.

يَسْـَٔلُونَكَ مَاذَآ أُحِلَّ لَهُمْ قُلْ أُحِلَّ لَكُمُ ٱلطَّيِّبَـٰتُ وَمَا عَلَّمْتُم مِّنَ ٱلْجَوَارِحِ مُكَلِّبِينَ تُعَلِّمُونَهُنَّ مِمَّا عَلَّمَكُمُ ٱللَّهُ فَكُلُواْ مِمَّآ أَمْسَكْنَ عَلَيْكُمْ وَٱذْكُرُواْ ٱسْمَ ٱللَّهِ عَلَيْهِ وَٱتَّقُواْ ٱللَّهَ إِنَّ ٱللَّهَ سَرِيعُ ٱلْحِسَابِ

4. Yas-aloonaka ma_tha_ o_hilla lahum qul o_hilla lakumu al_ttayyib_atu wam_a AAallamtum mina aljaw_ari_hi mukallibeena tuAAallimoonahunna mimma AAallamakumu Allahu fakuloo mimma amsakna AAalaykum wao_thkuroo isma Allahi AAalayhi wa_ittaqoo All_aha inna Allaha sareeAAu al_his_abi

5:4. They ask you as to what is permitted to them. Say, "Permitted to you are the good, wholesome things. And eat of what the animals trained by you as hounds – you teach them of what Allah has taught you – hunt for you and over which you mention Allah's name. And fear Allah! Indeed, Allah is quick in account-keeping.

ٱلْيَوْمَ أُحِلَّ لَكُمُ ٱلطَّيِّبَـٰتُ وَطَعَامُ ٱلَّذِينَ أُوتُواْ ٱلْكِتَـٰبَ حِلٌّ لَّكُمْ وَطَعَامُكُمْ حِلٌّ لَّهُمْ وَٱلْمُحْصَنَـٰتُ مِنَ ٱلْمُؤْمِنَـٰتِ وَٱلْمُحْصَنَـٰتُ مِنَ ٱلَّذِينَ أُوتُواْ ٱلْكِتَـٰبَ مِن قَبْلِكُمْ إِذَآ ءَاتَيْتُمُوهُنَّ أُجُورَهُنَّ مُحْصِنِينَ غَيْرَ مُسَـٰفِحِينَ وَلَا مُتَّخِذِىٓ أَخْدَانٍ وَمَن يَكْفُرْ بِٱلْإِيمَـٰنِ فَقَدْ حَبِطَ عَمَلُهُۥ وَهُوَ فِى ٱلْءَاخِرَةِ مِنَ ٱلْخَـٰسِرِينَ

5. Alyawma o_hilla lakumu al_ttayyib_atu wataAA_amu alla_theena ootoo alkit_aba _hillun lakum wataAA_amukum _hillun lahum waalmu_hsan_atu mina almu/min_ati waalmu_hsan_atu mina alla_theena ootoo alkit_aba min qablikum i_tha ataytumoohunna ojoorahunna mu_hsineena ghayra mus_afi_heena wala muttakhi_thee akhd_anin waman yakfur bial-eem_ani faqad _habi_ta AAamaluhu wahuwa fee al-_akhirati mina alkh_asireena

5:5. This day all the good wholesome things are permitted to you. And the food of those who have been given the Book is lawful for you and your food is lawful for them. And lawful for you are the chaste women from among the believers and the chaste women from among those who had been given the Book before you, when you have given them their dues as chaste women in marriage ties, and not for indulgence in extramarital sex or as live-in girlfriends. And he, who has suppressed Faith, has surely wasted his deeds; and, in the Hereafter, he shall be one of those doomed!

يَـٰٓأَيُّهَا ٱلَّذِينَ ءَامَنُوٓاْ إِذَا قُمْتُمْ إِلَى ٱلصَّلَوٰةِ فَٱغْسِلُواْ وُجُوهَكُمْ وَأَيْدِيَكُمْ

إِلَى ٱلْمَرَافِقِ وَٱمْسَحُواْ بِرُءُوسِكُمْ وَأَرْجُلَكُمْ إِلَى ٱلْكَعْبَيْنِ

وَإِن كُنتُمْ جُنُبًا فَٱطَّهَّرُواْ وَإِن كُنتُم مَّرْضَىٰٓ أَوْ عَلَىٰ سَفَرٍ أَوْ

جَآءَ أَحَدٌ مِّنكُم مِّنَ ٱلْغَآئِطِ أَوْ لَـٰمَسْتُمُ ٱلنِّسَآءَ فَلَمْ تَجِدُواْ

مَآءً فَتَيَمَّمُواْ صَعِيدًا طَيِّبًا فَٱمْسَحُواْ بِوُجُوهِكُمْ وَأَيْدِيكُم مِّنْهُ

مَا يُرِيدُ ٱللَّهُ لِيَجْعَلَ عَلَيْكُم مِّنْ حَرَجٍ وَلَـٰكِن يُرِيدُ لِيُطَهِّرَكُمْ وَلِيُتِمَّ

نِعْمَتَهُۥ عَلَيْكُمْ لَعَلَّكُمْ تَشْكُرُونَ ۝

6. Ya ayyuha allatheena amanoo itha qumtum ila alssalati faighsiloo wujoohakum waaydiyakum ila almarafiqi waimsahoo biruoosikum waarjulakum ila alkaAAbayni wa-in kuntum junuban faittahharoo wa-in kuntum marda aw AAala safarin aw jaa ahadun minkum mina algha-iti aw lamastumu alnnisaa falam tajidoo maan fatayammamoo saAAeedan tayyiban faimsahoo biwujoohikum waaydeekum minhu ma yureedu Allahu liyajAAala AAalaykum min harajin walakin yureedu liyutahhirakum waliyutimma niAAmatahu AAalaykum laAAallakum tashkuroona

5:6. O you who believe! When you get up for prayer, wash your faces and your hands up to the elbows – and wipe your heads – and your feet up to the ankles.[7] And if you are unclean, then cleanse yourselves. And if you are ill or on a journey, or any of you has come from the privy, or you have had sexual contacts with women, and you find no water, simulate washing then with clean earth, and wipe your faces and your hands therewith. Allah does not want to place you in difficulty, but He wants to keep you clean and to complete His Favour upon you, so that you may be grateful.

---

7. **This is the divine order for ablution (*wudu*) before a *salah*. As may be seen from the divine wording, the order is for ablution before <u>every</u> *salah*. But Muslims here in the Indian subcontinent are in the habit of considering a *wudu* made for one *salah* as valid for another coming hours later, during which interval**

they may attend to worldly work or engage in gossip with friends. This is one of many instances wherein today's Muslims go blatantly against specific divine instructions. No wonder then that they are devoid of Allah's Favour upon them. Please see the next Verse also in this context. The Muslims of today are breaking their covenant with Allah when they disobey the instructions.

7. Waothkuroo niAAmata Allahi AAalaykum wameethaqahu allathee wathaqakum bihi ith qultum samiAAna waataAAna waittaqoo Allaha inna Allaha AAaleemun bithati alssudoori

5:7. And remember Allah's Favour upon you and His Covenant with which He bound you, when you said, "We hear and we obey." And fear Allah. Indeed, Allah knows the secrets of the minds.

8. Ya ayyuha allatheena amanoo koonoo qawwameena lillahi shuhadaa bialqisti wala yajrimannakum shanaanu qawmin AAala alla taAAdiloo iAAdiloo huwa aqrabu lilttaqwa waittaqoo Allaha inna Allaha khabeerun bima taAAmaloona

5:8. O you who believe! Be firm as just witnesses for Allah. And let not enmity and hatred for people induce you to commit the crime of being unjust. Be just! It is conducive to piety. And fear Allah! Indeed, Allah is aware of what you do.

9. WaAAada Allahu allatheena amanoo waAAamiloo alssalihati lahum maghfiratun waajrun AAatheemun

5:9. Allah has promised forgiveness and a great reward for those who believe and do good deeds.

10. Waallatheena kafaroo wakaththaboo bi-ayatina ola-ika as-habu aljaheemi

5:10. And those who suppress the Truth and deny our Verses/Signs – those shall be the dwellers of the Fire.

يَـٰٓأَيُّهَا ٱلَّذِينَ ءَامَنُوا۟ ٱذْكُرُوا۟ نِعْمَتَ ٱللَّهِ عَلَيْكُمْ إِذْ هَمَّ قَوْمٌ أَن يَبْسُطُوٓا۟ إِلَيْكُمْ أَيْدِيَهُمْ فَكَفَّ أَيْدِيَهُمْ عَنكُمْ وَٱتَّقُوا۟ ٱللَّهَ وَعَلَى ٱللَّهِ فَلْيَتَوَكَّلِ ٱلْمُؤْمِنُونَ ﴿١١﴾

11. Ya ayyuha allatheena amanoo othkuroo niAAmata Allahi AAalaykum ith hamma qawmun an yabsutoo ilaykum aydiyahum fakaffa aydiyahum AAankum waittaqoo Allaha waAAala Allahi falyatawakkali almu/minoona

5:11. O you who believe! Remember Allah's Favour upon you when people had planned to raise their hands against you, but He stayed their hands from you.[8] And fear Allah! And in Allah let the believers put their trust.

8. Reference here is obviously to events during the time the Qur'aan was revealed. But many Muslims today may recall instances in their own personal lives when they were miraculously saved from attacks intended against them by others. I myself am aware of such instances in my life. Although we are guilty of disobedience to Him in many matters, Allah still protects us sometimes so that we remember this and come back to the blessed path of complete obedience and submission to Him, putting our complete trust in Him.

وَلَقَدْ أَخَذَ ٱللَّهُ مِيثَـٰقَ بَنِىٓ إِسْرَٰٓءِيلَ وَبَعَثْنَا مِنْهُمُ ٱثْنَىْ عَشَرَ نَقِيبًا وَقَالَ ٱللَّهُ إِنِّى مَعَكُمْ لَئِنْ أَقَمْتُمُ ٱلصَّلَوٰةَ وَءَاتَيْتُمُ ٱلزَّكَوٰةَ وَءَامَنتُم بِرُسُلِى وَعَزَّرْتُمُوهُمْ وَأَقْرَضْتُمُ ٱللَّهَ قَرْضًا حَسَنًا لَّأُكَفِّرَنَّ عَنكُمْ سَيِّـَٔاتِكُمْ وَلَأُدْخِلَنَّكُمْ جَنَّـٰتٍ تَجْرِى مِن تَحْتِهَا ٱلْأَنْهَـٰرُ فَمَن كَفَرَ بَعْدَ ذَٰلِكَ مِنكُمْ فَقَدْ ضَلَّ سَوَآءَ ٱلسَّبِيلِ ﴿١٢﴾

12. Walaqad akhatha Allahu meethaqa banee isra-eela wabaAAathna minhumu ithnay AAashara naqeeban waqala Allahu innee maAAakum la-in aqamtumu alssalata waataytumu alzzakata waamantum birusulee waAAazzartumoohum waaqradtumu Allaha qardan hasanan laokaffiranna AAankum sayyi-atikum walaodkhilannakum jannatin tajree min tahtiha al-anharu faman kafara baAAda thalika minkum faqad dalla sawaa alssabeeli

---

5:12. And Allah did take a covenant from the Children of Israel, and We raised up among them twelve chieftains. And Allah said, "I am indeed with you. If you establish prayer and give charity and believe in My Messengers and assist them and lend a good loan to Allah[9], I shall certainly condone your shortcomings, and shall certainly admit you to Gardens beneath which rivers flow. But whoever has suppressed the Truth from among you after that, he has surely lost the right way."

---

9. A similar phrase is used in <u>Verse 2:245</u>. **Kindly go through the study note under that Verse.**

فَبِمَا نَقْضِهِم مِّيثَـٰقَهُمْ لَعَنَّـٰهُمْ وَجَعَلْنَا قُلُوبَهُمْ قَـٰسِيَةً يُحَرِّفُونَ ٱلْكَلِمَ عَن مَّوَاضِعِهِۦ وَنَسُواْ حَظًّا مِّمَّا ذُكِّرُواْ بِهِۦ وَلَا تَزَالُ تَطَّلِعُ عَلَىٰ خَآئِنَةٍ مِّنْهُمْ إِلَّا قَلِيلًا مِّنْهُمْ فَٱعْفُ عَنْهُمْ وَٱصْفَحْ إِنَّ ٱللَّهَ يُحِبُّ ٱلْمُحْسِنِينَ ﴿١٣﴾

13. Fabima naqdihim meethaqahum laAAannahum wajaAAalna quloobahum qasiyatan yuharrifoona alkalima AAan mawadiAAihi wanasoo haththan mimma thukkiroo bihi wala tazalu tattaliAAu AAala kha-inatin minhum illa qaleelan minhum faoAAfu AAanhum waisfah inna Allaha yuhibbu almuhsineena

---

5:13. And then, because of their breach of their covenant, We cursed them and made their hearts hard. They pervert the Word from its contextual sense[10] and they have forgotten a part of what they were reminded of. And you will not cease to find treachery in them, except in a few of them. But then leave them alone and overlook. Allah does indeed love those who do good deeds.

---

10. Alas! Many Muslims of today are trying to do the same thing with the Qur'aan. Had it not been for the divine protection of the original text in Arabic, they might have succeeded in corrupting it.

وَمِنَ ٱلَّذِينَ قَالُوٓاْ إِنَّا نَصَـٰرَىٰٓ أَخَذْنَا مِيثَـٰقَهُمْ فَنَسُواْ حَظًّا مِّمَّا ذُكِّرُواْ بِهِۦ فَأَغْرَيْنَا بَيْنَهُمُ ٱلْعَدَاوَةَ وَٱلْبَغْضَآءَ إِلَىٰ يَوْمِ ٱلْقِيَـٰمَةِ وَسَوْفَ يُنَبِّئُهُمُ ٱللَّهُ بِمَا كَانُواْ يَصْنَعُونَ ۝

14. Wamina allatheena qaloo inna nasara akhathna meethaqahum fanasoo haththan mimma thukkiroo bihi faaghrayna baynahumu alAAadawata waalbaghdaa ila yawmi alqiyamati wasawfa yunabbi-ohumu Allahu bima kanoo yasnaAAoona

5:14. And from those who call themselves Christians, We took their covenant. Then they forgot a part of what they were reminded of. So then, We made mutual enmity and hatred stick to them till the Day of Resurrection. And Allah will inform them what work they did.

يَـٰٓأَهْلَ ٱلْكِتَـٰبِ قَدْ جَآءَكُمْ رَسُولُنَا يُبَيِّنُ لَكُمْ كَثِيرًا مِّمَّا كُنتُمْ تُخْفُونَ مِنَ ٱلْكِتَـٰبِ وَيَعْفُواْ عَن كَثِيرٍ قَدْ جَآءَكُم مِّنَ ٱللَّهِ نُورٌ وَكِتَـٰبٌ مُّبِينٌ

15. Ya ahla alkitabi qad jaakum rasooluna yubayyinu lakum katheeran mimma kuntum tukhfoona mina alkitabi wayaAAfoo AAan katheerin qad jaakum mina Allahi noorun wakitabun mubeenun

---

5:15. O people of the Book! Our Messenger has surely come to you explaining to you much of what you concealed and effaced from the Book. Surely, from Allah has come to you light, and a clear Book.

يَهْدِى بِهِ ٱللَّهُ مَنِ ٱتَّبَعَ رِضْوَٰنَهُۥ سُبُلَ ٱلسَّلَٰمِ وَيُخْرِجُهُم مِّنَ ٱلظُّلُمَٰتِ إِلَى ٱلنُّورِ بِإِذْنِهِۦ وَيَهْدِيهِمْ إِلَىٰ صِرَٰطٍ مُّسْتَقِيمٍ ﴿١٦﴾

16. Yahdee bihi Allahu mani ittabaAAa ridwanahu subula alssalami wayukhrijuhum mina al*thth*ulumati ila alnnoori bi-ithnihi wayahdeehim ila siratin mustaqeemin

5:16. With it Allah guides him, who seeks His pleasure, to ways of peace. And He takes them out of darknesses to light by His will. And He guides them to the Straight Path.

لَّقَدْ كَفَرَ ٱلَّذِينَ قَالُوٓاْ إِنَّ ٱللَّهَ هُوَ ٱلْمَسِيحُ ٱبْنُ مَرْيَمَ قُلْ فَمَن يَمْلِكُ مِنَ ٱللَّهِ شَيْـًٔا إِنْ أَرَادَ أَن يُهْلِكَ ٱلْمَسِيحَ ٱبْنَ مَرْيَمَ وَأُمَّهُۥ وَمَن فِى ٱلْأَرْضِ جَمِيعًا وَلِلَّهِ مُلْكُ ٱلسَّمَٰوَٰتِ وَٱلْأَرْضِ وَمَا بَيْنَهُمَا يَخْلُقُ مَا يَشَآءُ وَٱللَّهُ عَلَىٰ كُلِّ شَىْءٍ قَدِيرٌ ﴿١٧﴾

17. Laqad kafara alla*th*eena qaloo inna Allaha huwa almasee*h*u ibnu maryama qul faman yamliku mina Allahi shay-an in arada an yuhlika almasee*h*a ibna maryama waommahu waman fee al-ardi jameeAAan walillahi mulku alssamawati waal-ardi wama baynahuma yakhluqu ma yashao waAllahu AAala kulli shay-in qadeerun

5:17. Surely, they suppress the Truth who say, "The Messiah, son of Mary, is indeed Allah." Say, "Who then could have power over anything against Allah if He wished to destroy the Messiah, son of Mary, and his mother, and anyone on the entire earth? And to Allah belongs the kingdom of the heavens and the earth and all that is between them. He creates what He wills. And Allah can do anything.

وَقَالَتِ ٱلْيَهُودُ وَٱلنَّصَـٰرَىٰ نَحْنُ أَبْنَـٰٓؤُاْ ٱللَّهِ وَأَحِبَّـٰٓؤُهُۥ ۚ قُلْ فَلِمَ يُعَذِّبُكُم بِذُنُوبِكُم ۖ بَلْ أَنتُم بَشَرٌ مِّمَّنْ خَلَقَ ۚ يَغْفِرُ لِمَن يَشَآءُ وَيُعَذِّبُ مَن يَشَآءُ ۚ وَلِلَّهِ مُلْكُ ٱلسَّمَـٰوَٰتِ وَٱلْأَرْضِ وَمَا بَيْنَهُمَا ۖ وَإِلَيْهِ ٱلْمَصِيرُ ۝

18. Waqalati alyahoodu waalnnasara nahnu abnao Allahi waahibbaohu qul falima yuAAaththibukum bithunoobikum bal antum basharun mimman khalaqa yaghfiru liman yashao wayuAAaththibu man yashao walillahi mulku alssamawati waal-ardi wama baynahuma wa-ilayhi almaseeru

---

5:18. And the Jews and the Christians say, "We are the children of Allah and His loved ones." Say, "Why does He then punish you for your sins? Nay, you are but human beings from among those whom He has created. He forgives whom He wills and punishes whom He wills. And to Allah belongs the absolute authority over the heavens and the earth and over all that is between them. And to Him is the journey's end."

يَـٰٓأَهْلَ ٱلْكِتَـٰبِ قَدْ جَآءَكُمْ رَسُولُنَا يُبَيِّنُ لَكُمْ عَلَىٰ فَتْرَةٍ مِّنَ ٱلرُّسُلِ أَن تَقُولُواْ مَا جَآءَنَا مِنْ بَشِيرٍ وَلَا نَذِيرٍ ۖ فَقَدْ جَآءَكُم بَشِيرٌ وَنَذِيرٌ ۗ وَٱللَّهُ عَلَىٰ كُلِّ شَيْءٍ قَدِيرٌ ۝

19. Ya ahla alkitabi qad jaakum rasooluna yubayyinu lakum AAala fatratin mina alrrusuli an taqooloo ma jaana min basheerin wala natheerin faqad jaakum basheerun wanatheerun waAllahu AAala kulli shay-in qadeerun

---

5:19. O people of the Book! Surely, Our Messenger has come to you to explain things to you, after a break in sending the Messengers, lest you say, "No one had come to us as a messenger of good news or as a warner." Surely, now, there has come to you a Messenger of good news and a Warner. And Allah can do anything.

$$\text{وَإِذْ قَالَ مُوسَىٰ لِقَوْمِهِ يَٰقَوْمِ ٱذْكُرُواْ نِعْمَةَ ٱللَّهِ}$$

$$\text{عَلَيْكُمْ إِذْ جَعَلَ فِيكُمْ أَنۢبِيَآءَ وَجَعَلَكُم مُّلُوكًا وَءَاتَىٰكُم مَّا}$$

$$\text{لَمْ يُؤْتِ أَحَدًا مِّنَ ٱلْعَٰلَمِينَ ۝}$$

20. Wa-ith qala moosa liqawmihi ya qawmi othkuroo niAAmata Allahi AAalaykum ith jaAAala feekum anbiyaa wajaAAalakum mulookan waatakum ma lam yu/ti ahadan mina alAAalameena

5:20. And when Moses said to his people, "O my people! Remember Allah's Favour upon you when He raised Prophets among you and made you kings and gave you what He had not given to any of the worlds[11]."

11. For the meaning of *aalameen*, refer study note 1.5.

$$\text{يَٰقَوْمِ ٱدْخُلُواْ ٱلْأَرْضَ ٱلْمُقَدَّسَةَ ٱلَّتِى كَتَبَ ٱللَّهُ لَكُمْ}$$

$$\text{وَلَا تَرْتَدُّواْ عَلَىٰ أَدْبَارِكُمْ فَتَنقَلِبُواْ خَٰسِرِينَ ۝}$$

21. Ya qawmi odkhuloo al-arda almuqaddasata allatee kataba Allahu lakum wala tartaddoo AAala adbarikum fatanqaliboo khasireena

5:21. "O my people! Enter the holy land which Allah has assigned to you[12, 13] and turn not on your backs; for, then, you will turn back doomed."

12. It is based on this divine statement, which obviously the Torah also contains, that the State of Israel has now been created. The Jews claim that they have a divine right to the land, which was almost entirely inhabited by the Arabs at the beginning of the twentieth century. There were hardly any Jews living there then. They had been scattered all over the world as small minorities. The Allied Forces, which had defeated the Germans in World War II, had promised to the Jews, who had suffered greatly in Hitler's Germany, to give them a land of their own. And so was the State of Israel created in 1948. And the scattered Jews flocked to the new State from all over the world. The land with the original boundaries of Israel was not enough, and the State managed to occupy surrounding Arab territory in conflicts and wars that ensued. The Arabs were thus turned into refugees in their own land.

13. But, whatever the circumstances under which Israel stands now created, the coming into existence of the new State is a confirmation of the divine statement that the land was assigned to the Jews. Therefore, they are there now. They were there before also, forty years after they were first told to enter the land,

as the Verses, following this Verse, indicate. Under David and Solomon, the land prospered and expanded. But, thereafter, the Jews relapsed into the same rebellious mood as depicted in Verses below. They were punished, their State was destroyed, and they were scattered to live as small minorities in different parts of the world. [Refer Verses 17.4 & 17.5] They are brought together now as foretold in Verse 17.104. And if they become arrogant again, they are again destined for destruction. [Verse 17.7]

قَالُواْ يَـٰمُوسَىٰٓ إِنَّ فِيهَا قَوۡمًا جَبَّارِينَ وَإِنَّا لَن نَّدۡخُلَهَا حَتَّىٰ يَخۡرُجُواْ مِنۡهَا فَإِن يَخۡرُجُواْ مِنۡهَا فَإِنَّا دَٰخِلُونَ ۝

22. Qaloo ya moosa inna feeha qawman jabbareena wa-inna lan nadkhulaha hatta yakhrujoo minha fa-in yakhrujoo minha fa-inna dakhiloona

5:22. They said, "O Moses! In it indeed live a cruel people. And we shall indeed not enter it until they go out from it. And if they go out from it, then indeed we shall enter.

قَالَ رَجُلَانِ مِنَ ٱلَّذِينَ يَخَافُونَ أَنۡعَمَ ٱللَّهُ عَلَيۡهِمَا ٱدۡخُلُواْ عَلَيۡهِمُ ٱلۡبَابَ فَإِذَا دَخَلۡتُمُوهُ فَإِنَّكُمۡ غَٰلِبُونَ وَعَلَى ٱللَّهِ فَتَوَكَّلُوٓاْ إِن كُنتُم مُّؤۡمِنِينَ ۝

23. Qala rajulani mina allatheena yakhafoona anAAama Allahu AAalayhima odkhuloo AAalayhimu albaba fa-itha dakhaltumoohu fa-innakum ghaliboona waAAala Allahi fatawakkaloo in kuntum mu/mineena

5:23. Two men of those who feared and upon both of whom Allah had bestowed favour, said, "Enter upon them by the gate, and when you enter it, you shall indeed be victorious. And upon Allah put your trust, if you do believe."

قَالُواْ يَـٰمُوسَىٰٓ إِنَّا لَن نَّدۡخُلَهَآ أَبَدًا مَّا دَامُواْ فِيهَا فَٱذۡهَبۡ أَنتَ وَرَبُّكَ فَقَٰتِلَآ إِنَّا هَـٰهُنَا قَٰعِدُونَ ۝

24. Qaloo ya moosa inna lan nadkhulaha abadan ma damoo feeha fa-ithhab anta warabbuka faqatila inna hahuna qaAAidoona

5:24. They said, "O Moses! We shall never enter it so long as they are in it. Go then, you and your Lord, and fight you both with them. We shall indeed sit right here!"

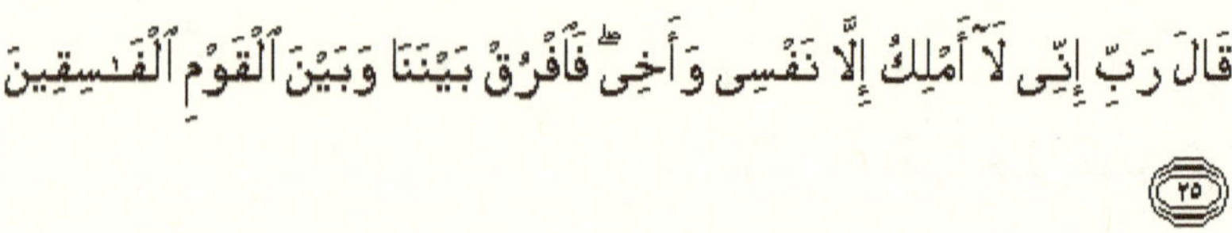

25. Qala rabbi innee la amliku illa nafsee waakhee faofruq baynana wabayna alqawmi alfasiqeena

5:25. He [Moses] said, "My Lord! I have indeed no control but on my own self and on my brother. Make a distinction, then, between us and the transgressing people."

26. Qala fa-innaha muharramatun AAalayhim arbaAAeena sanatan yateehoona fee al-ardi fala ta/sa AAala alqawmi alfasiqeena

5:26. Allah said, "So it is forbidden to them for forty years, during which time they shall suffer, wandering from place to place on the earth. Be not sad then for the transgressing people."

27. Waotlu AAalayhim nabaa ibnay adama bialhaqqi ith qarraba qurbanan fatuqubbila min ahadihima walam yutaqabbal mina al-akhari qala laaqtulannaka qala innama yataqabbalu Allahu mina almuttaqeena

5:27. And relate to them the story of the two sons of Adam with truth. When each offered a sacrifice, the sacrifice from one of them was accepted and the sacrifice from the other was not. The latter said, "I will certainly kill you." The former said, "Allah accepts offerings only from the pious."[14]

---

14. This story about the two sons of Adam is continued in Verses, immediately following.

لَئِنۢ بَسَطتَ إِلَىَّ يَدَكَ لِتَقْتُلَنِى مَآ أَنَا۠ بِبَاسِطٍ يَدِىَ إِلَيْكَ لِأَقْتُلَكَ إِنِّىٓ أَخَافُ ٱللَّهَ رَبَّ ٱلْعَـٰلَمِينَ ﴿٢٨﴾

28. La-in basatta ilayya yadaka litaqtulanee ma ana bibasitin yadiya ilayka li-aqtulaka innee akhafu Allaha rabba alAAalameena

5:28. [15]"If you do raise your hand against me to kill me, I am not going to raise my hand against you to kill you. Indeed, I fear Allah, the Lord of the worlds."

---

15. This Verse continues with the story of the two sons of Adam, which was started in the preceding Verse. And the quote here (continued in the next Verse 29 also) is how one son addressed the other, who threatened to kill the former.

إِنِّىٓ أُرِيدُ أَن تَبُوٓأَ بِإِثْمِى وَإِثْمِكَ فَتَكُونَ مِنْ أَصْحَـٰبِ ٱلنَّارِ وَذَٰلِكَ جَزَٰٓؤُاْ ٱلظَّـٰلِمِينَ ﴿٢٩﴾

29. Innee oreedu an taboo-a bi-ithmee wa-ithmika fatakoona min as-habi alnnari wathalika jazao alththalimeena

5:29. "Indeed do I wish that you bear the burden of my sin, as well as of your sin, and so you be of the inmates of the Fire. And that is the reward of the unjust."

فَطَوَّعَتْ لَهُۥ نَفْسُهُۥ قَتْلَ أَخِيهِ فَقَتَلَهُۥ فَأَصْبَحَ مِنَ ٱلْخَـٰسِرِينَ

30. FatawwaAAat lahu nafsuhu qatla akheehi faqatalahu faasbaha mina alkhasireena

5:30. Then his self incited him to kill his brother, so he killed him. And he became one of those, doomed.[16]

---

16. **This is perhaps the 2nd sin committed in the history of mankind. The first was when Adam went to the tree in Paradise, in disobedience to the express command of Allah Almighty (see Verses 2:35 & 2.36). Adam then had to suffer the ignominy of being ousted from Paradise. [The Muslims today are suffering ignominy also, because they are disobeying various divine commands given in the Qur'aan.] Now this 2nd sin has its genesis in the human trait of jealousy. One of the sons of Adam was jealous of his brother and killed him. And in today's world, jealousy related crimes are aplenty. Allah asked the Prophet to relate to the Children of Israel this story of the two sons of Adam, as a pointer to the Jews' sense of jealousy at someone, other than among themselves, was being made a Prophet.**

فَبَعَثَ ٱللَّهُ غُرَابًا يَبْحَثُ فِى ٱلْأَرْضِ لِيُرِيَهُۥ كَيْفَ يُوَٰرِى سَوْءَةَ أَخِيهِ قَالَ يَـٰوَيْلَتَىٰٓ أَعَجَزْتُ أَنْ أَكُونَ مِثْلَ هَـٰذَا ٱلْغُرَابِ فَأُوَٰرِىَ سَوْءَةَ أَخِى فَأَصْبَحَ مِنَ ٱلنَّـٰدِمِينَ

31. FabaAAatha Allahu ghuraban yabhathu fee al-ardi liyuriyahu kayfa yuwaree saw-ata akheehi qala ya waylata aAAajaztu an akoona mithla hatha alghurabi faowariya saw-ata akhee faasbaha mina alnnadimeena

5:31. Then Allah sent a crow digging the earth to show him how to dispose of the dead body of his brother. He said, "Woe to me! Have I not the competence even to be like this crow to dispose of the dead body of my brother?" And he was ashamed[17]

---

17. **The incomplete sentence gets completed in the next Verse.**

مِنْ أَجْلِ ذَٰلِكَ كَتَبْنَا عَلَىٰ بَنِىٓ إِسْرَٰٓءِيلَ أَنَّهُۥ مَن قَتَلَ نَفْسًۢا بِغَيْرِ نَفْسٍ أَوْ فَسَادٍ فِى ٱلْأَرْضِ فَكَأَنَّمَا قَتَلَ ٱلنَّاسَ جَمِيعًا وَمَنْ أَحْيَاهَا فَكَأَنَّمَآ أَحْيَا ٱلنَّاسَ جَمِيعًا ۚ وَلَقَدْ جَآءَتْهُمْ رُسُلُنَا بِٱلْبَيِّنَٰتِ ثُمَّ إِنَّ كَثِيرًا مِّنْهُم بَعْدَ ذَٰلِكَ فِى ٱلْأَرْضِ لَمُسْرِفُونَ ﴿٣٢﴾

32. Min ajli thalika katabna AAala banee isra-eela annahu man qatala nafsan bighayri nafsin aw fasadin fee al-ardi fakaannama qatala alnnasa jameeAAan waman ahyaha fakaannama ahya alnnasa jameeAAan walaqad jaat-hum rusuluna bialbayyinati thumma inna katheeran minhum baAAda thalika fee al-ardi lamusrifoona

5:32. on that ground. We ordained for the Children of Israel that if one killed a person – not in retaliation for killing another person or for spreading mischief on earth – it is as if he/she killed the entire mankind. And one who saved a life, it is as if he/she saved the entire mankind. And certainly, Our Messengers came to them with clear signs. Then indeed, thereafter, many of them did commit transgression on the earth.

إِنَّمَا جَزَٰٓؤُاْ ٱلَّذِينَ يُحَارِبُونَ ٱللَّهَ وَرَسُولَهُۥ وَيَسْعَوْنَ فِى ٱلْأَرْضِ فَسَادًا أَن يُقَتَّلُوٓاْ أَوْ يُصَلَّبُوٓاْ أَوْ تُقَطَّعَ أَيْدِيهِمْ وَأَرْجُلُهُم مِّنْ خِلَٰفٍ أَوْ يُنفَوْاْ مِنَ ٱلْأَرْضِ ۚ ذَٰلِكَ لَهُمْ خِزْىٌ فِى ٱلدُّنْيَا ۖ وَلَهُمْ فِى ٱلْأَخِرَةِ عَذَابٌ عَظِيمٌ ﴿٣٣﴾

33. Innama jazao allatheena yuhariboona Allaha warasoolahu wayasAAawna fee al-ardi fasadan an yuqattaloo aw yusallaboo aw tuqattaAAa aydeehim waarjuluhum min khilafin aw yunfaw mina al-ardi thalika lahum khizyun fee alddunya walahum fee al-akhirati AAathabun AAatheemun

5:33. The reward for those who wage war against Allah and His Messenger and strive to spread mischief on earth is only that they should be killed, or crucified, or their hands and their feet should be cut off on opposite sides, or they should be excommunicated.[18] That is, for them, a disgrace in this world, and, in the Hereafter, they shall suffer a grave punishment.

18. No eyebrows need be raised at the harshness of the punishments prescribed. All modern-day countries prescribe harsh punishments for those who wage war against the State. But Islam has a mercy clause for those who repent before being overpowered. See the next Verse.

إِلَّا ٱلَّذِينَ تَابُواْ مِن قَبْلِ أَن تَقْدِرُواْ عَلَيْهِمْ فَٱعْلَمُوٓاْ أَنَّ ٱللَّهَ غَفُورٌ رَّحِيمٌ

34. Illa allatheena taboo min qabli an taqdiroo AAalayhim faiAAlamoo anna Allaha ghafoorun raheemun

5:34. Except for those who repent before you overpower them. So be aware that Allah is Forgiving, Merciful.

يَٰٓأَيُّهَا ٱلَّذِينَ ءَامَنُواْ ٱتَّقُواْ ٱللَّهَ وَٱبْتَغُوٓاْ إِلَيْهِ ٱلْوَسِيلَةَ وَجَٰهِدُواْ فِى سَبِيلِهِۦ لَعَلَّكُمْ تُفْلِحُونَ ٣٥

35. Ya ayyuha allatheena amanoo ittaqoo Allaha waibtaghoo ilayhi alwaseelata wajahidoo fee sabeelihi laAAallakum tuflihoona

5:35. O you who believe! Fear Allah and seek means of approach to Him and struggle in His Path, so that you get success.[19]

19. The Arabic word *alwaseelata* (means of approach) has been grossly misunderstood by many Muslims of today. They think that in the light of this Verse, they can invoke the good offices of the Prophet (peace be upon him) and other dead pious men, for conferring of worldly benefits to them and for redressal of their worldly woes. Attention of such Muslims is invited to Verses 17:56 and 17:57 wherein the futility of invoking anyone other than Allah, is clarified. And in Verse 35:22, the Qur'aan categorically tells mankind, "And you are in no position to make those to hear who are in the graves." The 'means of approach' to Allah are those means which were employed by those great men themselves. They had persistently struggled in Allah's Path as indicated at the end of this Verse itself. 'Struggling in Allah's Path' is therefore the means. And 'struggling in Allah's Path' does not mean suicide attacks on soft targets as some may mistakenly believe! It is, on the other hand, to "believe, and do righteous deeds, and admonish with the Truth and admonish with Patience" as enunciated in *Surah* 103. And 'righteous deeds' are deeds that Allah Almighty commands mankind to do through His Message, the Qur'aan.

إِنَّ ٱلَّذِينَ كَفَرُواْ لَوْ أَنَّ لَهُم مَّا فِى ٱلْأَرْضِ جَمِيعًا وَمِثْلَهُۥ مَعَهُۥ لِيَفْتَدُواْ بِهِۦ مِنْ عَذَابِ يَوْمِ ٱلْقِيَٰمَةِ مَا تُقُبِّلَ مِنْهُمْ وَلَهُمْ عَذَابٌ أَلِيمٌ ﴿٣٦﴾

36. Inna allatheena kafaroo law anna lahum ma fee al-ardi jameeAAan wamithlahu maAAahu liyaftadoo bihi min AAathabi yawmi alqiyamati ma tuqubbila minhum walahum AAathabun aleemun

5:36. Indeed, if those who suppress the Truth had all that is in the earth, and the like of it besides, to offer as ransom against the punishment on the Day of Resurrection, it shall not be accepted from them. And for them there shall be a painful punishment.

يُرِيدُونَ أَن يَخْرُجُواْ مِنَ ٱلنَّارِ وَمَا هُم بِخَٰرِجِينَ مِنْهَا وَلَهُمْ عَذَابٌ مُّقِيمٌ ﴿٣٧﴾

37. Yureedoona an yakhrujoo mina alnnari wama hum bikharijeena minha walahum AAathabun muqeemun

5:37. They will long to go out of the Fire, and they shall find no way out there from. And, for them, it is a lasting punishment.

وَٱلسَّارِقُ وَٱلسَّارِقَةُ فَٱقْطَعُوٓاْ أَيْدِيَهُمَا جَزَآءً بِمَا كَسَبَا نَكَٰلًا مِّنَ ٱللَّهِ وَٱللَّهُ عَزِيزٌ حَكِيمٌ ﴿٣٨﴾

38. Waalssariqu waalssariqatu faiqtaAAoo aydiyahuma jazaan bima kasaba nakalan mina Allahi waAllahu AAazeezun hakeemun

5:38. And cut off the hand each of the man who steals and the woman who steals, as an exemplary punishment from Allah for what they have earned. And Allah is Omnipotent, Wise.[20]

20. In view of the next Verse, this punishment is to be meted out only to such an incorrigible thief who is unrepentant for his crime or indulges in it repeatedly despite declaring his repentance of earlier crimes. The punishment to such a thief has necessarily to be exemplary, so that others, seeing his amputated arm, are effectively discouraged from committing the crime. Modern-day governments, in the name of humanitarianism, have very light penal provisions of imprisonment for a limited period. A hardened criminal takes it in his stride, goes to prison, and duly resumes his criminal activity afresh after being released. And, with his ill-gotten wealth, he may grease the palms of the police, and thus evade imprisonment again. And seeing his apparent prosperity, others may emulate him. Allah-given law is always better than man-made laws.

فَمَن تَابَ مِنۢ بَعْدِ ظُلْمِهِۦ وَأَصْلَحَ فَإِنَّ ٱللَّهَ يَتُوبُ عَلَيْهِ إِنَّ ٱللَّهَ غَفُورٌ رَّحِيمٌ ﴿٣٩﴾

39. Faman taba min baAAdi *th*ulmihi waa*sla*ha fa-inna All*a*ha yatoobu AAalayhi inna All*a*ha ghafoorun ra*h*eem**un**

5:39. And he who repents after he has committed his crime and reforms himself, then, indeed, Allah will accept his repentance. And Allah is indeed Forgiving, Merciful.

أَلَمْ تَعْلَمْ أَنَّ ٱللَّهَ لَهُۥ مُلْكُ ٱلسَّمَٰوَٰتِ وَٱلْأَرْضِ يُعَذِّبُ مَن يَشَآءُ وَيَغْفِرُ لِمَن يَشَآءُ وَٱللَّهُ عَلَىٰ كُلِّ شَىْءٍ قَدِيرٌ ﴿٤٠﴾

40. Alam taAAlam anna All*a*ha lahu mulku alssam*a*w*a*ti waal-ar*d*i yuAAa*ththi*bu man yash*a*o wayaghfiru liman yash*a*o waAll*a*hu AAal*a* kulli shay-in qadeer**un**

5:40. Don't you know that to Allah belongs the absolute sovereignty over the heavens and the earth? He punishes whom He wills and forgives whom He wills. And Allah has power over all things.

۞ يَـٰٓأَيُّهَا ٱلرَّسُولُ لَا يَحْزُنكَ ٱلَّذِينَ يُسَـٰرِعُونَ فِى ٱلْكُفْرِ مِنَ ٱلَّذِينَ قَالُوٓاْ

ءَامَنَّا بِأَفْوَٰهِهِمْ وَلَمْ تُؤْمِن قُلُوبُهُمْ وَمِنَ ٱلَّذِينَ هَادُواْ سَمَّـٰعُونَ لِلْكَذِبِ

سَمَّـٰعُونَ لِقَوْمٍ ءَاخَرِينَ لَمْ يَأْتُوكَ يُحَرِّفُونَ ٱلْكَلِمَ مِنۢ بَعْدِ مَوَاضِعِهِۦ

يَقُولُونَ إِنْ أُوتِيتُمْ هَـٰذَا فَخُذُوهُ وَإِن لَّمْ تُؤْتَوْهُ فَٱحْذَرُواْ وَمَن يُرِدِ ٱللَّهُ

فِتْنَتَهُۥ فَلَن تَمْلِكَ لَهُۥ مِنَ ٱللَّهِ شَيْـًٔا أُوْلَـٰٓئِكَ ٱلَّذِينَ لَمْ يُرِدِ ٱللَّهُ أَن يُطَهِّرَ

قُلُوبَهُمْ لَهُمْ فِى ٱلدُّنْيَا خِزْىٌ وَلَهُمْ فِى ٱلْأَخِرَةِ عَذَابٌ عَظِيمٌ ﴿٤١﴾

41. Ya ayyuha alrrasoolu la yahzunka allatheena yusariAAoona fee alkufri mina allatheena qaloo amanna bi-afwahihim walam tu/min quloobuhum wamina allatheena hadoo sammaAAoona lilkathibi sammaAAoona liqawmin akhareena lam ya/tooka yuharrifoona alkalima min baAAdi mawadiAAihi yaqooloona in ooteetum hatha fakhuthoohu wa-in lam tu/twhu faihtharoo waman yuridi Allahu fitnatahu falan tamlika lahu mina Allahi shay-an ola-ika allatheena lam yuridi Allahu an yutahhira quloobahum lahum fee alddunya khizyun walahum fee al-akhirati AAathabun AAatheemun

5:41. O Messenger! Let not those make you sad, who are quick in suppressing the Truth from among those who say, with their mouths, "We believe" and their hearts do not believe, and from among those who are Jews. They listen to falsehood. They listen to others who do not come to you. They transpose the word after it had been placed in its proper context, saying, "If you are given this, take it, and if you are not given this, beware!" And if Allah wills to put anyone to distress and hardship, you can do nothing for him against Allah. Allah does not want to purify the hearts of such people. Disgrace it is for them in this world, and a grave punishment for them in the Hereafter!

سَمَّـٰعُونَ لِلْكَذِبِ أَكَّـٰلُونَ لِلسُّحْتِ فَإِن جَآءُوكَ فَٱحْكُم بَيْنَهُمْ أَوْ أَعْرِضْ

عَنْهُمْ وَإِن تُعْرِضْ عَنْهُمْ فَلَن يَضُرُّوكَ شَيْـًٔا وَإِنْ حَكَمْتَ فَٱحْكُم

بَيْنَهُم بِٱلْقِسْطِ إِنَّ ٱللَّهَ يُحِبُّ ٱلْمُقْسِطِينَ ﴿٤٢﴾

42. SammaAAoona lilkathibi akkaloona lilssuhti fa-in jaooka faohkum baynahum aw aAArid AAanhum wa-in tuAArid AAanhum falan yadurrooka shay-an wa-in hakamta faohkum baynahum bialqisti inna Allaha yuhibbu almuqsiteena

5:42. They listen to falsehood. They eat what is forbidden. So, if they come to you, judge between them or ignore them. And if you ignore them, they won't do any harm to you. And if you judge, judge between them fairly. Indeed, Allah loves those who are just.

وَكَيْفَ يُحَكِّمُونَكَ وَعِندَهُمُ ٱلتَّوْرَىٰةُ فِيهَا حُكْمُ ٱللَّهِ ثُمَّ يَتَوَلَّوْنَ مِنۢ بَعْدِ ذَٰلِكَ وَمَآ أُو۟لَـٰٓئِكَ بِٱلْمُؤْمِنِينَ ﴿٤٣﴾

43. Wakayfa yuhakkimoonaka waAAindahumu alttawratu feeha hukmu Allahi thumma yatawallawna min baAAdi thalika wama ola-ika bialmu/mineena

5:43. And how could they make you a judge? And they have the Torah, wherein is Allah's Judgment, and yet they turn away thereafter! And such as these are no believers! [21]

21. Had the Jews really believed in the Torah, they need not have come to the Prophet. They would have got Allah's judgement therein itself. This should not be construed to mean that the Jews did not need to believe in Muhammad (peace be upon him) as a duly accredited Prophet of Allah and in His last Message, the Qur'aan. The Torah itself contains such clear evidence about the coming of Prophet Muhammad that true belief in the Torah would automatically lead to belief in Prophet Muhammad and in the Qur'aan. That is why the Qur'aan says in Verse 6:20 that those who were given the Book earlier, know about the Prophet or about the Qur'aan as they know about their own sons.

إِنَّآ أَنزَلْنَا ٱلتَّوْرَىٰةَ فِيهَا هُدًى وَنُورٌ يَحْكُمُ بِهَا ٱلنَّبِيُّونَ ٱلَّذِينَ أَسْلَمُوا۟ لِلَّذِينَ هَادُوا۟ وَٱلرَّبَّـٰنِيُّونَ وَٱلْأَحْبَارُ بِمَا ٱسْتُحْفِظُوا۟ مِن كِتَـٰبِ ٱللَّهِ وَكَانُوا۟ عَلَيْهِ شُهَدَآءَ فَلَا تَخْشَوُا۟ ٱلنَّاسَ وَٱخْشَوْنِ وَلَا تَشْتَرُوا۟ بِـَٔايَـٰتِى ثَمَنًا قَلِيلًا وَمَن لَّمْ يَحْكُم بِمَآ أَنزَلَ ٱللَّهُ فَأُو۟لَـٰٓئِكَ هُمُ ٱلْكَـٰفِرُونَ

44. Inna anzalna alttawrata feeha hudan wanoorun yahkumu biha alnnabiyyoona allatheena aslamoo lillatheena hadoo waalrrabbaniyyoona waal-ahbaru bima istuhfithoo min kitabi Allahi wakanoo AAalayhi shuhadaa fala takhshawoo alnnasa waikhshawni wala tashtaroo bi-ayatee thamanan qaleelan waman lam yahkum bima anzala Allahu faola-ika humu alkafiroona

5:44. We did indeed send down the Torah, with guidance and light therein. Therewith, the Prophets, who submitted themselves to Allah, and the Rabbis and the doctors in religious law, required to guard part of the Book of Allah and be witnesses thereto, judged for the Jews. Therefore, fear the people not and fear Me, and do not buy a small benefit in exchange for My Verses/signs.[22] And they, who judge not by what Allah has sent down, are the suppressors of the Truth.

22. This divine directive is not just for the Jews or for the Prophet. It is for every human being who must make a decision or a judgement.

وَكَتَبْنَا عَلَيْهِمْ فِيهَآ أَنَّ ٱلنَّفْسَ بِٱلنَّفْسِ وَٱلْعَيْنَ بِٱلْعَيْنِ وَٱلْأَنفَ بِٱلْأَنفِ وَٱلْأُذُنَ بِٱلْأُذُنِ وَٱلسِّنَّ بِٱلسِّنِّ وَٱلْجُرُوحَ قِصَاصٌ فَمَن تَصَدَّقَ بِهِۦ فَهُوَ كَفَّارَةٌ لَّهُۥ وَمَن لَّمْ يَحْكُم بِمَآ أَنزَلَ ٱللَّهُ فَأُوْلَٰٓئِكَ هُمُ ٱلظَّٰلِمُونَ ﴿٤٥﴾

45. Wakatabna AAalayhim feeha anna alnnafsa bialnnafsi waalAAayna bialAAayni waal-anfa bial-anfi waalothuna bialothuni waalssinna bialssinni waaljurooha qisasun faman tasaddaqa bihi fahuwa kaffaratun lahu waman lam yahkum bima anzala Allahu faola-ika humu alththalimoona

5:45. And We ordained for them therein that life is for life, and eye for eye, and nose for nose, and ear for ear, and tooth for tooth, and a wound is a retaliation for a wound. But if one foregoes the retaliation by way of charity, it shall be expiation for him. And they, who judge not by what Allah has sent down, are the oppressors.

وَقَفَّيْنَا عَلَىٰٓ ءَاثَـٰرِهِم بِعِيسَى ٱبْنِ مَرْيَمَ مُصَدِّقًا لِّمَا

بَيْنَ يَدَيْهِ مِنَ ٱلتَّوْرَىٰةِ وَءَاتَيْنَـٰهُ ٱلْإِنجِيلَ فِيهِ هُدًى

وَنُورٌ وَمُصَدِّقًا لِّمَا بَيْنَ يَدَيْهِ مِنَ ٱلتَّوْرَىٰةِ وَهُدًى وَمَوْعِظَةً

لِّلْمُتَّقِينَ ۝

46. Waqaffayna AAala atharihim biAAeesa ibni maryama musaddiqan lima bayna yadayhi mina alttawrati waataynahu al-injeela feehi hudan wanoorun wamusaddiqan lima bayna yadayhi mina alttawrati wahudan wamawAAithatan lilmuttaqeena

---

5:46. And We caused Jesus, son of Mary, to follow in their footsteps, confirming what was before him of the Torah. And We gave him the Gospel containing guidance and light and confirming what was before it of the Torah and guidance and admonition for those who fear Allah.

وَلْيَحْكُمْ أَهْلُ ٱلْإِنجِيلِ بِمَآ أَنزَلَ ٱللَّهُ فِيهِ وَمَن لَّمْ يَحْكُم بِمَآ

أَنزَلَ ٱللَّهُ فَأُو۟لَـٰٓئِكَ هُمُ ٱلْفَـٰسِقُونَ ۝

47. Walyahkum ahlu al-injeeli bima anzala Allahu feehi waman lam yahkum bima anzala Allahu faola-ika humu alfasiqoona

---

5:47. And the followers of the Gospel ought to judge by what Allah revealed in it.[23] And they, who judge not by what Allah has sent down, are the transgressors/profligates.

---

23. And had the followers of Gospel judged by what was revealed in it, they would have believed in the Qur'aan when it came to them and acted thereupon.

وَأَنزَلْنَآ إِلَيْكَ ٱلْكِتَـٰبَ بِٱلْحَقِّ مُصَدِّقًا لِّمَا بَيْنَ يَدَيْهِ مِنَ ٱلْكِتَـٰبِ وَمُهَيْمِنًا عَلَيْهِ ۖ فَٱحْكُم بَيْنَهُم بِمَآ أَنزَلَ ٱللَّهُ ۖ وَلَا تَتَّبِعْ أَهْوَآءَهُمْ عَمَّا جَآءَكَ مِنَ ٱلْحَقِّ ۚ لِكُلٍّ جَعَلْنَا مِنكُمْ شِرْعَةً وَمِنْهَاجًا ۚ وَلَوْ شَآءَ ٱللَّهُ لَجَعَلَكُمْ أُمَّةً وَٰحِدَةً وَلَـٰكِن لِّيَبْلُوَكُمْ فِى مَآ ءَاتَىٰكُمْ ۖ فَٱسْتَبِقُوا۟ ٱلْخَيْرَٰتِ ۚ إِلَى ٱللَّهِ مَرْجِعُكُمْ جَمِيعًا فَيُنَبِّئُكُم بِمَا كُنتُمْ فِيهِ تَخْتَلِفُونَ ﴿٤٨﴾

48. Waanzalna ilayka alkitaba bialhaqqi musaddiqan lima bayna yadayhi mina alkitabi wamuhayminan AAalayhi faohkum baynahum bima anzala Allahu wala tattabiAA ahwaahum AAamma jaaka mina alhaqqi likullin jaAAalna minkum shirAAatan waminhajan walaw shaa Allahu lajaAAalakum ommatan wahidatan walakin liyabluwakum feema atakum faistabiqoo alkhayrati ila Allahi marjiAAukum jameeAAan fayunabbi-okum bima kuntum feehi takhtalifoona

5:48. And We have sent down to you the Book with the truth, to confirm what has come before it of the Book and to act as an authority thereupon. So, judge among them by what Allah has sent down, and follow not their vain desires which deviate from the truth that has come to you. For all of you, We have generated social customs and ways of life. And had Allah so willed, He would have made you a single community, but He wanted to test you in what He has given you, so compete with one another in doing good deeds.[24] To Allah is the return of all of you. He will then explain to you what you differed in.

24. **This Verse makes it clear that different customs and ways of life matter not, provided the broad divine commands are adhered to. Adhering to divine commands is what good deeds are all about.**

وَأَنِ ٱحْكُم بَيْنَهُم بِمَآ أَنزَلَ ٱللَّهُ وَلَا تَتَّبِعْ أَهْوَآءَهُمْ وَٱحْذَرْهُمْ أَن يَفْتِنُوكَ عَن بَعْضِ مَآ أَنزَلَ ٱللَّهُ إِلَيْكَ ۖ فَإِن تَوَلَّوْا۟ فَٱعْلَمْ أَنَّمَا يُرِيدُ ٱللَّهُ أَن يُصِيبَهُم بِبَعْضِ ذُنُوبِهِمْ ۗ وَإِنَّ كَثِيرًا مِّنَ ٱلنَّاسِ لَفَـٰسِقُونَ ﴿٤٩﴾

49. Waani ohkum baynahum bima anzala Allahu wala tattabiAA ahwaahum waihtharhum an yaftinooka AAan baAAdi ma anzala Allahu ilayka fa-in tawallaw faiAAlam annama yureedu Allahu an yuseebahum bibaAAdi thunoobihim wa-inna katheeran mina alnnasi lafasiqoona

5:49. And so you do judge among them by what Allah has sent down, and follow not their vain desires, and be cautious of them lest they tempt you away from some part of what Allah has enjoined upon you. If they then turn away, know that it is Allah's Will to afflict them with hardship for some of their sins. And a great number of the people are indeed the transgressors/profligates.

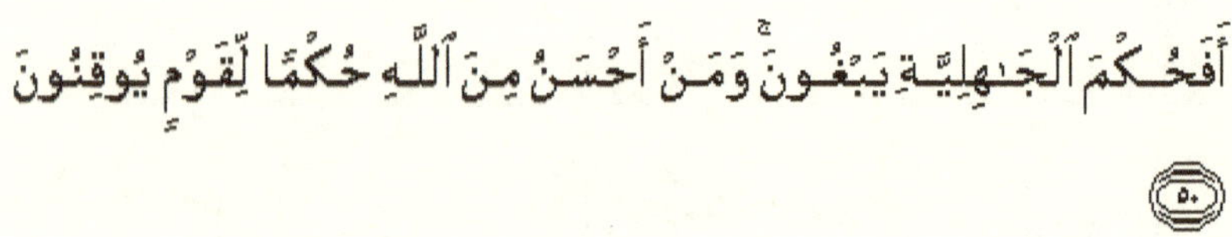

50. Afahukma aljahiliyyati yabghoona waman ahsanu mina Allahu hukman liqawmin yooqinoona

5:50. Is it then that they desire the rule of the times of ignorance? And who is better to rule, for a people who are firm in Faith, than Allah?

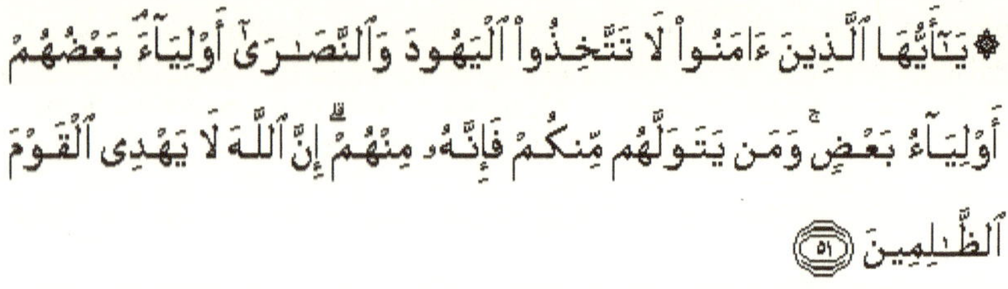

51. Ya ayyuha allatheena amanoo la tattakhithoo alyahooda waalnnasara awliyaa baAAduhum awliyao baAAdin waman yatawallahum minkum fa-innahu minhum inna Allaha la yahdee alqawma alththalimeena

5:51. O you who believe! Do not take the Jews and the Christians for close, intimate friends[25]. They are close to one another. And whoever amongst you is close to them, then, indeed he is one of them. Indeed, Allah does not guide the wrong-doers.

25. The Arabic term, which is translated here as 'close, intimate friends', is awliya. For the comprehensive Qur'aanic meaning of wali (singular of awliya) please refer study note 2:154.

فَتَرَى ٱلَّذِينَ فِى قُلُوبِهِم مَّرَضٌ يُسَـٰرِعُونَ فِيهِمْ يَقُولُونَ نَخْشَىٰٓ أَن تُصِيبَنَا دَآئِرَةٌ فَعَسَى ٱللَّهُ أَن يَأْتِيَ بِٱلْفَتْحِ أَوْ أَمْرٍ مِّنْ عِندِهِۦ فَيُصْبِحُوا۟ عَلَىٰ مَآ أَسَرُّوا۟ فِىٓ أَنفُسِهِمْ نَـٰدِمِينَ ۝

52. Fatara allatheena fee quloobihim maradun yusariAAoona feehim yaqooloona nakhsha an tuseebana da-iratun faAAasa Allahu an ya/tiya bialfathi aw amrin min AAindihi fayusbihoo AAala ma asarroo fee anfusihim nadimeena

5:52. And you will see those, in whose hearts is a disease, to be active in their company. They say, "We fear a turn of fortune afflicting us." And it may well be that Allah will bring about victory or such event, by His Will, that they become ashamed of their secret feelings.

وَيَقُولُ ٱلَّذِينَ ءَامَنُوٓا۟ أَهَـٰٓؤُلَآءِ ٱلَّذِينَ أَقْسَمُوا۟ بِٱللَّهِ جَهْدَ أَيْمَـٰنِهِمْ إِنَّهُمْ لَمَعَكُمْ حَبِطَتْ أَعْمَـٰلُهُمْ فَأَصْبَحُوا۟ خَـٰسِرِينَ ۝

53. Wayaqoolu allatheena amanoo ahaola-i allatheena aqsamoo biAllahi jahda aymanihim innahum lamaAAakum habitat aAAmaluhum faasbahoo khasireena

5:53. And those who believe say, "Are these the people who swore intensely by Allah that they were indeed with us? Their deeds have been in vain, and they are doomed."

يَـٰٓأَيُّهَا ٱلَّذِينَ ءَامَنُوا۟ مَن يَرْتَدَّ مِنكُمْ عَن دِينِهِۦ فَسَوْفَ يَأْتِى ٱللَّهُ بِقَوْمٍ يُحِبُّهُمْ وَيُحِبُّونَهُۥٓ أَذِلَّةٍ عَلَى ٱلْمُؤْمِنِينَ أَعِزَّةٍ عَلَى ٱلْكَـٰفِرِينَ يُجَـٰهِدُونَ فِى سَبِيلِ ٱللَّهِ وَلَا يَخَافُونَ لَوْمَةَ لَآئِمٍ ذَٰلِكَ فَضْلُ ٱللَّهِ يُؤْتِيهِ مَن يَشَآءُ وَٱللَّهُ وَٰسِعٌ عَلِيمٌ ۝

54. Ya ayyuha allatheena amanoo man yartadda minkum AAan deenihi fasawfa ya/tee Allahu biqawmin yuhibbuhum wayuhibboonahu athillatin AAala almu/mineena aAAizzatin AAala alkafireena yujahidoona fee sabeeli Allahi wala yakhafoona lawmata la-imin thalika fadlu Allahi yu/teehi man yashao waAllahu wasiAAun AAaleemun

5:54. O you who believe! If there be any from among you who turns back from his religion, then, Allah will bring a people whom He will love and who will love Him, humble with the believers, stern with those who suppress the Truth. They will strive in Allah's Path and will not fear the criticism of any critic. That is Allah's Favour which He gives to whom He wills. And Allah's knowledge encompasses everything.

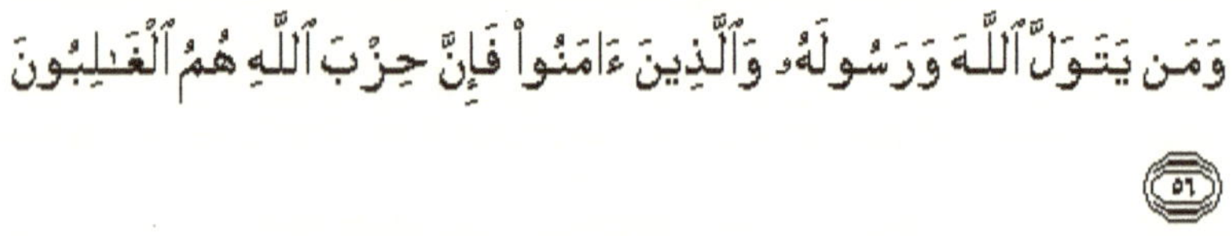

55. Innama waliyyukumu Allahu warasooluhu waallatheena amanoo allatheena yuqeemoona alssalata wayu/toona alzzakata wahum rakiAAoona

5:55. Your only close friends are Allah, His Messenger and those who believe, establish prayers, give charity and bow down in submission to Allah.

56. Waman yatawalla Allaha warasoolahu waallatheena amanoo fa-inna hizba Allahi humu alghaliboona

5:56. And the one who seeks closeness to Allah, His Messenger and those who believe, may rest assured that it is Allah's group that shall indeed be triumphant.[26]

26. Had majority of the Muslims today been so rest assured, they wouldn't find themselves in the unenviable position they are in.

يَٰٓأَيُّهَا ٱلَّذِينَ ءَامَنُوا۟ لَا تَتَّخِذُوا۟ ٱلَّذِينَ ٱتَّخَذُوا۟ دِينَكُمْ هُزُوًا وَلَعِبًا مِّنَ ٱلَّذِينَ أُوتُوا۟ ٱلْكِتَٰبَ مِن قَبْلِكُمْ وَٱلْكُفَّارَ أَوْلِيَآءَ وَٱتَّقُوا۟ ٱللَّهَ إِن كُنتُم مُّؤْمِنِينَ ۝٥٧

57. Ya ayyuha allatheena amanoo la tattakhithoo allatheena ittakhathoo deenakum huzuwan walaAAiban mina allatheena ootoo alkitaba min qablikum waalkuffara awliyaa waittaqoo Allaha in kuntum mu/mineena

5:57. O you who believe! Do not consider persons – from among those who were given the Book before you and from among the suppressors of Truth – who take your religion for a mockery and fun, as your close friends. And fear Allah if you do believe.

وَإِذَا نَادَيْتُمْ إِلَى ٱلصَّلَوٰةِ ٱتَّخَذُوهَا هُزُوًا وَلَعِبًا ذَٰلِكَ بِأَنَّهُمْ قَوْمٌ لَّا يَعْقِلُونَ ۝٥٨

58. Wa-itha nadaytum ila alssalati ittakhathooha huzuwan walaAAiban thalika bi-annahum qawmun la yaAAqiloona

5:58. And when you make a call for prayer they take it but as a mockery and fun. They do so because they are a people who understand not.

قُلْ يَٰٓأَهْلَ ٱلْكِتَٰبِ هَلْ تَنقِمُونَ مِنَّآ إِلَّآ أَنْ ءَامَنَّا بِٱللَّهِ وَمَآ أُنزِلَ إِلَيْنَا وَمَآ أُنزِلَ مِن قَبْلُ وَأَنَّ أَكْثَرَكُمْ فَٰسِقُونَ ۝٥٩

59. Qul ya ahla alkitabi hal tanqimoona minna illa an amanna biAllahi wama onzila ilayna wama onzila min qablu waanna aktharakum fasiqoona

5:59. Say, "O people of the Book! Do you take vengeance on us for no other reason than that we believe in Allah and in what is sent down to us and in what was sent down before, and [is it not a fact] that most of you are transgressors/profligates?"

قُلْ هَلْ أُنَبِّئُكُم بِشَرٍّ مِّن ذَٰلِكَ مَثُوبَةً عِندَ ٱللَّهِ مَن لَّعَنَهُ ٱللَّهُ وَغَضِبَ عَلَيْهِ وَجَعَلَ مِنْهُمُ ٱلْقِرَدَةَ وَٱلْخَنَازِيرَ وَعَبَدَ ٱلطَّٰغُوتَ أُوْلَٰئِكَ شَرٌّ مَّكَانًا وَأَضَلُّ عَن سَوَآءِ ٱلسَّبِيلِ ۝

60. Qul hal onabbi-okum bisharrin min thalika mathoobatan AAinda Allahi man laAAanahu Allahu waghadiba AAalayhi wajaAAala minhumu alqiradata waalkhanazeera waAAabada alttaghooti ola-ika sharrun makanan waadallu AAan sawa-i alssabeeli

5:60. Say, "Shall I inform you of a worse retribution than that from Allah? Those whom Allah has cursed and upon whom His wrath has fallen, and those of them whom He made apes and pigs, and those who worshipped the false god – those are the people in a worse position, and further astray from the Right Path."

وَإِذَا جَآءُوكُمْ قَالُوٓاْ ءَامَنَّا وَقَد دَّخَلُواْ بِٱلْكُفْرِ وَهُم قَدْ خَرَجُواْ بِهِۦ وَٱللَّهُ أَعْلَمُ بِمَا كَانُواْ يَكْتُمُونَ ۝

61. Wa-itha jaookum qaloo amanna waqad dakhaloo bialkufri wahum qad kharajoo bihi waAllahu aAAlamu bima kanoo yaktumoona

5:61. And when they came to you, they said, "We believe". And they in fact came in suppressing the Truth, and they in fact went out doing the same. And Allah knows what they were hiding.

وَتَرَىٰ كَثِيرًا مِّنْهُمْ يُسَٰرِعُونَ فِى ٱلْإِثْمِ وَٱلْعُدْوَٰنِ وَأَكْلِهِمُ ٱلسُّحْتَ لَبِئْسَ مَا كَانُواْ يَعْمَلُونَ ۝

62. Watara katheeran minhum yusariAAoona fee al-ithmi waalAAudwani waaklihimu alssuhta labi/sa ma kanoo yaAAmaloona

5:62. And you see many of them vie with one another in sin and hostility, and in their eating of what is unlawful. What they are doing is certainly bad.

لَوْلَا يَنْهَٰهُمُ ٱلرَّبَّٰنِيُّونَ وَٱلْأَحْبَارُ عَن قَوْلِهِمُ ٱلْإِثْمَ وَأَكْلِهِمُ ٱلسُّحْتَ

لَبِئْسَ مَا كَانُوا۟ يَصْنَعُونَ ۝

63. Lawla yanhahumu alrrabbaniyyoona waal-ahbaru AAan qawlihimu al-ithma waaklihimu alssuhta labi/sa ma kanoo yasnaAAoona

5:63. Why did the Rabbis and the Priests not prohibit them from their sinful utterances and from eating unlawful things? What they are bringing about is certainly bad.

وَقَالَتِ ٱلْيَهُودُ يَدُ ٱللَّهِ مَغْلُولَةٌ غُلَّتْ أَيْدِيهِمْ وَلُعِنُوا۟ بِمَا قَالُوا۟ بَلْ يَدَاهُ

مَبْسُوطَتَانِ يُنفِقُ كَيْفَ يَشَآءُ وَلَيَزِيدَنَّ كَثِيرًا مِّنْهُم مَّآ أُنزِلَ إِلَيْكَ

مِن رَّبِّكَ طُغْيَٰنًا وَكُفْرًا وَأَلْقَيْنَا بَيْنَهُمُ ٱلْعَدَٰوَةَ وَٱلْبَغْضَآءَ إِلَىٰ يَوْمِ

ٱلْقِيَٰمَةِ كُلَّمَآ أَوْقَدُوا۟ نَارًا لِّلْحَرْبِ أَطْفَأَهَا ٱللَّهُ وَيَسْعَوْنَ فِى ٱلْأَرْضِ

فَسَادًا وَٱللَّهُ لَا يُحِبُّ ٱلْمُفْسِدِينَ ۝

64. Waqalati alyahoodu yadu Allahi maghloolatun ghullat aydeehim waluAAinoo bima qaloo bal yadahu mabsootatani yunfiqu kayfa yashao walayazeedanna katheeran minhum ma onzila ilayka min rabbika tughyanan wakufran waalqayna baynahumu alAAadawata waalbaghdaa ila yawmi alqiyamati kullama awqadoo naran lilharbi atfaaha Allahu wayasAAawna fee al-ardi fasadan waAllahu la yuhibbu almufsideena

5:64. And the Jews say, "Allah's hand is bound!" Their hands are bound, and they are cursed for what they said. Nay, both His hands are spread out, He expends as He pleases. And what has been sent down to you from your Lord will certainly make many of them more steeped in insolence and suppression of the Truth. And We have put enmity and hatred amongst them until the Day of Resurrection. Every time they kindled the fire for war, Allah extinguished it.[27] And they strive for mischief on earth. And Allah does not love the mischief mongers.

27. Allah does thus control the activities of human beings. Had He left them to do as they pleased, humans would have long back been destroyed.

وَلَوْ أَنَّ أَهْلَ ٱلْكِتَـٰبِ ءَامَنُواْ وَٱتَّقَوْاْ لَكَفَّرْنَا عَنْهُمْ سَيِّـَٔاتِهِمْ وَلَأَدْخَلْنَـٰهُمْ جَنَّـٰتِ ٱلنَّعِيمِ ۝

65. Walaw anna ahla alkitabi amanoo waittaqaw lakaffarna AAanhum sayyi-atihim walaadkhalnahum jannati alnnaAAeemi

5:65. And if the people of the Book had indeed believed, and feared Allah, We would certainly have cleared their bad deeds from them and We would certainly have made them enter gardens of bliss.

وَلَوْ أَنَّهُمْ أَقَامُواْ ٱلتَّوْرَىٰةَ وَٱلْإِنجِيلَ وَمَآ أُنزِلَ إِلَيْهِم مِّن رَّبِّهِمْ لَأَكَلُواْ مِن فَوْقِهِمْ وَمِن تَحْتِ أَرْجُلِهِمْ مِّنْهُمْ أُمَّةٌ مُّقْتَصِدَةٌ وَكَثِيرٌ مِّنْهُمْ سَآءَ مَا يَعْمَلُونَ ۝

66. Walaw annahum aqamoo alttawrata waal-injeela wama onzila ilayhim min rabbihim laakaloo min fawqihim wamin tahti arjulihim minhum ommatun muqtasidatun wakatheerun minhum saa ma yaAAmaloona

5:66. And had they only stood by the Torah and the Gospel and that which is sent down to them from their Lord, they would certainly have got provision to eat from above them and from beneath their feet. Among them are people who keep to the right course. And what many of them do is bad.

يَـٰٓأَيُّهَا ٱلرَّسُولُ بَلِّغْ مَآ أُنزِلَ إِلَيْكَ مِن رَّبِّكَ وَإِن لَّمْ تَفْعَلْ فَمَا بَلَّغْتَ رِسَالَتَهُۥ وَٱللَّهُ يَعْصِمُكَ مِنَ ٱلنَّاسِ إِنَّ ٱللَّهَ لَا يَهْدِى ٱلْقَوْمَ ٱلْكَـٰفِرِينَ ۝

67. Ya ayyuha alrrasoolu balligh ma onzila ilayka min rabbika wa-in lam tafAAal fama ballaghta risalatahu waAllahu yaAAsimuka mina alnnasi inna Allaha la yahdee alqawma alkafireena

5:67. O Messenger! Deliver what has been sent down to you from your Lord. And if you do not do so, then you have not delivered His Message. And Allah will guard you against the people. Indeed, Allah guides not people that suppress the Truth.

قُل يَـٰٓأَهۡلَ ٱلۡكِتَـٰبِ لَسۡتُمۡ عَلَىٰ شَىۡءٍ حَتَّىٰ تُقِيمُواْ ٱلتَّوۡرَىٰةَ وَٱلۡإِنجِيلَ وَمَآ أُنزِلَ إِلَيۡكُم مِّن رَّبِّكُمۡ وَلَيَزِيدَنَّ كَثِيرًا مِّنۡهُم مَّآ أُنزِلَ إِلَيۡكَ مِن رَّبِّكَ طُغۡيَـٰنًا وَكُفۡرًا فَلَا تَأۡسَ عَلَى ٱلۡقَوۡمِ ٱلۡكَـٰفِرِينَ 

68. Qul ya ahla alkit<u>a</u>bi lastum AAal<u>a</u> shay-in <u>h</u>att<u>a</u> tuqeemoo alttawr<u>a</u>ta waal-injeela wam<u>a</u> onzila ilaykum min rabbikum walayazeedanna katheeran minhum m<u>a</u> onzila ilayka min rabbika <u>t</u>ughy<u>a</u>nan wakufran fal<u>a</u> ta/sa AAal<u>a</u> alqawmi alk<u>a</u>fireena

5:68. Say, "O followers of the Book! You stand on no basis till you stand by the Torah and the Gospel and that which is sent down to you from your Lord." And what has been sent down to you[28] from your Lord will certainly make many of them more steeped in insolence and suppression of the Truth. Grieve not therefore for the people who suppress the Truth.

28. I.e. to Prophet Muhammad (peace be upon him).

إِنَّ ٱلَّذِينَ ءَامَنُواْ وَٱلَّذِينَ هَادُواْ وَٱلصَّـٰبِـُٔونَ وَٱلنَّصَـٰرَىٰ مَنۡ ءَامَنَ بِٱللَّهِ وَٱلۡيَوۡمِ ٱلۡأَخِرِ وَعَمِلَ صَـٰلِحًا فَلَا خَوۡفٌ عَلَيۡهِمۡ وَلَا هُمۡ يَحۡزَنُونَ 

69. Inna alla<u>th</u>eena <u>a</u>manoo waalla<u>th</u>eena h<u>a</u>doo waalss<u>a</u>bi-oona waalna<u>sa</u>r<u>a</u> man <u>a</u>mana biAll<u>a</u>hi waalyawmi al-<u>a</u>khiri waAAamila <u>sa</u>li<u>h</u>an fal<u>a</u> khawfun AAalayhim wal<u>a</u> hum ya<u>h</u>zanoona

5:69. Indeed, those who believe, the Jews, the Saabioon and the Christians – whosoever believed in Allah and in the Last Day and acted righteously – fear then shall overpower them not; nor shall they grieve![29]

29. This Verse is almost verbatim the same as <u>Verse 2:62</u>**. Please therefore refer the study notes thereunder.**

لَقَدْ أَخَذْنَا مِيثَـٰقَ بَنِىٓ إِسْرَٰٓءِيلَ وَأَرْسَلْنَآ إِلَيْهِمْ رُسُلًا

كُلَّمَا جَآءَهُمْ رَسُولٌۢ بِمَا لَا تَهْوَىٰٓ أَنفُسُهُمْ فَرِيقًا كَذَّبُوا۟

وَفَرِيقًا يَقْتُلُونَ ۝

70. Laqad akhathna meethaqa banee isra-eela waarsalna ilayhim rusulan kullama jaahum rasoolun bima la tahwa anfusuhum fareeqan kaththaboo wafareeqan yaqtuloona

5:70. We did take the Covenant of the Children of Israel[30] and We sent to them Messengers. Whenever a Messenger came to them with what their hearts did not like, he was either contradicted or killed.

30. Please see Verses 2:63, 2:83 and 2:84 to know what the Covenant was about.

وَحَسِبُوٓا۟ أَلَّا تَكُونَ فِتْنَةٌ فَعَمُوا۟ وَصَمُّوا۟ ثُمَّ تَابَ ٱللَّهُ عَلَيْهِمْ

ثُمَّ عَمُوا۟ وَصَمُّوا۟ كَثِيرٌ مِّنْهُمْ وَٱللَّهُ بَصِيرٌۢ بِمَا يَعْمَلُونَ ۝

71. Wahasiboo alla takoona fitnatun faAAamoo wasammoo thumma taba Allahu AAalayhim thumma AAamoo wasammoo katheerun minhum waAllahu baseerun bima yaAAmaloona

5:71. And they thought that there would be no retribution, so they became blind and deaf. Then Allah forgave them, and thereafter too, many of them became blind and deaf. And Allah is watchful over what they do.

لَّقَدْ كَفَرَ ٱلَّذِينَ قَالُوٓاْ إِنَّ ٱللَّهَ هُوَ ٱلْمَسِيحُ ٱبْنُ مَرْيَمَ وَقَالَ ٱلْمَسِيحُ يَـٰبَنِىٓ إِسْرَٰٓءِيلَ ٱعْبُدُواْ ٱللَّهَ رَبِّى وَرَبَّكُمْ إِنَّهُۥ مَن يُشْرِكْ بِٱللَّهِ فَقَدْ حَرَّمَ ٱللَّهُ عَلَيْهِ ٱلْجَنَّةَ وَمَأْوَىٰهُ ٱلنَّارُ وَمَا لِلظَّـٰلِمِينَ مِنْ أَنصَارٍ ﴿٧٢﴾

72. Laqad kafara allatheena qaloo inna Allaha huwa almaseehu ibnu maryama waqala almaseehu ya banee isra-eela oAAbudoo Allaha rabbee warabbakum innahu man yushrik biAllahi faqad harrama Allahu AAalayhi aljannata wama/wahu alnnaru wama lilththalimeena min ansarin

5:72. They did certainly suppress the Truth, who said, "The Messiah, son of Mary, is indeed Allah." And the Messiah said, "O Children of Israel! Worship Allah, my Lord and your Lord. Whoever indeed associates others with Allah in his worship, then Allah has forbidden to him the Garden[31], and his abode is the Fire. And there shall be none to help the unjust."

31. It's a tragic paradox that the very Prophet who thus strongly advocated against association of anyone with Allah, himself got associated with Allah by his own so-called followers, the Christians! They are blissfully unaware that the Garden is forbidden to them in terms of what their own Prophet said. And they think that their Jesus has already given them their passports to Paradise!

لَّقَدْ كَفَرَ ٱلَّذِينَ قَالُوٓاْ إِنَّ ٱللَّهَ ثَالِثُ ثَلَـٰثَةٍ وَمَا مِنْ إِلَـٰهٍ إِلَّآ إِلَـٰهٌ وَٰحِدٌ وَإِن لَّمْ يَنتَهُواْ عَمَّا يَقُولُونَ لَيَمَسَّنَّ ٱلَّذِينَ كَفَرُواْ مِنْهُمْ عَذَابٌ أَلِيمٌ ﴿٧٣﴾

73. Laqad kafara allatheena qaloo inna Allaha thalithu thalathatin wama min ilahin illa ilahun wahidun wa-in lam yantahoo AAamma yaqooloona layamassanna allatheena kafaroo minhum AAathabun aleemun

5:73. They did certainly suppress the Truth, who said, "The third of the Trinity is indeed Allah." And there is none worthy of worship but the One Allah, and if they desist not from what they say, a painful punishment shall afflict those among them who suppress the Truth.

أَفَلَا يَتُوبُونَ إِلَى اللَّهِ وَيَسْتَغْفِرُونَهُ وَاللَّهُ غَفُورٌ رَّحِيمٌ

74. Afala yatooboona ila Allahi wayastaghfiroonahu waAllahu ghafoorun raheemun

5:74. Will they not then turn to Allah in repentance and ask for His forgiveness? And Allah is Forgiving, Merciful.

مَّا الْمَسِيحُ ابْنُ مَرْيَمَ إِلَّا رَسُولٌ قَدْ خَلَتْ مِن قَبْلِهِ الرُّسُلُ وَأُمُّهُ صِدِّيقَةٌ كَانَا يَأْكُلَانِ الطَّعَامَ انظُرْ كَيْفَ نُبَيِّنُ لَهُمُ الْآيَاتِ ثُمَّ انظُرْ أَنَّى يُؤْفَكُونَ

75. Ma almaseehu ibnu maryama illa rasoolun qad khalat min qablihi alrrusulu waommuhu siddeeqatun kana ya/kulani alttaAAama on_thur kayfa nubayyinu lahumu al-ayati thumma on_thur anna yu/fakoona

5:75. The Messiah, son of Mary, was but a Messenger. Messengers did come and pass away before him. And his mother was a truthful woman. They both used to eat food. See how We make the Verses/signs clear to them. Then see how they are turned away.

قُلْ أَتَعْبُدُونَ مِن دُونِ اللَّهِ مَا لَا يَمْلِكُ لَكُمْ ضَرًّا وَلَا نَفْعًا وَاللَّهُ هُوَ السَّمِيعُ الْعَلِيمُ

76. Qul ataAAbudoona min dooni Allahi ma la yamliku lakum _darran wala nafAAan waAllahu huwa alssameeAAu alAAaleemu

5:76. Say, "Do you worship, besides Allah, that which is incapable of inflicting any harm on you, or conferring any benefit? And Allah – He is the One listening, knowing."

قُلْ يَـٰٓأَهْلَ ٱلْكِتَـٰبِ لَا تَغْلُواْ فِى دِينِكُمْ غَيْرَ ٱلْحَقِّ وَلَا تَتَّبِعُوٓاْ أَهْوَآءَ قَوْمٍ قَدْ ضَلُّواْ مِن قَبْلُ وَأَضَلُّواْ كَثِيرًا وَضَلُّواْ عَن سَوَآءِ ٱلسَّبِيلِ ﴿٧٧﴾

77. Qul ya ahla alkitabi la taghloo fee deenikum ghayra alhaqqi wala tattabiAAoo ahwaa qawmin qad dalloo min qablu waadalloo katheeran wadalloo AAan sawa-i alssabeeli

5:77. Say, "O people of the Book! Commit no unjust excesses in your religion (way of life) and follow not the vain desires of people who went astray before, and who led many astray and (themselves) went astray from the Right Path."[32]

32. At the time of revelation of the Qur'aan, this divine directive was addressed to the Jews and the Christians. But now, it is equally applicable to the Muslims. They too are the people of the Book and they too are committing unjust excesses in their religion, as do the Christians and the Jews. Through the *ahaadeeth* and through the "learned" books of the *fuqaha* they have unjustly made additions to and subtractions from their Religion, and have thus polluted the pristine purity, clarity and beauty of Qur'aanic Islam.

لُعِنَ ٱلَّذِينَ كَفَرُواْ مِنۢ بَنِىٓ إِسْرَٰٓءِيلَ عَلَىٰ لِسَانِ دَاوُۥدَ وَعِيسَى ٱبْنِ مَرْيَمَ ذَٰلِكَ بِمَا عَصَواْ وَّكَانُواْ يَعْتَدُونَ ﴿٧٨﴾

78. LuAAina allatheena kafaroo min banee isra-eela AAala lisani dawooda waAAeesa ibni maryama thalika bima AAasaw wakanoo yaAAtadoona

5:78. Cursed by the tongue of David and Jesus, son of Mary, were those who suppressed the Truth from among the Children of Israel. That was because they disobeyed and were transgressors.

كَانُواْ لَا يَتَنَاهَوْنَ عَن مُّنكَرٍ فَعَلُوهُ لَبِئْسَ مَا كَانُواْ يَفْعَلُونَ ﴿٧٩﴾

79. Kanoo la yatanahawna AAan munkarin faAAaloohu labi/sa ma kanoo yafAAaloona

5:79. They were not forbidding one another from the forbidden things they did. What they did was certainly bad.[33]

---

33. This Verse, just as the preceding Verse, is about the Jews. But it is applicable to most Muslims of the present age also. They too do things that are forbidden in the Qur'aan. And they are not forbidding one another from doing those forbidden things. And, I am afraid, the next two Verses too are applicable to many a Muslim today!

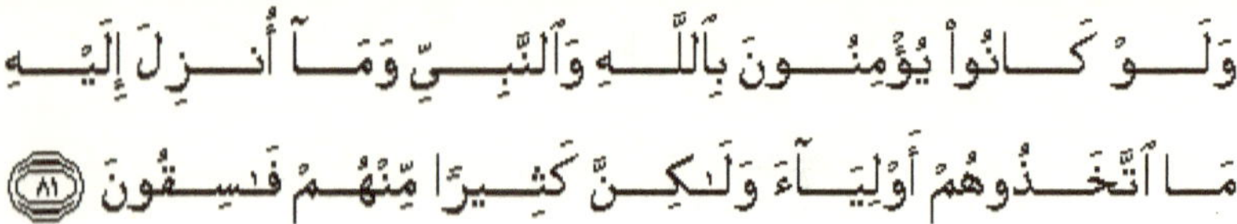

80. Tara katheeran minhum yatawallawna allatheena kafaroo labi/sa ma qaddamat lahum anfusuhum an sakhita Allahu AAalayhim wafee alAAathabi hum khalidoona

---

5:80. You see many of them being close to those who suppress the Truth. What their sensual selves have sent ahead for them is certainly so bad that Allah is displeased with them. And in punishment shall they abide.

---

81. Walaw kanoo yu/minoona biAllahi waalnnabiyyi wama onzila ilayhi ma ittakhathoohum awliyaa walakinna katheeran minhum fasiqoona

---

5:81. And had they believed in Allah, in the prophet and in what is sent down to him, they would not have taken them for close friends. But most of them are transgressors/profligates.

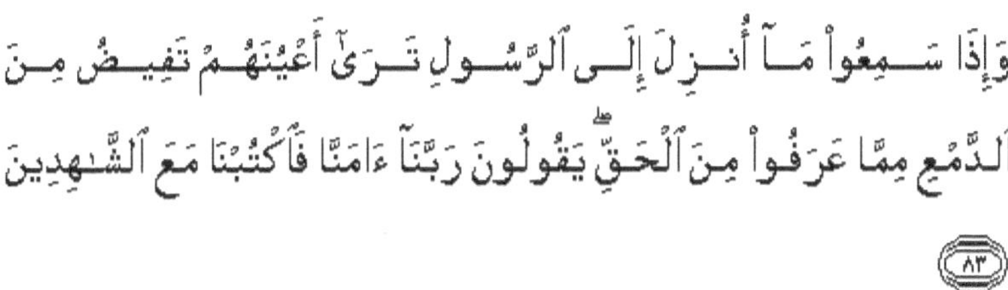

82. Latajidanna ashadda alnnasi AAadawatan lillatheena amanoo alyahooda waallatheena ashrakoo walatajidanna aqrabahum mawaddatan lillatheena amanoo allatheena qaloo inna nasara thalika bi-anna minhum qisseeseena waruhbanan waannahum la yastakbiroona

5:82. You will certainly find the Jews and the polytheists to be the bitterest people in hostility towards those who believe. And you will certainly find the nearest in friendship to those who believe, to be those who say, "We are Christians." That is because there are priests and monks among them who do not behave proudly.

83. Wa-itha samiAAoo ma onzila ila alrrasooli tara aAAyunahum tafeedu mina alddamAAi mimma AAarafoo mina alhaqqi yaqooloona rabbana amanna faoktubna maAAa alshshahideena

5:83. And when they[34] listen to what has been sent down upon the Messenger, you see their eyes overflowing with tears because of the truth they recognise. They say, "Our Lord! We believe, so enlist us among those who give witness."

34. 'they' here were the Christian priests and monks living at the time the Qur'aan was revealed, referred to in the preceding Verse 5:82 and who did not behave proudly. What these good people then said is recorded at the end of this Verse as well as in the next Verse.

وَمَا لَنَا لَا نُؤْمِنُ بِٱللَّهِ وَمَا جَآءَنَا مِنَ ٱلْحَقِّ وَنَطْمَعُ أَن يُدْخِلَنَا رَبُّنَا مَعَ ٱلْقَوْمِ ٱلصَّلِحِينَ ۝

84. Wama lana la nu/minu biAllahi wama jaana mina alhaqqi wanatmaAAu an yudkhilana rabbuna maAAa alqawmi alssaliheena

5:84. "And why should we not believe in Allah and in that which has come to us of the truth? And we earnestly desire that our Lord admits us to be with the righteous people."

فَأَثَـٰبَهُمُ ٱللَّهُ بِمَا قَالُوا۟ جَنَّـٰتٍ تَجْرِى مِن تَحْتِهَا ٱلْأَنْهَـٰرُ خَـٰلِدِينَ فِيهَا وَذَٰلِكَ جَزَآءُ ٱلْمُحْسِنِينَ ۝

85. Faathabahumu Allahu bima qaloo jannatin tajree min tahtiha al-anharu khalideena feeha wathalika jazao almuhsineena

5:85. Allah then would reward them, because of what they say, gardens, with rivers flowing underneath, to abide therein. And that is the reward of those who do good deeds.

وَٱلَّذِينَ كَفَرُوا۟ وَكَذَّبُوا۟ بِـَٔايَـٰتِنَا أُو۟لَـٰٓئِكَ أَصْحَـٰبُ ٱلْجَحِيمِ ۝

86. Waallatheena kafaroo wakaththaboo bi-ayatina ola-ika as-habu aljaheemi

5:86. And those who suppress the Truth and treat Our Verses/signs as lies – they are the dwellers of the Fire.

يَـٰٓأَيُّهَا ٱلَّذِينَ ءَامَنُوا۟ لَا تُحَرِّمُوا۟ طَيِّبَـٰتِ مَآ أَحَلَّ ٱللَّهُ لَكُمْ وَلَا تَعْتَدُوٓا۟ إِنَّ ٱللَّهَ لَا يُحِبُّ ٱلْمُعْتَدِينَ ۝

87. Ya ayyuha allatheena amanoo la tuharrimoo tayyibati ma ahalla Allahu lakum wala taAAtadoo inna Allaha la yuhibbu almuAAtadeena

5:87. O you who believe! Forbid not the good, wholesome things which Allah has made lawful for you, and transgress not! Indeed, Allah loves not those who transgress.

وَكُلُواْ مِمَّا رَزَقَكُمُ ٱللَّهُ حَلَٰلًا طَيِّبًا وَٱتَّقُواْ ٱللَّهَ ٱلَّذِىٓ أَنتُم بِهِۦ مُؤْمِنُونَ ۝

88. Wakuloo mimma razaqakumu Allahu halalan tayyiban waittaqoo Allaha allathee antum bihi mu/minoona

5:88. And eat of the lawful and good, wholesome things that Allah has provided for you, and fear Allah, Whom you believe.

لَا يُؤَاخِذُكُمُ ٱللَّهُ بِٱللَّغْوِ فِىٓ أَيْمَٰنِكُمْ وَلَٰكِن يُؤَاخِذُكُم بِمَا عَقَّدتُّمُ ٱلْأَيْمَٰنَ فَكَفَّٰرَتُهُۥٓ إِطْعَامُ عَشَرَةِ مَسَٰكِينَ مِنْ أَوْسَطِ مَا تُطْعِمُونَ أَهْلِيكُمْ أَوْ كِسْوَتُهُمْ أَوْ تَحْرِيرُ رَقَبَةٍ فَمَن لَّمْ يَجِدْ فَصِيَامُ ثَلَٰثَةِ أَيَّامٍ ذَٰلِكَ كَفَّٰرَةُ أَيْمَٰنِكُمْ إِذَا حَلَفْتُمْ وَٱحْفَظُوٓاْ أَيْمَٰنَكُمْ كَذَٰلِكَ يُبَيِّنُ ٱللَّهُ لَكُمْ ءَايَٰتِهِۦ لَعَلَّكُمْ تَشْكُرُونَ ۝

89. La yu-akhithukumu Allahu biallaghwi fee aymanikum walakin yu-akhithukum bima AAaqqadtumu al-aymana fakaffaratuhu itAAamu AAasharati masakeena min awsati ma tutAAimoona ahleekum aw kiswatuhum aw tahreeru raqabatin faman lam yajid fasiyamu thalathati ayyamin thalika kaffaratu aymanikum itha halaftum waihfathoo aymanakum kathalika yubayyinu Allahu lakum ayatihi laAAallakum tashkuroona

5:89. Allah does not call you to account for anything trivial in your oaths, but He calls you to account for the binding terms of your oaths. The expiation of it, then, is the feeding of ten poor persons with the average food you feed your families with, or their clothing, or the freeing of a neck[35]. And for the one, who cannot afford, three days of fasting. That is the expiation of your oaths when you take them. And guard your oaths! Thus, does Allah make clear to you His Verses, so that you may feel grateful.

35. I.e. freeing a human being from bondage. In modern times too, we have bonded labour. The have-nots' poor financial condition becomes a breeding ground for their exploitation by the rich. The poor get immersed in their debts and thus become bonded labour for the rich. To help such poor people to be free of their debts would be equivalent to freeing their necks.

يَٰٓأَيُّهَا ٱلَّذِينَ ءَامَنُوٓاْ إِنَّمَا ٱلْخَمْرُ وَٱلْمَيْسِرُ وَٱلْأَنصَابُ وَٱلْأَزْلَٰمُ رِجْسٌ مِّنْ عَمَلِ ٱلشَّيْطَٰنِ فَٱجْتَنِبُوهُ لَعَلَّكُمْ تُفْلِحُونَ ﴿٩٠﴾

90. Ya ayyuha allatheena amanoo innama alkhamru waalmaysiru waal-ansabu waal-azlamu rijsun min AAamali alshshaytani fajtaniboohu laAAallakum tuflihoona

5:90. O you who believe! Intoxicants, games of chance, animals sacrificed at the altars of idols and divining by arrows[36] are just aspects of an abomination from among Satan's doings. Shun it then, to attain salvation.

36. Please refer study note 5:5 for the meaning of the corresponding Arabic term *al-azlamu*

إِنَّمَا يُرِيدُ ٱلشَّيْطَٰنُ أَن يُوقِعَ بَيْنَكُمُ ٱلْعَدَٰوَةَ وَٱلْبَغْضَآءَ فِى ٱلْخَمْرِ وَٱلْمَيْسِرِ وَيَصُدَّكُمْ عَن ذِكْرِ ٱللَّهِ وَعَنِ ٱلصَّلَوٰةِ فَهَلْ أَنتُم مُّنتَهُونَ ﴿٩١﴾

91. Innama yureedu alshshaytanu an yooqiAAa baynakumu alAAadawata waalbaghdaa fee alkhamri waalmaysiri wayasuddakum AAan thikri Allahi waAAani alssalati fahal antum muntahoona

5:91. The Satan only desires to cause enmity and hatred in your midst by means of intoxicants and games of chance, and to keep you off remembrance of Allah, and off prayer. Won't you then desist?

$$\text{وَأَطِيعُوا۟ ٱللَّهَ وَأَطِيعُوا۟ ٱلرَّسُولَ وَٱحْذَرُوا۟ فَإِن تَوَلَّيْتُمْ فَٱعْلَمُوٓا۟ أَنَّمَا عَلَىٰ}$$

$$\text{رَسُولِنَا ٱلْبَلَـٰغُ ٱلْمُبِينُ ﴿٩٢﴾}$$

92. WaateeAAoo Allaha waateeAAoo alrrasoola waihtharoo fa-in tawallaytum faiAAlamoo annama AAala rasoolina albalaghu almubeenu

5:92. And obey Allah and obey the Messenger[37] and beware! If you then turn back, know that the responsibility on Our Messenger is but clear conveyance of the divine Message.

37. About the directive to obey the Messenger, please see footnotes 3:144 to 3:146 on Verse 3.132.

$$\text{لَيْسَ عَلَى ٱلَّذِينَ ءَامَنُوا۟ وَعَمِلُوا۟ ٱلصَّـٰلِحَـٰتِ جُنَاحٌ فِيمَا}$$

$$\text{طَعِمُوٓا۟ إِذَا مَا ٱتَّقَوا۟ وَّءَامَنُوا۟ وَعَمِلُوا۟ ٱلصَّـٰلِحَـٰتِ ثُمَّ ٱتَّقَوا۟ وَّءَامَنُوا۟}$$

$$\text{ثُمَّ ٱتَّقَوا۟ وَّأَحْسَنُوا۟ وَٱللَّهُ يُحِبُّ ٱلْمُحْسِنِينَ ﴿٩٣﴾}$$

93. Laysa AAala allatheena amanoo waAAamiloo alssalihati junahun feema taAAimoo itha ma ittaqaw waamanoo waAAamiloo alssalihati thumma ittaqaw waamanoo thumma ittaqaw waahsanoo waAllahu yuhibbu almuhsineena

5:93. Upon those who believed and did good deeds, there is no sin in what they had eaten earlier, so long as they feared Allah, and believed, and did good deeds. Then they feared Allah and believed. Then they feared Allah and did good work[38]. And Allah loves those who do good work.

38. Good work includes not only performing religious duties like praying and fasting as ordained, but also doing one's worldly work like, say, carpentry, to the best of one's abilities.

يَـٰٓأَيُّهَا ٱلَّذِينَ ءَامَنُوا۟ لَيَبْلُوَنَّكُمُ ٱللَّهُ بِشَىْءٍ مِّنَ ٱلصَّيْدِ تَنَالُهُۥ أَيْدِيكُمْ وَرِمَاحُكُمْ لِيَعْلَمَ ٱللَّهُ مَن يَخَافُهُۥ بِٱلْغَيْبِ فَمَنِ ٱعْتَدَىٰ بَعْدَ ذَٰلِكَ فَلَهُۥ عَذَابٌ أَلِيمٌ ۝

94. Y<u>a</u> ayyuh<u>a</u> alla<u>th</u>eena <u>a</u>manoo layabluwannakumu All<u>a</u>hu bishay-in mina al<u>ss</u>aydi tan<u>a</u>luhu aydeekum warim<u>a</u>hukum liyaAAlama All<u>a</u>hu man yakh<u>a</u>fuhu bialghaybi famani iAAtad<u>a</u> baAAda <u>tha</u>lika falahu AAa<u>th</u>abun aleem**un**

5:94. O you who believe! Allah will certainly test you in respect of game within reach of your hands and your lances, that Allah might know who fears Him unseen. A painful punishment then for the one, who transgresses after this.[39]

---

39. This Verse was revealed obviously with reference to the next Verse prohibiting hunting while in the state of *Ihram*.

يَـٰٓأَيُّهَا ٱلَّذِينَ ءَامَنُوا۟ لَا تَقْتُلُوا۟ ٱلصَّيْدَ وَأَنتُمْ حُرُمٌ وَمَن قَتَلَهُۥ مِنكُم مُّتَعَمِّدًا فَجَزَآءٌ مِّثْلُ مَا قَتَلَ مِنَ ٱلنَّعَمِ يَحْكُمُ بِهِۦ ذَوَا عَدْلٍ مِّنكُمْ هَدْيًۢا بَـٰلِغَ ٱلْكَعْبَةِ أَوْ كَفَّـٰرَةٌ طَعَامُ مَسَـٰكِينَ أَوْ عَدْلُ ذَٰلِكَ صِيَامًا لِّيَذُوقَ وَبَالَ أَمْرِهِۦ عَفَا ٱللَّهُ عَمَّا سَلَفَ وَمَنْ عَادَ فَيَنتَقِمُ ٱللَّهُ مِنْهُ وَٱللَّهُ عَزِيزٌ ذُو ٱنتِقَامٍ ۝

95. Y<u>a</u> ayyuh<u>a</u> alla<u>th</u>eena <u>a</u>manoo l<u>a</u> taqtuloo al<u>ss</u>ayda waantum <u>h</u>urumun waman qatalahu minkum mutaAAammidan fajaz<u>a</u>on mithlu m<u>a</u> qatala mina alnnaAAami ya<u>h</u>kumu bihi <u>tha</u>w<u>a</u> AAadlin minkum hadyan b<u>a</u>ligha alkaAAbati aw kaff<u>a</u>ratun <u>ta</u>AA<u>a</u>mu mas<u>a</u>keena aw AAadlu <u>tha</u>lika <u>s</u>iy<u>a</u>man liya<u>th</u>ooqa wab<u>a</u>la amrihi AAaf<u>a</u> All<u>a</u>hu AAamm<u>a</u> salafa waman AA<u>a</u>da fayantaqimu All<u>a</u>hu minhu waAll<u>a</u>hu AAazeezun <u>th</u>oo intiq<u>a</u>m**in**

5:95. O you who believe! Kill not the game while you are in the state of *Ihram*. And whoever among you kills it intentionally, the penalty is the like of what he killed, from the cattle, as adjudged by two just persons among you, as an offering to be brought to the Kaabah – Or the expiation therefor is the feeding of the poor or commensurate fasting – so that whoever killed the game, may taste the burden of his deed. Allah has forgiven what is past. And whoever does it again, Allah will take retribution from him. And Allah is Omnipotent, Capable to take retribution.

أُحِلَّ لَكُمْ صَيْدُ ٱلْبَحْرِ وَطَعَامُهُۥ مَتَٰعًا لَّكُمْ وَلِلسَّيَّارَةِ وَحُرِّمَ عَلَيْكُمْ صَيْدُ ٱلْبَرِّ مَا دُمْتُمْ حُرُمًا وَٱتَّقُوا۟ ٱللَّهَ ٱلَّذِىٓ إِلَيْهِ تُحْشَرُونَ ﴿٩٦﴾

96. Ohilla lakum saydu albahri wataAAamuhu mataAAan lakum walilssayyarati wahurrima AAalaykum saydu albarri ma dumtum huruman waittaqoo Allaha allathee ilayhi tuhsharoona

5:96. Lawful to you is the sea game and its food – a provision for you and for the travellers – and the land game is forbidden to you so long as you are in the state of *Ihram*. And fear Allah, to Whom you shall be gathered.

۞ جَعَلَ ٱللَّهُ ٱلْكَعْبَةَ ٱلْبَيْتَ ٱلْحَرَامَ قِيَٰمًا لِّلنَّاسِ وَٱلشَّهْرَ ٱلْحَرَامَ وَٱلْهَدْىَ وَٱلْقَلَٰٓئِدَ ذَٰلِكَ لِتَعْلَمُوٓا۟ أَنَّ ٱللَّهَ يَعْلَمُ مَا فِى ٱلسَّمَٰوَٰتِ وَمَا فِى ٱلْأَرْضِ وَأَنَّ ٱللَّهَ بِكُلِّ شَىْءٍ عَلِيمٌ ﴿٩٧﴾

97. JaAAala Allahu alkaAAabata albayta alharama qiyaman lilnnasi waalshshahra alharama waalhadya waalqala-ida thalika litaAAlamoo anna Allaha yaAAlamu ma fee alssamawati wama fee al-ardi waanna Allaha bikulli shay-in AAaleemun

5:97. Allah has made the sacred house of the Kaabah a symbol for the people to stand by, so also the sacred month, the offerings and the animals with garlands. It is a symbolic recognition that Allah has knowledge of all that is in the heavens and all that is in the earth, and that Allah is aware of all things.

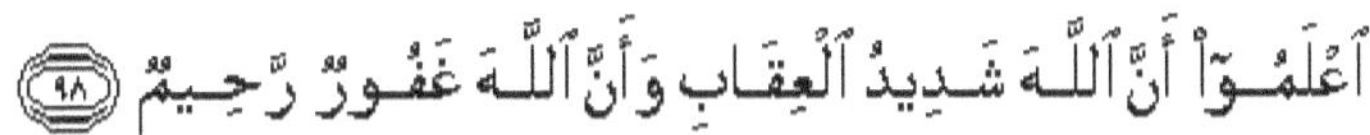

ٱعْلَمُوٓا۟ أَنَّ ٱللَّهَ شَدِيدُ ٱلْعِقَابِ وَأَنَّ ٱللَّهَ غَفُورٌ رَّحِيمٌ ﴿٩٨﴾

98. IAAlamoo anna Allaha shadeedu alAAiqabi waanna Allaha ghafoorun raheemun

---

5:98. Know that Allah is severe in punishment, and that Allah is Forgiving, Merciful.

مَّا عَلَى ٱلرَّسُولِ إِلَّا ٱلْبَلَـٰغُ ۗ وَٱللَّهُ يَعْلَمُ مَا تُبْدُونَ وَمَا تَكْتُمُونَ ﴿٩٩﴾

99. Ma AAala alrrasooli illa albalaghu waAllahu yaAAlamu ma tubdoona wama taktumoona

---

5:99. The Messenger's responsibility is but to deliver. And Allah knows what you reveal, and what you conceal.

قُل لَّا يَسْتَوِى ٱلْخَبِيثُ وَٱلطَّيِّبُ وَلَوْ أَعْجَبَكَ كَثْرَةُ ٱلْخَبِيثِ ۚ فَٱتَّقُوا۟ ٱللَّهَ يَـٰٓأُو۟لِى ٱلْأَلْبَـٰبِ لَعَلَّكُمْ تُفْلِحُونَ ﴿١٠٠﴾

100. Qul la yastawee alkhabeethu waalttayyibu walaw aAAjabaka kathratu alkhabeethi faittaqoo Allaha ya olee al-albabi laAAallakum tuflihoona

---

5:100. Say, "The impure and the pure are not the same, although many of the the impure things may please you. So, O those endowed with insight, fear Allah to become successful!"

يَٰٓأَيُّهَا ٱلَّذِينَ ءَامَنُوا۟ لَا تَسْـَٔلُوا۟ عَنْ أَشْيَآءَ إِن تُبْدَ لَكُمْ تَسُؤْكُمْ وَإِن

تَسْـَٔلُوا۟ عَنْهَا حِينَ يُنَزَّلُ ٱلْقُرْءَانُ تُبْدَ لَكُمْ عَفَا ٱللَّهُ عَنْهَا وَٱللَّهُ غَفُورٌ

حَلِيمٌ ۝ ١٠١

101. Ya ayyuha allatheena amanoo la tas-aloo AAan ashyaa in tubda lakum tasu/kum wa-in tas-aloo AAanha heena yunazzalu alqur-anu tubda lakum AAafa Allahu AAanha waAllahu ghafoorun haleemun

---

5:101. O you who believe! Do not put questions about things, which, if clarified to you, may cause difficulties for you. And if you put questions about them when the Qur'aan is being revealed, they may be clarified to you. Allah has absolved you of any obligation thereon.[40] And Allah is Forgiving, Kind.

---

40. This Verse makes it clear that in matters in which the Qur'aan is silent, mankind has freedom of action.

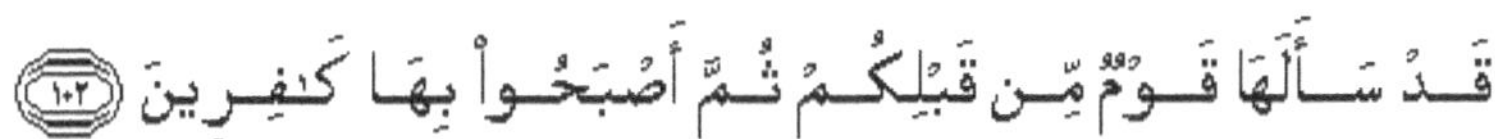

قَدْ سَأَلَهَا قَوْمٌ مِّن قَبْلِكُمْ ثُمَّ أَصْبَحُوا۟ بِهَا كَٰفِرِينَ ۝ ١٠٢

102. Qad saalaha qawmun min qablikum thumma asbahoo biha kafireena

---

5:102. A people before you did ask such questions, and then became suppressors of the Truth, on that account.[41]

---

41. People referred to here are the Children of Israel. (See Verses 2:67 to 2:71)

مَا جَعَلَ ٱللَّهُ مِنۢ بَحِيرَةٍ وَلَا سَآئِبَةٍ وَلَا وَصِيلَةٍ وَلَا حَامٍ وَلَٰكِنَّ ٱلَّذِينَ كَفَرُواْ يَفْتَرُونَ عَلَى ٱللَّهِ ٱلْكَذِبَ ۖ وَأَكْثَرُهُمْ لَا يَعْقِلُونَ ۝

103. Ma jaAAala Allahu min baheeratin wala sa-ibatin wala waseelatin wala hamin walakinna allatheena kafaroo yaftaroona AAala Allahi alkathiba waaktharuhum la yaAAqiloona

---

5:103. Allah has not made any *bahirah, saibah, wasilah* or *ham*[42], but those who suppress the Truth fabricate the lie against Allah. And most of them understand not.

---

42. Obviously, these are names of some superstitious things the Arabs did during their earlier days of ignorance. As the next Verse indicates, those Arabs were just following what they found their fathers doing.

وَإِذَا قِيلَ لَهُمْ تَعَالَوْاْ إِلَىٰ مَآ أَنزَلَ ٱللَّهُ وَإِلَى ٱلرَّسُولِ قَالُواْ حَسْبُنَا مَا وَجَدْنَا عَلَيْهِ ءَابَآءَنَآ ۚ أَوَلَوْ كَانَ ءَابَآؤُهُمْ لَا يَعْلَمُونَ شَيْئًا وَلَا يَهْتَدُونَ ۝

104. Wa-itha qeela lahum taAAalaw ila ma anzala Allahu wa-ila alrrasooli qaloo hasbuna ma wajadna AAalayhi abaana awa law kana abaohum la yaAAlamoona shay-an wala yahtadoona

---

5:104. And when it is said to them, "Come to what Allah has sent down and to the Messenger", they say, "What we found our fathers with, is sufficient for us". What! Even though their fathers knew nothing and followed not the right guidance!?

$$\text{يَٰٓأَيُّهَا ٱلَّذِينَ ءَامَنُواْ عَلَيْكُمْ أَنفُسَكُمْ ۖ لَا يَضُرُّكُم مَّن ضَلَّ إِذَا ٱهْتَدَيْتُمْ ۚ إِلَى ٱللَّهِ مَرْجِعُكُمْ جَمِيعًا فَيُنَبِّئُكُم بِمَا كُنتُمْ تَعْمَلُونَ ۝}$$

105. Ya ayyuha allatheena amanoo AAalaykum anfusakum la yadurrukum man dalla itha ihtadaytum ila Allahi marjiAAukum jameeAAan fayunabbi-okum bima kuntum taAAmaloona

---

5:105. O you who believe! You are responsible for your own selves. He who errs cannot hurt you when you are on the right path.[43] To Allah you all are to return, when He will inform you of what you did.

---

43. Muslims would not be in the doldrums, they are in today, had they unshakeable faith in the divine statement of this Verse.

$$\text{يَٰٓأَيُّهَا ٱلَّذِينَ ءَامَنُواْ شَهَٰدَةُ بَيْنِكُمْ إِذَا حَضَرَ أَحَدَكُمُ ٱلْمَوْتُ حِينَ ٱلْوَصِيَّةِ ٱثْنَانِ ذَوَا عَدْلٍ مِّنكُمْ أَوْ ءَاخَرَانِ مِنْ غَيْرِكُمْ إِنْ أَنتُمْ ضَرَبْتُمْ فِى ٱلْأَرْضِ فَأَصَٰبَتْكُم مُّصِيبَةُ ٱلْمَوْتِ ۚ تَحْبِسُونَهُمَا مِنۢ بَعْدِ ٱلصَّلَوٰةِ فَيُقْسِمَانِ بِٱللَّهِ إِنِ ٱرْتَبْتُمْ لَا نَشْتَرِى بِهِۦ ثَمَنًا وَلَوْ كَانَ ذَا قُرْبَىٰ وَلَا نَكْتُمُ شَهَٰدَةَ ٱللَّهِ إِنَّآ إِذًا لَّمِنَ ٱلْءَاثِمِينَ ۝}$$

106. Ya ayyuha allatheena amanoo shahadatu baynikum itha hadara ahadakumu almawtu heena alwasiyyati ithnani thawa AAadlin minkum aw akharani min ghayrikum in antum darabtum fee al-ardi faasabatkum museebatu almawti tahbisoonahuma min baAAdi alssalati fayuqsimani biAllahi ini irtabtum la nashtaree bihi thamanan walaw kana tha qurba wala naktumu shahadata Allahi inna ithan lamina al-athimeena

---

5:106. O you who believe! When death approaches any of you, call to witness among you, at the time of making the will, two just persons from among you, or two from among others than you, if you are travelling in the land and death befalls you. Detain the two after the prayer, then, if you are in doubt, they shall both swear by Allah, "We will not sell it for a price – and even though it is for a relative – and we will not hide the testimony. By Allah, then, certainly, we should be among the sinners."

فَإِنْ عُثِرَ عَلَىٰٓ أَنَّهُمَا ٱسْتَحَقَّآ إِثْمًا فَـَٔاخَرَانِ يَقُومَانِ مَقَامَهُمَا مِنَ ٱلَّذِينَ ٱسْتَحَقَّ عَلَيْهِمُ ٱلْأَوْلَيَٰنِ فَيُقْسِمَانِ بِٱللَّهِ لَشَهَٰدَتُنَآ أَحَقُّ مِن شَهَٰدَتِهِمَا وَمَا ٱعْتَدَيْنَآ إِنَّآ إِذًا لَّمِنَ ٱلظَّٰلِمِينَ ۝

107. Fa-in AAuthira AAala annahuma istahaqqa ithman faakharani yaqoomani maqamahuma mina allatheena istahaqqa AAalayhimu al-awlayani fayuqsimani biAllahi lashahadatuna ahaqqu min shahadatihima wama iAAtadayna inna ithan lamina alththalimeena

5:107. Then if it becomes known that they both have been guilty of a sin, two others shall stand up in their place from among those, nearest in kin, who have a rightful claim. Then the two should swear by Allah, "Certainly our testimony is truer than the testimony of those two, and we have not committed any trespass. We should then indeed be of those who oppress."

ذَٰلِكَ أَدْنَىٰٓ أَن يَأْتُوا۟ بِٱلشَّهَٰدَةِ عَلَىٰ وَجْهِهَآ أَوْ يَخَافُوٓا۟ أَن تُرَدَّ أَيْمَٰنٌ بَعْدَ أَيْمَٰنِهِمْ وَٱتَّقُوا۟ ٱللَّهَ وَٱسْمَعُوا۟ وَٱللَّهُ لَا يَهْدِى ٱلْقَوْمَ ٱلْفَٰسِقِينَ ۝

108. Thalika adna an ya/too bialshshahadati AAala wajhiha aw yakhafoo an turadda aymanun baAAda aymanihim waittaqoo Allaha waismaAAoo waAllahu la yahdee alqawma alfasiqeena

5:108. That should make the testimony more transparent. Or else, they may fear rejection of other testimonies after theirs. And fear Allah and listen. And Allah does not guide the transgressing people.

يَوْمَ يَجْمَعُ ٱللَّهُ ٱلرُّسُلَ فَيَقُولُ مَاذَآ أُجِبْتُمْ قَالُواْ لَا عِلْمَ لَنَآ إِنَّكَ أَنتَ عَلَّـٰمُ ٱلْغُيُوبِ ﴿١٠٩﴾

109. Yawma yajmaAAu Allahu alrrusula fayaqoolu matha ojibtum qaloo la AAilma lana innaka anta AAallamu alghuyoobi

5:109. The day when Allah will assemble the Messengers, then ask them, "What response did you get?", they will say, "We have no knowledge. Indeed! You are the Knower of the unseen things."

إِذْ قَالَ ٱللَّهُ يَـٰعِيسَى ٱبْنَ مَرْيَمَ ٱذْكُرْ نِعْمَتِى عَلَيْكَ وَعَلَىٰ وَٰلِدَتِكَ إِذْ أَيَّدتُّكَ بِرُوحِ ٱلْقُدُسِ تُكَلِّمُ ٱلنَّاسَ فِى ٱلْمَهْدِ وَكَهْلًا وَإِذْ عَلَّمْتُكَ ٱلْكِتَـٰبَ وَٱلْحِكْمَةَ وَٱلتَّوْرَٰةَ وَٱلْإِنجِيلَ وَإِذْ تَخْلُقُ مِنَ ٱلطِّينِ كَهَيْـَٔةِ ٱلطَّيْرِ بِإِذْنِى فَتَنفُخُ فِيهَا فَتَكُونُ طَيْرًا بِإِذْنِى وَتُبْرِئُ ٱلْأَكْمَهَ وَٱلْأَبْرَصَ بِإِذْنِى وَإِذْ تُخْرِجُ ٱلْمَوْتَىٰ بِإِذْنِى وَإِذْ كَفَفْتُ بَنِى إِسْرَٰٓئِيلَ عَنكَ إِذْ جِئْتَهُم بِٱلْبَيِّنَـٰتِ فَقَالَ ٱلَّذِينَ كَفَرُواْ مِنْهُمْ إِنْ هَـٰذَآ إِلَّا سِحْرٌ مُّبِينٌ ﴿١١٠﴾

110. Ith qala Allahu ya AAeesa ibna maryama othkur niAAmatee AAalayka waAAala walidatika ith ayyadtuka biroohi alqudusi tukallimu alnnasa fee almahdi wakahlan wa-ith AAallamtuka alkitaba waalhikmata waalttawrata waal-injeela wa-ith takhluqu mina altteeni kahay-ati alttayri bi-ithnee fatanfukhu feeha fatakoonu tayran bi-ithnee watubri-o al-akmaha waal-abrasa bi-ithnee wa-ith tukhriju almawta bi-ithnee wa-ith kafaftu banee isra-eela AAanka ith ji/tahum bialbayyinati faqala allatheena kafaroo minhum in hatha illa sihrun mubeenun

5:110. When Allah will say,"O Jesus, son of Mary! Remember My Favour on you and on your mother, when I supported you with the holy Spirit, you spoke to the people in the cradle and as an adult, and when I taught you the Book and the wisdom and the Torah and the Gospel, and when you made out of clay a bird-like figure by My permission, then you breathed into it and it became a bird by My permission, and you healed the blind and the leprous by My permission, and when you brought out the dead by My permission, and when I restrained the children of Israel from you as you came to them with clear signs, but those who suppressed the Truth from among them said, 'This is nothing but pure magic'."

وَإِذْ أَوْحَيْتُ إِلَى ٱلْحَوَارِيِّــنَ أَنْ ءَامِنُواْ بِى وَبِرَسُولِى قَالُوٓاْ ءَامَنَّا وَٱشْهَدْ بِأَنَّنَا مُسْلِمُونَ ۝

111. Wa-ith awhaytu ila alhawariyyeena an aminoo bee wabirasoolee qaloo amanna waishhad bi-annana muslimoona

5:111. And when I inspired the disciples[44] to believe in Me and in My Messenger, they said, "We do believe and bear witness that we do submit."

44. As the next Verse indicates, these were Jesus' disciples.

إِذْ قَالَ ٱلْحَــوَارِيُّونَ يَٰعِيسَــى ٱبْـنَ مَـرْيَمَ هَـلْ يَسْـتَطِيعُ رَبُّـكَ أَن يُنَزِّلَ عَلَيْنَا مَآئِدَةً مِّـنَ ٱلسَّـمَآءِ قَالَ ٱتَّقُـواْ ٱللَّـهَ إِن كُنتُم مُّؤْمِنِينَ ۝

112. Ith qala alhawariyyoona ya AAeesa ibna maryama hal yastateeAAu rabbuka an yunazzila AAalayna ma-idatan mina alssama-i qala ittaqoo Allaha in kuntum mu/mineena

5:112. When the disciples asked, "O Jesus, son of Mary! Can your Lord send down to us a table spread with food from heaven?" He said, "Fear Allah, if you are believers."

قَالُواْ نُرِيدُ أَن نَّأْكُلَ مِنْهَا وَتَطْمَئِنَّ قُلُوبُنَا وَنَعْلَمَ أَن قَدْ صَدَقْتَنَا وَنَكُونَ عَلَيْهَا مِنَ ٱلشَّـٰهِدِينَ ﴿١١٣﴾

113. Qaloo nureedu an na/kula minha watatma-inna quloobuna wanaAAlama an qad sadaqtana wanakoona AAalayha mina alshshahideena

5:113. They said, "We wish to eat there from, satisfy our minds, know that you have indeed told us the truth and be of the witnesses to it."

قَالَ عِيسَى ٱبْنُ مَرْيَمَ ٱللَّهُمَّ رَبَّنَآ أَنزِلْ عَلَيْنَا مَآئِدَةً مِّنَ ٱلسَّمَآءِ تَكُونُ لَنَا عِيدًا لِّأَوَّلِنَا وَءَاخِرِنَا وَءَايَةً مِّنكَ وَٱرْزُقْنَا وَأَنتَ خَيْرُ ٱلرَّازِقِينَ ﴿١١٤﴾

114. Qala AAeesa ibnu maryama allahumma rabbana anzil AAalayna ma-idatan mina alssama-i takoonu lana AAeedan li-awwalina waakhirina waayatan minka waorzuqna waanta khayru alrraziqeena

5:114. Jesus, son of Mary, said, "O Allah, our Lord! Send down to us from the heaven a table spread with food which should be to us – to the first of us and to the last of us – a festival, and a sign from You. And give us food, and You are the Best of the givers of food."

قَالَ ٱللَّهُ إِنِّى مُنَزِّلُهَا عَلَيْكُمْ فَمَن يَكْفُرْ بَعْدُ مِنكُمْ فَإِنِّىٓ أُعَذِّبُهُۥ عَذَابًا لَّآ أُعَذِّبُهُۥٓ أَحَدًا مِّنَ ٱلْعَٰلَمِينَ ۝١١٥

115. Qala Allahu innee munazziluha AAalaykum faman yakfur baAAdu minkum fa-innee oAAaththibuhu AAathaban la oAAaththibuhu ahadan mina alAAalameena

5:115. Allah said, "I am indeed going to send it down to you, but then if anyone thereafter suppresses the Truth from amongst you, I will indeed give him such punishment as I have not given to anyone in the worlds."

وَإِذْ قَالَ ٱللَّهُ يَٰعِيسَى ٱبْنَ مَرْيَمَ ءَأَنتَ قُلْتَ لِلنَّاسِ ٱتَّخِذُونِى وَأُمِّىَ إِلَٰهَيْنِ مِن دُونِ ٱللَّهِ قَالَ سُبْحَٰنَكَ مَا يَكُونُ لِىٓ أَنْ أَقُولَ مَا لَيْسَ لِى بِحَقٍّ إِن كُنتُ قُلْتُهُۥ فَقَدْ عَلِمْتَهُۥ تَعْلَمُ مَا فِى نَفْسِى وَلَآ أَعْلَمُ مَا فِى نَفْسِكَ إِنَّكَ أَنتَ عَلَّٰمُ ٱلْغُيُوبِ ۝١١٦

116. Wa-ith qala Allahu ya AAeesa ibna maryama aanta qulta lilnnasi ittakhithoonee waommiya ilahayni min dooni Allahi qala subhanaka ma yakoonu lee an aqoola ma laysa lee bihaqqin in kuntu qultuhu faqad AAalimtahu taAAlamu ma fee nafsee wala aAAlamu ma fee nafsika innaka anta AAallamu alghuyoobi

5:116. And when Allah will say, "O Jesus, son of Mary! Did you tell mankind to take you and your mother for two gods besides Allah?" He (Jesus) will say, "Glory be to You, I couldn't say anything that I had no right to. If I had said it, You would indeed have known it. You know what is in my mind, and I do not know what is in Your mind. You are indeed the Knower of the things unseen."

مَا قُلْتُ لَهُمْ إِلَّا مَا أَمَرْتَنِي بِهِۦٓ أَنِ ٱعْبُدُواْ ٱللَّهَ رَبِّى وَرَبَّكُمْ وَكُنتُ عَلَيْهِمْ شَهِيدًا مَّا دُمْتُ فِيهِمْ فَلَمَّا تَوَفَّيْتَنِى كُنتَ أَنتَ ٱلرَّقِيبَ عَلَيْهِمْ وَأَنتَ عَلَىٰ كُلِّ شَىْءٍ شَهِيدٌ ﴿١١٧﴾

117. Ma qultu lahum illa ma amartanee bihi ani oAAbudoo Allaha rabbee warabbakum wakuntu AAalayhim shaheedan ma dumtu feehim falamma tawaffaytanee kunta anta alrraqeeba AAalayhim waanta AAala kulli shay-in shaheed**un**

5:117. "I did not tell them anything except what You enjoined me with: 'Worship Allah, my Lord and your Lord.' And I was a witness over them so long as I remained among them, but when You caused me to die, You were the Guard over them.[45] And You are Witness over all things."

---

45. The scenario here is Allah's Court on Judgement Day in the Hereafter. Prophet Jesus (peace be upon him) is in the witness box. The Almighty, All-knowing Judge is questioning him. From Verse 5:116 above to Verse 5:119 below is a transcript of that interrogation. And this part of the transcript – recorded in this Verse 5:117 – gives the lie to the popular belief among Muslims about a 2nd coming of Jesus to this earth.

إِن تُعَذِّبْهُمْ فَإِنَّهُمْ عِبَادُكَ وَإِن تَغْفِرْ لَهُمْ فَإِنَّكَ أَنتَ ٱلْعَزِيزُ ٱلْحَكِيمُ ﴿١١٨﴾

118. In tuAAaththibhum fa-innahum AAibaduka wa-in taghfir lahum fa-innaka anta alAAazeezu alhakeem**u**

5:118. "If You punish them, then indeed they are Your worshippers; and if You forgive them, then indeed You are the Omnipotent, the Wise."

قَالَ ٱللَّهُ هَـٰذَا يَوْمُ يَنفَعُ ٱلصَّـٰدِقِينَ صِدْقُهُمْ لَهُمْ جَنَّـٰتٌ تَجْرِى مِن تَحْتِهَا ٱلْأَنْهَـٰرُ خَـٰلِدِينَ فِيهَا أَبَدًا رَّضِىَ ٱللَّهُ عَنْهُمْ وَرَضُوا۟ عَنْهُ ذَٰلِكَ ٱلْفَوْزُ ٱلْعَظِيمُ ﴿١١٩﴾

119. Qala Allahu hatha yawmu yanfaAAu alssadiqeena sidquhum lahum jannatun tajree min tahtiha al-anharu khalideena feeha abadan radiya Allahu AAanhum waradoo AAanhu thalika alfawzu alAAatheemu

---

5:119. Allah will say, "This day, their truthfulness shall benefit the truthful ones. For them are gardens beneath which rivers flow, to abide in them for ever." Allah is well pleased with them and they are well pleased with Allah. That is the highest success.

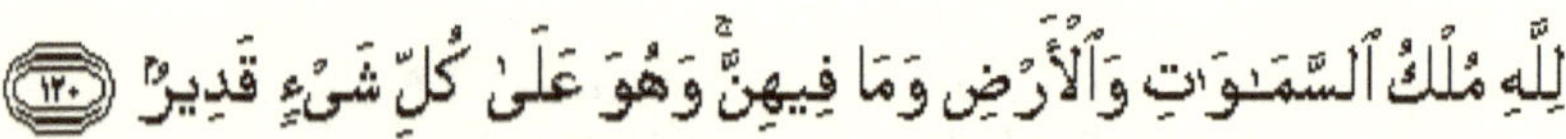

لِلَّهِ مُلْكُ ٱلسَّمَـٰوَٰتِ وَٱلْأَرْضِ وَمَا فِيهِنَّ وَهُوَ عَلَىٰ كُلِّ شَىْءٍ قَدِيرٌ ﴿١٢٠﴾

120. Lillahi mulku alssamawati waal-ardi wama feehinna wahuwa AAala kulli shay-in qadeerun

---

5:120. The absolute sovereignty over the heavens and the earth and over what is in them belongs to Allah; and He has power over all things!

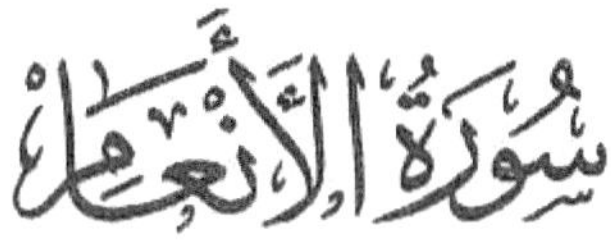

Chapter 6: Al-An'am (The Cattle)

In the Name of Allah, the Gracious, the Merciful

1. Alhamdu lillahi allathee khalaqa alssamawati waal-arda wajaAAala alththulumati waalnnoora thumma allatheena kafaroo birabbihim yaAAdiloona

---

6:1. The praise is for Allah, Who created the heavens and the earth and made the darknesses and the light. Yet, those who suppress the Truth sit in judgement over the attributes of their Lord!

---

2. Huwa allathee khalaqakum min teenin thumma qada ajalan waajalun musamman AAindahu thumma antum tamtaroona

---

6:2. He it is Who created you from clay, and then decreed a term. And it is a term denominated[1] with Him. But, then, you are in doubt.

---

1. Allah knows how long every individual shall live in this world. He also knows when this world itself, as we know it, will come to an end.

$$\text{وَهُوَ ٱللَّهُ فِى ٱلسَّمَـٰوَٰتِ وَفِى ٱلْأَرْضِ ۖ يَعْلَمُ سِرَّكُمْ وَجَهْرَكُمْ وَيَعْلَمُ مَا تَكْسِبُونَ ﴿٣﴾}$$

3. Wahuwa Allahu fee alssamawati wafee al-ardi yaAAlamu sirrakum wajahrakum wayaAAlamu ma taksiboona

---

6:3. And it is Allah Who pervades the heavens and the earth. He knows what you conceal and what you reveal, and He knows what you earn.

$$\text{وَمَا تَأْتِيهِم مِّنْ ءَايَةٍ مِّنْ ءَايَـٰتِ رَبِّهِمْ إِلَّا كَانُوا عَنْهَا مُعْرِضِينَ ﴿٤﴾}$$

4. Wama ta/teehim min ayatin min ayati rabbihim illa kanoo AAanha muAArideena

---

6:4. And no sign/Verse has ever come to them, of the signs/Verses of their Lord, from which they have not turned aside.

فَقَدْ كَذَّبُواْ بِالْحَقِّ لَمَّا جَآءَهُمْ فَسَوْفَ يَأْتِيهِمْ أَنْبَتَؤُاْ مَا كَانُواْ بِهِۦ يَسْتَهْزِءُونَ ۝

5. Faqad kaththaboo bialhaqqi lamma jaahum fasawfa ya/teehim anbao ma kanoo bihi yastahzi-oona

---

6:5. They did reject the truth when it came to them. And the details of what they mocked at will soon come to them.

أَلَمْ يَرَوْاْ كَمْ أَهْلَكْنَا مِن قَبْلِهِم مِّن قَرْنٍ مَّكَّنَّـٰهُمْ فِى الْأَرْضِ مَا لَمْ نُمَكِّن لَّكُمْ وَأَرْسَلْنَا السَّمَآءَ عَلَيْهِم مِّدْرَارًا وَجَعَلْنَا الْأَنْهَـٰرَ تَجْرِى مِن تَحْتِهِمْ فَأَهْلَكْنَـٰهُم بِذُنُوبِهِمْ وَأَنشَأْنَا مِنْ بَعْدِهِمْ قَرْنًا ءَاخَرِينَ ۝

6. Alam yaraw kam ahlakna min qablihim min qarnin makkannahum fee al-ardi ma lam numakkin lakum waarsalna alssamaa AAalayhim midraran wajaAAalna al-anhara tajree min tahtihim faahlaknahum bithunoobihim waansha/na min baAAdihim qarnan akhareena

---

6:6. Do they not see how many a generation We destroyed before them? We have not established you as firmly as We had established them on the earth. And We made the sky pour rain on them in abundance, and We made the rivers flow beneath them. Then We destroyed them because of their sins and raised up, after them, other generations.

وَلَوْ نَزَّلْنَا عَلَيْكَ كِتَـٰبًا فِى قِرْطَاسٍ فَلَمَسُوهُ بِأَيْدِيهِمْ لَقَالَ الَّذِينَ كَفَرُواْ إِنْ هَـٰذَآ إِلَّا سِحْرٌ مُّبِينٌ ۝

7. Walaw nazzalna AAalayka kitaban fee qirtasin falamasoohu bi-aydeehim laqala allatheena kafaroo in hatha illa sihrun mubeenun

6:7. And even if We had sent to you a book on paper so that they could touch it with their hands, those who suppress the Truth would certainly have said, "This is nothing but pure magic."

وَقَالُواْ لَوْلَا أُنزِلَ عَلَيْهِ مَلَكٌ وَلَوْ أَنزَلْنَا مَلَكًا لَّقُضِىَ ٱلْأَمْرُ ثُمَّ لَا يُنظَرُونَ

8. Waqaloo lawla onzila AAalayhi malakun walaw anzalna malakan laqudiya al-amru thumma la yuntharoona

6:8. And they say, "Why has not an angel been sent down to him?" And had We sent down an angel, the matter would have certainly been decided then and there, and they would have been given no respite.

وَلَوْ جَعَلْنَـٰهُ مَلَكًا لَّجَعَلْنَـٰهُ رَجُلًا وَلَلَبَسْنَا عَلَيْهِم مَّا يَلْبِسُونَ

9. Walaw jaAAalnahu malakan lajaAAalnahu rajulan walalabasna AAalayhim ma yalbisoona

6:9. And had We sent an angel as the Messenger, We would certainly have made him (appear as) a man, and We would certainly have made them as confused as they are now.

وَلَقَدِ ٱسْتُهْزِئَ بِرُسُلٍ مِّن قَبْلِكَ فَحَاقَ بِٱلَّذِينَ سَخِرُوا۟ مِنْهُم مَّا كَانُوا۟ بِهِۦ يَسْتَهْزِءُونَ ﴿١٠﴾

10. Walaqadi istuhzi-a birusulin min qablika fahaqa biallatheena sakhiroo minhum ma kanoo bihi yastahzi-oona

---

6:10. And, certainly, Messengers before you were mocked at, but the very thing, they made fun of, surrounded those who, among them, mocked!

قُلْ سِيرُوا۟ فِى ٱلْأَرْضِ ثُمَّ ٱنظُرُوا۟ كَيْفَ كَانَ عَٰقِبَةُ ٱلْمُكَذِّبِينَ ﴿١١﴾

11. Qul seeroo fee al-ardi thumma onthuroo kayfa kana AAaqibatu almukaththibeena

---

6:11. Say, "Travel on earth and then see what end the rejecters met with."

قُل لِّمَن مَّا فِى ٱلسَّمَٰوَٰتِ وَٱلْأَرْضِ قُل لِّلَّهِ كَتَبَ عَلَىٰ نَفْسِهِ ٱلرَّحْمَةَ لَيَجْمَعَنَّكُمْ إِلَىٰ يَوْمِ ٱلْقِيَٰمَةِ لَا رَيْبَ فِيهِ ٱلَّذِينَ خَسِرُوٓا۟ أَنفُسَهُمْ فَهُمْ لَا يُؤْمِنُونَ ﴿١٢﴾

12. Qul liman ma fee alssamawati waal-ardi qul lillahi kataba AAala nafsihi alrrahmata layajmaAAannakum ila yawmi alqiyamati la rayba feehi allatheena khasiroo anfusahum fahum la yu/minoona

6:12. Ask, "To whom does all that is in the heavens and the earth belong?" Say, "To Allah. He has made mercy an obligatory attribute of Him Himself. He will certainly gather you on the Resurrection Day, wherein there is no doubt. Those, who have lost their souls, believe not."

وَلَهُۥ مَا سَكَنَ فِى ٱلَّيْلِ وَٱلنَّهَارِ وَهُوَ ٱلسَّمِيعُ ٱلْعَلِيمُ ۝

13. Walahu ma sakana fee allayli waalnnahari wahuwa alssameeAAu alAAaleemu

6:13. "And to Him belongs what lives by the night and the day. And He is the One Who hears, the One Who knows."

قُلْ أَغَيْرَ ٱللَّهِ أَتَّخِذُ وَلِيًّا فَاطِرِ ٱلسَّمَـٰوَٰتِ وَٱلْأَرْضِ وَهُوَ يُطْعِمُ وَلَا يُطْعَمُ قُلْ إِنِّىٓ أُمِرْتُ أَنْ أَكُونَ أَوَّلَ مَنْ أَسْلَمَ وَلَا تَكُونَنَّ مِنَ ٱلْمُشْرِكِينَ ۝

14. Qul aghayra Allahi attakhithu waliyyan fatiri alssamawati waal-ardi wahuwa yutAAimu wala yutAAamu qul innee omirtu an akoona awwala man aslama wala takoonanna mina almushrikeena

6:14. Say, "Shall I take for a *wali*[2] anyone instead of Allah, Creator of the heavens and the earth, and Who feeds and is not fed?" Say, "I am indeed commanded to be the first among those who submit." And be not you, of the polytheists!

2. For the comprehensive meaning of this Arabic word, please see study notes 2:154 and 2:155 **on Verse 2:107.**

قُلْ إِنِّيٓ أَخَافُ إِنْ عَصَيْتُ رَبِّى عَذَابَ يَوْمٍ عَظِيمٍ ﴿١٥﴾

15. Qul innee akhafu in AAasaytu rabbee AAathaba yawmin AAatheemin

---

6:15. Say, "I do indeed fear punishment on a dreadful Day, if I disobey my Lord."

مَّن يُصْرَفْ عَنْهُ يَوْمَئِذٍ فَقَدْ رَحِمَهُۥ وَذَٰلِكَ ٱلْفَوْزُ ٱلْمُبِينُ ﴿١٦﴾

16. Man yusraf AAanhu yawma-ithin faqad rahimahu wathalika alfawzu almubeenu

---

6:16. He/she from whom it[3] is averted on that day, Allah surely has shown mercy to him/her. And that is the most manifest success.

---

3. The punishment mentioned in the preceding Verse.

وَإِن يَمْسَسْكَ ٱللَّهُ بِضُرٍّ فَلَا كَاشِفَ لَهُۥٓ إِلَّا هُوَ وَإِن يَمْسَسْكَ بِخَيْرٍ فَهُوَ عَلَىٰ كُلِّ شَىْءٍ قَدِيرٌ ﴿١٧﴾

17. Wa-in yamsaska Allahu bidurrin fala kashifa lahu illa huwa wa-in yamsaska bikhayrin fahuwa AAala kulli shay-in qadeerun

6:17. And if Allah afflicts you with some harm, there is none to take it off but He. And if He gives you something good, then He it is Who can do anything.

وَهُوَ ٱلْقَاهِرُ فَوْقَ عِبَادِهِۦ وَهُوَ ٱلْحَكِيمُ ٱلْخَبِيرُ ۝

18. Wahuwa alqahiru fawqa AAibadihi wahuwa alhakeemu alkhabeeru

6:18. And He it is Who has Supreme Power over His creatures. And He is the Wise, the One Who knows about all things.

قُلْ أَيُّ شَيْءٍ أَكْبَرُ شَهَٰدَةً قُلِ ٱللَّهُ شَهِيدٌ بَيْنِى وَبَيْنَكُمْ وَأُوحِىَ إِلَىَّ هَٰذَا ٱلْقُرْءَانُ لِأُنذِرَكُم بِهِۦ وَمَنۢ بَلَغَ أَئِنَّكُمْ لَتَشْهَدُونَ أَنَّ مَعَ ٱللَّهِ ءَالِهَةً أُخْرَىٰ قُل لَّآ أَشْهَدُ قُلْ إِنَّمَا هُوَ إِلَٰهٌ وَٰحِدٌ وَإِنَّنِى بَرِىٓءٌ مِّمَّا تُشْرِكُونَ ۝

19. Qul ayyu shay-in akbaru shah_a_datan quli All_a_hu shaheedun baynee wabaynakum waoo_h_iya ilayya _hatha_ alqur-_a_nu li-on_th_irakum bihi waman balagha a-innakum latash_h_adoona anna maAAa All_a_hi _a_lihatan okhr_a_ qul l_a_ ash_h_adu qul innam_a_ huwa il_a_hun w_ah_idun wa-innanee baree-on mimm_a_ tushrikoon_a_

6:19. Ask them what thing is the weightiest in testimony? Say, "Allah! HE is witness between you and me. And this Qur'aan has been revealed to me so that I may, therewith, warn you and warn whomsoever it reaches. Do you really bear witness that there are other gods with Allah?" Say, "I do not bear witness." Say, "HE is the One and Only Being worthy of worship, and, indeed, I am free of the belief in those whom you set up as partners to Allah."

ٱلَّذِينَ ءَاتَيْنَـٰهُمُ ٱلْكِتَـٰبَ يَعْرِفُونَهُۥ كَمَا يَعْرِفُونَ أَبْنَآءَهُمُ ٱلَّذِينَ خَسِرُوٓاْ أَنفُسَهُمْ فَهُمْ لَا يُؤْمِنُونَ ۝

20. Allatheena ataynahumu alkitaba yaAArifoonahu kama yaAArifoona abnaahum allatheena khasiroo anfusahum fahum la yu/minoona

6:20. Those whom We have given the Book recognize him[4] as they recognize their sons. Those who have lost their souls – they will not believe!

4. I.e. Muhammad as the duly appointed Prophet and Messenger from Allah.

وَمَنْ أَظْلَمُ مِمَّنِ ٱفْتَرَىٰ عَلَى ٱللَّهِ كَذِبًا أَوْ كَذَّبَ بِـَٔايَـٰتِهِۦٓ إِنَّهُۥ لَا يُفْلِحُ ٱلظَّـٰلِمُونَ ۝

21. Waman athlamu mimmani iftara AAala Allahi kathiban aw kaththaba bi-ayatihi innahu la yuflihu alththalimoona

6:21. And who is more unjust than he who forges a lie about Allah or rejects His Verses/signs? Indeed, the unjust will not be successful!

وَيَوْمَ نَحْشُرُهُمْ جَمِيعًا ثُمَّ نَقُولُ لِلَّذِينَ أَشْرَكُوٓاْ أَيْنَ شُرَكَآؤُكُمُ ٱلَّذِينَ كُنتُمْ تَزْعُمُونَ ۝

22. Wayawma na<u>h</u>shuruhum jameeAAan thumma naqoolu lilla<u>th</u>eena ashrakoo ayna shuraka<u>o</u>kumu alla<u>th</u>eena kuntum tazAAumoona

---

6:22. And, one day, We shall gather them all together, then ask those who associated others with Allah, "Where are your associates you surmised?"

ثُمَّ لَمْ تَكُن فِتْنَتُهُمْ إِلَّا أَن قَالُوا۟ وَٱللَّهِ رَبِّنَا مَا كُنَّا مُشْرِكِينَ ﴿٢٣﴾

23. Thumma lam takun fitnatuhum ill<u>a</u> an q<u>a</u>loo waAll<u>a</u>hi rabbin<u>a</u> m<u>a</u> kunn<u>a</u> mushrikeena

---

6:23. They will then be left with no excuse but to say, "By Allah, our Lord, we were not polytheists."

ٱنظُرْ كَيْفَ كَذَبُوا۟ عَلَىٰ أَنفُسِهِمْ وَضَلَّ عَنْهُم مَّا كَانُوا۟ يَفْتَرُونَ ﴿٢٤﴾

24. On<u>th</u>ur kayfa ka<u>th</u>aboo AAal<u>a</u> anfusihim wa<u>d</u>alla AAanhum m<u>a</u> k<u>a</u>noo yaftaroona

---

6:24. See how they would lie against their own selves, and how that which they forged would desert them.

وَمِنْهُم مَّن يَسْتَمِعُ إِلَيْكَ وَجَعَلْنَا عَلَىٰ قُلُوبِهِمْ أَكِنَّةً أَن يَفْقَهُوهُ وَفِىٓ ءَاذَانِهِمْ وَقْرًا وَإِن يَرَوْاْ كُلَّ ءَايَةٍ لَّا يُؤْمِنُواْ بِهَا حَتَّىٰٓ إِذَا جَآءُوكَ يُجَٰدِلُونَكَ يَقُولُ ٱلَّذِينَ كَفَرُوٓاْ إِنْ هَٰذَآ إِلَّآ أَسَٰطِيرُ ٱلْأَوَّلِينَ ۝

25. Waminhum man yastamiAAu ilayka wajaAAalna AAala quloobihim akinnatan an yafqahoohu wafee athanihim waqran wa-in yaraw kulla ayatin la yu/minoo biha hatta itha jaooka yujadiloonaka yaqoolu allatheena kafaroo in hatha illa asateeru al-awwaleena

---

6:25. And of them there are some who come to hear you, and We have put veils over their minds and deafness in their ears, so they do not understand what you tell them. And even if they see every Sign, they will not believe in it. So much so, that when they come to you to argue with you, those, who suppress the Truth, say, "These are nothing but tales of the ealier people."

وَهُمْ يَنْهَوْنَ عَنْهُ وَيَنْئَوْنَ عَنْهُ وَإِن يُهْلِكُونَ إِلَّآ أَنفُسَهُمْ وَمَا يَشْعُرُونَ ۝

26. Wahum yanhawna AAanhu wayan-awna AAanhu wa-in yuhlikoona illa anfusahum wama yashAAuroona

---

6:26. And they prevent others from it[5] and they keep themselves away from it[5], and they destroy not but their own selves and they perceive not.

---

5. I.e. the divine Message the Prophet was conveying to the people.

وَلَوْ تَرَىٰ إِذْ وُقِفُواْ عَلَى ٱلنَّارِ فَقَالُواْ يَٰلَيْتَنَا نُرَدُّ وَلَا نُكَذِّبَ بِـَٔايَٰتِ رَبِّنَا وَنَكُونَ مِنَ ٱلْمُؤْمِنِينَ ﴿٢٧﴾

27. Walaw tara ith wuqifoo AAala alnnari faqaloo ya laytana nuraddu wala nukaththiba bi-ayati rabbina wanakoona mina almu/mineena

6:27. And if you could but see the scene when they would be held over the fire! They would then say, "Would that we were sent back! We would not then reject the Verses/signs of our Lord and we would be of the believers."

بَلْ بَدَا لَهُم مَّا كَانُواْ يُخْفُونَ مِن قَبْلُ وَلَوْ رُدُّواْ لَعَادُواْ لِمَا نُهُواْ عَنْهُ وَإِنَّهُمْ لَكَٰذِبُونَ ﴿٢٨﴾

28. Bal bada lahum ma kanoo yukhfoona min qablu walaw ruddoo laAAadoo lima nuhoo AAanhu wa-innahum lakathiboona

6:28. Nay! What they concealed before would just become manifest to them. And were they to be sent back, they would certainly commit that which they are forbidden, and certainly indeed they are liars.

وَقَالُواْ إِنْ هِىَ إِلَّا حَيَاتُنَا ٱلدُّنْيَا وَمَا نَحْنُ بِمَبْعُوثِينَ ﴿٢٩﴾

29. Waqaloo in hiya illa hayatuna alddunya wama nahnu bimabAAootheena

6:29. And they say, "There is nothing but our life of this world, and we shall not be resurrected."

وَلَوْ تَرَىٰ إِذْ وُقِفُواْ عَلَىٰ رَبِّهِمْ قَالَ أَلَيْسَ هَـٰذَا بِٱلْحَقِّ قَالُواْ بَلَىٰ

وَرَبِّنَا قَالَ فَذُوقُواْ ٱلْعَذَابَ بِمَا كُنتُمْ تَكْفُرُونَ ﴿٣٠﴾

30. Walaw tara ith wuqifoo AAala rabbihim qala alaysa hatha bialhaqqi qaloo bala warabbina qala fathooqoo alAAathaba bima kuntum takfuroona

6:30. And if you could but see the scene when they would be standing before their Lord! HE will ask, "Is not this the Truth?" They will say, "Yes, and by our Lord!" HE will say, "Taste then the punishment for being suppresors of the Truth."

قَدْ خَسِرَ ٱلَّذِينَ كَذَّبُواْ بِلِقَآءِ ٱللَّهِ حَتَّىٰ إِذَا

جَآءَتْهُمُ ٱلسَّاعَةُ بَغْتَةً قَالُواْ يَـٰحَسْرَتَنَا عَلَىٰ مَا فَرَّطْنَا فِيهَا وَهُمْ

يَحْمِلُونَ أَوْزَارَهُمْ عَلَىٰ ظُهُورِهِمْ أَلَا سَآءَ مَا يَزِرُونَ ﴿٣١﴾

31. Qad khasira allatheena kaththaboo biliqa-i Allahi hatta itha jaat-humu alssaAAatu baghtatan qaloo ya hasratana AAala ma farratna feeha wahum yahmiloona awzarahum AAala thuhoorihim ala saa ma yaziroona

6:31. They surely are doomed, who deny their appointment with Allah. Until, when, suddenly, the Hour dawns on them, they say, "Alas for us that we gave no thought to it!" And they bear their burdens on their backs. It is evil, what they bear; isn't it?

وَمَا ٱلْحَيَوٰةُ ٱلدُّنْيَآ إِلَّا لَعِبٌ وَلَهْوٌ وَلَلدَّارُ ٱلْأَخِرَةُ خَيْرٌ لِّلَّذِينَ يَتَّقُونَ أَفَلَا تَعْقِلُونَ ۝

32. Wama alhayatu alddunya illa laAAibun walahwun walalddaru al-akhirati khayrun lillatheena yattaqoona afala taAAqiloona

---

6:32. And the life of this world is nothing but play and pastime. And, certainly, the abode of the Hereafter is better for those who fear Allah. Don't you then understand?

قَدْ نَعْلَمُ إِنَّهُۥ لَيَحْزُنُكَ ٱلَّذِى يَقُولُونَ فَإِنَّهُمْ لَا يُكَذِّبُونَكَ وَلَكِنَّ ٱلظَّٰلِمِينَ بِـَٔايَٰتِ ٱللَّهِ يَجْحَدُونَ ۝

33. Qad naAAlamu innahu layahzunuka allathee yaqooloona fa-innahum la yukaththiboonaka walakinna alththalimeena bi-ayati Allahi yajhadoona

---

6:33. We do know indeed that what they say certainly grieves you. Still, surely, it is not you that they reject, but it is Allah's Verses/signs that the wicked people deny!

وَلَقَدْ كُذِّبَتْ رُسُلٌ مِّن قَبْلِكَ فَصَبَرُوا۟ عَلَىٰ مَا كُذِّبُوا۟ وَأُوذُوا۟ حَتَّىٰ أَتَىٰهُمْ نَصْرُنَا وَلَا مُبَدِّلَ لِكَلِمَٰتِ ٱللَّهِ وَلَقَدْ جَآءَكَ مِن نَّبَإِى۟ ٱلْمُرْسَلِينَ ۝

34. Walaqad kuththibat rusulun min qablika fasabaroo AAala ma kuththiboo waoothoo hatta atahum nasruna wala mubaddila likalimati Allahi walaqad jaaka min naba-i almursaleena

---

6:34. And surely Messengers before you were rejected, but they bore their rejection and persecution with patience, until Our help reached them. And none can change Allah's Words. And, surely, some of the tales of the Messengers have come to you.

وَإِن كَانَ كَبُرَ عَلَيْكَ إِعْرَاضُهُمْ فَإِنِ ٱسْتَطَعْتَ أَن تَبْتَغِىَ نَفَقًا فِى ٱلْأَرْضِ أَوْ سُلَّمًا فِى ٱلسَّمَآءِ فَتَأْتِيَهُم بِـَٔايَةٍ وَلَوْ شَآءَ ٱللَّهُ لَجَمَعَهُمْ عَلَى ٱلْهُدَىٰ فَلَا تَكُونَنَّ مِنَ ٱلْجَٰهِلِينَ ﴿٣٥﴾

35. Wa-in kana kabura AAalayka iAAraduhum fa-ini istataAAta an tabtaghiya nafaqan fee al-ardi aw sullaman fee alssama-i fata/tiyahum bi-ayatin walaw shaa Allahu lajamaAAahum AAala alhuda fala takoonanna mina aljahileena

6:35. And if their aversion is hard on you, then, if you can, seek an opening deep into the earth or a ladder [link] up into the heavens, and then bring them a sign. And if Allah had so willed, He would certainly have gathered them all on guidance. Be not then of those who are ignorant.[6]

6. This is an obvious reprimand from Allah to His Messenger. HE has put this on record here to let mankind know that His Messengers too are His creatures, and not His partners in Creation. The Messengers too, being human, were prone to errors. What this Verse reveals to us is that the Prophet (peace be upon him) ardently desired Allah to give him a sign to show to his people to convince them of his being His accredited Messenger. But Allah had other plans. HE did not want His last Messenger to mankind to be recognised based on any obvious sign like those given to his predecessors, Jesus and Moses. Those signs, in any case, had yielded little results. HE, in His Wisdom, knew that His last Messenger was being sent at the threshold of an era of proliferation of knowledge. Allah now wanted His last Messenger to be recognised based on the intellect He had granted mankind. HE wanted the people to use this intellect, and the knowledge they are now getting, to scrutinise the character of the person sent as the last Messenger and to scrutinise the Message he was conveying to them. Allah here reminds His Messenger that He knows what to do to guide His creatures. Nothing – not even the ardent personal desire of His Messenger – can come in the way of His plans.

۞ إِنَّمَا يَسْتَجِيبُ ٱلَّذِينَ يَسْمَعُونَ وَٱلْمَوْتَىٰ يَبْعَثُهُمُ ٱللَّهُ ثُمَّ إِلَيْهِ يُرْجَعُونَ ﴿٣٦﴾

36. Innama yastajeebu alla<u>th</u>eena yasmaAAoona waalmaw<u>t</u>a yabAAathuhumu All<u>a</u>hu thumma ilayhi yurjaAAoona

---

6:36. Only those respond, who hear! And as for the dead, Allah will resurrect them, then to Him they shall be returned.[7]

---

7. Implied in this Verse is the fact that the dead can't hear. Reference in this context is invited to Verse 35:22 wherein we are informed that "... And you are in no position to make those to hear who are in the graves." Besides the dead, 'those in the graves' would include persons killed in the way of Allah whom Allah has directed us not to consider as 'dead' vide <u>Verse 2:154</u>**. In the immediate context of this Verse here, however, the non-believers may have been referred to here as the 'dead', since they were unable to comprehend the divine Message being conveyed to them by the Prophet (peace upon him).**

وَقَالُوا۟ لَوْلَا نُزِّلَ عَلَيْهِ ءَايَةٌ مِّن رَّبِّهِۦ قُلْ إِنَّ ٱللَّهَ قَادِرٌ عَلَىٰ أَن يُنَزِّلَ ءَايَةً وَلَٰكِنَّ أَكْثَرَهُمْ لَا يَعْلَمُونَ ﴿٣٧﴾

37. Waq<u>a</u>loo lawl<u>a</u> nuzzila AAalayhi <u>a</u>yatun min rabbihi qul inna All<u>a</u>ha q<u>a</u>dirun AAal<u>a</u> an yunazzila <u>a</u>yatan wal<u>a</u>kinna aktharahum l<u>a</u> yaAAlamoona

---

6:37. And they say, "Why is a sign not sent down upon him from his Lord?" Say, "Allah can indeed send down a sign." But most of them would not know it as a sign![8]

---

8. Most of the Messengers preceding Prophet Muhammad were given the signs, but most of their respective people would not recognise them as such and had continued in their wayward behaviour. It was therefore in the divine scheme of things that the *Ummah* of the last Messenger would not be given an obviously miraculous sign as such. The *Ummah* had to use, instead, its Allah-given faculty of Intelligence to fathom the sign in the circumstances of the life of the Messenger in their midst, and in the Verses of the Qur'aan in the process of being revealed. This divine strategy proved to be more effective since Prophet Muhammad's mission was eminently more successful than most other Prophetic missions.

وَمَا مِن دَآبَّةٍ فِى ٱلْأَرْضِ وَلَا طَـٰٓئِرٍ يَطِيرُ بِجَنَاحَيْهِ إِلَّآ أُمَمٌ أَمْثَالُكُم مَّا فَرَّطْنَا فِى ٱلْكِتَـٰبِ مِن شَىْءٍ ثُمَّ إِلَىٰ رَبِّهِمْ يُحْشَرُونَ ﴿٣٨﴾

38. Wama min dabbatin fee al-ardi wala ta-irin yateeru bijanahayhi illa omamun amthalukum ma farratna fee alkitabi min shay-in thumma ila rabbihim yuhsharoona

6:38. And there is no creature crawling on earth or bird flying with its two wings but lives in communities like yours. – We have neglected nothing in the Book.[9] – Then unto their Lord shall they be gathered.

9. The Qur'aan has been referred to as the Book (*alkitaab*) at several places throughout therein. Allah thus tells us that everything necessary for the guidance of mankind has been put down in the Qur'aan.

وَٱلَّذِينَ كَذَّبُوا۟ بِـَٔايَـٰتِنَا صُمٌّ وَبُكْمٌ فِى ٱلظُّلُمَـٰتِ مَن يَشَإِ ٱللَّهُ يُضْلِلْهُ وَمَن يَشَأْ يَجْعَلْهُ عَلَىٰ صِرَٰطٍ مُّسْتَقِيمٍ ﴿٣٩﴾

39. Waallatheena kaththaboo bi-ayatina summun wabukmun fee alththulumati man yasha-i Allahu yudlilhu waman yasha/ yajAAalhu AAala siratin mustaqeemin

6:39. And they who reject Our Verses/signs are deaf and dumb in darknesses. Allah sends astray whom He wills. And He puts on the Straight Path whom He wills.

قُلْ أَرَءَيْتَكُم إِنْ أَتَىٰكُمْ عَذَابُ ٱللَّهِ أَوْ أَتَتْكُمُ ٱلسَّاعَةُ أَغَيْرَ ٱللَّهِ تَدْعُونَ إِن كُنتُمْ صَـٰدِقِينَ ﴿٤٠﴾

40. Qul araaytakum in atakum AAathabu Allahi aw atatkumu alssaAAatu aghayra Allahi tadAAoona in kuntum sadiqeena

6:40. Say, "You see, if Allah's punishment comes upon you or the Hour comes upon you, would you then, honestly, pray to any one other than Allah?"

بَلْ إِيَّاهُ تَدْعُونَ فَيَكْشِفُ مَا تَدْعُونَ إِلَيْهِ إِن شَاءَ وَتَنسَوْنَ مَا تُشْرِكُونَ

۝

41. Bal iyyahu tadAAoona fayakshifu ma tadAAoona ilayhi in shaa watansawna ma tushrikoona

6:41. Nay, to Him only you would pray! He would then, if He wills, remove the distress, the removal of which you prayed for, and you would then forget the others you worshipped besides Him.

وَلَقَدْ أَرْسَلْنَآ إِلَىٰ أُمَمٍ مِّن قَبْلِكَ فَأَخَذْنَٰهُم بِالْبَأْسَآءِ وَالضَّرَّآءِ لَعَلَّهُمْ يَتَضَرَّعُونَ ۝

42. Walaqad arsalna ila omamin min qablika faakhathnahum bialba/sa-i waalddarra-i laAAallahum yatadarraAAoona

6:42. And certainly We did send down Messengers and Messages to peoples before you. We then seized them with distress and affliction in order that they might humble themselves.

فَلَوْلَآ إِذْ جَآءَهُم بَأْسُنَا تَضَرَّعُواْ وَلَٰكِن قَسَتْ قُلُوبُهُمْ وَزَيَّنَ لَهُمُ الشَّيْطَٰنُ مَا كَانُواْ يَعْمَلُونَ ۝

43. Falawla ith jaahum ba/suna tadarraAAoo walakin qasat quloobuhum wazayyana lahumu alshshaytanu ma kanoo yaAAmaloona

6:43. Then why did they not, when Our punishment came to them, humble themselves? But their hearts hardened, and the Satan made what they did, look fair to them.

فَلَمَّا نَسُواْ مَا ذُكِّرُواْ بِهِۦ فَتَحْنَا عَلَيْهِمْ أَبْوَٰبَ كُلِّ شَىْءٍ حَتَّىٰٓ إِذَا فَرِحُواْ بِمَآ أُوتُوٓاْ أَخَذْنَٰهُم بَغْتَةً فَإِذَا هُم مُّبْلِسُونَ ۝

44. Falamma nasoo ma _th_ukkiroo bihi fata_h_na AAalayhim abwaba kulli shay-in _h_atta i_th_a fari_h_oo bima ootoo akha_th_na_h_um baghtatan fa-i_th_a hum mublisoon**a**

6:44. Then when they forgot what they had been reminded of, We opened for them the doors of all things. Until, when they were engrossed in rejoicing what they were given, We seized them suddenly. Then it was when they were driven to desperation and despair.

فَقُطِعَ دَابِرُ ٱلْقَوْمِ ٱلَّذِينَ ظَلَمُواْ وَٱلْحَمْدُ لِلَّهِ رَبِّ ٱلْعَٰلَمِينَ ۝

45. Faqu_t_iAAa _d_abiru alqawmi alla_th_eena _th_alamoo waal_h_amdu lill_a_hi rabbi alAA_a_lameen**a**

6:45. And the roots of the wicked people were cut off. And all praise to Allah, the Lord of the worlds!

قُلْ أَرَءَيْتُمْ إِنْ أَخَذَ ٱللَّهُ سَمْعَكُمْ وَأَبْصَٰرَكُمْ وَخَتَمَ عَلَىٰ قُلُوبِكُم مَّنْ إِلَٰهٌ غَيْرُ ٱللَّهِ يَأْتِيكُم بِهِۦٓ ٱنظُرْ كَيْفَ نُصَرِّفُ ٱلْأَيَٰتِ ثُمَّ هُمْ يَصْدِفُونَ

46. Qul araaytum in akha_th_a All_a_hu samAAakum waab_s_arakum wakhatama AAal_a_ quloobikum man il_a_hun ghayru All_a_hi ya/teekum bihi on_th_ur kayfa nu_s_arrifu al-_a_yati thumma hum ya_s_difoon**a**

6:46. Say, "You see, if Allah took away your hearing and your sight, and put seals on your hearts, which god, other than Allah, can restore it to you?" Look, how We explain the Verses/signs, yet they turn away!

قُلْ أَرَءَيْتَكُمْ إِنْ أَتَنكُمْ عَذَابُ ٱللَّهِ بَغْتَةً أَوْ جَهْرَةً هَلْ يُهْلَكُ إِلَّا ٱلْقَوْمُ ٱلظَّٰلِمُونَ ﴿٤٧﴾

47. Qul araaytakum in atakum AAathabu Allahi baghtatan aw jahratan hal yuhlaku illa alqawmu al_ththa_limoona

6:47. Say, "You see, if Allah's punishment were to come to you, suddenly or with due notice, would any but the wicked people be destroyed?"[10, 11]

10. There is a divine reiteration here that when a natural calamity (like earthquake, hurricane, and tsunami) strikes, it is only the wicked people who are destroyed therein. However, I am aware that a few years back several small children were killed in an earthquake. Can we then conclude that the small children killed were wicked? Most of them were primary school children and may therefore have been under the age of 10! Whatever might have been the moral condition of their parents, the children can, by no stretch of imagination, be called wicked. And anyone who considers the Qur'aanic Verse to be wrong, he/she immediately falls outside the pail of Islam. How should the believers consider the occurrence of that episode then!?

11. Death is an inevitable occurrence in any human being's life. And we know of many known believers being killed in wars even during the Prophet's time. Being killed is not equivalent to being destroyed. The word in question used in this Verse is destroyed (*yuhlaku*). And wherever the Qur'aan has used this word, it is to denote the destruction of a person's soul by causing his/her body not only killed in this worldly life, but subjected to severe pynishment in the Hereafter, for the person's wanton acts of omission and commission against laid-down divine laws, in this worldly life. Therefore, we cannot say that the children killed in the earthquake were destroyed therein. But their killing was certainly a trial/punishment for the children's parents and near and dear relatives who survived the earthquake.

وَمَا نُرْسِلُ ٱلْمُرْسَلِينَ إِلَّا مُبَشِّرِينَ وَمُنذِرِينَ فَمَنْ ءَامَنَ وَأَصْلَحَ فَلَا خَوْفٌ عَلَيْهِمْ وَلَا هُمْ يَحْزَنُونَ ﴿٤٨﴾

48. Wama nursilu almursaleena illa mubashshireena wamun_th_ireena faman amana waaslaha fala khawfun AAalayhim wala hum ya_h_zanoona

6:48. And We did not send the Messengers but as harbingers of good news and warners. Then those who believe and mend their ways, they shall have no fear, nor shall they grieve.

وَٱلَّذِينَ كَذَّبُواْ بِـَٔايَـٰتِنَا يَمَسُّهُمُ ٱلْعَذَابُ بِمَا كَانُواْ يَفْسُقُونَ

49. Waallatheena kaththaboo bi-ayatina yamassuhumu alAAathabu bima kanoo yafsuqoona

6:49. And those who reject Our Verses/signs, punishment shall afflict them because they are committing transgression.

قُل لَّآ أَقُولُ لَكُمْ عِندِى خَزَآئِنُ ٱللَّهِ وَلَآ أَعْلَمُ ٱلْغَيْبَ وَلَآ أَقُولُ لَكُمْ إِنِّى مَلَكٌ إِنْ أَتَّبِعُ إِلَّا مَا يُوحَىٰٓ إِلَىَّ قُلْ هَلْ يَسْتَوِى ٱلْأَعْمَىٰ وَٱلْبَصِيرُ أَفَلَا تَتَفَكَّرُونَ

50. Qul la aqoolu lakum AAindee khaza-inu Allahi wala aAAlamu alghayba wala aqoolu lakum innee malakun in attabiAAu illa ma yooha ilayya qul hal yastawee al-aAAma waalbaseeru afala tatafakkaroona

6:50. Say, "I do not say to you, I have Allah's treasures with me, nor do I know the unseen, nor do I say to you that I am an angel. I do not but follow what is revealed to me." Say, "Are the blind and the seeing alike? Won't you then ponder?"

وَأَنذِرْ بِهِ ٱلَّذِينَ يَخَافُونَ أَن يُحْشَرُوٓاْ إِلَىٰ رَبِّهِمْ لَيْسَ لَهُم مِّن دُونِهِۦ وَلِىٌّ وَلَا شَفِيعٌ لَّعَلَّهُمْ يَتَّقُونَ

51. Waanthir bihi allatheena yakhafoona an yuhsharoo ila rabbihim laysa lahum min doonihi waliyyun wala shafeeAAun laAAallahum yattaqoona

6:51. And warn with it[12] those who fear that they shall be gathered to their Lord – there is no *wali*[13] for them, nor any intercessor besides Him – that they may be pious.

12. The Qur'aan.

13. Please see <u>study note 2:154</u> **on Verse 2:107.**

وَلَا تَطْرُدِ ٱلَّذِينَ يَدْعُونَ رَبَّهُم بِٱلْغَدَوٰةِ وَٱلْعَشِيِّ يُرِيدُونَ وَجْهَهُ

مَا عَلَيْكَ مِنْ حِسَابِهِم مِّن شَىْءٍ وَمَا مِنْ حِسَابِكَ عَلَيْهِم مِّن شَىْءٍ

فَتَطْرُدَهُمْ فَتَكُونَ مِنَ ٱلظَّـٰلِمِينَ ۝

52. Wala taṭrudi allatheena yadAAoona rabbahum bialghadati waalAAashiyyi yureedoona wajhahu ma AAalayka min ḥisabihim min shay-in wama min ḥisabika AAalayhim min shay-in fataṭrudahum fatakoona mina althṭthalimeena

6:52. And turn not away those who pray to their Lord, morning and evening, desiring His pleasure. Neither are you[14] responsible for anything in their account, nor are they responsible for anything in your[14] account. If you still turn them away, you should be among the wicked people.

---

14. The 2nd person pronoun used at both these places is in the singular, indicating that the addressee of the divine command in this Verse, in the first instance, was the Prophet.

وَكَذَٰلِكَ فَتَنَّا بَعْضَهُم بِبَعْضٍ لِّيَقُولُوٓاْ أَهَـٰٓؤُلَآءِ مَنَّ ٱللَّهُ عَلَيْهِم مِّنۢ

بَيْنِنَآ أَلَيْسَ ٱللَّهُ بِأَعْلَمَ بِٱلشَّـٰكِرِينَ ۝

53. Wakathalika fatanna baAAdahum bibaAAdin liyaqooloo ahaola-i manna Allahu AAalayhim min baynina alaysa Allahu bi-aAAlama bialshshakireena

6:53. And thus have We tried some of them through others, so that they say, "Are these the people[15] upon whom Allah has conferred benefits from amongst us?" Does not Allah know who the grateful are!?

---

15. This Verse, read with the preceding Verse 52, indicates that some poor believers had gathered around the Prophet. It is these poor people who are referred to here in this remark, made obviously by some rich persons of the community.

وَإِذَا جَاءَكَ ٱلَّذِينَ يُؤْمِنُونَ بِـَٔايَٰتِنَا فَقُلْ سَلَٰمٌ عَلَيْكُمْ ۖ كَتَبَ رَبُّكُمْ عَلَىٰ نَفْسِهِ ٱلرَّحْمَةَ ۖ أَنَّهُۥ مَنْ عَمِلَ مِنكُمْ سُوٓءًۢا بِجَهَٰلَةٍ ثُمَّ تَابَ مِنۢ بَعْدِهِۦ وَأَصْلَحَ فَأَنَّهُۥ غَفُورٌ رَّحِيمٌ ۝

54. Wa-itha jaaka allatheena yu/minoona bi-ayatina faqul salamun AAalaykum kataba rabbukum AAala nafsihi alrrahmata annahu man AAamila minkum soo-an bijahalatin thumma taba min baAAdihi waaslaha faannahu ghafoorun raheem**un**

6:54. And when those who believe in Our Verses/signs come to you, say, "Peace on you! Your Lord has made mandatory upon Himself the attribute of mercifulness. So, if any of you does a bad thing in ignorance, and thereafter repents and mends his/her ways, then He is indeed Forgiving, Merciful."

وَكَذَٰلِكَ نُفَصِّلُ ٱلْءَايَٰتِ وَلِتَسْتَبِينَ سَبِيلُ ٱلْمُجْرِمِينَ ۝

55. Wakathalika nufassilu al-ayati walitastabeena sabeelu almujrimeena

6:55. And thus do We explain the Verses/signs in detail to make the way of the guilty manifest.[16]

16. **The guilty is given every chance to mend himself (see preceding Verse). If he persists in his wayward behaviour, clearly, then, he is a wicked man deserving divine punishment.**

قُل إِنِّى نُهِيتُ أَنْ أَعْبُدَ ٱلَّذِينَ تَدْعُونَ مِن دُونِ ٱللَّهِ قُل لَّا أَتَّبِعُ أَهْوَآءَكُمْ قَدْ ضَلَلْتُ إِذًا وَمَآ أَنَا۠ مِنَ ٱلْمُهْتَدِينَ ۝

56. Qul innee nuheetu an aAAbuda alla_theena_ tadAAoona min dooni All_a_hi qul l_a_ attabiAAu ahw_a_akum qad _d_alaltu i_th_an wam_a_ an_a_ mina almuhtadeen_a_

6:56. Say, "I am indeed forbidden to worship those, other than Allah, whom you pray to." Say, "I follow not your desires. I should be gone astray otherwise, and I should not be of those who are guided."

قُل إِنِّى عَلَىٰ بَيِّنَةٍ مِّن رَّبِّى وَكَذَّبْتُم بِهِۦ مَا عِندِى مَا تَسْتَعْجِلُونَ بِهِۦ إِنِ ٱلْحُكْمُ إِلَّا لِلَّهِ يَقُصُّ ٱلْحَقَّ وَهُوَ خَيْرُ ٱلْفَٰصِلِينَ ۝

57. Qul innee AAal_a_ bayyinatin min rabbee waka_ththabtum bihi m_a_ AAindee m_a_ tastaAAjiloona bihi ini al_h_ukmu ill_a_ lill_a_hi yaqu_ss_u al_h_aqqa wahuwa khayru alf_as_ileen_a_

6:57. Say, "I stand on manifest authority from my Lord, and you deny it! I have no power over what you hasten for. The decision is for none but Allah to take. HE tells the truth and He is the Best of the judges."

قُل لَّوْ أَنَّ عِندِى مَا تَسْتَعْجِلُونَ بِهِۦ لَقُضِىَ ٱلْأَمْرُ بَيْنِى وَبَيْنَكُمْ وَٱللَّهُ أَعْلَمُ بِٱلظَّٰلِمِينَ ۝

58. Qul law anna AAindee m_a_ tastaAAjiloona bihi laqu_d_iya al-amru baynee wabaynakum waAll_a_hu aAAlamu bial_ththa_limeena

6:58. Say, "Had I the power over what you hasten for[17], the matter between you and me would have certainly been decided. And Allah knows the wicked people."

17. It was the Last Day, and then the Hereafter, which the non-believers wanted hastened!

۞ وَعِندَهُۥ مَفَاتِحُ ٱلْغَيْبِ لَا يَعْلَمُهَآ إِلَّا هُوَ وَيَعْلَمُ مَا فِى ٱلْبَرِّ وَٱلْبَحْرِ وَمَا تَسْقُطُ مِن وَرَقَةٍ إِلَّا يَعْلَمُهَا وَلَا حَبَّةٍ فِى ظُلُمَٰتِ ٱلْأَرْضِ وَلَا رَطْبٍ وَلَا يَابِسٍ إِلَّا فِى كِتَٰبٍ مُّبِينٍ ﴿٥٩﴾

59. WaAAindahu mafatihu alghaybi la yaAAlamuha illa huwa wayaAAlamu ma fee albarri waalbahri wama tasqutu min waraqatin illa yaAAlamuha wala habbatin fee thulumati al-ardi wala ratbin wala yabisin illa fee kitabin mubeenin

6:59. And with Him are the keys of the unseen – none knows them but He. And He knows what is there in the land and the sea. And not a leaf falls, but He knows it. And no grain in the dark recesses of the earth, or anything green or dry, but it is all recorded in a book manifest.[18]

18. Allah thus informs us that He causes everything happening, whether on a macro scale or micro, anywhere, is recorded. Allah's ways are inscrutable for the human mind, but the modern man, with his advanced knowledge, gets an inkling of His ways when he finds how, inter alia, his genealogy is recorded in his DNA!

وَهُوَ ٱلَّذِى يَتَوَفَّىٰكُم بِٱلَّيْلِ وَيَعْلَمُ مَا جَرَحْتُم بِٱلنَّهَارِ ثُمَّ يَبْعَثُكُمْ فِيهِ لِيُقْضَىٰٓ أَجَلٌ مُّسَمًّى ثُمَّ إِلَيْهِ مَرْجِعُكُمْ ثُمَّ يُنَبِّئُكُم بِمَا كُنتُمْ تَعْمَلُونَ

60. Wahuwa alla_thee_ yatawaffa_kum biallayli wayaAAlamu m_a_ jara_h_tum bialnnah_a_ri thumma yabAAathukum feehi liyuq_da_ ajalun musamman thumma ilayhi marjiAAukum thumma yunabbi-okum bim_a_ kuntum taAAmaloon_a_

6:60. And He it is Who takes your souls at night. And He knows what you strive for in the day, then raises you up therein to fulfill an appointed term. Then to Him is your return, when He will inform you of what you had been doing.

وَهُوَ ٱلْقَاهِرُ فَوْقَ عِبَادِهِۦ وَيُرْسِلُ عَلَيْكُمْ حَفَظَةً حَتَّىٰٓ إِذَا جَآءَ أَحَدَكُمُ ٱلْمَوْتُ تَوَفَّتْهُ رُسُلُنَا وَهُمْ لَا يُفَرِّطُونَ

61. Wahuwa alqa_h_iru fawqa AAiba_dihi wayursilu AAalaykum hafa_th_atan _h_att_a_ i_tha_ jaa a_h_adakumu almawtu tawaffat-hu rusulun_a_ wahum l_a_ yufarri_t_oon_a_

6:61. And He is the One Supreme above His subjects, and He sends guardians over you. Until when death comes to one of you, Our Messengers take his/her soul up, and they make no mistake.

ثُمَّ رُدُّوٓاْ إِلَى ٱللَّهِ مَوْلَىٰهُمُ ٱلْحَقِّ أَلَا لَهُ ٱلْحُكْمُ وَهُوَ أَسْرَعُ ٱلْحَسِبِينَ

62. Thumma ruddoo il<u>a</u> All<u>a</u>hi mawl<u>a</u>humu al<u>h</u>aqqi al<u>a</u> lahu al<u>h</u>ukmu wahuwa asraAAu al<u>h</u>asibeena

6:62. They are then returned to their True Master. Isn't His, the Command and isn't He, quick in taking account?

قُلْ مَن يُنَجِّيكُم مِّن ظُلُمَـٰتِ ٱلْبَرِّ وَٱلْبَحْرِ تَدْعُونَهُۥ تَضَرُّعًا وَخُفْيَةً لَّئِنْ أَنجَىٰنَا مِنْ هَـٰذِهِۦ لَنَكُونَنَّ مِنَ ٱلشَّـٰكِرِينَ ۝

63. Qul man yunajjeekum min <u>th</u>ulum<u>a</u>ti albarri wa<u>a</u>lba<u>h</u>ri tadAAoonahu ta<u>d</u>arruAAan wakhufyatan la-in anj<u>a</u>n<u>a</u> min h<u>ath</u>ihi lanakoonanna mina alshsh<u>a</u>kireena

6:63. Say, "Who is it that delivers you from darknesses of the land and the sea when you pray to Him in humility and secrecy, 'If He delivers us from this, we should certainly be of the grateful ones'?"

قُلِ ٱللَّهُ يُنَجِّيكُم مِّنْهَا وَمِن كُلِّ كَرْبٍ ثُمَّ أَنتُمْ تُشْرِكُونَ ۝

64. Quli All<u>a</u>hu yunajjeekum minh<u>a</u> wamin kulli karbin thumma antum tushrikoona

6:64. Say, "Allah delivers you from those and from every distress, but, then, you go and worship others besides Allah!

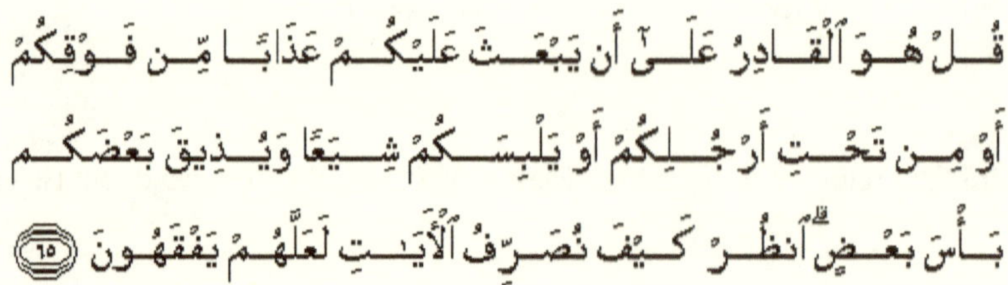

65. Qul huwa alqadiru AAala an yabAAatha AAalaykum AAathaban min fawqikum aw min tahti arjulikum aw yalbisakum shiyaAAan wayutheeqa baAAdakum ba/sa baAAdin onthur kayfa nusarrifu al-ayati laAAallahum yafqahoona

---

6:65. Say, "He has the power to send punishment upon you from above you or from beneath your feet, or to clothe you in sectarian garbs and make some of you taste the hostility of others."[19] See how variously We do explain the Verses/signs so that they may understand.

---

19. It is not only through earthquakes and other such natural calamities that Allah punishes mankind. HE punishes them through sectarian conflicts among them as well, as this Verse informs us.

---

66. Wakaththaba bihi qawmuka wahuwa alhaqqu qul lastu AAalaykum biwakeelin

---

6:66. And your people have declared it[20] to be a lie, and it is the Truth. Say, "I am not given the responsibility of managing your affairs."

---

20. 'It' here connotes not only what is stated in the preceding Verses, but also the Qur'aan as a whole.

لِّكُلِّ نَبَإٍ مُّسْتَقَرٌّ وَسَوْفَ تَعْلَمُونَ ۝

67. Likulli naba-in mustaqarrun wasawfa taAAalmoon**a**

6:67. And you will in time come to know that every information given[21] is based on Truth.

---

21. Given in the preceding Verses and in the Qur'aan as a whole.

وَإِذَا رَأَيْتَ ٱلَّذِينَ يَخُوضُونَ فِىٓ ءَايَٰتِنَا فَأَعْرِضْ عَنْهُمْ حَتَّىٰ يَخُوضُوا۟

فِى حَدِيثٍ غَيْرِهِۦ ۚ وَإِمَّا يُنسِيَنَّكَ ٱلشَّيْطَٰنُ فَلَا تَقْعُدْ بَعْدَ ٱلذِّكْرَىٰ

مَعَ ٱلْقَوْمِ ٱلظَّٰلِمِينَ ۝

68. Wa-i**tha** raayta alla**th**eena yakhoo**d**oona fee **a**yati**na** faaAAri**d** AAanhum **h**atta yakhoo**d**oo fee **h**adeethin ghayrihi wa-imm**a** yunsiyannaka alshshay**t**anu fal**a** taqAAud baAAda al**thth**ikr**a** maAAa alqawmi al**ththa**limeen**a**

6:68. And when you see people denying and ridiculing Our Verses/signs, withdraw from them until they enter another topic of talk. And if the Satan causes you to forget, then, after remembering the divine directive, sit not in the company of the wicked people.

وَمَا عَلَى ٱلَّذِينَ يَتَّقُونَ مِنْ حِسَابِهِم مِّن شَىْءٍ وَلَٰكِن ذِكْرَىٰ لَعَلَّهُمْ

يَتَّقُونَ ۝

69. Wama AAala allatheena yattaqoona min hisabihim min shay-in walakin thikra laAAallahum yattaqoona

6:69. And those who fear Allah shall not be responsible for anything in those wicked people's account, but their responsibility it is to remind the wicked people, so that the latter may also fear Allah.

وَذَرِ ٱلَّذِينَ ٱتَّخَذُواْ دِينَهُمْ لَعِبًا وَلَهْوًا وَغَرَّتْهُمُ ٱلْحَيَوٰةُ ٱلدُّنْيَا ۚ وَذَكِّرْ بِهِ أَن تُبْسَلَ نَفْسٌ بِمَا كَسَبَتْ لَيْسَ لَهَا مِن دُونِ ٱللَّهِ وَلِيٌّ وَلَا شَفِيعٌ وَإِن تَعْدِلْ كُلَّ عَدْلٍ لَّا يُؤْخَذْ مِنْهَا ۗ أُوْلَٰٓئِكَ ٱلَّذِينَ أُبْسِلُواْ بِمَا كَسَبُواْ ۖ لَهُمْ شَرَابٌ مِّنْ حَمِيمٍ وَعَذَابٌ أَلِيمٌ بِمَا كَانُواْ يَكْفُرُونَ ﴿٧٠﴾

70. Wathari allatheena ittakhathoo deenahum laAAiban walahwan wagharrat-humu alhayatu alddunya wathakkir bihi an tubsala nafsun bima kasabat laysa laha min dooni Allahi waliyyun wala shafeeAAun wa-in taAAdil kulla AAadlin la yu/khath minha ola-ika allatheena obsiloo bima kasaboo lahum sharabun min hameemin waAAathabun aleemun bima kanoo yakfuroona

6:70. And leave alone those who have taken their religion (way of life) as just play and pastime, and whom this world's life has deceived. But do remind them with it[22] lest an individual self is given up to destruction for what it has earned. It shall not have, other than Allah, any *wali* nor an intercessor, and even if it offers all possible ransom, it shall not be accepted from it. These are they who shall be given up to destruction for what they earned. For them will be a drink of boiling water and a painful punishment, because they had been suppressing the Truth.

22. The Qur'aanic teachings.

قُلْ أَنَدْعُواْ مِن دُونِ ٱللَّهِ مَا لَا يَنفَعُنَا وَلَا يَضُرُّنَا وَنُرَدُّ عَلَىٰٓ أَعْقَابِنَا بَعْدَ إِذْ هَدَىٰنَا ٱللَّهُ كَٱلَّذِى ٱسْتَهْوَتْهُ ٱلشَّيَـٰطِينُ فِى ٱلْأَرْضِ حَيْرَانَ لَهُۥٓ أَصْحَـٰبٌ يَدْعُونَهُۥٓ إِلَى ٱلْهُدَى ٱئْتِنَا قُلْ إِنَّ هُدَى ٱللَّهِ هُوَ ٱلْهُدَىٰ وَأُمِرْنَا لِنُسْلِمَ لِرَبِّ ٱلْعَـٰلَمِينَ ۝

71. Qul anadAAoo min dooni All<u>a</u>hi m<u>a</u> l<u>a</u> yanfaAAun<u>a</u> wal<u>a</u> ya<u>d</u>urrun<u>a</u> wanuraddu AAal<u>a</u> aAAq<u>a</u>bin<u>a</u> baAAda i<u>th</u> had<u>a</u>n<u>a</u> All<u>a</u>hu ka<u>a</u>lla<u>th</u>ee istahwat-hu alshshay<u>at</u>eenu fee al-ar<u>d</u>i <u>h</u>ayr<u>a</u>na lahu a<u>s</u>-<u>h</u>abun yadAAoonahu il<u>a</u> alhud<u>a</u> i/tin<u>a</u> qul inna hud<u>a</u> All<u>a</u>hi huwa alhud<u>a</u> waomirn<u>a</u> linuslima lirabbi alAA<u>a</u>lameena

---

6:71. Say, "Shall we pray to someone – other than Allah – who can do us neither good nor harm, and shall we turn back on our heels, after Allah has guided us, like him whom the devils have made to move about perplexed in the earth and who has companions calling him to their guidance?" Say, "Indeed, Allah's guidance is the guidance.[23] And we are commanded to submit to the Lord of the worlds."

---

23. In other words, no other guidance that adds to or subtracts from Allah's guidance has any divine sanction. And what is Allah's guidance? The essentials of this guidance are as stipulated in the Qur'aan. Anyone acting <u>honestly</u> within the framework of those stipulations can be said to be abiding by Allah's guidance. But most Muslims today have abandoned this divine framework. And the tragic fact is that they do not know that they have abandoned it! Because they do not understand what the Qur'aan says. They take no pains to understand it. They just go by what others say it contains.

وَأَنْ أَقِيمُواْ ٱلصَّلَوٰةَ وَٱتَّقُوهُ وَهُوَ ٱلَّذِىٓ إِلَيْهِ تُحْشَرُونَ ۝

72. Waan aqeemoo al<u>ss</u>al<u>a</u>ta wa<u>i</u>ttaqoohu wahuwa alla<u>th</u>ee ilayhi tu<u>h</u>sharoona

---

6:72. "And that we should establish prayer and fear Him." And He it is to Whom you shall be gathered.

وَهُوَ ٱلَّذِى خَلَقَ ٱلسَّمَـٰوَٰتِ وَٱلْأَرْضَ بِٱلْحَقِّ وَيَوْمَ يَقُولُ كُن فَيَكُونُ قَوْلُهُ ٱلْحَقُّ وَلَهُ ٱلْمُلْكُ يَوْمَ يُنفَخُ فِى ٱلصُّورِ عَـٰلِمُ ٱلْغَيْبِ وَٱلشَّهَـٰدَةِ وَهُوَ ٱلْحَكِيمُ ٱلْخَبِيرُ ﴿٧٣﴾

73. Wahuwa alla_thee_ khalaqa alssama_w_ati waal-ar_da_ bial_h_aqqi wayawma yaqoolu kun fayakoonu qawluhu al_h_aqqu walahu almulku yawma yunfakhu fee al_ss_oori AAalimu alghaybi waalshshah_a_dati wahuwa al_h_akeemu alkhabee**ru**

6:73. And He it is, as a matter of fact, Who has created the heavens and the earth. And the time He says, 'Be', it is! His word is the truth. And His is the Sovereignty, the day the Trumpet is blown.[24] HE is the Knower of the unseen and the seen. And He is the Wise, the Aware.

24. Allah's sovereignty it is over the heavens and the earth, always. But He has delegated some of His sovereign powers temporarily to mankind, just to test them. HE resumes these delegated powers also, when the Trumpet is blown to herald the the Last Day.

۞ وَإِذْ قَالَ إِبْرَٰهِيمُ لِأَبِيهِ ءَازَرَ أَتَتَّخِذُ أَصْنَامًا ءَالِهَةً إِنِّى أَرَىٰكَ وَقَوْمَكَ فِى ضَلَـٰلٍ مُّبِينٍ ﴿٧٤﴾

74. Wa-i_th_ qala ibra_h_eemu li-abeehi _a_zara atattakhi_th_u a_s_naman alihatan innee ar_a_ka waqawmaka fee _d_alalin mubee**nin**

6:74. And when Abraham told his father, Azar, "Do you take idols as gods? I do indeed see you and your people in manifest error."

وَكَذَٰلِكَ نُرِىٓ إِبْرَٰهِيمَ مَلَكُوتَ ٱلسَّمَٰوَٰتِ وَٱلْأَرْضِ وَلِيَكُونَ مِنَ ٱلْمُوقِنِينَ ﴿٧٥﴾

75. Wakathalika nuree ibraheema malakoota alssamawati waal-ardi waliyakoona mina almooqineena

6:75. And thus did We show to Abraham the Reality of sovereignty over the heavens and the earth so that he was of those, strong in Faith.

فَلَمَّا جَنَّ عَلَيْهِ ٱلَّيْلُ رَءَا كَوْكَبًا قَالَ هَٰذَا رَبِّى فَلَمَّآ أَفَلَ قَالَ لَآ أُحِبُّ ٱلْأَفِلِينَ ﴿٧٦﴾

76. Falamma janna AAalayhi allaylu raa kawkaban qala hatha rabbee falamma afala qala la ohibbu al-afileena

6:76. So when the night fell on him, he saw a star. He said, "This is my Lord." But when it set, he said, "I do not love things that set."

فَلَمَّا رَءَا ٱلْقَمَرَ بَازِغًا قَالَ هَٰذَا رَبِّى فَلَمَّآ أَفَلَ قَالَ لَئِن لَّمْ يَهْدِنِى رَبِّى لَأَكُونَنَّ مِنَ ٱلْقَوْمِ ٱلضَّآلِّينَ ﴿٧٧﴾

77. Falamma raa alqamara bazighan qala hatha rabbee falamma afala qala la-in lam yahdinee rabbee laakoonanna mina alqawmi alddalleena

6:77. Then when he saw the moon rising, he said, "This is my Lord." But when it set, he said, "If my Lord does not guide me, I shall certainly be of the people gone astray."

فَلَمَّا رَءَا ٱلشَّمْسَ بَازِغَةً قَالَ هَـٰذَا رَبِّى هَـٰذَآ أَكْبَرُ فَلَمَّآ أَفَلَتْ قَالَ يَـٰقَوْمِ إِنِّى بَرِىٓءٌ مِّمَّا تُشْرِكُونَ ۝

78. Falamma raa alshshamsa bazighatan qala hatha rabbee hatha akbaru falamma afalat qala ya qawmi innee baree-on mimma tushrikoona

---

6:78. Then when he saw the sun rising up, he said, "This is my Lord. This is the greatest. But when it set, he said, "O my people! I am indeed absolved of worshipping those, other than Allah, whom you worship."

إِنِّى وَجَّهْتُ وَجْهِىَ لِلَّذِى فَطَرَ ٱلسَّمَـٰوَٰتِ وَٱلْأَرْضَ حَنِيفًا وَمَآ أَنَا۠ مِنَ ٱلْمُشْرِكِينَ ۝

79. Innee wajjahtu wajhiya lillathee fatara alssamawati waal-arda haneefan wama ana mina almushrikeena

---

6:79. "I have indeed turned my face wholeheartedly to Him Who has created the heavens and the earth, and I am not of those who worship others besides Allah."

وَحَآجَّهُۥ قَوْمُهُۥ قَالَ أَتُحَٰجُّوٓنِّى فِى ٱللَّهِ وَقَدْ هَدَٰنِ وَلَآ أَخَافُ مَا تُشْرِكُونَ بِهِۦٓ إِلَّآ أَن يَشَآءَ رَبِّى شَيْـًٔا وَسِعَ رَبِّى كُلَّ شَىْءٍ عِلْمًا أَفَلَا تَتَذَكَّرُونَ ۝

80. Wahajjahu qawmuhu qala atuhajjoonnee fee Allahi waqad hadani wala akhafu ma tushrikoona bihi illa an yashaa rabbee shay-an wasiAAa rabbee kulla shay-in AAilman afala tatathakkaroona

---

6:80. And his people quarrelled with him. He said, "Do you quarrel with me about Allah, Who certainly has guided me? And I do not fear those you worship besides Him in anything except what my Lord wills. My Lord comprehends all things in His knowledge. Don't you remember?"

وَكَيْفَ أَخَافُ مَآ أَشْرَكْتُمْ وَلَا تَخَافُونَ أَنَّكُمْ أَشْرَكْتُم بِٱللَّهِ مَا لَمْ يُنَزِّلْ بِهِۦ عَلَيْكُمْ سُلْطَٰنًا فَأَىُّ ٱلْفَرِيقَيْنِ أَحَقُّ بِٱلْأَمْنِ إِن كُنتُمْ تَعْلَمُونَ

81. Wakayfa akhafu ma ashraktum wala takhafoona annakum ashraktum biAllahi ma lam yunazzil bihi AAalaykum sultanan faayyu alfareeqayni ahaqqu bial-amni in kuntum taAAlamoona

---

6:81. "And why should I fear those whom you worship besides Allah, when you do not fear that you worship that, besides Allah, for which He has not sent down to you any authority. Then tell me if you do know which of the two parties has a greater claim to security?"

ٱلَّذِينَ ءَامَنُوا۟ وَلَمْ يَلْبِسُوٓا۟ إِيمَٰنَهُم بِظُلْمٍ أُو۟لَٰٓئِكَ لَهُمُ ٱلْأَمْنُ وَهُم مُّهْتَدُونَ ۝

82. Allatheena amanoo walam yalbisoo eemanahum bithulmin ola-ika lahumu al-amnu wahum muhtadoona

6:82. "Those who believe, and do not obscure their belief with wickedness, those are they who shall have the security and those are they who are guided."

وَتِلْكَ حُجَّتُنَآ ءَاتَيْنَٰهَآ إِبْرَٰهِيمَ عَلَىٰ قَوْمِهِۦ نَرْفَعُ دَرَجَٰتٍ مَّن نَّشَآءُ إِنَّ رَبَّكَ حَكِيمٌ عَلِيمٌ ۝

83. Watilka hujjatuna ataynaha ibraheema AAala qawmihi narfaAAu darajatin man nashao inna rabbaka hakeemun AAaleemun

6:83. And that was Our argument which we gave to Abraham against his people. We raise whom We will in rank. Indeed, your Lord is Wise, Knowledgeable!

وَوَهَبْنَا لَهُۥ إِسْحَٰقَ وَيَعْقُوبَ كُلًّا هَدَيْنَا وَنُوحًا هَدَيْنَا مِن قَبْلُ وَمِن ذُرِّيَّتِهِۦ دَاوُۥدَ وَسُلَيْمَٰنَ وَأَيُّوبَ وَيُوسُفَ وَمُوسَىٰ وَهَٰرُونَ وَكَذَٰلِكَ نَجْزِى ٱلْمُحْسِنِينَ ۝

84. Wawahabna lahu ishaqa wayaAAqooba kullan hadayna wanoohan hadayna min qablu wamin thurriyyatihi dawooda wasulaymana waayyooba wayoosufa wamoosa waharoona wakathalika najzee almuhsineena

6:84. And We gave him Isaac and Jacob. We guided everyone. And, before that, We guided Noah, and of his progeny, David and Solomon and Job and Joseph and Moses and Aaron. And thus, do We reward those who do good.

وَزَكَرِيَّا وَيَحْيَىٰ وَعِيسَىٰ وَإِلْيَاسَ كُلٌّ مِّنَ ٱلصَّٰلِحِينَ ۝

85. Wazakariyya wayahya waAAeesa wailyasa kullun mina alssaliheena

6:85. And Zachariya and John and Jesus and Elias, all of them righteous men!

وَإِسْمَٰعِيلَ وَٱلْيَسَعَ وَيُونُسَ وَلُوطًا وَكُلًّا فَضَّلْنَا عَلَى ٱلْعَٰلَمِينَ ۝

86. Wa-ismaAAeela wailyasaAAa wayoonusa walootan wakullan faddalna AAala alAAalameena

6:86. And Ishmael and Elisha and Jonah and Lot, and to all of them We gave favours over the worlds.

وَمِنْ ءَابَآئِهِمْ وَذُرِّيَّٰتِهِمْ وَإِخْوَٰنِهِمْ وَٱجْتَبَيْنَٰهُمْ وَهَدَيْنَٰهُمْ إِلَىٰ صِرَٰطٍ مُّسْتَقِيمٍ ۝

87. Wamin aba-ihim wathurriyyatihim wa-ikhwanihim waijtabaynahum wahadaynahum ila siratin mustaqeemin

6:87. And from among their fathers and their progeny and their brethren, We chose some and guided to the Straight Path.

ذَٰلِكَ هُدَى ٱللَّهِ يَهۡدِى بِهِۦ مَن يَشَآءُ مِنۡ عِبَادِهِۦۚ وَلَوۡ أَشۡرَكُواْ لَحَبِطَ عَنۡهُم مَّا كَانُواْ يَعۡمَلُونَ ۝

88. Thalika huda Allahi yahdee bihi man yashao min AAibadihi walaw ashrakoo lahabita AAanhum ma kanoo yaAAmaloona

6:88. That is Allah's guidance. He guides thereby whom He wills of His subjects. And if they worship other gods, certainly, what they did would become useless for them.

أُوْلَـٰٓئِكَ ٱلَّذِينَ ءَاتَيۡنَٰهُمُ ٱلۡكِتَٰبَ وَٱلۡحُكۡمَ وَٱلنُّبُوَّةَۚ فَإِن يَكۡفُرۡ بِهَا هَـٰٓؤُلَآءِ فَقَدۡ وَكَّلۡنَا بِهَا قَوۡمًا لَّيۡسُواْ بِهَا بِكَٰفِرِينَ ۝

89. Ola-ika allatheena ataynahumu alkitaba waalhukma waalnnubuwwata fa-in yakfur biha haola-i faqad wakkalna biha qawman laysoo biha bikafireena

6:89. They are those whom We gave the Book and the authority and the prophecy. As their peoples suppressed and denied the Truth thereof, We then entrusted it to a people who do not suppress and deny the Truth in it.

أُوْلَٰٓئِكَ ٱلَّذِينَ هَدَى ٱللَّهُ فَبِهُدَىٰهُمُ ٱقْتَدِهْ قُل لَّآ أَسْـَٔلُكُمْ عَلَيْهِ أَجْرًا إِنْ هُوَ إِلَّا ذِكْرَىٰ لِلْعَٰلَمِينَ ۝

90. Ola-ika alla<u>th</u>eena hada<u> </u>All<u>a</u>hu fabihuda<u>h</u>umu iqtadih qul l<u>a</u> as-alukum AAalayhi ajran in huwa ill<u>a</u> <u>th</u>ikr<u>a</u> lilAA<u>a</u>lameena

---

6:90. They are those whom Allah had guided. Follow their guidance then! [25] Say, "I do not ask you for any reward for it[26]. It is the Book of Guidance, to be referred to often, not just for you but for all the worlds[27]."

---

25. It may please be carefully noted that what Allah tells mankind here is for them to follow His chosen Prophets and Messengers only. All those who are mentioned by their names in the foregoing Verses were all Prophets and/or Messengers. This divine command to mankind is to follow the Prophets only - and not others. This Verse does not give any mandatory command for them to follow the others, howsoever learned and pious they may have been.

26. The Qur'aan.

27. Till the Last Day.

وَمَا قَدَرُواْ ٱللَّهَ حَقَّ قَدْرِهِۦٓ إِذْ قَالُواْ مَآ أَنزَلَ ٱللَّهُ عَلَىٰ بَشَرٍ مِّن شَىْءٍ قُلْ مَنْ أَنزَلَ ٱلْكِتَٰبَ ٱلَّذِى جَآءَ بِهِۦ مُوسَىٰ نُورًا وَهُدًى لِّلنَّاسِ تَجْعَلُونَهُۥ قَرَاطِيسَ تُبْدُونَهَا وَتُخْفُونَ كَثِيرًا وَعُلِّمْتُم مَّا لَمْ تَعْلَمُوٓاْ أَنتُمْ وَلَآ ءَابَآؤُكُمْ قُلِ ٱللَّهُ ثُمَّ ذَرْهُمْ فِى خَوْضِهِمْ يَلْعَبُونَ ۝

91. Wam<u>a</u> qadaroo All<u>a</u>ha <u>h</u>aqqa qadrihi i<u>th</u> q<u>a</u>loo m<u>a</u> anzala All<u>a</u>hu AAal<u>a</u> basharin min shay-in qul man anzala alkit<u>a</u>ba alla<u>th</u>ee j<u>a</u>a bihi moos<u>a</u> nooran wahudan lilnn<u>a</u>si tajAAaloonahu qar<u>a</u>teesa tubdoonah<u>a</u> watukhfoona katheeran waAAullimtum m<u>a</u> lam taAAlamoo antum wal<u>a</u> <u>aba</u>okum quli All<u>a</u>hu thumma <u>th</u>arhum fee khaw<u>d</u>ihim yalAAaboon<u>a</u>

6:91. And they do not appreciate Allah's unique Majesty and Power as it should be appreciated, when they say, "Allah has not sent down any revelation upon man." Say, "Who revealed the Book that Moses brought, a light and guidance to men, which you made into sheets you show – while you conceal much – and you were taught what you or your fathers did not know?" Say, "Allah!" Then leave them to play with their vain talk in which the Truth is suppressed and ridiculed.

وَهَـٰذَا كِـتَـٰبٌ أَنزَلْنَـٰهُ مُبَـارَكٌ مُصَـدِّقُ ٱلَّـذِى بَيْـنَ يَدَيْـهِ وَلِتُنذِرَ أُمَّ ٱلْقُرَىٰ وَمَـنْ حَوْلَهَا وَٱلَّذِينَ يُؤْمِنُونَ بِٱلْأَخِرَةِ يُؤْمِنُونَ بِهِۦ وَهُمْ عَلَىٰ صَلَاتِهِمْ يُحَافِظُونَ ﴿٩٢﴾

92. Wahatha kitabun anzalnahu mubarakun musaddiqu allathee bayna yadayhi walitunthira omma alqura waman hawlaha waallatheena yu/minoona bial-akhirati yu/minoona bihi wahum AAala salatihim yuhafithoona

6:92. And We have sent down this blessed Book, confirming that which is before it, so that you may warn the Mother City[28] and settlements around it. And those who believe in the Hereafter believe in it, and they guard their prayers.

28. Makkah.

وَمَنْ أَظْلَمُ مِمَّنِ ٱفْتَرَىٰ عَلَى ٱللَّهِ كَذِبًا أَوْ قَالَ أُوحِىَ إِلَىَّ وَلَمْ يُوحَ إِلَيْهِ شَىْءٌ وَمَن قَالَ سَأُنزِلُ مِثْلَ مَآ أَنزَلَ ٱللَّهُ وَلَوْ تَرَىٰ إِذِ ٱلظَّٰلِمُونَ فِى غَمَرَٰتِ ٱلْمَوْتِ وَٱلْمَلَٰٓئِكَةُ بَاسِطُوٓاْ أَيْدِيهِمْ أَخْرِجُوٓاْ أَنفُسَكُمُ ٱلْيَوْمَ تُجْزَوْنَ عَذَابَ ٱلْهُونِ بِمَا كُنتُمْ تَقُولُونَ عَلَى ٱللَّهِ غَيْرَ ٱلْحَقِّ وَكُنتُمْ عَنْ ءَايَٰتِهِۦ تَسْتَكْبِرُونَ ۝

93. Waman a_th_lamu mimmani iftara AAala Allahi ka_th_iban aw qala ooh_iya ilayya walam yooh_a ilayhi shay-on waman qala saonzilu mithla ma anzala Allahu walaw tara i_th_i al_ththa_limoona fee ghamar_a_ti almawti waalmal_a-ikatu b_a_si_t_oo aydeehim akhrijoo anfusakumu alyawma tujzawna AAa_th_aba alhooni bima kuntum taqooloona AAala Allahi ghayra al_h_aqqi wakuntum AAan _a_y_a_tihi tastakbiroon_a_

6:93. And who can be more wicked than he who forges a lie against Allah, or says, 'It has been revealed to me' while nothing has been revealed to him, and who says, "I shall reveal the like of what Allah has revealed"? And if you could but see the wicked people when they are in the throes of death and the angels stretch out their hands saying, "Take out your lives! It's time you are recompensed with a contemptible punishment for speaking false things about Allah and for being too proud to accept His Verses/signs."

وَلَقَدْ جِئْتُمُونَا فُرَٰدَىٰ كَمَا خَلَقْنَٰكُمْ أَوَّلَ مَرَّةٍ وَتَرَكْتُم مَّا خَوَّلْنَٰكُمْ وَرَآءَ ظُهُورِكُمْ وَمَا نَرَىٰ مَعَكُمْ شُفَعَآءَكُمُ ٱلَّذِينَ زَعَمْتُمْ أَنَّهُمْ فِيكُمْ شُرَكَٰٓؤُاْ لَقَد تَّقَطَّعَ بَيْنَكُمْ وَضَلَّ عَنكُم مَّا كُنتُمْ تَزْعُمُونَ ۝

94. Walaqad ji/tumoona fur_a_da kam_a_ khalaqn_a_kum awwala marratin wataraktum m_a_ khawwaln_a_kum war_a_a _th_uhoorikum wam_a_ nara maAAakum shufaAA_a_akumu alla_th_eena zaAAamtum annahum feekum shurak_a_o laqad taqa_tt_aAAa baynakum wa_d_alla AAankum m_a_ kuntum tazAAumoon_a_

6:94. And certainly you have come to Us alone just as We had created you the first time. And you have left behind your backs the things which We had given you. And We do

101

not see with you your intercessors about whom you had asserted that they were gods besides Allah for you. Certainly, the ties between you are cut off and what you had been asserting has deserted you.

۞ إِنَّ ٱللَّهَ فَالِقُ ٱلْحَبِّ وَٱلنَّوَىٰ يُخْرِجُ ٱلْحَيَّ مِنَ ٱلْمَيِّتِ وَمُخْرِجُ ٱلْمَيِّتِ مِنَ ٱلْحَيِّ ذَٰلِكُمُ ٱللَّهُ فَأَنَّىٰ تُؤْفَكُونَ ﴿٩٥﴾

95. Inna Allaha faliqu alhabbi waalnnawa yukhriju alhayya mina almayyiti wamukhriju almayyiti mina alhayyi thalikumu Allahu faanna tu/fakoona

---

6:95. Indeed, Allah causes the grain and the date stone to split. He brings forth the living from the dead and He is the One Who brings forth the dead from the living. That One is Allah! How are you then turned away from the Truth?

فَالِقُ ٱلْإِصْبَاحِ وَجَعَلَ ٱلَّيْلَ سَكَنًا وَٱلشَّمْسَ وَٱلْقَمَرَ حُسْبَانًا ذَٰلِكَ تَقْدِيرُ ٱلْعَزِيزِ ٱلْعَلِيمِ ﴿٩٦﴾

96. Faliqu al-isbahi wajaAAala allayla sakanan waalshshamsa waalqamara husbanan thalika taqdeeru alAAazeezi alAAaleemi

---

6:96. He causes the daybreaks. And He has made the night for rest, and the sun and the moon for timekeeping. That is the setting arranged by the Omnipotent, the Knowledgeable.

وَهُوَ ٱلَّذِى جَعَلَ لَكُمُ ٱلنُّجُومَ لِتَهْتَدُواْ بِهَا فِى ظُلُمَـٰتِ ٱلْبَرِّ وَٱلْبَحْرِ ۗ قَدْ فَصَّلْنَا ٱلْأَيَـٰتِ لِقَوْمٍ يَعْلَمُونَ ﴿٩٧﴾

97. Wahuwa allathee jaAAala lakumu alnnujooma litahtadoo biha fee thulumati albarri waalbahri qad fassalna al-ayati liqawmin yaAAlamoona

---

6:97. And He it is Who has made the stars for you that you may find your way thereby in the darkness of the land and the sea. We have certainly made the Verses/signs plain for people who know.

وَهُوَ ٱلَّذِىٓ أَنشَأَكُم مِّن نَّفْسٍ وَٰحِدَةٍ فَمُسْتَقَرٌّ وَمُسْتَوْدَعٌ ۗ قَدْ فَصَّلْنَا ٱلْأَيَـٰتِ لِقَوْمٍ يَفْقَهُونَ ﴿٩٨﴾

98. Wahuwa allathee anshaakum min nafsin wahidatin famustaqarrun wamustawdaAAun qad fassalna al-ayati liqawmin yafqahoona

---

6:98. And He it is Who has brought you into being from a single human being, then there is for you a domicile and a depository.[29] We have certainly made the Verses/signs plain for people who understand.

---

29. 'Domicile' is a human being's sojourn on this earth as a living being. And the 'depository' is the earth itself wherein the remains of a human being get deposited, after his/her death. The latter term could also connote the depository, with Allah Almighty, wherein souls of all dead persons are deposited till the persons are resurrected on the Day of Resurrection.

وَهُوَ ٱلَّذِىٓ أَنزَلَ مِنَ ٱلسَّمَآءِ مَآءً فَأَخْرَجْنَا بِهِۦ نَبَاتَ كُلِّ شَىْءٍ فَأَخْرَجْنَا مِنْهُ خَضِرًا نُّخْرِجُ مِنْهُ حَبًّا مُّتَرَاكِبًا وَمِنَ ٱلنَّخْلِ مِن طَلْعِهَا قِنْوَانٌ دَانِيَةٌ وَجَنَّـٰتٍ مِّنْ أَعْنَابٍ وَٱلزَّيْتُونَ وَٱلرُّمَّانَ مُشْتَبِهًا وَغَيْرَ مُتَشَـٰبِهٍ ٱنظُرُوٓا۟ إِلَىٰ ثَمَرِهِۦٓ إِذَآ أَثْمَرَ وَيَنْعِهِۦٓ إِنَّ فِى ذَٰلِكُمْ لَأَيَـٰتٍ لِّقَوْمٍ يُؤْمِنُونَ ۝

99. Wahuwa allathee anzala mina alssama-i maan faakhrajna bihi nabata kulli shay-in faakhrajna minhu khadiran nukhriju minhu habban mutarakiban wamina alnnakhli min talAAiha qinwanun daniyatun wajannatin min aAAnabin waalzzaytoona waalrrummana mushtabihan waghayra mutashabihin onthuroo ila thamarihi itha athmara wayanAAihi inna fee thalikum laayatin liqawmin yu/minoona

---

6:99. And He it is Who sends down water from the sky. Then We bring forth with it every kind of growth. Then We bring forth from it greenery from which We produce grain clustered in ears. And of the palm-tree – of its sheaths – come forth clusters of dates within reach. And gardens of grapes and olives and pomegranates, alike and unlike – look at its fruit when it bears fruit and when it ripens. Indeed, there are signs in these things for people who believe.

وَجَعَلُوا۟ لِلَّهِ شُرَكَآءَ ٱلْجِنَّ وَخَلَقَهُمْ وَخَرَقُوا۟ لَهُۥ بَنِينَ وَبَنَـٰتٍ بِغَيْرِ عِلْمٍ سُبْحَـٰنَهُۥ وَتَعَـٰلَىٰ عَمَّا يَصِفُونَ ۝

100. WajaAAaloo lillahi shurakaa aljinna wakhalaqahum wakharaqoo lahu baneena wabanatin bighayri AAilmin subhanahu wataAAala AAamma yasifoona

---

6:100. And they worship the jinn as associates of Allah, and He created them! And, without knowledge, they falsely attribute sons and daughters to Him. Glorified is He! He is far too high and exalted above what they ascribe to Him.

بَـدِيعُ ٱلسَّمَـوَتِ وَٱلْأَرْضِ أَنَّىٰ يَكُونُ لَـهُ وَلَـدٌ وَلَمْ تَكُن لَّـهُ صَـٰحِبَةٌ وَخَلَقَ كُلَّ شَىْءٍ وَهُوَ بِكُلِّ شَىْءٍ عَلِيمٌ

101. BadeeAAu alssamawati waal-ardi anna yakoonu lahu waladun walam takun lahu sahibatun wakhalaqa kulla shay-in wahuwa bikulli shay-in AAaleemun

6:101. The One to bring into being the heavens and the earth! How could He have a son when He has no consort? And He Himself created everything, and He is the One Who knows all things!

ذَٰلِكُمُ ٱللَّهُ رَبُّكُمْ لَا إِلَـهَ إِلَّا هُوَ خَـٰلِقُ كُلِّ شَىْءٍ فَٱعْبُدُوهُ وَهُوَ عَلَىٰ كُلِّ شَىْءٍ وَكِيلٌ

102. Thalikumu Allahu rabbukum la ilaha illa huwa khaliqu kulli shay-in faoAAbudoohu wahuwa AAala kulli shay-in wakeelun

6:102. That One is Allah, your Lord! There is no god but Him. HE is the Creator of all things, so worship Him! And He is the One Who looks after all things.

لَّا تُدْرِكُهُ ٱلْأَبْصَـٰرُ وَهُوَ يُدْرِكُ ٱلْأَبْصَـٰرَ وَهُوَ ٱللَّطِيفُ ٱلْخَبِيرُ

103. La tudrikuhu al-absaru wahuwa yudriku al-absara wahuwa allateefu alkhabeeru

6:103. No vision can grasp Him, and He grasps all visions. And He is Aware of the minutest detail.

قَدْ جَاءَكُم بَصَآئِرُ مِن رَّبِّكُمْ فَمَنْ أَبْصَرَ فَلِنَفْسِهِۦ وَمَنْ عَمِىَ فَعَلَيْهَا وَمَآ أَنَا عَلَيْكُم بِحَفِيظٍ ۝

104. Qad jaakum basa-iru min rabbikum faman absara falinafsihi waman AAamiya faAAalayha wama ana AAalaykum bihafeethin

6:104. "Evidences have certainly come to you from your Lord. Whoever then sees the evidences, it is for his own good; and whoever is blind to them, it is to his own detriment! And I am not a guardian over you."

وَكَذَالِكَ نُصَرِّفُ ٱلْآيَاتِ وَلِيَقُولُواْ دَرَسْتَ وَلِنُبَيِّنَهُۥ لِقَوْمٍ يَعْلَمُونَ ۝

105. Wakathalika nusarrifu al-ayati waliyaqooloo darasta walinubayyinahu liqawmin yaAAlamoona

6:105. And thus do We variously explain the Verses/signs so that they say, "You have repeated [what you had already said before]" and that We may make it clear to people who know.[30]

30. The Qur'aan itself explains here why certain things therein are apparently repeated. The divine purpose is to make those things clearer with additional information, or, just to hammer the things more securely into the forgetful human minds.

ٱتَّبِعْ مَآ أُوحِىَ إِلَيْكَ مِن رَّبِّكَ لَآ إِلَـٰهَ إِلَّا هُوَ وَأَعْرِضْ عَنِ ٱلْمُشْرِكِينَ ۝١٠٦

106. IttabiAA ma oohiya ilayka min rabbika la ilaha illa huwa waaAArid AAani almushrikeena

---

6:106. Follow what is revealed to you from your Lord! There is no god but Him. And turn away from those who worship others besides Allah.

وَلَوْ شَآءَ ٱللَّهُ مَآ أَشْرَكُوا۟ وَمَا جَعَلْنَـٰكَ عَلَيْهِمْ حَفِيظًا وَمَآ أَنتَ عَلَيْهِم بِوَكِيلٍ ۝١٠٧

107. Walaw shaa Allahu ma ashrakoo wama jaAAalnaka AAalayhim hafeethan wama anta AAalayhim biwakeelin

---

6:107. Had Allah so willed, they would not have worshipped others besides Him. And We have not appointed you[31] as a caretaker over them. And you are not there to look after all their affairs.

---

31. 2nd person pronoun here is in the singular, indicating that the addressee is the Prophet.

وَلَا تَسُبُّواْ ٱلَّذِينَ يَدْعُونَ مِن دُونِ ٱللَّهِ فَيَسُبُّواْ ٱللَّهَ عَدْوًا بِغَيْرِ عِلْمٍ كَذَٰلِكَ زَيَّنَّا لِكُلِّ أُمَّةٍ عَمَلَهُمْ ثُمَّ إِلَىٰ رَبِّهِم مَّرْجِعُهُمْ فَيُنَبِّئُهُم بِمَا كَانُواْ يَعْمَلُونَ ۝

108. Wala tasubboo allatheena yadAAoona min dooni Allahi fayasubboo Allaha AAadwan bighayri AAilmin kathalika zayyanna likulli ommatin AAamalahum thumma ila rabbihim marjiAAuhum fayunabbi-ohum bima kanoo yaAAmaloona

---

6:108. And do not abuse those whom they pray to, besides Allah, lest they should abuse Allah out of enmity and ignorance. To every people thus[32] We have made their own deeds look fair. Then to their Lord shall be their return when He will inform them of what they used to do.

---

32. When one community decries what another community does, the latter retaliates by condemning what the former does. As in the example given at the beginning of this Verse itself, Muslims may be inclined to abuse and ridicule the false gods non-Muslims pray to. Doing so may seem good to the Muslims as, to their minds, they are denigrating things that are falsely considered as divine. But those things prayed to may be icons of good people like Prophets and saints whom people, in their ignorance, consider worthy of worship, besides Allah! One example, which immediately comes to mind, is that of Jesus and his mother Mary, whom the Christians venerate and pray to. Can Muslims abuse either of these two? No – not at all! Both find mention in the Qur'aan as venerable persons. On the same basis, it would be wrong for Muslims to abuse gods of any other community. If Muslims would abuse them, the other communities would abuse Allah. By abusing Allah, they should certainly be inviting their own doom, but in the short life of this world they would be deluded into thinking that they have done a great thing!

وَأَقْسَمُواْ بِٱللَّهِ جَهْدَ أَيْمَٰنِهِمْ لَئِن جَآءَتْهُمْ ءَايَةٌ لَّيُؤْمِنُنَّ بِهَا قُلْ إِنَّمَا ٱلْءَايَٰتُ عِندَ ٱللَّهِ وَمَا يُشْعِرُكُمْ أَنَّهَآ إِذَا جَآءَتْ لَا يُؤْمِنُونَ ۝

109. Waaqsamoo biAllahi jahda aymanihim la-in jaat-hum ayatun layu/minunna biha qul innama al-ayatu AAinda Allahi wama yushAAirukum annaha itha jaat la yu/minoona

6:109. And they swear by Allah, with the strongest of their oaths, that if a Sign comes to them, they will certainly believe therein. Say, "Allah does certainly have the Signs." And you know not that when it (a Sign) does indeed come, they will not believe[33]

33. The sentence continues into the next Verse.

وَنُقَلِّبُ أَفْئِدَتَهُمْ وَأَبْصَـٰرَهُمْ كَمَا لَمْ يُؤْمِنُوا بِهِۦٓ أَوَّلَ مَرَّةٍ وَنَذَرُهُمْ فِى طُغْيَـٰنِهِمْ يَعْمَهُونَ ﴿١١٠﴾

110. Wanuqallibu af-idatahum waabsarahum kama lam yu/minoo bihi awwala marratin wanatharuhum fee tughyanihim yaAAmahoona

6:110. and We will turn their hearts and their sights away, as they fail to believe in it the first thing after its occurrence, and We will leave them to wander blindly in their transgression![34]

34. Please see study note 8 above, in this context.

۞ وَلَوْ أَنَّنَا نَزَّلْنَا إِلَيْهِمُ ٱلْمَلَـٰٓئِكَةَ وَكَلَّمَهُمُ ٱلْمَوْتَىٰ وَحَشَرْنَا عَلَيْهِمْ كُلَّ شَىْءٍ قُبُلًا مَّا كَانُوا لِيُؤْمِنُوٓا إِلَّآ أَن يَشَآءَ ٱللَّهُ وَلَـٰكِنَّ أَكْثَرَهُمْ يَجْهَلُونَ ﴿١١١﴾

111. Walaw annana nazzalna ilayhimu almala-ikata wakallamahumu almawta wahasharna AAalayhim kulla shay-in qubulan ma kanoo liyu/minoo illa an yashaa Allahu walakinna aktharahum yajhaloona

6:111. And even if We had sent down to them the angels and the dead had spoken to them and We had brought together all things before them, they would not have believed unless Allah willed, but most of them are ignorant.

وَكَذَٰلِكَ جَعَلْنَا لِكُلِّ نَبِيٍّ عَدُوًّا شَيَـٰطِينَ ٱلْإِنسِ وَٱلْجِنِّ يُوحِى بَعْضُهُمْ إِلَىٰ بَعْضٍ زُخْرُفَ ٱلْقَوْلِ غُرُورًا وَلَوْ شَآءَ رَبُّكَ مَا فَعَلُوهُ فَذَرْهُمْ وَمَا يَفْتَرُونَ ۝

112. Wakathalika jaAAalna likulli nabiyyin AAaduwwan shayateena al-insi waaljinni yoohee baAAduhum ila baAAdin zukhrufa alqawli ghurooran walaw shaa rabbuka ma faAAaloohu fatharhum wama yaftaroona

6:112. And thus, did We make *shayateen*[35], from among mankind and jinn, hostile to every prophet – they deceive one another with sweet talk. And had your Lord so willed they would not have done it. Leave them then alone with what they fabricate.

35. Please see study notes 2:33 to 2:35 **on Verse 2:36.**

وَلِتَصْغَىٰ إِلَيْهِ أَفْئِدَةُ ٱلَّذِينَ لَا يُؤْمِنُونَ بِٱلْآخِرَةِ وَلِيَرْضَوْهُ وَلِيَقْتَرِفُوا۟ مَا هُم مُّقْتَرِفُونَ ۝

113. Walitasgha ilayhi af-idatu allatheena la yu/minoona bial-akhirati waliyardawhu waliyaqtarifoo ma hum muqtarifoona

6:113. [36]So that the hearts of those who do not believe in the Hereafter may get inclined to what they fabricate and that they may be well pleased with it and that they may earn what they earn.

36. This Verse is in continuation of the last sentence in the preceding Verse.

أَفَغَيْرَ ٱللَّهِ أَبْتَغِى حَكَمًا وَهُوَ ٱلَّذِىٓ أَنزَلَ إِلَيْكُمُ ٱلْكِتَـٰبَ مُفَصَّلًا وَٱلَّذِينَ

ءَاتَيْنَـٰهُمُ ٱلْكِتَـٰبَ يَعْلَمُونَ أَنَّهُۥ مُنَزَّلٌ مِّن رَّبِّكَ بِٱلْحَقِّ فَلَا تَكُونَنَّ مِنَ

ٱلْمُمْتَرِينَ ﴿١١٤﴾

114. Afaghayra Allahi abtaghee _hakaman_ wahuwa allathee anzala ilaykumu alkitaba mufassalan waallatheena ataynahumu alkitaba yaAAlamoona annahu munazzalun min rabbika bialhaqqi fala takoonanna mina almumtareena

6:114. Shall I[37] then seek a judge other than Allah? And He it is Who has revealed to you the Book explained in detail. And those whom We[38] have given the Book know that it is, in fact, revealed by your Lord. So be not[39] of those who doubt.

---

37. Whom does this pronoun in the first person singular refer to? If it were to refer to the Prophet, the Verse would have begun with the word _qul_ (say) as elsewhere in the Qur'aan. And the context of the sentence rules out that the pronoun could have referred to Allah. The only alternative left is that the pronoun refers to the angel conveying the Verse to the Prophet. But the angel must have made this statement in order that the same statement is reflected from the mind of every believer. The divine purpose is to make every believer believe that since Allah has given him/her a detailed Book of Guidance in the form of the Qur'aan he/she stands in need of no guide <u>other than</u> Him and His Book. In other words, it is the bounden duty of every believer to reject any guide in the form of a person or his book that advocates anything contrary to the divine Guidance given in the Qur'aan.

38. The revelation is from Allah, and He uses the angels to convey it to His human Messengers. That is why the pronoun used here is We.

39. The addressee here is an individual. That individual could be the Prophet or every believer, individually.

وَتَمَّتْ كَلِمَتُ رَبِّكَ صِدْقًا وَعَدْلًا لَّا مُبَدِّلَ لِكَلِمَـٰتِهِۦ وَهُوَ ٱلسَّمِيعُ ٱلْعَلِيمُ

115. Watammat kalimatu rabbika _sidqan_ waAAadlan la mubaddila likalimatihi wahuwa alssameeAAu alAAaleemu

6:115. And the word of your Lord is complete in truth and justice. None can change His words. And He is the One Who listens, the One Who knows!

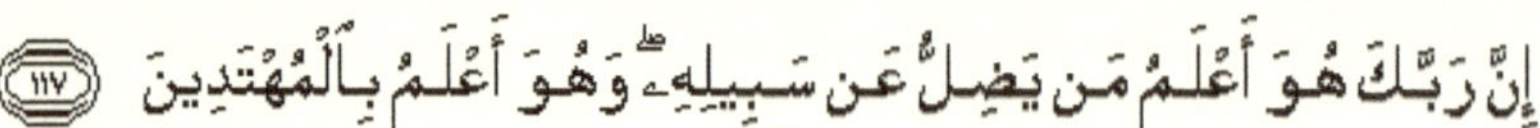

116. Wa-in tutiAA akthara man fee al-ardi yudillooka AAan sabeeli Allahi in yattabiAAoona illa alththanna wa-in hum illa yakhrusoona

6:116. And if you (singular in number) obey most of those on the earth, they will lead you astray from Allah's Path. They follow nothing, but conjecture and they do nothing but guess.

117. Inna rabbaka huwa aAAlamu man yadillu AAan sabeelihi wahuwa aAAlamu bialmuhtadeena

6:117. It is your Lord, indeed, Who knows who goes astray from His Path. And He it is Who knows those who follow the Guidance.

118. Fakuloo mimma thukira ismu Allahi AAalayhi in kuntum bi-ayatihi mu/mineena

6:118. Eat then of that[40] on which Allah's name has been mentioned, if you do believe in His Verses/signs.

40. Many a translator has made an interpolation to indicate that 'that' here refers to non-veg items of food. The translators thus make an unwarranted assumption that they are, by making the interpolation, clarifying what the divine Verse had left unclarified! The translators' assumption is clearly unwarranted in view of Verse 115 above. So, the clear implication of this Verse 118 is that the believers ought to take Allah's Name before partaking of any food, veg or non-veg.

وَمَا لَكُمْ أَلَّا تَأْكُلُواْ مِمَّا ذُكِرَ ٱسْمُ ٱللَّهِ عَلَيْهِ وَقَدْ فَصَّلَ لَكُم مَّا حَرَّمَ عَلَيْكُمْ إِلَّا مَا ٱضْطُرِرْتُمْ إِلَيْهِ وَإِنَّ كَثِيرًا لَّيُضِلُّونَ بِأَهْوَآئِهِم بِغَيْرِ عِلْمٍ إِنَّ رَبَّكَ هُوَ أَعْلَمُ بِٱلْمُعْتَدِينَ ﴿١١٩﴾

119. Wama lakum alla ta/kuloo mimma thukira ismu Allahi AAalayhi waqad fassala lakum ma harrama AAalaykum illa ma idturirtum ilayhi wa-inna katheeran layudilloona bi-ahwa-ihim bighayri AAilmin inna rabbaka huwa aAAlamu bialmuAAtadeena

6:119. And why should you not eat of that on which Allah's name has been mentioned, and He has already made plain for you what He has forbidden – except under compelling circumstances – to you? And, indeed, many do unknowingly lead people astray by their own personal likes and dislikes. Indeed, your Lord it is Who knows those who transgress.

وَذَرُواْ ظَٰهِرَ ٱلْإِثْمِ وَبَاطِنَهُۥ إِنَّ ٱلَّذِينَ يَكْسِبُونَ ٱلْإِثْمَ سَيُجْزَوْنَ بِمَا كَانُواْ يَقْتَرِفُونَ ﴿١٢٠﴾

120. Watharoo thahira al-ithmi wabatinahu inna allatheena yaksiboona al-ithma sayujzawna bima kanoo yaqtarifoona

6:120. And desist from committing a sin openly and from secret approaches to it.[41] Indeed, they who strive for the perpetration of any sinful act shall be recompensed for what they earned.

41. A sin is normally committed secretly. Therefore, committing a sin openly could only mean that the sin is in fact committed. And committing the interior (*batin*) of a sin could mean doing something which would lead to that sin. *batinahu* is therefore translated here 'as secret approaches to it'. Refer also, in this context, to Verse 151 below, wherein mankind is specifically directed not to even come near indecencies.

وَلَا تَأْكُلُواْ مِمَّا لَمْ يُذْكَرِ ٱسْمُ ٱللَّهِ عَلَيْهِ وَإِنَّهُۥ لَفِسْقٌ وَإِنَّ ٱلشَّيَـٰطِينَ لَيُوحُونَ إِلَىٰٓ أَوْلِيَآئِهِمْ لِيُجَـٰدِلُوكُمْ وَإِنْ أَطَعْتُمُوهُمْ إِنَّكُمْ لَمُشْرِكُونَ

121. Wala ta/kuloo mimma lam yuthkari ismu Allahi AAalayhi wa-innahu lafisqun wa-inna alshshayateena layoohoona ila awliya-ihim liyujadilookum wa-in ataAAtumoohum innakum lamushrikoona

6:121. And eat not of that on which Allah's name has not been mentioned and doing so would indeed be a rebellion against Allah. And the devils do indeed inspire their friends to contend with you. And if you obey them, you shall certainly be those who worship others besides Allah.

أَوَمَن كَانَ مَيْتًا فَأَحْيَيْنَـٰهُ وَجَعَلْنَا لَهُۥ نُورًا يَمْشِى بِهِۦ فِى ٱلنَّاسِ كَمَن مَّثَلُهُۥ فِى ٱلظُّلُمَـٰتِ لَيْسَ بِخَارِجٍ مِّنْهَا كَذَٰلِكَ زُيِّنَ لِلْكَـٰفِرِينَ مَا كَانُواْ يَعْمَلُونَ ١٢٢

122. Awa man kana maytan faahyaynahu wajaAAalna lahu nooran yamshee bihi fee alnnasi kaman mathaluhu fee alththulumati laysa bikharijin minha kathalika zuyyina lilkafireena ma kanoo yaAAmaloona

6:122. Is he whom We raised from the dead and for whom we made a light by which he walks among the people, like him who is in darkness from which there is no way out? Thus, what the suppressors of Truth do has been made to look fair to them.[42]

---

42. The suppressors of Truth are happy with the moral darkness in which they live. They therefore seek no way out there from.

وَكَذَٰلِكَ جَعَلْنَا فِى كُلِّ قَرْيَةٍ أَكَـٰبِرَ مُجْرِمِيهَا لِيَمْكُرُوا۟ فِيهَا ۖ وَمَا يَمْكُرُونَ إِلَّا بِأَنفُسِهِمْ وَمَا يَشْعُرُونَ ۝١٢٣

123. Waka_tha_lika jaAAaln_a_ fee kulli qaryatin ak_a_bira mujrimeeh_a_ liyamkuroo feeh_a_ wam_a_ yamkuroona ill_a_ bi-anfusihim wam_a_ yashAAuroon_a_

6:123. And thus[43] have We made, in every human settlement, the biggest of the criminals to plot therein. And they plot not but against their own selves, and they perceive this not.

43. I.e. by making their evil deeds look good to the criminals.

وَإِذَا جَاءَتْهُمْ ءَايَةٌ قَالُوا۟ لَن نُّؤْمِنَ حَتَّىٰ نُؤْتَىٰ مِثْلَ مَا أُوتِىَ رُسُلُ ٱللَّهِ ٱللَّهُ أَعْلَمُ حَيْثُ يَجْعَلُ رِسَالَتَهُۥ ۗ سَيُصِيبُ ٱلَّذِينَ أَجْرَمُوا۟ صَغَارٌ عِندَ ٱللَّهِ وَعَذَابٌ شَدِيدٌۢ بِمَا كَانُوا۟ يَمْكُرُونَ ۝١٢٤

124. Wa-i_tha_ j_a_at-hum ayatun qaloo lan nu/mina _h_atta nu/t_a_ mithla m_a_ ootiya rusulu All_a_hi All_a_hu aAAlamu _h_aythu yajAAalu ris_a_latahu sayu_s_eebu alla_th_eena ajramoo _s_a_gh_a_run AAinda All_a_hi waAAa_th_abun shadeedun bim_a_ k_a_noo yamkuroon_a_

6:124. And when a Verse/sign comes to them they say, "We will not believe till we are given the like of what Allah's Messengers are given. Allah knows with whom to place His Message. The criminals shall get disgrace and severe punishment from Allah because they plotted against the divine scheme of things.

فَمَن يُرِدِ ٱللَّهُ أَن يَهْدِيَهُۥ يَشْرَحْ صَدْرَهُۥ لِلْإِسْلَٰمِ ۖ وَمَن يُرِدْ أَن يُضِلَّهُۥ يَجْعَلْ صَدْرَهُۥ ضَيِّقًا حَرَجًا كَأَنَّمَا يَصَّعَّدُ فِى ٱلسَّمَاءِ ۚ كَذَٰلِكَ يَجْعَلُ ٱللَّهُ ٱلرِّجْسَ عَلَى ٱلَّذِينَ لَا يُؤْمِنُونَ ۝١٢٥

125. Faman yuridi All_a_hu an yahdiyahu yashra_h_ _s_adrahu lil-isl_a_mi waman yurid an yu_d_illahu yajAAal _s_adrahu _d_ayyiqan _h_arajan kaannam_a_ yassaAAAAadu fee alssam_a_-i ka_th_alika yajAAalu All_a_hu alrrijsa AAal_a_ alla_th_eena l_a_ yu/minoona

6:125. And whomsoever Allah wills to guide, He opens his mind for Islam, and whomsoever He wills to send astray, He makes his mind narrow and restricted as though he were ascending into the sky.[44] Thus does Allah lay disgrace on those who do not believe.

44. When one climbs a mountain, a stairway or a tree, one feels the gravitational pull restricting or trying to prevent one's upward movement. A man who has gone astray similarly feels some restrictive force trying to prevent him from accepting Islam.

وَهَـٰذَا صِرَٰطُ رَبِّكَ مُسْتَقِيمًا قَدْ فَصَّلْنَا الْأَيَـٰتِ لِقَوْمٍ يَذَّكَّرُونَ ۝

126. Wahatha siratu rabbika mustaqeeman qad fassalna al-ayati liqawmin yaththakkaroona

6:126. And this[45] is the Straight Path of your Lord. WE have certainly explained the Verses/signs plainly for a people who ponder.

45. The Path of Islam as enunciated in the Qur'aan.

لَهُمْ دَارُ ٱلسَّلَـٰمِ عِندَ رَبِّهِمْ وَهُوَ وَلِيُّهُم بِمَا كَانُوا۟ يَعْمَلُونَ ۝

127. Lahum daru alssalami AAinda rabbihim wahuwa waliyyuhum bima kanoo yaAAmaloona

6:127. For them, there shall be the home of peace with their Lord, and He will be their *Wali*[46] because of their deeds.

46. Refer study note 2:154 on Verse 2:107.

وَيَوْمَ يَحْشُرُهُمْ جَمِيعًا يَـٰمَعْشَرَ ٱلْجِنِّ قَدِ ٱسْتَكْثَرْتُم مِّنَ ٱلْإِنسِ وَقَالَ أَوْلِيَآؤُهُم مِّنَ ٱلْإِنسِ رَبَّنَا ٱسْتَمْتَعَ بَعْضُنَا بِبَعْضٍ وَبَلَغْنَآ أَجَلَنَا ٱلَّذِىٓ أَجَّلْتَ لَنَا قَالَ ٱلنَّارُ مَثْوَىٰكُمْ خَـٰلِدِينَ فِيهَآ إِلَّا مَا شَآءَ ٱللَّهُ إِنَّ رَبَّكَ حَكِيمٌ عَلِيمٌ ﴿١٢٨﴾

128. Wayawma ya<u>h</u>shuruhum jameeAAan y<u>a</u> maAAshara aljinni qadi istakthartum mina al-insi waq<u>a</u>la awliy<u>a</u>ohum mina al-insi rabban<u>a</u> istamtaAAa baAA<u>d</u>una bibaAA<u>d</u>in wabalaghn<u>a</u> ajalan<u>a</u> alla<u>th</u>ee a<u>jj</u>alta lan<u>a</u> q<u>a</u>la alnn<u>a</u>ru mathw<u>a</u>kum kh<u>a</u>lideena feeh<u>a</u> ill<u>a</u> m<u>a</u> sh<u>a</u>a All<u>a</u>hu inna rabbaka <u>h</u>akeemun AAaleem**un**

6:128. And on the Day when He shall gather them all together, "O assembly of jinn! You did frequent some among mankind." And their *awliya*[47] from among mankind shall say, "Our Lord! We did benefit one another, and we have reached our destination You fixed for us." HE shall say, "The Fire shall be your abode. You shall dwell therein forever, except as Allah wills. Indeed, your Lord is Wise, Knowledgeable."

---

47. Plural of *wali*.

وَكَذَٰلِكَ نُوَلِّى بَعْضَ ٱلظَّـٰلِمِينَ بَعْضًا بِمَا كَانُوا۟ يَكْسِبُونَ ﴿١٢٩﴾

129. Waka<u>th</u>alika nuwallee baAA<u>d</u>a al<u>ththa</u>limeena baAA<u>d</u>an bim<u>a</u> k<u>a</u>noo yaksiboon<u>a</u>

6:129. And thus, do We make the wrongdoers *awliya* of one another because of what they earned.

يَـٰمَعْشَرَ ٱلْجِنِّ وَٱلْإِنسِ أَلَمْ يَأْتِكُمْ رُسُلٌ مِّنكُمْ يَقُصُّونَ عَلَيْكُمْ ءَايَـٰتِى

وَيُنذِرُونَكُمْ لِقَآءَ يَوْمِكُمْ هَـٰذَا قَالُواْ شَهِدْنَا عَلَىٰٓ أَنفُسِنَا وَغَرَّتْهُمُ

ٱلْحَيَوٰةُ ٱلدُّنْيَا وَشَهِدُواْ عَلَىٰٓ أَنفُسِهِمْ أَنَّهُمْ كَانُواْ كَـٰفِرِينَ ﴿١٣٠﴾

130. Y_a maAAshara aljinni waal-insi alam ya/tikum rusulun minkum yaqu_ss_oona AAalaykum _a_y_a_tee wayun_th_iroonakum liqaa yawmikum _ha_tha qaloo shahidn_a AAal_a anfusin_a wagharrat-humu al_ha_y_a_tu aldduny_a washahidoo AAal_a anfusihim annahum k_a_noo k_a_fireena

---

6:130. "O assembly of jinn and mankind! Did there not come to you Messengers from amongst you, recounting to you My Verses/signs and warning you of your appointment for this Day?" They shall say, "We bear witness against our own selves." And the life of this world deceived them, and they shall bear witness against their own selves that they were suppressing the Truth.

ذَٰلِكَ أَن لَّمْ يَكُن رَّبُّكَ مُهْلِكَ ٱلْقُرَىٰ بِظُلْمٍ وَأَهْلُهَا غَـٰفِلُونَ ﴿١٣١﴾

131. _Th_alika an lam yakun rabbuka muhlika alqur_a_ bi_zh_ulmin waahluh_a gh_a_filoona

---

6:131. The Messengers were sent because your Lord would not destroy human settlements oppressively, while their inhabitants were unaware.

وَلِكُلٍّ دَرَجَـٰتٌ مِّمَّا عَمِلُواْ وَمَا رَبُّكَ بِغَـٰفِلٍ عَمَّا يَعْمَلُونَ ﴿١٣٢﴾

132. Walikullin daraj_a_tun mimm_a AAamiloo wam_a rabbuka bigh_a_filin AAamm_a yaAAmaloona

---

6:132. And all have ranks according to what they do. And your Lord is not unaware of what they do.

وَرَبُّكَ ٱلْغَنِىُّ ذُو ٱلرَّحْمَةِ إِن يَشَأْ يُذْهِبْكُمْ وَيَسْتَخْلِفْ مِنۢ بَعْدِكُم مَّا يَشَآءُ كَمَآ أَنشَأَكُم مِّن ذُرِّيَّةِ قَوْمٍ ءَاخَرِينَ ﴿١٣٣﴾

133. Warabbuka alghaniyyu <u>th</u>oo alrra<u>h</u>mati in yasha/ yu<u>th</u>hibkum wayastakhlif min baAAdikum m<u>a</u> yash<u>a</u>o kam<u>a</u> anshaakum min <u>th</u>urriyyati qawmin akhareena

133. And your Lord is the Self-sufficient One, Mercy being (one of His) Attributes. If He so wills, He may destroy you, and make whom He wills successors after you, just as He raised you up from the seed of another people.

إِنَّ مَا تُوعَدُونَ لَآتٍ وَمَآ أَنتُم بِمُعْجِزِينَ ﴿١٣٤﴾

134. Inna m<u>a</u> tooAAadoona la<u>a</u>tin wam<u>a</u> antum bimuAAjizeena

6:134. Indeed, that which you are promised must come to pass, and you are in no position to prevent it.

قُلْ يَٰقَوْمِ ٱعْمَلُوا۟ عَلَىٰ مَكَانَتِكُمْ إِنِّى عَامِلٌ فَسَوْفَ تَعْلَمُونَ مَن تَكُونُ لَهُۥ عَٰقِبَةُ ٱلدَّارِ إِنَّهُۥ لَا يُفْلِحُ ٱلظَّٰلِمُونَ ﴿١٣٥﴾

135. Qul y<u>a</u> qawmi iAAmaloo AAal<u>a</u> mak<u>a</u>natikum innee AA<u>a</u>milun fasawfa taAAlamoona man takoonu lahu AA<u>a</u>qibatu aldd<u>a</u>ri innahu l<u>a</u> yufli<u>h</u>u al<u>thth</u>alimoona

6:135. Say, "O my people! You do your best and I do what I do. You will duly come to know for which of us the final abode[48] will be. Surely, the wicked persons shall not be successful."

48. From the context it is apparent that the abode meant here is the abode in Paradise.

وَجَعَلُواْ لِلَّهِ مِمَّا ذَرَأَ مِنَ ٱلْحَرْثِ وَٱلْأَنْعَـٰمِ نَصِيبًا فَقَالُواْ هَـٰذَا لِلَّهِ بِزَعْمِهِمْ وَهَـٰذَا لِشُرَكَآبِنَا فَمَا كَانَ لِشُرَكَآبِهِمْ فَلَا يَصِلُ إِلَى ٱللَّهِ وَمَا كَانَ لِلَّهِ فَهُوَ يَصِلُ إِلَىٰ شُرَكَآبِهِمْ سَآءَ مَا يَحْكُمُونَ ﴿١٣٦﴾

136. WajaAAaloo lillahi mimma tharaa mina alharthi waal-anAAami naseeban faqaloo hatha lillahi bizaAAmihim wahatha lishuraka-ina fama kana lishuraka-ihim fala yasilu ila Allahi wama kana lillahi fahuwa yasilu ila shuraka-ihim saa ma yahkumoona

6:136. And they assign to Allah a share out of what He has created of tilth and cattle! And they arbitrarily apportion, "This is for Allah, and this for those whom we worship besides Allah." Then what is apportioned for those whom they worship besides Allah, does not reach Allah. And what is apportioned for Allah, reaches those others they worship! Evil is the way they judge!

وَكَذَٰلِكَ زَيَّنَ لِكَثِيرٍ مِّنَ ٱلْمُشْرِكِينَ قَتْلَ أَوْلَـٰدِهِمْ شُرَكَآؤُهُمْ لِيُرْدُوهُمْ وَلِيَلْبِسُواْ عَلَيْهِمْ دِينَهُمْ وَلَوْ شَآءَ ٱللَّهُ مَا فَعَلُوهُ فَذَرْهُمْ وَمَا يَفْتَرُونَ ﴿١٣٧﴾

137. Wakathalika zayyana likatheerin mina almushrikeena qatla awladihim shurakaohum liyurdoohum waliyalbisoo AAalayhim deenahum walaw shaa Allahu ma faAAaloohu fatharhum wama yaftaroona

6:137. And thus those, other than Allah, whom they worship have made killing of their children look fair to most of the polytheists, to lead them to their own destruction and cause confusion in their religion. And if Allah had willed, they would not have done it. So, leave them and their fabrications alone.

وَقَالُواْ هَـٰذِهِۦٓ أَنْعَـٰمٌ وَحَرْثٌ حِجْرٌ لَّا يَطْعَمُهَآ إِلَّا مَن نَّشَآءُ بِزَعْمِهِمْ وَأَنْعَـٰمٌ حُرِّمَتْ ظُهُورُهَا وَأَنْعَـٰمٌ لَّا يَذْكُرُونَ ٱسْمَ ٱللَّهِ عَلَيْهَا ٱفْتِرَآءً عَلَيْهِ سَيَجْزِيهِم بِمَا كَانُواْ يَفْتَرُونَ ۝١٣٨

138. Waqaloo hathihi anAAamun waharthun hijrun la yatAAamuha illa man nashao bizaAAmihim waanAAamun hurrimat thuhooruha waanAAamun la yathkuroona isma Allahi AAalayha iftiraan AAalayhi sayajzeehim bima kanoo yaftaroona

6:138. And they arbitrarily say, "These cattle and tilth are prohibited. None shall eat them except such as we please." And they say there are cattle whose backs are forbidden, and cattle on which they would not mention Allah's name, fabricating a lie against Him. HE shall requite them for what they used to fabricate.

وَقَالُواْ مَا فِى بُطُونِ هَـٰذِهِ ٱلْأَنْعَـٰمِ خَالِصَةٌ لِّذُكُورِنَا وَمُحَرَّمٌ عَلَىٰٓ أَزْوَٰجِنَا وَإِن يَكُن مَّيْتَةً فَهُمْ فِيهِ شُرَكَآءُ سَيَجْزِيهِمْ وَصْفَهُمْ إِنَّهُۥ حَكِيمٌ عَلِيمٌ

139. Waqaloo ma fee butooni hathihi al-anAAami khalisatun lithukoorina wamuharramun AAala azwajina wa-in yakun maytatan fahum feehi shurakao sayajzeehim wasfahum innahu hakeemun AAaleemun

6:139. And they say, "What is in the wombs of these cattle is especially for our males, and forbidden to our females. And if it be stillborn, then they share therein." HE will 'reward' them for their prescriptions. He is indeed Wise, Knowledgeable.

قَدْ خَسِرَ ٱلَّذِينَ قَتَلُوٓاْ أَوْلَـٰدَهُمْ سَفَهًۢا بِغَيْرِ عِلْمٍ وَحَرَّمُواْ مَا رَزَقَهُمُ ٱللَّهُ ٱفْتِرَآءً عَلَى ٱللَّهِ قَدْ ضَلُّواْ وَمَا كَانُواْ مُهْتَدِينَ

140. Qad khasira allatheena qataloo awladahum safahan bighayri AAilmin waharramoo ma razaqahumu Allahu iftiraan AAala Allahi qad dalloo wama kanoo muhtadeena

6:140. Doomed surely are they who have killed their children[49] foolishly without knowledge, and have forbidden what Allah has provided for them, fabricating a lie against Allah. They have surely gone astray and are not those who follow divine Guidance.

49. People in the modern age too kill their children, but in the wombs!

وَهُوَ ٱلَّذِىٓ أَنشَأَ جَنَّٰتٍ مَّعْرُوشَٰتٍ وَغَيْرَ مَعْرُوشَٰتٍ وَٱلنَّخْلَ وَٱلزَّرْعَ مُخْتَلِفًا أُكُلُهُۥ وَٱلزَّيْتُونَ وَٱلرُّمَّانَ مُتَشَٰبِهًا وَغَيْرَ مُتَشَٰبِهٍ كُلُوا۟ مِن ثَمَرِهِۦٓ إِذَآ أَثْمَرَ وَءَاتُوا۟ حَقَّهُۥ يَوْمَ حَصَادِهِۦ وَلَا تُسْرِفُوٓا۟ إِنَّهُۥ لَا يُحِبُّ ٱلْمُسْرِفِينَ ﴿١٤١﴾

141. Wahuwa allathee anshaa jannatin maAArooshatin waghayra maAArooshatin waalnnakhla waalzzarAAa mukhtalifan okuluhu waalzzaytoona waalrrummana mutashabihan waghayra mutashabihin kuloo min thamarihi itha athmara waatoo haqqahu yawma hasadihi wala tusrifoo innahu la yuhibbu almusrifeena

6:141. And He it is Who produces gardens, trellised and untrellised, and date palms and seed-produce of which the fruits are of various sorts, and olives and pomegranates, like and unlike. Eat of its fruit when it bears fruit, and pay its due[50] on the day of harvest, and squander not! Indeed, He loves not the squanderers.

50. The Creator expects His subjects to give something to the poor and needy from the fruits, which He grants them by His grace. They should not make the mistake of thinking that the fruits are the result of their labours alone. Without Allah's grace, all their labours could come to naught.

وَمِنَ ٱلْأَنْعَٰمِ حَمُولَةً وَفَرْشًا كُلُوا۟ مِمَّا رَزَقَكُمُ ٱللَّهُ وَلَا تَتَّبِعُوا۟ خُطُوَٰتِ ٱلشَّيْطَٰنِ إِنَّهُۥ لَكُمْ عَدُوٌّ مُّبِينٌ ﴿١٤٢﴾

142. Wamina al-anAAami hamoolatan wafarshan kuloo mimma razaqakumu Allahu wala tattabiAAoo khutuwati alshshaytani innahu lakum AAaduwwun mubeenun

6:142. And of cattle there are those that are beasts of burden and those to be laid down on the ground for slaughter and food. Eat of what Allah has provided for you and follow not the footsteps of Satan. Indeed, he is to you an open enemy.

ثَمَٰنِيَةَ أَزْوَٰجٍ مِّنَ ٱلضَّأْنِ ٱثْنَيْنِ وَمِنَ ٱلْمَعْزِ ٱثْنَيْنِ قُلْ ءَآلذَّكَرَيْنِ

حَرَّمَ أَمِ ٱلْأُنثَيَيْنِ أَمَّا ٱشْتَمَلَتْ عَلَيْهِ أَرْحَامُ ٱلْأُنثَيَيْنِ نَبِّـُٔونِى

بِعِلْمٍ إِن كُنتُمْ صَٰدِقِينَ ﴿١٤٣﴾

143. Thama_niyata azwa_jin mina aldda/ni ithnayni wamina almaAAzi ithnayni qul al_ththa_karayni _harrama ami alonthayayni amm_a ishtamalat AAalayhi ar_hamu alonthayayni nabbi-oonee biAAilmin in kuntum _sadiqeena

6:143. Of eight cattle in pairs, consider two of sheep and two of goats. Ask them, "Which ones has He forbidden – the two males or the two females or that which the wombs of the two females contain? Inform me, with knowledge, if you are truthful."

وَمِنَ ٱلْإِبِلِ ٱثْنَيْنِ وَمِنَ ٱلْبَقَرِ ٱثْنَيْنِ قُلْ ءَآلذَّكَرَيْنِ حَرَّمَ أَمِ ٱلْأُنثَيَيْنِ

أَمَّا ٱشْتَمَلَتْ عَلَيْهِ أَرْحَامُ ٱلْأُنثَيَيْنِ أَمْ كُنتُمْ شُهَدَآءَ إِذْ وَصَّىٰكُمُ ٱللَّهُ

بِهَٰذَا فَمَنْ أَظْلَمُ مِمَّنِ ٱفْتَرَىٰ عَلَى ٱللَّهِ كَذِبًا لِّيُضِلَّ ٱلنَّاسَ بِغَيْرِ عِلْمٍ

إِنَّ ٱللَّهَ لَا يَهْدِى ٱلْقَوْمَ ٱلظَّٰلِمِينَ ﴿١٤٤﴾

144. Wamina al-ibili ithnayni wamina albaqari ithnayni qul al_ththa_karayni _harrama ami alonthayayni amm_a ishtamalat AAalayhi ar_hamu alonthayayni am kuntum shuhada_a ith wa_s_sakumu All_ahu bi_hatha faman a_thlamu mimmani iftar_a AAal_a All_ahi ka_thiban liyu_dilla alnn_asa bighayri AAilmin inna Allaha l_a yahdee alqawma al_ththa_limeena

6:144. And consider two of camels and two of cows. Ask, "Which ones has He forbidden – the two males or the two females or that which the wombs of the two females contain? Were you witnesses when Allah enjoined this on you? Who, then, can be more unjust than he who, without knowledge, fabricates a lie against Allah, to lead mankind astray? Indeed, Allah does not guide the people who are unjust! [51]

51. In this Verse, and the preceding one, Allah exposes the arbitrariness and falsehood of the disbelievers, claiming – as per their own whims, fancies or superstitious beliefs – that certain cattle are forbidden for certain people. Refer Verses 138 and 139 above, in this context.

قُل لَّآ أَجِدُ فِى مَآ أُوحِىَ إِلَىَّ مُحَرَّمًا عَلَىٰ طَاعِمٍ يَطْعَمُهُۥٓ إِلَّآ أَن يَكُونَ مَيْتَةً أَوْ دَمًا مَّسْفُوحًا أَوْ لَحْمَ خِنزِيرٍ فَإِنَّهُۥ رِجْسٌ أَوْ فِسْقًا أُهِلَّ لِغَيْرِ ٱللَّهِ بِهِۦ ۚ فَمَنِ ٱضْطُرَّ غَيْرَ بَاغٍ وَلَا عَادٍ فَإِنَّ رَبَّكَ غَفُورٌ رَّحِيمٌ ﴿١٤٥﴾

145. Qul la ajidu feema oohiya ilayya muharraman AAala taAAimin yatAAamuhu illa an yakoona maytatan aw daman masfoohan aw lahma khinzeerin fa-innahu rijsun aw fisqan ohilla lighayri Allahi bihi famani idturra ghayra baghin wala AAadin fa-inna rabbaka ghafoorun raheemun

6:145. Say, "I do not find in that which has been revealed to me anything forbidden for anyone to eat except that which has died of itself, or blood poured forth, or flesh of swine – for that indeed is unclean – or that which is a transgression, on which a name other than Allah has been invoked. But then whoever is driven by necessity, without being disobedient or transgressing, then indeed your Lord is Forgiving, Merciful.

وَعَلَى ٱلَّذِينَ هَادُوا۟ حَرَّمْنَا كُلَّ ذِى ظُفُرٍ ۖ وَمِنَ ٱلْبَقَرِ وَٱلْغَنَمِ حَرَّمْنَا عَلَيْهِمْ شُحُومَهُمَآ إِلَّا مَا حَمَلَتْ ظُهُورُهُمَآ أَوِ ٱلْحَوَايَآ أَوْ مَا ٱخْتَلَطَ بِعَظْمٍ ۚ ذَٰلِكَ جَزَيْنَٰهُم بِبَغْيِهِمْ ۖ وَإِنَّا لَصَٰدِقُونَ ﴿١٤٦﴾

146. WaAAala allatheena hadoo harramna kulla thee thufurin wamina albaqari waalghanami harramna AAalayhim shuhoomahuma illa ma hamalat thuhooruhuma awi alhawaya aw ma ikhtalata biAAathmin thalika jazaynahum bibaghyihim wa-inna lasadiqoona

6:146. And to those who were Jews We had forbidden every animal having claws. And of oxen and sheep We had forbidden to them the fat of both, except such as was on their backs or in the entrails or what was mixed with bones. That was a punishment We gave them on account of their rebellion, and We are indeed Truthful.

فَإِن كَذَّبُوكَ فَقُل رَّبُّكُمْ ذُو رَحْمَةٍ وَاسِعَةٍ وَلَا يُرَدُّ بَأْسُهُ عَنِ ٱلْقَوْمِ ٱلْمُجْرِمِينَ ۝

147. Fa-in kaththabooka faqul rabbukum thoo rahmatin wasiAAatin wala yuraddu ba/suhu AAani alqawmi almujrimeena

6:147. Then if they deny you, say, "Your Lord is the Embodiment of vast mercy. And His punishment cannot be averted from the criminals."

سَيَقُولُ ٱلَّذِينَ أَشْرَكُواْ لَوْ شَاءَ ٱللَّهُ مَا أَشْرَكْنَا وَلَا ءَابَاؤُنَا وَلَا حَرَّمْنَا مِن شَيْءٍ كَذَلِكَ كَذَّبَ ٱلَّذِينَ مِن قَبْلِهِم حَتَّىٰ ذَاقُواْ بَأْسَنَا قُلْ هَلْ عِندَكُم مِّنْ عِلْمٍ فَتُخْرِجُوهُ لَنَآ إِن تَتَّبِعُونَ إِلَّا ٱلظَّنَّ وَإِنْ أَنتُمْ إِلَّا تَخْرُصُونَ ۝

148. Sayaqoolu allatheena ashrakoo law shaa Allahu ma ashrakna wala abaona wala harramna min shay-in kathalika kaththaba allatheena min qablihim hatta thaqoo ba/sana qul hal AAindakum min AAilmin fatukhrijoohu lana in tattabiAAoona illa alththanna wa-in antum illa takhrusoona

6:148. Those, who worship others besides Allah, will say, "If Allah had willed, we and our fathers would not have worshipped others besides Him, nor would we have forbidden anything." Thus, did those before them deny until they tasted Our punishment. Say, "Have you any knowledge that you can put forth for us? You follow nothing, but conjecture and you do nothing, but guess!"

قُلْ فَلِلَّهِ ٱلْحُجَّةُ ٱلْبَالِغَةُ فَلَوْ شَاءَ لَهَدَىٰكُمْ أَجْمَعِينَ ۝

149. Qul falillahi alhujjatu albalighatu falaw shaa lahadakum ajmaAAeena

6:149. Say, "With Allah then is the conclusive argument. And had He so willed, He would certainly have guided you all."

قُل هَلُمَّ شُهَدَآءَكُمُ الَّذِينَ يَشْهَدُونَ أَنَّ اللَّهَ حَرَّمَ هَٰذَا ۖ فَإِن شَهِدُوا فَلَا تَشْهَدْ مَعَهُمْ ۚ وَلَا تَتَّبِعْ أَهْوَآءَ الَّذِينَ كَذَّبُوا بِـَٔايَٰتِنَا وَالَّذِينَ لَا يُؤْمِنُونَ بِالْأَخِرَةِ وَهُم بِرَبِّهِمْ يَعْدِلُونَ ۝

150. Qul halumma shuhadaakumu alla_theena yashhadoona anna Alla_ha _harrama _hatha fa-in shahidoo fala tashhad maAAahum wala tattabiAA ahwaa alla_theena ka_th_thaboo bi-ayatina waalla_theena la yu/minoona bial-akhirati wahum birabbihim yaAAdiloona

6:150. Say, "Produce your witnesses who can testify that Allah has forbidden this." Then if they testify, do not testify with them. And follow not the desires of those who reject Our Verses/signs and who do not believe in the Hereafter and hold others as equals to their Lord!

۞ قُل تَعَالَوْا أَتْلُ مَا حَرَّمَ رَبُّكُمْ عَلَيْكُمْ ۖ أَلَّا تُشْرِكُوا بِهِ شَيْـًٔا ۖ وَبِالْوَٰلِدَيْنِ إِحْسَٰنًا ۖ وَلَا تَقْتُلُوٓا أَوْلَٰدَكُم مِّنْ إِمْلَٰقٍ ۖ نَّحْنُ نَرْزُقُكُمْ وَإِيَّاهُمْ ۖ وَلَا تَقْرَبُوا الْفَوَٰحِشَ مَا ظَهَرَ مِنْهَا وَمَا بَطَنَ ۖ وَلَا تَقْتُلُوا النَّفْسَ الَّتِى حَرَّمَ اللَّهُ إِلَّا بِالْحَقِّ ۚ ذَٰلِكُمْ وَصَّىٰكُم بِهِ لَعَلَّكُمْ تَعْقِلُونَ ۝

151. Qul taAAalaw atlu ma _harrama rabbukum AAalaykum alla tushrikoo bihi shay-an wabialwalidayni i_hsanan wala taqtuloo awladakum min imlaqin na_hnu narzuqukum wa-iyya_hum wala taqraboo alfawa_hisha ma _thahara minha wama ba_tana wala taqtuloo alnnafsa allatee _harrama Alla_hu illa bial_haqqi _thalikum wassakum bihi laAAallakum taAAqiloona

6:151. Say, "Come, I will recite what your Lord has forbidden to you. He has enjoined that you do not worship anything besides Him, that you be good and kind to your parents, that you do not kill your children because of poverty – We provide sustenance for you, and for them – that you do not come near indecencies, whether done openly or in secrecy, and that you do not kill anyone, which act Allah has forbidden, except for the requirements of justice. This He has enjoined you with, that you may understand[52]".

---

52. Understand the propriety of the things divinely ordained.

وَلَا تَقْرَبُوا۟ مَالَ ٱلْيَتِيمِ إِلَّا بِٱلَّتِى هِىَ أَحْسَنُ حَتَّىٰ يَبْلُغَ أَشُدَّهُۥ وَأَوْفُوا۟

ٱلْكَيْلَ وَٱلْمِيزَانَ بِٱلْقِسْطِ لَا نُكَلِّفُ نَفْسًا إِلَّا وُسْعَهَا وَإِذَا قُلْتُمْ فَٱعْدِلُوا۟

وَلَوْ كَانَ ذَا قُرْبَىٰ وَبِعَهْدِ ٱللَّهِ أَوْفُوا۟ ذَٰلِكُمْ وَصَّىٰكُم بِهِۦ لَعَلَّكُمْ

تَذَكَّرُونَ ۝١٥٢

152. Wala taqraboo mala alyateemi illa biallatee hiya ahsanu hatta yablugha ashuddahu waawfoo alkayla waalmeezana bialqisti la nukallifu nafsan illa wusAAaha wa-itha qultum faiAAdiloo walaw kana tha qurba wabiAAahdi Allahi awfoo thalikum wassakum bihi laAAallakum tathakkaroona

6:152. "And approach not the property of the orphan, but in the morally most appropriate manner, [53] until he/she attains maturity. And give full measure and weight, with justice. We do not burden a person beyond one's capacity. And be just when you speak, even if it be to a near and dear one. And fulfill your obligation to Allah. This He has enjoined you with, that you may remember."

53. The obvious hint here is that the trustee of the orphan's property should not use the property for the trustee's own use and aggrandisement.

وَأَنَّ هَٰذَا صِرَٰطِى مُسْتَقِيمًا فَٱتَّبِعُوهُ وَلَا تَتَّبِعُوا۟ ٱلسُّبُلَ فَتَفَرَّقَ بِكُمْ عَن

سَبِيلِهِۦ ذَٰلِكُمْ وَصَّىٰكُم بِهِۦ لَعَلَّكُمْ تَتَّقُونَ ۝١٥٣

153. Waanna hatha siratee mustaqeeman faittabiAAoohu wala tattabiAAoo alssubula fatafarraqa bikum AAan sabeelihi thalikum wassakum bihi laAAallakum tattaqoona

6:153. And this then is My Straight Path, so follow it. And follow not the paths that alienate you from His Path.[54] This He has enjoined you with, that you may be pious.

54. The Path, that Allah Almighty calls His own and indicates it through the demonstrative pronoun 'this', is obviously that shown by the Qur'aan. We follow that Path, only by following the do's and don'ts

mentioned in the Qur'aan. And it is repeatedly asserted in the Qur'aan that the divine commandments therein meant to be followed by mankind are variously explained for easy understanding of all those who fear Allah. And, yet, many Muslims today commit blasphemy by believing that understanding the Qur'aan is the prerogative of the very few, who are well-versed in Arabic, are aware of the innumerable *ahaadeeth* and have deeply studied the various works of *fuqhaa* besides! Such Muslims are, in effect, following the other paths that alienate them from Allah's Path. The alienation effected is reflected first in their disbelief that the common man, who is a *muttaqi*, can understand the Qur'aan. The man-influenced *ahaadeeth* have led the Muslims further away from the pure divine Path. (Refer <u>study notes 3:35 to 3:37</u> on Verse 3:31). They are unfortunately following a *deen* other than that approved by Allah Ta'ala in <u>Verse 5:3</u>.

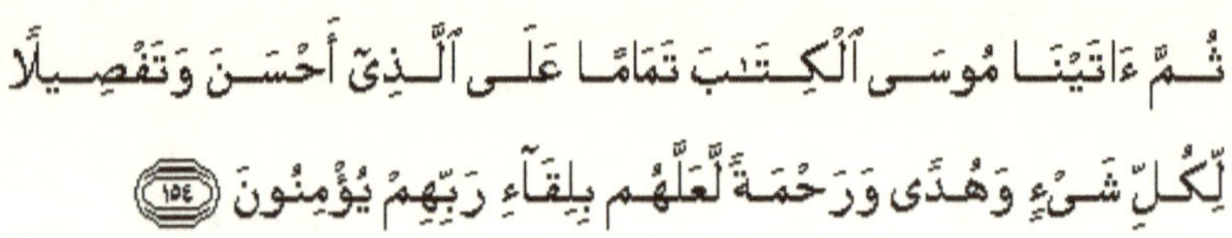

154. Thumma atayna moosa alkitaba tamaman AAala allathee ahsana watafseelan likulli shay-in wahudan warahmatan laAAallahum biliqa-i rabbihim yu/minoona

6:154. Also, We gave Moses the complete Book for those who would do good deeds, with details on every thing, and as a guidance and a mercy, so that they should believe that they were scheduled to meet their Lord.[55]

55. The purpose of the mention here of the Book (Torah) given to Moses is to warn the Muslims against following in the footsteps of Moses' people. They were given a completed Book, complete in all respects to lead them on the divine Straight Path. Yet they resorted to open belligerence and intransigence even when Moses was living with them. This is recorded in <u>Verses 2:55 onwards</u> of Qur'aanic Chapter 2. They thus chose to follow paths other than that shown to them in the Torah. Therefore, the Jews lost political power and got dispersed to all parts of the world to live there as small minorities. They have been given political power again now, but, surely, they are under divine test. As the Jews had been in a state of ignominy till recently, so are the Muslims now. They too have abandoned the Qur'aanic Path and have thus become the favourite whipping boys of all and sundry, all over the world.

155. Wahatha kitabun anzalnahu mubarakun faittabiAAoohu waittaqoo laAAallakum turhamoona

6:155. And We have sent down this Book[56] as a blessing. Follow it then and fear Allah so that mercy is shown to you.

56. The Qur'aan.

أَن تَقُولُوٓاْ إِنَّمَآ أُنزِلَ ٱلْكِتَـٰبُ عَلَىٰ طَآئِفَتَيْنِ مِن قَبْلِنَا وَإِن كُنَّا عَن دِرَاسَتِهِمْ لَغَـٰفِلِينَ ﴿١٥٦﴾

156. An taqooloo innama onzila alkitabu AAala ta-ifatayni min qablina wa-in kunna AAan dirasatihim laghafileena

6:156. Lest you say, "The Book was sent down only to two groups[57] before us, and We were truly unaware of lessons therein."

57. The Jews and the Christians.

أَوْ تَقُولُواْ لَوْ أَنَّآ أُنزِلَ عَلَيْنَا ٱلْكِتَـٰبُ لَكُنَّآ أَهْدَىٰ مِنْهُمْ فَقَدْ جَآءَكُم بَيِّنَةٌ مِّن رَّبِّكُمْ وَهُدًى وَرَحْمَةٌ فَمَنْ أَظْلَمُ مِمَّن كَذَّبَ بِـَٔايَـٰتِ ٱللَّهِ وَصَدَفَ عَنْهَا سَنَجْزِى ٱلَّذِينَ يَصْدِفُونَ عَنْ ءَايَـٰتِنَا سُوٓءَ ٱلْعَذَابِ بِمَا كَانُواْ يَصْدِفُونَ ﴿١٥٧﴾

157. Aw taqooloo law anna onzila AAalayna alkitabu lakunna ahda minhum faqad jaakum bayyinatun min rabbikum wahudan warahmatun faman athlamu mimman kaththaba bi-ayati Allahi wasadafa AAanha sanajzee allatheena yasdifoona AAan ayatina soo-a alAAathabi bima kanoo yasdifoona

6:157. Or lest you say, "If only the Book had been sent down to us, we would certainly have been guided better than they." So now, surely, there has come to you a Clarification, Guidance and Mercy from your Lord.[58] Who then is more unjust than he who rejects Allah's Verses/signs, and turns away there from? We will repay those who turn away from Our Verses/signs with an evil punishment because of their turning away.

58. The Qur'aan embodies the Clarification, Guidance and Mercy, all from the Compassionate and Understanding Creator.

هَلْ يَنظُرُونَ إِلَّا أَن تَأْتِيَهُمُ ٱلْمَلَـٰٓئِكَةُ أَوْ يَأْتِيَ رَبُّكَ أَوْ يَأْتِيَ بَعْضُ ءَايَـٰتِ رَبِّكَ يَوْمَ يَأْتِى بَعْضُ ءَايَـٰتِ رَبِّكَ لَا يَنفَعُ نَفْسًا إِيمَـٰنُهَا لَمْ تَكُنْ ءَامَنَتْ مِن قَبْلُ أَوْ كَسَبَتْ فِىٓ إِيمَـٰنِهَا خَيْرًا ۗ قُلِ ٱنتَظِرُوٓا۟ إِنَّا مُنتَظِرُونَ ۝

158. Hal yan*th*uroona illa an ta/tiyahumu almala-ikatu aw ya/tiya rabbuka aw ya/tiya baAA*d*u a*y*ati rabbika yawma ya/tee baAA*d*u a*y*ati rabbika l*a* yanfaAAu nafsan eem*a*nuh*a* lam takun *a*manat min qablu aw kasabat fee eem*a*nih*a* khayran quli inta*th*iroo inn*a* munta*th*iroona

6:158. Are they waiting for nothing but that the angels should come to them or that your Lord should come, or that some of the signs of your Lord should come? The day when some of the signs of your Lord do come, one's belief then shall be of no benefit to anyone who had already not attained faith or earned good points through one's faith before! Say, "Just you wait! We too are waiting."

إِنَّ ٱلَّذِينَ فَرَّقُوا۟ دِينَهُمْ وَكَانُوا۟ شِيَعًا لَّسْتَ مِنْهُمْ فِى شَىْءٍ ۚ إِنَّمَآ أَمْرُهُمْ إِلَى ٱللَّهِ ثُمَّ يُنَبِّئُهُم بِمَا كَانُوا۟ يَفْعَلُونَ ۝

159. Inna alla*th*eena farraqoo deenahum wak*a*noo shiyaAAan lasta minhum fee shay-in innam*a* amruhum il*a* All*a*hi thumma yunabbi-ohum bim*a* k*a*noo yafAAaloona

6:159. You have indeed no concern with those who divide their religion into sects. Their matter goes to Allah, Who will then tell them what they did.[59]

59. This is a strong divine condemnation of those who cause divisions in the Allah-approved Religion of Islam. And yet there are divisions galore in Islam! How are these divisions caused and by whom? As far as my understanding goes, the first division was caused based on the controversy over the *ahaadeeth* reporting the last sermon of the Prophet, peace upon him. As per some *ahaadeeth*, the Prophet was reported to have said that he was leaving behind his Sunnah, besides the Qur'aan. There are some who dispute this and say that it was not the Sunnah, but Ahle-Bayt. Thus, arose the two sects, Sunnis and Shias, the latter sect adopting the very word, Allah Ta'ala used to condemn the schism, to identify

themselves by! Herein lies a clear pointer to the answer to the question, how and by whom. It is through the man-influenced, error-prone *ahaadeeth* that Satan has helped Muslims bring about the divisions! When will the Muslims realise this and save themselves from certain doom?

مَن جَآءَ بِٱلْحَسَنَةِ فَلَهُۥ عَشْرُ أَمْثَالِهَا ۖ وَمَن جَآءَ بِٱلسَّيِّئَةِ فَلَا يُجْزَىٰٓ إِلَّا مِثْلَهَا وَهُمْ لَا يُظْلَمُونَ ﴿١٦٠﴾

160. Man jaa bialhasanati falahu AAashru amthaliha waman jaa bialssayyi-ati fala yujza illa mithlaha wahum la yuthlamoona

6:160. One who comes up with a good deed, shall have the credit of ten like it, and one who comes up with an evil deed, shall have the recompense of only the like thereof and they shall not be wronged.

قُلْ إِنَّنِى هَدَىٰنِى رَبِّىٓ إِلَىٰ صِرَٰطٍ مُّسْتَقِيمٍ دِينًا قِيَمًا مِّلَّةَ إِبْرَٰهِيمَ حَنِيفًا ۚ وَمَا كَانَ مِنَ ٱلْمُشْرِكِينَ ﴿١٦١﴾

161. Qul innanee hadanee rabbee ila siratin mustaqeemin deenan qiyaman millata ibraheema haneefan wama kana mina almushrikeena

6:161. Say, "As for me, my Lord has indeed guided me to the Straight Path of the right religion – the creed of Abraham[60], the upright man; and he was not of those who worship others besides Allah."

---

60. Abraham's creed was to submit to the Lord of the worlds. See <u>Verse 2:131</u>.

قُلْ إِنَّ صَلَاتِى وَنُسُكِى وَمَحْيَاىَ وَمَمَاتِى لِلَّهِ رَبِّ ٱلْعَٰلَمِينَ ﴿١٦٢﴾

162. Qul inna salatee wanusukee wamahyaya wamamatee lillahi rabbi alAAalameena

---

6:162. Say, "Indeed, my prayer, my sacrifice, my life and my death are all for Allah, the Lord of the worlds."

لَا شَرِيكَ لَهُۥ وَبِذَٰلِكَ أُمِرْتُ وَأَنَا۠ أَوَّلُ ٱلْمُسْلِمِينَ ١٦٣

163. La shareeka lahu wabi<u>th</u>alika omirtu waan<u>a</u> awwalu almuslimeen<u>a</u>

6:163. "He has no associate whom I should worship. And that am I commanded with, and I am the first of those who submit!"

قُلْ أَغَيْرَ ٱللَّهِ أَبْغِى رَبًّا وَهُوَ رَبُّ كُلِّ شَىْءٍ وَلَا تَكْسِبُ كُلُّ نَفْسٍ إِلَّا عَلَيْهَا وَلَا تَزِرُ وَازِرَةٌ وِزْرَ أُخْرَىٰ ثُمَّ إِلَىٰ رَبِّكُم مَّرْجِعُكُمْ فَيُنَبِّئُكُم بِمَا كُنتُمْ فِيهِ تَخْتَلِفُونَ ١٦٤

164. Qul aghayra All<u>a</u>hi abghee rabban wahuwa rabbu kulli shay-in wal<u>a</u> taksibu kullu nafsin ill<u>a</u> AAalayh<u>a</u> wal<u>a</u> taziru w<u>a</u>ziratun wizra okhr<u>a</u> thumma il<u>a</u> rabbikum marjiAAukum fayunabbi-okum bim<u>a</u> kuntum feehi takhtalifoon<u>a</u>

6:164. Say, "Shall I seek a lord other than Allah? And He is the Lord of all things! And none earns anything but for one's own self. And no bearer of burden shall bear the burden of another. Then to your Lord is your return. He will then explain to you the things in which you differed."

وَهُوَ ٱلَّذِى جَعَلَكُمْ خَلَٰٓئِفَ ٱلْأَرْضِ وَرَفَعَ بَعْضَكُمْ فَوْقَ بَعْضٍ دَرَجَٰتٍ لِّيَبْلُوَكُمْ فِى مَآ ءَاتَىٰكُمْ إِنَّ رَبَّكَ سَرِيعُ ٱلْعِقَابِ وَإِنَّهُۥ لَغَفُورٌ رَّحِيمٌ

١٦٥

165. Wahuwa alla<u>th</u>ee jaAAalakum khal<u>a</u>-ifa al-ar<u>d</u>i warafaAAa baAA<u>d</u>akum fawqa baAA<u>d</u>in darajatin liyabluwakum fee m<u>a</u> <u>a</u>t<u>a</u>kum inna rabbaka sareeAAu alAAiq<u>a</u>bi wa-innahu lagha<u>f</u>oorun ra<u>h</u>eem<u>un</u>

6:165. And He it is Who has made you His representatives on earth and raised some of you above others in ranks so that He may test you in what He has given you. Indeed, your Lord is swift in retribution, and He is indeed Forgiving, Merciful!

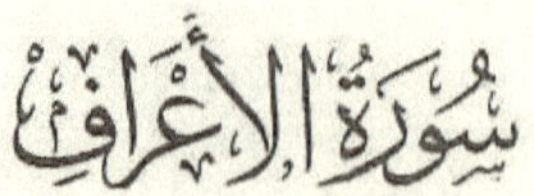

Chapter 7: Al-Auraf (The Heights)

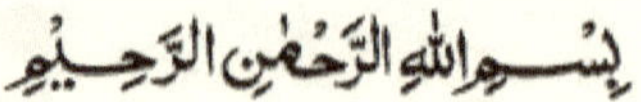

In the Name of Allah, the Gracious, the Merciful

1. Alif-l<u>a</u>m-meem-<u>sad</u>

7:1. Alif L<u>a</u>m Meem <u>Sad</u>[1]

---

1. These are some of those initials which we find mysteriously placed at the beginning of some Qur'aanic Chapters. See <u>study note 2:1</u> **on Verse 2:1.**

كِتَـٰبٌ أُنزِلَ إِلَيْكَ فَلَا يَكُن فِى صَدْرِكَ حَرَجٌ مِّنْهُ لِتُنذِرَ بِهِۦ وَذِكْرَىٰ لِلْمُؤْمِنِينَ ۝

2. Kit<u>a</u>bun onzila ilayka fal<u>a</u> yakun fee <u>s</u>adrika <u>h</u>arajun minhu litun<u>th</u>ira bihi wa<u>th</u>ikr<u>a</u> lilmu/mineena

---

7:2. A Book sent down upon you – let there be no reservations in your mind on that account – which you may warn thereby. And [it's] a Reference Book, containing things to be remembered, for the believers.[2]

---

2. The Book referred to in this Verse is obviously the Qur'aan.

ٱتَّبِعُواْ مَآ أُنزِلَ إِلَيْكُم مِّن رَّبِّكُمْ وَلَا تَتَّبِعُواْ مِن دُونِهِۦٓ أَوْلِيَآءَ قَلِيلًا مَّا تَذَكَّرُونَ ۝

3. IttabiAAoo ma onzila ilaykum min rabbikum wala tattabiAAoo min doonihi awliyaa qaleelan ma tathakkaroona

---

7:3. Follow what has been sent down to you from your Lord and follow not any *awliya*[3] besides Him. Little do you remember!

---

3. Refer study notes 2:154 and 2:155 on Verse 2:107**. By considering the man-influenced, error-prone** *ahaadeeth* **as sacrosanct as the Qur'aanic Verses, Muslims are but following** *awliya* **besides Allah. As to why** *ahaadeeth* **could be man-influenced and error-prone, please refer study notes 3:35 to 3:37 on** Verse 3:31**.**

وَكَم مِّن قَرْيَةٍ أَهْلَكْنَـٰهَا فَجَآءَهَا بَأْسُنَا بَيَـٰتًا أَوْ هُمْ قَآئِلُونَ ۝

4. Wakam min qaryatin ahlaknaha fajaaha ba/suna bayatan aw hum qa-iloona

---

7:4. And in many a human settlement that We have destroyed, Our punishment came to it by night or while its inhabitants were having their midday nap.[4]

---

4. The punishment came at a time when the inhabitants were not in a position even to attempt an escape!

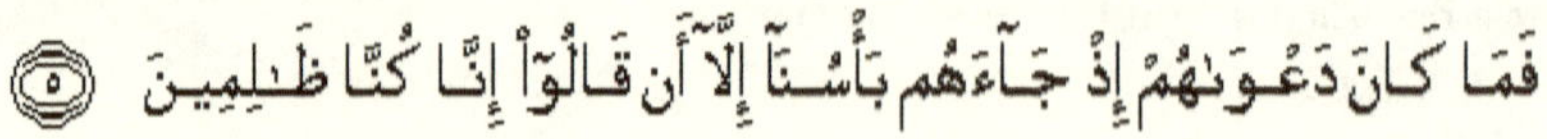

فَمَا كَانَ دَعْوَىٰهُمْ إِذْ جَاءَهُم بَأْسُنَآ إِلَّا أَن قَالُوٓاْ إِنَّا كُنَّا ظَٰلِمِينَ ۝

5. Fama kana daAAwahum ith jaahum ba/suna illa an qaloo inna kunna _tha_limeen**a**

7:5. They could say nothing – when Our punishment came to them – but that, "We were indeed in the wrong!"

فَلَنَسْـَٔلَنَّ ٱلَّذِينَ أُرْسِلَ إِلَيْهِمْ وَلَنَسْـَٔلَنَّ ٱلْمُرْسَلِينَ ۝

6. Falanas-alanna alla_the_ena orsila ilayhim walanas-alanna almursaleen**a**

7:6. Then, surely, We shall question those to whom the divine Message was sent, and, surely, We shall question the Messengers.

فَلَنَقُصَّنَّ عَلَيْهِم بِعِلْمٍ وَمَا كُنَّا غَآئِبِينَ ۝

7. Falanaqu_ss_anna AAalayhim biAAilmin wama kunna gha-ibeen**a**

7:7. Then, surely, We shall narrate to them with knowledge, and We were never absent.

وَٱلْوَزْنُ يَوْمَئِذٍ ٱلْحَقُّ فَمَن ثَقُلَتْ مَوَٰزِينُهُۥ فَأُوْلَـٰٓئِكَ هُمُ ٱلْمُفْلِحُونَ

8. Waalwaznu yawma-ithini alhaqqu faman thaqulat mawazeenuhu faola-ika humu almuflihoona

7:8. And the weight that day shall be the genuine one.[5] Those then whose scale will be heavy, those shall be successful.

5. Obviously good deeds in this world shall be the weights. The better the good deed, the heavier shall its weight be.

وَمَنْ خَفَّتْ مَوَٰزِينُهُۥ فَأُوْلَـٰٓئِكَ ٱلَّذِينَ خَسِرُوٓاْ أَنفُسَهُم بِمَا كَانُواْ بِـَٔايَـٰتِنَا يَظْلِمُونَ

9. Waman khaffat mawazeenuhu faola-ika allatheena khasiroo anfusahum bima kanoo bi-ayatina yathlimoona

7:9. And those whose scale is light, those are they who have caused their own doom because they wronged Our Verses/signs.

وَلَقَدْ مَكَّنَّـٰكُمْ فِى ٱلْأَرْضِ وَجَعَلْنَا لَكُمْ فِيهَا مَعَـٰيِشَ قَلِيلًا مَّا تَشْكُرُونَ

10. Walaqad makkannakum fee al-ardi wajaAAalna lakum feeha maAAayisha qaleelan ma tashkuroona

---

7:10. And We did provide for your boarding and lodging on earth and created in it means of livelihood for you. You give but little thanks.

وَلَقَدْ خَلَقْنَـٰكُمْ ثُمَّ صَوَّرْنَـٰكُمْ ثُمَّ قُلْنَا لِلْمَلَـٰٓئِكَةِ ٱسْجُدُوا۟ لِءَادَمَ فَسَجَدُوٓا۟ إِلَّآ إِبْلِيسَ لَمْ يَكُن مِّنَ ٱلسَّـٰجِدِينَ ﴿١١﴾

11. Walaqad khalaqnakum thumma sawwarnakum thumma qulna lilmala-ikati osjudoo li-adama fasajadoo illa ibleesa lam yakun mina alssajideena

---

7:11. And We did create you, then fashioned you, and then We said to the angels, "Prostrate to Adam." They then prostrated, but *Iblees*[6] did not! He wouldn't be of those who prostrate.

---

6. Refer study notes 2:27 to 2:30 on <u>Verse 2:34</u>.

قَالَ مَا مَنَعَكَ أَلَّا تَسْجُدَ إِذْ أَمَرْتُكَ قَالَ أَنَا۠ خَيْرٌ مِّنْهُ خَلَقْتَنِى مِن نَّارٍ وَخَلَقْتَهُۥ مِن طِينٍ ﴿١٢﴾

12. Qala ma manaAAaka alla tasjuda ith amartuka qala ana khayrun minhu khalaqtanee min narin wakhalaqtahu min teenin

---

7:12. Allah asked, "What prevented you from prostrating when I commanded you?" *Iblees* said, "I am better than he. You created me of fire, and You created him of dust."

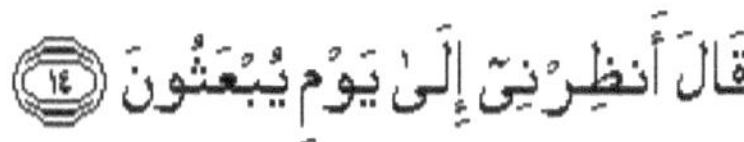

13. Q_ala faihbi_t minh_a fam_a yakoonu laka an tatakabbara feeh_a faokhruj innaka mina al_ssaghireena

---

7:13. Allah said, "Down you go then from here! You cannot behave arrogantly here. Get out! You are indeed of those who have belittled themselves."

14. Q_ala an_thirnee il_a yawmi yubAAathoona

7:14. *Iblees* said, "Grant me respite till the Day they are raised up."

---

15. Q_ala innaka mina almun_thareena

7:15. Allah said, "You are indeed one of those to whom respite is granted."

قَالَ فَبِمَآ أَغْوَيْتَنِى لَأَقْعُدَنَّ لَهُمْ صِرَاطَكَ ٱلْمُسْتَقِيمَ ﴿١٦﴾

16. Qala fabima aghwaytanee laaqAAudanna lahum sirataka almustaqeema

7:16. *Iblees* said, "Since You have led me astray, I will certainly lie in wait for them[7] in Your Straight Path."

7. Mankind.

ثُمَّ لَآتِيَنَّهُم مِّنْ بَيْنِ أَيْدِيهِمْ وَمِنْ خَلْفِهِمْ وَعَنْ أَيْمَـٰنِهِمْ وَعَن شَمَآئِلِهِمْ وَلَا تَجِدُ أَكْثَرَهُمْ شَـٰكِرِينَ ﴿١٧﴾

17. Thumma laatiyannahum min bayni aydeehim wamin khalfihim waAAan aymanihim waAAan shama-ilihim wala tajidu aktharahum shakireena

7:17. "Then I will certainly come to them from the front and from behind them, and from the right and from the left of them. And You shall not find a great number of them grateful."

قَالَ ٱخْرُجْ مِنْهَا مَذْءُومًا مَّدْحُورًا لَّمَن تَبِعَكَ مِنْهُمْ لَأَمْلَأَنَّ جَهَنَّمَ مِنكُمْ أَجْمَعِينَ ﴿١٨﴾

18. Qala okhruj minha mathooman madhooran laman tabiAAaka minhum laamlaanna jahannama minkum ajmaAAeena

7:18. Allah said, "Get out of here, as one rebuked and expelled! I will certainly fill Hell with you all – you and whoever of them will follow you."

وَيَـٰٓـَٔادَمُ ٱسْكُنْ أَنتَ وَزَوْجُكَ ٱلْجَنَّةَ فَكُلَا مِنْ حَيْثُ شِئْتُمَا وَلَا تَقْرَبَا هَـٰذِهِ ٱلشَّجَرَةَ فَتَكُونَا مِنَ ٱلظَّـٰلِمِينَ ۝

19. Waya adamu oskun anta wazawjuka aljannata fakula min haythu shi/tuma wala taqraba hathihi alshshajarata fatakoona mina al*ththa*limeena

7:19. "And O Adam! Dwell you and your wife in the Garden. Eat whatever you like and go not near this tree! Otherwise, you will be of the wicked people."

فَوَسْوَسَ لَهُمَا ٱلشَّيْطَـٰنُ لِيُبْدِىَ لَهُمَا مَا وُۥرِىَ عَنْهُمَا مِن سَوْءَٰتِهِمَا وَقَالَ مَا نَهَٮٰكُمَا رَبُّكُمَا عَنْ هَـٰذِهِ ٱلشَّجَرَةِ إِلَّآ أَن تَكُونَا مَلَكَيْنِ أَوْ تَكُونَا مِنَ ٱلْخَـٰلِدِينَ ۝

20. Fawaswasa lahuma alshshaytanu liyubdiya lahuma ma wooriya AAanhuma min saw-atihima waqala ma nahakuma rabbukuma AAan hathihi alshshajarati illa an takoona malakayni aw takoona mina alkhalideena

7:20. And the Satan then tempted them both to lay bare to them what had been hidden from them of their carnal desires. And he said, "Your Lord forbade you from this tree lest you two should become angels or of the immortal beings."

وَقَاسَمَهُمَآ إِنِّى لَكُمَا لَمِنَ ٱلنَّٰصِحِينَ ۝

21. Waqasamahuma innee lakuma lamina alnnasiheena

7:21. And he swore to them both, "I am indeed one of your sincere advisers."

فَدَلَّىٰهُمَا بِغُرُورٍ فَلَمَّا ذَاقَا ٱلشَّجَرَةَ بَدَتْ لَهُمَا سَوْءَٰتُهُمَا وَطَفِقَا يَخْصِفَانِ عَلَيْهِمَا مِن وَرَقِ ٱلْجَنَّةِ وَنَادَىٰهُمَا رَبُّهُمَآ أَلَمْ أَنْهَكُمَا عَن تِلْكُمَا ٱلشَّجَرَةِ وَأَقُل لَّكُمَآ إِنَّ ٱلشَّيْطَٰنَ لَكُمَا عَدُوٌّ مُّبِينٌ ۝

22. Fadallahuma bighuroorin falamma thaqa alshshajarata badat lahuma saw-atuhuma watafiqa yakhsifani AAalayhima min waraqi aljannati wanadahuma rabbuhuma alam anhakuma AAan tilkuma alshshajarati waaqul lakuma inna alshshaytana lakuma AAaduwwun mubeenun

---

7:22. So he misled them both by deceit. And when they tasted of the tree, their carnal desires became manifest to them, and they both began to cover themselves with the leaves of the garden. And their Lord called out to them, "Did I not forbid you both from that tree and tell you that the Satan is an open enemy to you both?"

قَالَا رَبَّنَا ظَلَمْنَآ أَنفُسَنَا وَإِن لَّمْ تَغْفِرْ لَنَا وَتَرْحَمْنَا لَنَكُونَنَّ مِنَ ٱلْخَٰسِرِينَ ۝

23. Qala rabbana thalamna anfusana wa-in lam taghfir lana watarhamna lanakoonanna mina alkhasireena

---

7:23. They said, "Our Lord! We have wronged ourselves. And if You forgive us not, and have mercy on us not, we shall certainly be of the losers."

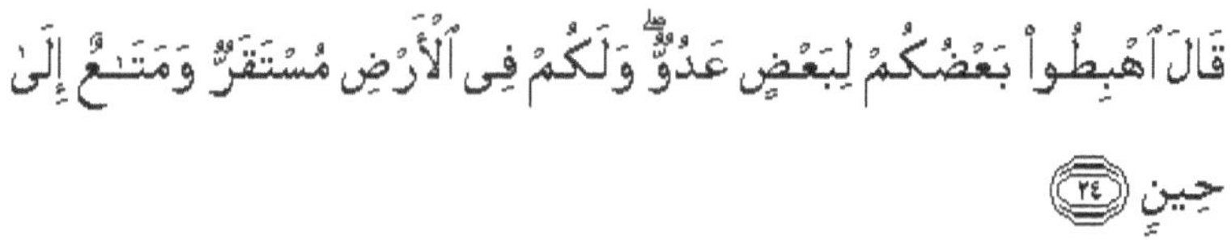

24. Qala ihbitoo baAAdukum libaAAdin AAaduwwun walakum fee al-ardi mustaqarrun wamataAAun ila heenin

7:24. HE said, "Down you go! Some of you would be inimical to some others. And there is for you in the earth provision for lodging and boarding, for a period."

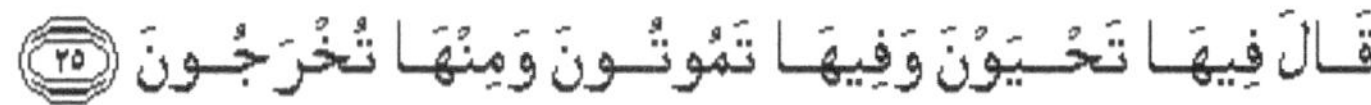

25. Qala feeha tahyawna wafeeha tamootoona waminha tukhrajoona

7:25. HE said, "Therein shall you live, and therein shall you die, and there from shall you be raised."[8]

8. Verses 19 to 25 herein above, give an encapsulated history of mankind till Resurrection Day. The first couple of human beings started their lives in the utopian pleasantness of Paradise. There, the Lord had put just one restriction on them, with a due warning against disobeying the restriction order. But they were given the capability to disobey. And under the influence of their avowed enemy, the Satan, they disobeyed! Thus, did the first human sin happen. And the first couple was duly punished by being banished from Paradise. They and their progeny are put on test again, on this earth, with some restrictions divinely placed on them. They may regain Paradise only if they pass the test. So here, in this encapsulated history of mankind, Allah Almighty gives us His Law of Crime and Punishment for mankind. Anyone who goes against Allah's directives commits a crime. He is then liable to Allah's punishment here in this world itself and/or in the Hereafter.

يَـٰبَنِىٓ ءَادَمَ قَدْ أَنزَلْنَا عَلَيْكُمْ لِبَاسًا يُوَٰرِى سَوْءَٰتِكُمْ وَرِيشًا ۖ وَلِبَاسُ ٱلتَّقْوَىٰ ذَٰلِكَ خَيْرٌ ۚ ذَٰلِكَ مِنْ ءَايَـٰتِ ٱللَّهِ لَعَلَّهُمْ يَذَّكَّرُونَ ﴿٢٦﴾

26. Ya banee adama qad anzalna AAalaykum libasan yuwaree saw-atikum wareeshan walibasu alttaqwa thalika khayrun thalika min ayati Allahi laAAallahum yaththakkaroona

7:26. O Children of Adam! We have certainly sent down to you clothing to hide and keep in control your carnal desires and to adorn yourself with. And the clothing of piety is the one that is better. That is among Allah's Verses/signs for them to remember.

يَـٰبَنِىٓ ءَادَمَ لَا يَفْتِنَنَّكُمُ ٱلشَّيْطَـٰنُ كَمَآ أَخْرَجَ أَبَوَيْكُم مِّنَ ٱلْجَنَّةِ يَنزِعُ عَنْهُمَا لِبَاسَهُمَا لِيُرِيَهُمَا سَوْءَٰتِهِمَآ ۗ إِنَّهُۥ يَرَىٰكُمْ هُوَ وَقَبِيلُهُۥ مِنْ حَيْثُ لَا تَرَوْنَهُمْ ۗ إِنَّا جَعَلْنَا ٱلشَّيَـٰطِينَ أَوْلِيَآءَ لِلَّذِينَ لَا يُؤْمِنُونَ ﴿٢٧﴾

27. Ya banee adama la yaftinannakumu alshshaytanu kama akhraja abawaykum mina aljannati yanziAAu AAanhuma libasahuma liyuriyahuma saw-atihima innahu yarakum huwa waqabeeluhu min haythu la tarawnahum inna jaAAalna alshshayateena awliyaa lillatheena la yu/minoona

7:27. O Children of Adam! Let not the Satan tempt you just as he did to your parents, causing their expulsion from the Garden and stripping them both of their clothing to expose to them their carnal desires. Indeed, he and his tribe see you from where you cannot see them. We have indeed made the devils to be the *awliya*[9] of those who believe not.

9. Refer study notes 2.154 and 2.155 on Verse 2.107.

وَإِذَا فَعَلُواْ فَٰحِشَةً قَالُواْ وَجَدْنَا عَلَيْهَآ ءَابَآءَنَا وَٱللَّهُ أَمَرَنَا بِهَا قُلْ إِنَّ ٱللَّهَ لَا يَأْمُرُ بِٱلْفَحْشَآءِ أَتَقُولُونَ عَلَى ٱللَّهِ مَا لَا تَعْلَمُونَ ۝

28. Wa-itha faAAaloo fahishatan qaloo wajadna AAalayha abaana waAllahu amarana biha qul inna Allaha la ya/muru bialfahsha-i ataqooloona AAala Allahi ma la taAAlamoona

7:28. And when they commit an indecency they say, "We found our fathers doing this, and Allah has enjoined it on us." Say, "Allah does indeed not enjoin indecency. Do you say what you know not about Allah?"

قُلْ أَمَرَ رَبِّى بِٱلْقِسْطِ وَأَقِيمُواْ وُجُوهَكُمْ عِندَ كُلِّ مَسْجِدٍ وَٱدْعُوهُ مُخْلِصِينَ لَهُ ٱلدِّينَ كَمَا بَدَأَكُمْ تَعُودُونَ ۝

29. Qul amara rabbee bialqisti waaqeemoo wujoohakum AAinda kulli masjidin waodAAoohu mukhliseena lahu alddeena kama badaakum taAAoodoona

7:29. Say, "My Lord has enjoined justice. And you should pray to Him, in complete attention and devotion, at every place of worship, and keep the Religion pure for Him. Just as He brought you into being in the beginning, so shall you return [to life again]!"

فَرِيقًا هَدَىٰ وَفَرِيقًا حَقَّ عَلَيْهِمُ ٱلضَّلَٰلَةُ إِنَّهُمُ ٱتَّخَذُواْ ٱلشَّيَٰطِينَ أَوْلِيَآءَ مِن دُونِ ٱللَّهِ وَيَحْسَبُونَ أَنَّهُم مُّهْتَدُونَ ۝

30. Fareeqan hada wafareeqan haqqa AAalayhimu alddalalatu innahumu ittakhathoo alshshayateena awliyaa min dooni Allahi wayahsaboona annahum muhtadoona

---

7:30. Some He guided, and some deserved to go astray. They indeed took the devils, instead of Allah, as their *awliya*, and thought that they were guided!

يَـٰبَنِىٓ ءَادَمَ خُـذُواْ زِينَتَكُـمْ عِنـدَ كُـلِّ مَسْـجِدٍ وَكُلُـواْ وَٱشْـرَبُواْ وَلَا تُسْـرِفُوٓاْ إِنَّـهُ لَا يُحِـبُّ ٱلْمُسْـرِفِينَ ۝

31. Ya banee adama khuthoo zeenatakum AAinda kulli masjidin wakuloo waishraboo wala tusrifoo innahu la yuhibbu almusrifeena

---

7:31. O Children of Adam! Be well-dressed, clean and tidy at every place of worship, [10] and [11] and eat and drink, but indulge not in extravagance. HE does not indeed like those who indulge in extravagance.

---

10. I would like to mention here the insistence of some traditionalists – who consider the *ahaadeeth* more sacrosanct than even the Qur'aanic Verses – that Muslims should keep the lower ends of their pyjamas and trousers above the ankles. A *hadeeth* [*Sahih Bukhari* Volume 7, *hadeeth* No. 678] tells them that if the garment extends below the ankles, the wearer goes to Hell. And this vital information is not there in the Qur'aan! Therefore, the traditionalists believe that without the *ahaadeeth*, Islam is incomplete. The Qur'aan, on the other hand, reiterates, "... We have neglected nothing in the Book ..." (Verse 6:38) and that "... We have certainly explained, <u>in this Qur'aan</u>, every kind of example ..." (Verse 17:89). How could the Qur'aan then neglect to mention a thing that would lead a man to Hell!? It cannot, and it does not, because, Allah Almighty, the Author of the Book, cannot be wrong in saying that the Qur'aan has neglected nothing! We are then left with the only conclusion that there is something wrong with the *hadeeth*, which is man-influenced and therefore error-prone.

11. As this Verse and the one immediately following (7:32) clearly tells us, Allah does not want us to look shabby or uncouth in our dress. One of the purposes of our dress is to make us look better. Allah does not prohibit us this adornment. HE wouldn't wish us to wear short trousers if these make us look comical. What Allah desires, however, is that we be clean. HE certainly wouldn't like our trousers to be so long as to collect dirt from the ground as we walk on.

قُلْ مَنْ حَرَّمَ زِينَةَ ٱللَّهِ ٱلَّتِىٓ أَخْرَجَ لِعِبَادِهِۦ وَٱلطَّيِّبَـٰتِ مِنَ ٱلرِّزْقِ قُلْ هِىَ لِلَّذِينَ ءَامَنُواْ فِى ٱلْحَيَوٰةِ ٱلدُّنْيَا خَالِصَةً يَوْمَ ٱلْقِيَـٰمَةِ كَذَٰلِكَ نُفَصِّلُ ٱلْأَيَـٰتِ لِقَوْمٍ يَعْلَمُونَ ﴿٣٢﴾

32. Qul man harrama zeenata Allahi allatee akhraja liAAibadihi waalttayyibati mina alrrizqi qul hiya lillatheena amanoo fee alhayati alddunya khalisatan yawma alqiyamati kathalika nufassilu al-ayati liqawmin yaAAlamoona

---

7:32. Say, "Who has prohibited Allah's decorations and the wholesome provisions which He has brought forth for His subjects?" Say, "These are for the believers in the life of this world, and exclusively for them, [12] on the Resurrection Day." Thus, do We make the Verses/signs clear for people who know.

---

12. As noted in the preceding study notes, this Verse makes it abundantly clear that Allah does not want the believers to deprive themselves of the good things of this life. The good things are also available to the non-believers in this world but will not be available for them in the Hereafter.

قُلْ إِنَّمَا حَرَّمَ رَبِّىَ ٱلْفَوَٰحِشَ مَا ظَهَرَ مِنْهَا وَمَا بَطَنَ وَٱلْإِثْمَ وَٱلْبَغْىَ بِغَيْرِ ٱلْحَقِّ وَأَن تُشْرِكُواْ بِٱللَّهِ مَا لَمْ يُنَزِّلْ بِهِۦ سُلْطَـٰنًا وَأَن تَقُولُواْ عَلَى ٱللَّهِ مَا لَا تَعْلَمُونَ ﴿٣٣﴾

33. Qul innama harrama rabbiya alfawahisha ma thahara minha wama batana waal-ithma waalbaghya bighayri alhaqqi waan tushrikoo biAllahi ma lam yunazzil bihi sultanan waan taqooloo AAala Allahi ma la taAAlamoona

---

7:33. Say, "My Lord has prohibited only indecencies[13], those of them that are apparent as well as those that are concealed, and sin and unjustified rebellion, and that you worship others besides Allah, for which He has not sent down any authority, and that you say about Allah that which you know not."

---

13. In Verses 17:32 and 27:54, sexual behaviour like adultery, sodomy and homosexuality are termed as *faahishah*, singular of *fawaahish* translated here as indecencies.

وَلِكُلِّ أُمَّةٍ أَجَلٌ فَإِذَا جَاءَ أَجَلُهُمْ لَا يَسْتَأْخِرُونَ سَاعَةً وَلَا يَسْتَقْدِمُونَ ﴿٣٤﴾

34. Walikulli ommatin ajalun fa-itha jaa ajaluhum la yasta/khiroona saAAatan wala yastaqdimoona

---

7:34. And for every community there is an end. So when their end comes, not a moment can they delay it nor advance it.

يَٰبَنِىٓ ءَادَمَ إِمَّا يَأْتِيَنَّكُمْ رُسُلٌ مِّنكُمْ يَقُصُّونَ عَلَيْكُمْ ءَايَٰتِى فَمَنِ ٱتَّقَىٰ وَأَصْلَحَ فَلَا خَوْفٌ عَلَيْهِمْ وَلَا هُمْ يَحْزَنُونَ ﴿٣٥﴾

35. Ya banee adama imma ya/tiyannakum rusulun minkum yaqussoona AAalaykum ayatee famani ittaqa waaslaha fala khawfun AAalayhim wala hum yahzanoona

---

7:35. O Children of Adam! As and when Messengers come to you from amongst you relating to you My Verses/signs, then on those who take heed and mend themselves, there shall be no fear, nor shall they grieve.

وَٱلَّذِينَ كَذَّبُواْ بِـَٔايَـٰتِنَا وَٱسْتَكْبَرُواْ عَنْهَآ أُوْلَـٰٓئِكَ أَصْحَـٰبُ ٱلنَّارِ هُمْ فِيهَا خَـٰلِدُونَ ۩

36. Waallatheena kaththaboo bi-ayatina waistakbaroo AAanha ola-ika as-habu alnnari hum feeha khalidoona

7:36. And as for those who reject Our Verses/signs and arrogantly turn away from them, they will be the dwellers of the Fire and will abide therein forever.

فَمَنْ أَظْلَمُ مِمَّنِ ٱفْتَرَىٰ عَلَى ٱللَّهِ كَذِبًا أَوْ كَذَّبَ بِـَٔايَـٰتِهِۦٓ أُوْلَـٰٓئِكَ يَنَالُهُمْ نَصِيبُهُم مِّنَ ٱلْكِتَـٰبِ حَتَّىٰٓ إِذَا جَآءَتْهُمْ رُسُلُنَا يَتَوَفَّوْنَهُمْ قَالُوٓاْ أَيْنَ مَا كُنتُمْ تَدْعُونَ مِن دُونِ ٱللَّهِ قَالُواْ ضَلُّواْ عَنَّا وَشَهِدُواْ عَلَىٰٓ أَنفُسِهِمْ أَنَّهُمْ كَانُواْ كَـٰفِرِينَ ۩

37. Faman athlamu mimmani iftara AAala Allahi kathiban aw kaththaba bi-ayatihi ola-ika yanaluhum naseebuhum mina alkitabi hatta itha jaat-hum rusuluna yatawaffawnahum qaloo ayna ma kuntum tadAAoona min dooni Allahi qaloo dalloo AAanna washahidoo AAala anfusihim annahum kanoo kafireena

7:37. Who is then more wicked than he who concocts a lie against Allah or rejects His Verses/signs? Such persons get what is destined for them in this life, until, Our Messengers come to them causing them to die and ask, "Where are those whom you used to invoke and worship besides Allah?" They would say, "They have deserted us." And they shall bear witness against themselves that they were suppressors of the Truth.

قَالَ ٱدْخُلُواْ فِىٓ أُمَمٍ قَدْ خَلَتْ مِن قَبْلِكُم مِّنَ ٱلْجِنِّ وَٱلْإِنسِ فِى ٱلنَّارِ كُلَّمَا دَخَلَتْ أُمَّةٌ لَّعَنَتْ أُخْتَهَا حَتَّىٰٓ إِذَا ٱدَّارَكُواْ فِيهَا جَمِيعًا قَالَتْ أُخْرَىٰهُمْ لِأُولَىٰهُمْ رَبَّنَا هَٰٓؤُلَآءِ أَضَلُّونَا فَـَٔاتِهِمْ عَذَابًا ضِعْفًا مِّنَ ٱلنَّارِ قَالَ لِكُلٍّ ضِعْفٌ وَلَٰكِن لَّا تَعْلَمُونَ ﴿٣٨﴾

38. Qala odkhuloo fee omamin qad khalat min qablikum mina aljinni waal-insi fee alnnari kullama dakhalat ommatun laAAanat okhtaha hatta itha iddarakoo feeha jameeAAan qalat okhrahum li-oolahum rabbana haola-i adalloona faatihim AAathaban diAAfan mina alnnari qala likullin diAAfun walakin la taAAlamoona

---

7:38. He[14] will say, "Enter the Fire among communities of jinn and humans that have passed away before you." Every time a community enters, it curses its sister community, until when they all will have reached it, the community that followed shall say about the community that preceded it, "Our Lord! These led us astray, so give them a double punishment of the Fire." He[14] will say, "It's double[15] for everyone, but you know not."

---

14. 'He' here could be Allah or one of the angels.

15. One, for themselves going astray; and two, for leading others astray.

وَقَالَتْ أُولَىٰهُمْ لِأُخْرَىٰهُمْ فَمَا كَانَ لَكُمْ عَلَيْنَا مِن فَضْلٍ فَذُوقُواْ ٱلْعَذَابَ بِمَا كُنتُمْ تَكْسِبُونَ ﴿٣٩﴾

39. Waqalat oolahum li-okhrahum fama kana lakum AAalayna min fadlin fathooqoo alAAathaba bima kuntum taksiboona

---

7:39. And the community that preceded will say to the community that followed, "So you have no preference over us. You taste then the punishment for what you used to earn."

إِنَّ ٱلَّذِينَ كَذَّبُواْ بِـَٔايَـٰتِنَا وَٱسْتَكْبَرُواْ عَنْهَا لَا تُفَتَّحُ لَهُمْ أَبْوَٰبُ ٱلسَّمَآءِ وَلَا يَدْخُلُونَ ٱلْجَنَّةَ حَتَّىٰ يَلِجَ ٱلْجَمَلُ فِى سَمِّ ٱلْخِيَاطِ وَكَذَٰلِكَ نَجْزِى ٱلْمُجْرِمِينَ ۝

40. Inna allatheena kaththaboo bi-ayatina waistakbaroo AAanha la tufattahu lahum abwabu alssama-i wala yadkhuloona aljannata hatta yalija aljamalu fee sammi alkhiyati wakathalika najzee almujrimeena

7:40. Indeed, the doors of heaven shall not be opened for those who reject Our Verses/signs and arrogantly turn away from them, nor shall they enter Paradise until the cable [thick rope] passes through the eye of the needle[16]. And thus, do We reward the sinners.

16. This idiomatically expressed clause means: nor shall they ever enter Paradise.

لَهُم مِّن جَهَنَّمَ مِهَادٌ وَمِن فَوْقِهِمْ غَوَاشٍ وَكَذَٰلِكَ نَجْزِى ٱلظَّـٰلِمِينَ ۝

41. Lahum min jahannama mihadun wamin fawqihim ghawashin wakathalika najzee alththalimeena

7:41. For them shall there be a bed of Hell and over them coverings thereof. And thus, do We reward the wicked people.

وَٱلَّذِينَ ءَامَنُواْ وَعَمِلُواْ ٱلصَّـٰلِحَـٰتِ لَا نُكَلِّفُ نَفْسًا إِلَّا وُسْعَهَآ أُوْلَـٰٓئِكَ أَصْحَـٰبُ ٱلْجَنَّةِ هُمْ فِيهَا خَـٰلِدُونَ ۝

42. Waallatheena amanoo waAAamiloo alssalihati la nukallifu nafsan illa wusAAaha ola-ika as-habu aljannati hum feeha khalidoona

---

7:42. And as for those who believe and do good deeds, We burden not anyone beyond one's capacity. They will be the dwellers of Paradise and will abide therein forever.

وَنَزَعْنَا مَا فِى صُدُورِهِم مِّنْ غِلٍّ تَجْرِى مِن تَحْتِهِمُ ٱلْأَنْهَـٰرُ وَقَالُواْ ٱلْحَمْدُ لِلَّهِ ٱلَّذِى هَدَىٰنَا لِهَـٰذَا وَمَا كُنَّا لِنَهْتَدِىَ لَوْلَآ أَنْ هَدَىٰنَا ٱللَّهُ لَقَدْ جَآءَتْ رُسُلُ رَبِّنَا بِٱلْحَقِّ وَنُودُوٓاْ أَن تِلْكُمُ ٱلْجَنَّةُ أُورِثْتُمُوهَا بِمَا كُنتُمْ تَعْمَلُونَ ۝

43. WanazaAAna ma fee sudoorihim min ghillin tajree min tahtihimu al-anharu waqaloo alhamdu lillahi allathee hadana lihatha wama kunna linahtadiya lawla an hadana Allahu laqad jaat rusulu rabbina bialhaqqi wanoodoo an tilkumu aljannatu oorithtumooha bima kuntum taAAmaloona

---

7:43. And We will remove any ill-feeling they had in their minds, and beneath them the rivers shall flow. And they will say, "All praise is due to Allah Who guided us to this! And had Allah not guided us we would never have found the way. Messengers of our Lord had certainly brought the Truth. And it shall be announced to them, "This is the Paradise for you. You have inherited it because of what you used to do."

وَنَادَىٰٓ أَصْحَـٰبُ ٱلْجَنَّةِ أَصْحَـٰبَ ٱلنَّارِ أَن قَدْ وَجَدْنَا مَا وَعَدَنَا رَبُّنَا حَقًّا فَهَلْ وَجَدتُّم مَّا وَعَدَ رَبُّكُمْ حَقًّا قَالُوا۟ نَعَمْ فَأَذَّنَ مُؤَذِّنٌۢ بَيْنَهُمْ أَن لَّعْنَةُ ٱللَّهِ عَلَى ٱلظَّـٰلِمِينَ ۝

44. Wan<u>ada</u> a<u>s-h</u>abu aljannati a<u>s-h</u>aba alnn<u>a</u>ri an qad wajadn<u>a</u> m<u>a</u> waAAadan<u>a</u> rabbun<u>a</u> <u>h</u>aqqan fahal wajadtum m<u>a</u> waAAada rabbukum <u>h</u>aqqan q<u>a</u>loo naAAam faa<u>ththa</u>na mu-a<u>ththi</u>nun baynahum an laAAnatu All<u>a</u>hi AAal<u>a</u> al<u>ththa</u>limeena

---

7:44. And the dwellers of Paradise will call out to the dwellers of the Fire, "We have indeed found what our Lord promised us to be true. Have you too found what your Lord promised to be true?" They will say, "Yes!" Then an announcer in between them will announce, "Allah's curse is on the wicked people."

ٱلَّذِينَ يَصُدُّونَ عَن سَبِيلِ ٱللَّهِ وَيَبْغُونَهَا عِوَجًا وَهُم بِٱلْءَاخِرَةِ كَـٰفِرُونَ ۝

45. Alla<u>th</u>eena ya<u>s</u>uddoona AAan sabeeli All<u>a</u>hi wayabghoonah<u>a</u> AAiwajan wahum bial-<u>a</u>khirati k<u>a</u>firoona

---

7:45. [17]"On those who hindered people from Allah's Path and sought to distort it. And they believed not in the Hereafter."

---

17. This Verse describes the wicked people (_alththalimeen_) mentioned at the end of the preceding Verse.

وَبَيْنَهُمَا حِجَابٌ وَعَلَى ٱلْأَعْرَافِ رِجَالٌ يَعْرِفُونَ كُلًّا بِسِيمَنهُمْ وَنَادَوْاْ أَصْحَـٰبَ ٱلْجَنَّةِ أَن سَلَـٰمٌ عَلَيْكُمْ لَمْ يَدْخُلُوهَا وَهُمْ يَطْمَعُونَ ۝

46. Wabaynahuma hijabun waAAala al-aAArafi rijalun yaAArifoona kullan biseemahum wanadaw as-haba aljannati an salamun AAalaykum lam yadkhulooha wahum yatmaAAoona

---

7:46. And between the two there shall be a veil. And on the heights, there will be men who will recognise all others by their distinguishing features. And they will greet the dwellers of Paradise, "Peace on you." They[18] will not have yet entered it but will hope to!

---

18. The men on the heights. These appear to be those whose fate is not yet declared. They are obviouly placed on some high ground from which they can see the dwellers of both Paradise and Hell.

۞ وَإِذَا صُرِفَتْ أَبْصَـٰرُهُمْ تِلْقَآءَ أَصْحَـٰبِ ٱلنَّارِ قَالُواْ رَبَّنَا لَا تَجْعَلْنَا مَعَ ٱلْقَوْمِ ٱلظَّـٰلِمِينَ ۝

47. Wa-itha surifat absaruhum tilqaa as-habi alnnari qaloo rabbana la tajAAalna maAAa alqawmi alththalimeena

---

7:47. And when their eyes will be turned towards the dwellers of the Fire, they will say, "Our Lord! Place us not with the wicked people."

وَنَادَىٰ أَصْحَـٰبُ ٱلْأَعْرَافِ رِجَالًا يَعْرِفُونَهُم بِسِيمَنهُمْ قَالُواْ مَآ أَغْنَىٰ عَنكُمْ جَمْعُكُمْ وَمَا كُنتُمْ تَسْتَكْبِرُونَ ۝

48. Wan<u>a</u>d<u>a</u> a<u>s</u>-<u>h</u>abu al-aAAr<u>a</u>fi rij<u>a</u>lan yaAArifoonahum biseem<u>a</u>hum q<u>a</u>loo m<u>a</u> aghn<u>a</u> AAankum jamAAukum wam<u>a</u> kuntum tastakbiroon<u>a</u>

7:48. And the dwellers of the heights will call out to men whom they will recognise by their distinguishing features, "Of no avail were to you the wealth you amassed and the things you took pride in!"

أَهَـٰٓؤُلَآءِ ٱلَّـذِينَ أَقْسَـمْتُمْ لَا يَنَـالُهُمُ ٱللَّـهُ بِرَحْمَـةٍ ٱدْخُـلُوا۟ ٱلْجَنَّـةَ لَا خَـوْفٌ عَلَيْكُـمْ وَلَآ أَنتُـمْ تَحْـزَنُونَ ۝

49. Ah<u>aola</u>-i alla<u>thee</u>na aqsamtum l<u>a</u> yan<u>a</u>luhumu All<u>a</u>hu bira<u>h</u>matin odkhuloo aljannata l<u>a</u> khawfun AAalaykum wal<u>a</u> antum ta<u>h</u>zanoon<u>a</u>

7:49. "Are these – who were told, 'Enter Paradise! You shall have no fear, nor shall you grieve' – the same about whom you swore that Allah will not bestow mercy on them?"

وَنَـادَىٰٓ أَصْحَـٰبُ ٱلنَّارِ أَصْحَـٰبَ ٱلْجَنَّـةِ أَنْ أَفِيضُـوا۟ عَلَيْنَـا مِـنَ ٱلْمَـآءِ أَوْ مِمَّـا رَزَقَكُـمُ ٱللَّـهُ قَـالُوٓا۟ إِنَّ ٱللَّـهَ حَرَّمَهُمَـا عَلَـى ٱلْكَـٰفِـرِينَ ۝

50. Wan<u>a</u>d<u>a</u> a<u>s</u>-<u>h</u>abu aln<u>a</u>ri a<u>s</u>-<u>h</u>aba aljannati an afee<u>d</u>oo AAalayn<u>a</u> mina alm<u>a</u>-i aw mimm<u>a</u> razaqakumu All<u>a</u>hu q<u>a</u>loo inna All<u>a</u>ha <u>h</u>arramahum<u>a</u> AAal<u>a</u> alk<u>a</u>fireen<u>a</u>

7:50. And the dwellers of the Fire will call out to the dwellers of Paradise, "Let some water or some of the provisions Allah has given you overflow to us!" They will say, "Allah has indeed prohibited them both upon those who suppressed the Truth."

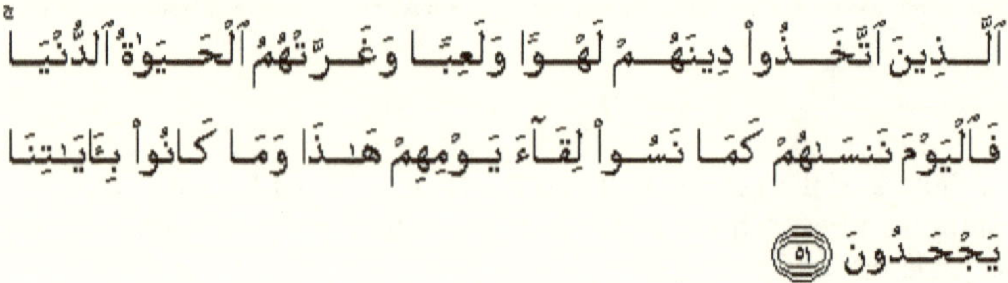

51. Alla<u>th</u>eena ittakha<u>th</u>oo deenahum lahwan walaAAiban wagharrat-humu al<u>h</u>ay<u>a</u>tu aldduny<u>a</u> faalyawma nans<u>a</u>hum kam<u>a</u> nasoo liq<u>a</u>a yawmihim h<u>atha</u> wam<u>a</u> k<u>a</u>noo bi-<u>a</u>y<u>a</u>tin<u>a</u> yaj<u>h</u>adoon**a**

7:51. "Who[19] took their religion as just sport and pastime and their worldly life deceived them." So today We forget them, as they forgot their appointment for this day and denied Our Verses/signs.

---

19. I.e., the dwellers of the Fire. Refer preceding Verse.

---

52. Walaqad ji/n<u>a</u>hum bikit<u>a</u>bin fa<u>ss</u>aln<u>a</u>hu AAal<u>a</u> AAilmin hudan wara<u>h</u>matan liqawmin yu/minoon**a**

7:52. And certainly We have brought them a Book[20], which We have explained based on knowledge, and which is a guidance and a mercy for people who believe.

---

20. The Qur'aan. It embodies the Clarification, Guidance and Mercy, all from the Compassionate and Understanding Creator.

هَلْ يَنظُرُونَ إِلَّا تَأْوِيلَهُۥ يَوْمَ يَأْتِى تَأْوِيلُهُۥ يَقُولُ ٱلَّذِينَ نَسُوهُ مِن قَبْلُ

قَدْ جَآءَتْ رُسُلُ رَبِّنَا بِٱلْحَقِّ فَهَل لَّنَا مِن شُفَعَآءَ فَيَشْفَعُواْ لَنَآ أَوْ نُرَدُّ

فَنَعْمَلَ غَيْرَ ٱلَّذِى كُنَّا نَعْمَلُ قَدْ خَسِرُوٓاْ أَنفُسَهُمْ وَضَلَّ عَنْهُم مَّا كَانُواْ

يَفْتَرُونَ ۝

53. Hal yan_th_uroona illa ta/weelahu yawma ya/tee ta/weeluhu yaqoolu alla_th_eena nasoohu min qablu qad _j_aat rusulu rabbina bial_h_aqqi fahal lana min shufaAAaa fayashfaAAoo lana aw nuraddu fanaAAmala ghayra alla_th_ee kunna naAAmalu qad khasiroo anfusahum wa_d_alla AAanhum ma kanoo yaftaroona

7:53. Are they waiting for it[21] to occur first? On the day it occurs, those who had forgotten about it before, will say, "Messengers of our Lord had indeed come with the Truth! Are there for us then any intercessors to intercede on our behalf? Or could we be sent back so that we do things other than what we used to do?" Indeed, they have doomed themselves and that which they concocted has deserted them!

21. The Day of Resurrection.

إِنَّ رَبَّكُمُ ٱللَّهُ ٱلَّذِى خَلَقَ ٱلسَّمَٰوَٰتِ وَٱلْأَرْضَ فِى سِتَّةِ أَيَّامٍ ثُمَّ ٱسْتَوَىٰ عَلَى

ٱلْعَرْشِ يُغْشِى ٱلَّيْلَ ٱلنَّهَارَ يَطْلُبُهُۥ حَثِيثًا وَٱلشَّمْسَ وَٱلْقَمَرَ وَٱلنُّجُومَ

مُسَخَّرَٰتٍ بِأَمْرِهِۦ أَلَا لَهُ ٱلْخَلْقُ وَٱلْأَمْرُ تَبَارَكَ ٱللَّهُ رَبُّ ٱلْعَٰلَمِينَ ۝

54. Inna rabbakumu Allahu alla_th_ee khalaqa alssamawati waal-ar_d_a fee sittati ayyamin thumma istawa AAala alAAarshi yughshee allayla alnnahara ya_t_lubuhu _h_atheethan waalshshamsa waalqamara waalnnujooma musakhkhara_t_in bi-amrihi ala lahu alkhalqu waal-amru tabaraka Allahu rabbu alAAalameena

7:54. Surely your Lord is Allah, Who created the heavens and the earth in six periods of time, and Who then ascended the Throne. He brings the night as a cover over the day, the night pursuing the day incessantly. And the sun and the moon and the stars are subservient to His command. Aren't the Creation and the Command His? Blessed is Allah, the Lord of the worlds!

اُدْعُواْ رَبَّكُمْ تَضَرُّعًا وَخُفْيَةً إِنَّهُ لَا يُحِبُّ الْمُعْتَدِينَ ۝

55. OdAAoo rabbakum tadarruAAan wakhufyatan innahu la yuhibbu almuAAtadeena

7:55. Invoke your Lord in humility and secrecy. He does not indeed like those who transgress the limits.

وَلَا تُفْسِدُواْ فِى ٱلْأَرْضِ بَعْدَ إِصْلَـٰحِهَا وَٱدْعُوهُ خَوْفًا وَطَمَعًا إِنَّ رَحْمَتَ ٱللَّهِ قَرِيبٌ مِّنَ ٱلْمُحْسِنِينَ ۝

56. Wala tufsidoo fee al-ardi baAAda islahiha waodAAoohu khawfan watamaAAan inna rahmata Allahi qareebun mina almuhsineena

7:56. And make no mischief on the earth after its reformation and invoke Him with fear and hope. Allah's Mercy is ever near those who are good.

وَهُوَ ٱلَّذِى يُرْسِلُ ٱلرِّيَـٰحَ بُشْرًۢا بَيْنَ يَدَىْ رَحْمَتِهِ حَتَّىٰ إِذَآ أَقَلَّتْ سَحَابًا ثِقَالًا سُقْنَـٰهُ لِبَلَدٍ مَّيِّتٍ فَأَنزَلْنَا بِهِ ٱلْمَآءَ فَأَخْرَجْنَا بِهِ مِن كُلِّ ٱلثَّمَرَٰتِ كَذَٰلِكَ نُخْرِجُ ٱلْمَوْتَىٰ لَعَلَّكُمْ تَذَكَّرُونَ ۝

57. Wahuwa allathee yursilu alrriyaha bushran bayna yaday rahmatihi hatta itha aqallat sahaban thiqalan suqnahu libaladin mayyitin faanzalna bihi almaa faakhrajna bihi min kulli alththamarati kathalika nukhriju almawta laAAallakum tathakkaroona

7:57. And He it is Who sends the winds heralding the good news of His mercy, until, when it carries a heavily laden cloud, We make it serve as a water-carrier for a dead land. We then send water down on it and bring out with it all kinds of fruits. Thus, shall We raise the dead, may you remember!

وَٱلْبَلَدُ ٱلطَّيِّبُ يَخْرُجُ نَبَاتُهُۥ بِإِذْنِ رَبِّهِۦ ۖ وَٱلَّذِى خَبُثَ لَا يَخْرُجُ إِلَّا نَكِدًا ۚ كَذَٰلِكَ نُصَرِّفُ ٱلْآيَٰتِ لِقَوْمٍ يَشْكُرُونَ ۝

58. Waalbaladu alttayyibu yakhruju nabatuhu bi-ithni rabbihi waallathee khabutha la yakhruju illa nakidan kathalika nusarrifu al-ayati liqawmin yashkuroona

7:58. And as for the good land, its vegetation springs forth by the permission of its Lord, and as for the infertile one, its vegetation comes forth but scantily. We thus variously explain the Verses/signs for people who are grateful.

لَقَدْ أَرْسَلْنَا نُوحًا إِلَىٰ قَوْمِهِۦ فَقَالَ يَٰقَوْمِ ٱعْبُدُوا۟ ٱللَّهَ مَا لَكُم مِّنْ إِلَٰهٍ غَيْرُهُۥٓ إِنِّىٓ أَخَافُ عَلَيْكُمْ عَذَابَ يَوْمٍ عَظِيمٍ ۝

59. Laqad arsalna noohan ila qawmihi faqala ya qawmi oAAbudoo Allaha ma lakum min ilahin ghayruhu innee akhafu AAalaykum AAathaba yawmin AAatheemin

7:59. We did send Noah to his people. He told them, "O my people! Worship Allah, you have no god other than Him! I do indeed fear for you the punishment of a dreadful Day."

قَالَ ٱلْمَلَأُ مِن قَوْمِهِۦٓ إِنَّا لَنَرَىٰكَ فِى ضَلَٰلٍ مُّبِينٍ ۝

60. Qala almalao min qawmihi inna lanaraka fee dalalin mubeenin

7:60. The leaders of his people said, "We do indeed see you to be in clear error."

قَالَ يَٰقَوْمِ لَيْسَ بِى ضَلَٰلَةٌ وَلَٰكِنِّى رَسُولٌ مِّن رَّبِّ ٱلْعَٰلَمِينَ ۝

61. Qala ya qawmi laysa bee dalalatun walakinnee rasoolun min rabbi alAAalameena

7:61. He said, "O my people! There is no error in me, but I am a Messenger from the Lord of the worlds."

أُبَلِّغُكُمْ رِسَٰلَٰتِ رَبِّى وَأَنصَحُ لَكُمْ وَأَعْلَمُ مِنَ ٱللَّهِ مَا لَا تَعْلَمُونَ ۝

62. Oballighukum risalati rabbee waansahu lakum waaAAlamu mina Allahi ma la taAAlamoona

7:62. "I deliver to you Messages of my Lord, and I advise you, and I know from Allah what you know not."

أَوَعَجِبْتُمْ أَن جَآءَكُمْ ذِكْرٌ مِّن رَّبِّكُمْ عَلَىٰ رَجُلٍ مِّنكُمْ لِيُنذِرَكُمْ وَلِتَتَّقُواْ وَلَعَلَّكُمْ تُرْحَمُونَ ﴿٦٣﴾

63. Awa AAajibtum an jaakum thikrun min rabbikum AAala rajulin minkum liyunthirakum walitattaqoo walaAAallakum turhamoona

---

7:63. "Does it surprise you that a Reminder has come to you from your Lord through a man, from amongst you, so that he may warn you and you may fear Allah, and so that you may be treated with Mercy?"

فَكَذَّبُوهُ فَأَنجَيْنَـٰهُ وَٱلَّذِينَ مَعَهُۥ فِى ٱلْفُلْكِ وَأَغْرَقْنَا ٱلَّذِينَ كَذَّبُواْ بِـَٔايَـٰتِنَآ إِنَّهُمْ كَانُواْ قَوْمًا عَمِينَ ﴿٦٤﴾

64. Fakaththaboohu faanjaynahu waallatheena maAAahu fee alfulki waaghraqna allatheena kaththaboo bi-ayatina innahum kanoo qawman AAameena

---

7:64. And they refused to believe him, and We saved him and those with him in the Ark, and We drowned those who refused to believe in Our Verses/signs. They were indeed a blind people.

وَإِلَىٰ عَادٍ أَخَاهُمْ هُودًا قَالَ يَـٰقَوْمِ ٱعْبُدُواْ ٱللَّـهَ مَا لَكُم مِّنْ إِلَـٰهٍ غَيْرُهُۥٓ أَفَلَا تَتَّقُونَ ﴿٦٥﴾

65. Wa-ila AAadin akhahum hoodan qala ya qawmi oAAbudoo Allaha ma lakum min ilahin ghayruhu afala tattaqoona

---

7:65. And to *AAad*[22] We sent their brother *Hood*. He said, "O my people! Worship Allah, you have no god other than Him. Will you not then guard yourselves against evil?"

---

22. A people who lived in ancient ages. They were very proud and arrogant (Verse 41:15). Their story is also narrated in Verses 11:50 to 11:60. One of them, Hood, was the Prophet sent to warn them.

قَالَ ٱلْمَلَأُ ٱلَّذِينَ كَفَرُواْ مِن قَوْمِهِۦٓ إِنَّا لَنَرَىٰكَ فِى سَفَاهَةٍ وَإِنَّا لَنَظُنُّكَ مِنَ ٱلْكَـٰذِبِينَ ﴿٦٦﴾

66. Qala almalao allatheena kafaroo min qawmihi inna lanaraka fee safahatin wa-inna lanathunnuka mina alkathibeena

---

7:66. The leaders of those who suppressed the Truth from among his people said, "We do indeed see you in folly, and we do indeed consider you to be among the liars."

قَالَ يَٰقَوْمِ لَيْسَ بِى سَفَاهَةٌ وَلَٰكِنِّى رَسُولٌ مِّن رَّبِّ ٱلْعَٰلَمِينَ ﴿٦٧﴾

67. Qala ya qawmi laysa bee safahatun walakinnee rasoolun min rabbi alAAalameena

---

7:67. He said, "O my people! There is no folly in me, but I am a Messenger of the Lord of the worlds."

68. Oballighukum risalati rabbee waana lakum nasihun ameen**un**

7:68. "I deliver to you Messages of my Lord and I am a trustworthy adviser to you."

---

69. Awa AAajibtum an jaakum thikrun min rabbikum AAala rajulin minkum liyunthirakum waothkuroo ith jaAAalakum khulafaa min baAAdi qawmi noohin wazadakum fee alkhalqi bastatan faothkuroo alaa Allahi laAAallakum tuflihoon**a**

7:69. "Does it surprise you that a Reminder has come to you from your Lord through a man, from amongst you, so that he may warn you? And remember when He made you His vicegerents[23] on earth after Noah's people and made you excel in construction activity[24]. So, remember Allah's Graces so that you may succeed."

---

23. Refer study notes 2:22 to 2:25 on <u>Verse 2:30</u> regarding the meaning of the Qur'aanic term *khaleefa/khalifa* singular of *khulafa*.

24. Refer Verses 26:128 and 26:129 to know more about those people's construction activity.

قَالُوٓاْ أَجِئْتَنَا لِنَعْبُدَ ٱللَّهَ وَحْدَهُۥ وَنَذَرَ مَا كَانَ يَعْبُدُ ءَابَآؤُنَا فَأْتِنَا بِمَا تَعِدُنَآ إِن كُنتَ مِنَ ٱلصَّٰدِقِينَ ۝

70. Qaloo aji/tana linaAAbuda Allaha wahdahu wanathara ma kana yaAAbudu abaona fa/tina bima taAAiduna in kunta mina alssadiqeena

7:70. They said, "Have you come to us to make us worship Allah alone and give up what our fathers used to worship? Then, if you are of the truthful ones, bring to us what you threaten us with."

قَالَ قَدْ وَقَعَ عَلَيْكُم مِّن رَّبِّكُمْ رِجْسٌ وَغَضَبٌ أَتُجَٰدِلُونَنِى فِىٓ أَسْمَآءٍ سَمَّيْتُمُوهَآ أَنتُمْ وَءَابَآؤُكُم مَّا نَزَّلَ ٱللَّهُ بِهَا مِن سُلْطَٰنٍ فَٱنتَظِرُوٓاْ إِنِّى مَعَكُم مِّنَ ٱلْمُنتَظِرِينَ ۝

71. Qala qad waqaAAa AAalaykum min rabbikum rijsun waghadabun atujadiloonanee fee asma-in sammaytumooha antum waabaokum ma nazzala Allahu biha min sultanin faintathiroo innee maAAakum mina almuntathireena

7:71. He said, "Disgrace and wrath from your Lord have indeed befallen you. Do you argue with me about names which you and your fathers have given, and for which Allah has not sent any authority? Then wait! I am with you, among those who wait."

فَأَنجَيْنَٰهُ وَٱلَّذِينَ مَعَهُۥ بِرَحْمَةٍ مِّنَّا وَقَطَعْنَا دَابِرَ ٱلَّذِينَ كَذَّبُواْ بِـَٔايَٰتِنَا وَمَا كَانُواْ مُؤْمِنِينَ ۝

72. Faanjaynahu waallatheena maAAahu birahmatin minna waqataAAna dabira allatheena kaththaboo bi-ayatina wama kanoo mu/mineena

7:72. We then saved him, and those with him, by Mercy from Us. And We cut off the roots of those who treated Our Verses/signs as lies. And they believed not!

وَإِلَىٰ ثَمُودَ أَخَاهُمْ صَٰلِحًا قَالَ يَٰقَوْمِ ٱعْبُدُواْ ٱللَّهَ مَا لَكُم

مِّنْ إِلَٰهٍ غَيْرُهُۥ قَدْ جَآءَتْكُم بَيِّنَةٌ مِّن رَّبِّكُمْ هَٰذِهِۦ نَاقَةُ ٱللَّهِ لَكُمْ

ءَايَةً فَذَرُوهَا تَأْكُلْ فِىٓ أَرْضِ ٱللَّهِ وَلَا تَمَسُّوهَا بِسُوٓءٍ فَيَأْخُذَكُمْ

عَذَابٌ أَلِيمٌ ﴿٧٣﴾

73. Wa-ila thamooda akhahum salihan qala ya qawmi oAAbudoo Allaha ma lakum min ilahin ghayruhu qad jaatkum bayyinatun min rabbikum hathihi naqatu Allahi lakum ayatan fatharooha ta/kul fee ardi Allahi wala tamassooha bisoo-in faya/khuthakum AAathabun aleemun

7:73. And to Thamood[25] We sent their brother Salih. He said, "O my people! Worship Allah, you have no god other than Him. Clear proof indeed has come to you from your Lord: this Allah's she-camel is a sign for you. Leave her alone then to graze on Allah's land, and harm her not, lest a painful punishment should seize you."

25. Another people of the ancient ages.

وَٱذْكُرُوٓاْ إِذْ جَعَلَكُمْ خُلَفَآءَ مِنۢ بَعْدِ عَادٍ وَبَوَّأَكُمْ

فِى ٱلْأَرْضِ تَتَّخِذُونَ مِن سُهُولِهَا قُصُورًا وَتَنْحِتُونَ ٱلْجِبَالَ بُيُوتًا

فَٱذْكُرُوٓاْ ءَالَآءَ ٱللَّهِ وَلَا تَعْثَوْاْ فِى ٱلْأَرْضِ مُفْسِدِينَ ﴿٧٤﴾

74. Wa<u>oth</u>kuroo i<u>th</u> jaAAalakum khula<u>faa</u> min baAAdi AA<u>a</u>din wabawwaakum fee al-ar<u>d</u>i tattakhi<u>th</u>oona min suhooli<u>ha</u> qu<u>s</u>ooran watan<u>h</u>itoona aljib<u>a</u>la buyootan f<u>aoth</u>kuroo <u>a</u>l<u>a</u>a All<u>a</u>hi wal<u>a</u> taAAa<u>th</u>aw fee al-ar<u>d</u>i mufsideen<u>a</u>

7:74. And remember when He made you His vicegerents after *AA<u>a</u>d* and settled you in the land. You build for yourselves palaces on its plains and carve out houses in the mountains. So, remember Allah's Graces, and do not go about making mischief on the earth.

قَالَ ٱلْمَلَأُ ٱلَّذِينَ ٱسْتَكْبَرُواْ مِن قَوْمِهِۦ لِلَّذِينَ ٱسْتُضْعِفُواْ لِمَنْ ءَامَنَ مِنْهُمْ أَتَعْلَمُونَ أَنَّ صَٰلِحًا مُّرْسَلٌ مِّن رَّبِّهِۦ قَالُوٓاْ إِنَّا بِمَآ أُرْسِلَ بِهِۦ مُؤْمِنُونَ

75. Q<u>a</u>la almalao alla<u>th</u>eena istakbaroo min qawmihi lilla<u>th</u>eena istu<u>d</u>AAifoo liman <u>a</u>mana minhum ataAAlamoona anna <u>sa</u>li<u>h</u>an mursalun min rabbihi q<u>a</u>loo inn<u>a</u> bim<u>a</u> orsila bihi mu/minoon<u>a</u>

7:75. The leaders of those who behaved arrogantly among his people said to those who believed, among the weak, "Do you know that Salih is sent by his Lord?" They said, "We are indeed believers in what he has been sent with."

قَالَ ٱلَّذِينَ ٱسْتَكْبَرُوٓاْ إِنَّا بِٱلَّذِىٓ ءَامَنتُم بِهِۦ كَٰفِرُونَ ٧٦

76. Q<u>a</u>la alla<u>th</u>eena istakbaroo inn<u>a</u> bi<u>a</u>lla<u>th</u>ee <u>a</u>mantum bihi k<u>a</u>firoon<u>a</u>

7:76. The arrogant ones said, "We do indeed reject what you believe in."

فَعَقَرُواْ ٱلنَّاقَةَ وَعَتَوْاْ عَنْ أَمْرِ رَبِّهِمْ وَقَالُواْ يَـٰصَـٰلِحُ ٱئْتِنَا بِمَا تَعِدُنَآ إِن كُـنتَ مِنَ ٱلْمُرْسَلِينَ ۝

77. FaAAaqaroo alnnaqata waAAataw AAan amri rabbihim waqaloo ya salihu i/tina bima taAAiduna in kunta mina almursaleena

7:77. Then they hamstrung the she-camel and behaved insolently towards the Command of their Lord. And they said, "O Salih! If you are one of the Messengers, then bring us what you threatened us with."

فَأَخَذَتْهُمُ ٱلرَّجْفَةُ فَأَصْبَحُواْ فِى دَارِهِمْ جَـٰثِمِينَ ۝

78. Faakhathat-humu alrrajfatu faasbahoo fee darihim jathimeena

7:78. Then the earthquake shook them, and they lay prostrate in their houses.

فَتَوَلَّىٰ عَنْهُمْ وَقَالَ يَـٰقَوْمِ لَقَدْ أَبْلَغْتُكُمْ رِسَالَةَ رَبِّى وَنَصَحْتُ لَكُمْ وَلَـٰكِن لَّا تُحِبُّونَ ٱلنَّـٰصِحِينَ ۝

79. Fatawalla AAanhum waqala ya qawmi laqad ablaghtukum risalata rabbee wanasahtu lakum walakin la tuhibboona alnnasiheena

7:79. Then he turned away from them and said, "O my people! I did certainly deliver to you the Message of my Lord, and I gave you advice, but you do not like those who advise."

وَلُوطًا إِذْ قَالَ لِقَوْمِهِ أَتَأْتُونَ ٱلْفَٰحِشَةَ مَا سَبَقَكُم بِهَا مِنْ أَحَدٍ مِّنَ ٱلْعَٰلَمِينَ ۝

80. Walootan ith qala liqawmihi ata/toona alfahishata ma sabaqakum biha min ahadin mina alAAalameena

---

7:80. And Lot[26], when he said to his people, "You commit the obscene offence that none in the worlds committed before you!?"

---

26. Another Prophet, a contemporary of Prophet Abraham. And please note the economical use of words in the Qur'aan. In the preceding Verses, Prophets Noah, Hood and Salih were described as having been sent to their respective peoples, so was Lot sent to his people to warn them. That entire expression is shortened here into just two words 'And Lot'

إِنَّكُمْ لَتَأْتُونَ ٱلرِّجَالَ شَهْوَةً مِّن دُونِ ٱلنِّسَاءِ بَلْ أَنتُمْ قَوْمٌ مُّسْرِفُونَ ۝

81. Innakum lata/toona alrrijala shahwatan min dooni alnnisa-i bal antum qawmun musrifoona

---

7:81. "You do come to men for sexual pleasure, instead of to women!? Nay! You are a people who transgress."

وَمَا كَانَ جَوَابَ قَوْمِهِ إِلَّا أَن قَالُوا أَخْرِجُوهُم مِّن قَرْيَتِكُمْ إِنَّهُمْ أُنَاسٌ يَتَطَهَّرُونَ ۝

82. Wama kana jawaba qawmihi illa an qaloo akhrijoohum min qaryatikum innahum onasun yatatahharoona

---

7:82. And the response of his people was but to say, "Drive them out of your place; they are men who want to cleanse themselves!"

فَأَنجَيْنَـٰهُ وَأَهْلَهُ إِلَّا امْرَأَتَهُ كَانَتْ مِنَ الْغَـٰبِرِينَ ۝

83. Faanjaynahu waahlahu illa imraatahu kanat mina alghabireena

---

7:83. We then saved him and his family, except for his wife; she was of those who remained behind.

وَأَمْطَرْنَا عَلَيْهِم مَّطَرًا فَانظُرْ كَيْفَ كَانَ عَـٰقِبَةُ الْمُجْرِمِينَ ۝

84. Waamtarna AAalayhim mataran faon_th_ur kayfa kana AAaqibatu almujrimeena

---

7:84. And We rained upon them a rain.[27] Look! What the sinners end up with.

---

27. Verses 11:82 and 11:83 explain that it was a rain of stones of baked clay, hitting marked targets, one after another. And the marked targets were the sinners among Lot's people!

وَإِلَىٰ مَدْيَنَ أَخَاهُمْ شُعَيْبًا قَالَ يَـٰقَوْمِ ٱعْبُدُوا۟ ٱللَّهَ مَا لَكُم مِّنْ إِلَـٰهٍ غَيْرُهُۥ قَدْ جَآءَتْكُم بَيِّنَةٌ مِّن رَّبِّكُمْ فَأَوْفُوا۟ ٱلْكَيْلَ وَٱلْمِيزَانَ وَلَا تَبْخَسُوا۟ ٱلنَّاسَ أَشْيَآءَهُمْ وَلَا تُفْسِدُوا۟ فِى ٱلْأَرْضِ بَعْدَ إِصْلَـٰحِهَا ذَٰلِكُمْ خَيْرٌ لَّكُمْ إِن كُنتُم مُّؤْمِنِينَ ﴿٨٥﴾

85. Wa-ila madyana akhahum shuAAayban qala ya qawmi oAAbudoo Allaha ma lakum min ilahin ghayruhu qad jaatkum bayyinatun min rabbikum faawfoo alkayla waalmeezana wala tabkhasoo alnnasa ashyaahum wala tufsidoo fee al-ardi baAAda islahiha thalikum khayrun lakum in kuntum mu/mineena

7:85. And to Midian[28] We sent their brother Shu'aib. He said, "O my people! Worship Allah, you have no god other than Him. Clear sign indeed has come to you from your Lord, [29] so give full measure and weight and do not cheat people in their things and make no mischief on the earth after its reformation. It is better for you if you do believe."

28. Another people of the pre-historic times.

29. The clear sign for the people of Midian was the annihilation of their predecessors, the people of Lot (see Verse 29:35).

وَلَا تَقْعُدُوا۟ بِكُلِّ صِرَٰطٍ تُوعِدُونَ وَتَصُدُّونَ عَن سَبِيلِ ٱللَّهِ مَنْ ءَامَنَ بِهِۦ وَتَبْغُونَهَا عِوَجًا وَٱذْكُرُوٓا۟ إِذْ كُنتُمْ قَلِيلًا فَكَثَّرَكُمْ وَٱنظُرُوا۟ كَيْفَ كَانَ عَـٰقِبَةُ ٱلْمُفْسِدِينَ ﴿٨٦﴾

86. Wala taqAAudoo bikulli siratin tooAAidoona watasuddoona AAan sabeeli Allahi man amana bihi watabghoonaha AAiwajan waothkuroo ith kuntum qaleelan fakaththarakum waonthuroo kayfa kana AAaqibatu almufsideena

7:86. "And do not lie in wait on every path, cajoling away and hindering one who believes in Allah from His way, seeking to make it crooked, complicated or difficult.[30] And remember when you were but few, He increased you in number. And look! What the mischief-makers end up with."

30. The Satan, of course, has vowed to do this. And there are his human friends who openly help him do this. But, mind you, there are religious leaders of the Muslims themselves who, in their Friday sermons, seek to make the Allah-given simple tenets of Islam complicated and difficult to observe. They too, unwittingly, help the Satan in his avowed mission!

وَإِن كَانَ طَآئِفَةٌ مِّنكُمْ ءَامَنُواْ بِٱلَّذِىٓ أُرْسِلْتُ بِهِۦ وَطَآئِفَةٌ لَّمْ يُؤْمِنُواْ فَٱصْبِرُواْ حَتَّىٰ يَحْكُمَ ٱللَّهُ بَيْنَنَا وَهُوَ خَيْرُ ٱلْحَـٰكِمِينَ ۞ ٨٧

87. Wa-in kana ta-ifatun minkum amanoo biallathee orsiltu bihi wata-ifatun lam yu/minoo faisbiroo hatta yahkuma Allahu baynana wahuwa khayru alhakimeena

7:87. "And if there is a section of you who believe in that which I am sent with, and another section who do not believe, then wait patiently until Allah judges between us. And He is the Best of judges."[31]

31. The principle enunciated in this Verse ought to be the guiding principle of mutual relationship between Muslims and non-Muslims even in this present age, and in all ages to come. That could help minimise the strife between the two sections.

❉ قَالَ ٱلْمَلَأُ ٱلَّذِينَ ٱسْتَكْبَرُواْ مِن قَوْمِهِۦ لَنُخْرِجَنَّكَ يَٰشُعَيْبُ وَٱلَّذِينَ ءَامَنُواْ مَعَكَ مِن قَرْيَتِنَآ أَوْ لَتَعُودُنَّ فِى مِلَّتِنَا قَالَ أَوَلَوْ كُنَّا كَٰرِهِينَ ۝

88. Qala almalao allatheena istakbaroo min qawmihi lanukhrijannaka ya shuAAaybu waallatheena amanoo maAAaka min qaryatina aw lataAAoodunna fee millatina qala awa law kunna kariheena

---

7:88. Those of the nobility among his[32] people, who were arrogant, said, "We will certainly drive you, and those who have believed with you, out, O Shu'aib, from our place, unless you return to our way of life." He said, "Even when we dislike it?"

---

32. Prophet Shu'aib's (peace be upon him). See preceding Verses.

قَدِ ٱفْتَرَيْنَا عَلَى ٱللَّهِ كَذِبًا إِنْ عُدْنَا فِى مِلَّتِكُم بَعْدَ إِذْ نَجَّىٰنَا ٱللَّهُ مِنْهَا وَمَا يَكُونُ لَنَآ أَن نَّعُودَ فِيهَآ إِلَّآ أَن يَشَآءَ ٱللَّهُ رَبُّنَا وَسِعَ رَبُّنَا كُلَّ شَىْءٍ عِلْمًا عَلَى ٱللَّهِ تَوَكَّلْنَا رَبَّنَا ٱفْتَحْ بَيْنَنَا وَبَيْنَ قَوْمِنَا بِٱلْحَقِّ وَأَنتَ خَيْرُ ٱلْفَٰتِحِينَ ۝

89. Qadi iftarayna AAala Allahi kathiban in AAudna fee millatikum baAAda ith najjana Allahu minha wama yakoonu lana an naAAooda feeha illa an yashaa Allahu rabbuna wasiAAa rabbuna kulla shay-in AAilman AAala Allahi tawakkalna rabbana iftah baynana wabayna qawmina bialhaqqi waanta khayru alfatiheena

---

7:89. [33]"We should be forging a lie against Allah if we return to your way of life after Allah has delivered us from it. And it befits us not that we should return to it, unless Allah, our Lord, so wishes. Our Lord comprehends all things in His knowledge. In Allah do we trust. Our Lord! Decide justly between us and our people. And You are the Best of judges."

---

33. This Verse is a continuation of Prophet Shu'aib's reply to his people.

وَقَالَ ٱلۡمَلَأُ ٱلَّذِينَ كَفَرُواْ مِن قَوۡمِهِۦ لَئِنِ ٱتَّبَعۡتُمۡ شُعَيۡبًا إِنَّكُمۡ إِذًا لَّخَـٰسِرُونَ ۝

90. Waqala almalao allatheena kafaroo min qawmihi la-ini ittabaAAtum shuAAayban innakum ithan lakhasiroona

---

7:90. And those of the nobility among his people, who suppressed the Truth, said, "If you follow Shu'aib, then surely you are doomed!"

فَأَخَذَتۡهُمُ ٱلرَّجۡفَةُ فَأَصۡبَحُواْ فِى دَارِهِمۡ جَـٰثِمِينَ ۝

91. Faakhathat-humu alrrajfatu faasbahoo fee darihim jathimeena

---

7:91. A violent shaking seized them then, and they lay lifeless in their abode.

ٱلَّذِينَ كَذَّبُواْ شُعَيۡبًا كَأَن لَّمۡ يَغۡنَوۡاْ فِيهَا ٱلَّذِينَ كَذَّبُواْ شُعَيۡبًا كَانُواْ هُمُ ٱلۡخَـٰسِرِينَ ۝

92. Alla<u>th</u>eena ka<u>ththaboo</u> shuAAayban kaan lam yaghnaw feeh<u>a</u> alla<u>th</u>eena ka<u>ththaboo</u> shuAAayban <u>k</u>anoo humu alkha<u>s</u>ireen<u>a</u>

7:92. Those who denied Shu'aib, they were as though they had never flourished therein; those who denied Shu'aib, they were the ones who were doomed.

فَتَوَلَّىٰ عَنْهُمْ وَقَالَ يَـٰقَوْمِ لَقَدْ أَبْلَغْتُكُمْ رِسَـٰلَـٰتِ رَبِّى
وَنَصَحْتُ لَكُمْ فَكَيْفَ ءَاسَىٰ عَلَىٰ قَوْمٍ كَـٰفِرِينَ ﴿٩٣﴾

93. Fatawall<u>a</u> AAanhum waqala y<u>a</u> qawmi laqad ablaghtukum risalati rabbee wana<u>s</u>a<u>h</u>tu lakum fakayfa <u>as</u>a AAal<u>a</u> qawmin k<u>a</u>fireen<u>a</u>

7:93. He then turned away from them and said, "O my people! I have indeed delivered to you the Messages of my Lord and I have given you good advice. How can I then grieve over people who suppressed the Truth?"

وَمَآ أَرْسَلْنَا فِى قَرْيَةٍ مِّن نَّبِىٍّ إِلَّآ أَخَذْنَآ أَهْلَهَا بِالْبَأْسَآءِ وَالضَّرَّآءِ
لَعَلَّهُمْ يَضَّرَّعُونَ ﴿٩٤﴾

94. Wam<u>a</u> arsaln<u>a</u> fee qaryatin min nabiyyin ill<u>a</u> akha<u>th</u>n<u>a</u> ahlah<u>a</u> bialba/s<u>a</u>-i waal<u>dd</u>arr<u>a</u>-i laAAallahum ya<u>dd</u>arraAAoon<u>a</u>

7:94. And We sent not a Prophet to a place, but We seized its people with adversity and distress so that they became compliant.

ثُمَّ بَدَّلْنَا مَكَانَ ٱلسَّيِّئَةِ ٱلْحَسَنَةَ حَتَّىٰ عَفَوا۟ وَّقَالُوا۟ قَدْ مَسَّ ءَابَآءَنَا ٱلضَّرَّآءُ وَٱلسَّرَّآءُ فَأَخَذْنَٰهُم بَغْتَةً وَهُمْ لَا يَشْعُرُونَ ۝

95. Thumma baddalna makana alssayyi-ati alhasanata hatta AAafaw waqaloo qad massa abaana alddarrao waalssarrao faakhathnahum baghtatan wahum la yashAAuroona

---

7:95. We then changed the bad condition to good until they grew in prosperity and said, "Distress and ease did befall our fathers." Then, all of a sudden, We caught them unawares.

وَلَوْ أَنَّ أَهْلَ ٱلْقُرَىٰ ءَامَنُوا۟ وَٱتَّقَوْا۟ لَفَتَحْنَا عَلَيْهِم بَرَكَٰتٍ مِّنَ ٱلسَّمَآءِ وَٱلْأَرْضِ وَلَٰكِن كَذَّبُوا۟ فَأَخَذْنَٰهُم بِمَا كَانُوا۟ يَكْسِبُونَ ۝

96. Walaw anna ahla alqura amanoo waittaqaw lafatahna AAalayhim barakatin mina alssama-i waal-ardi walakin kaththaboo faakhathnahum bima kanoo yaksiboona

---

7:96. And if the people of those places had believed and had been pious, We would certainly have opened up for them blessings from the heavens and the earth. But they denied the Truth! So We seized them because of what they had earned.

أَفَأَمِنَ أَهْلُ ٱلْقُرَىٰ أَن يَأْتِيَهُم بَأْسُنَا بَيَٰتًا وَهُمْ نَآئِمُونَ ۝

97. Afaamina ahlu alqura an ya/tiyahum ba/suna bayatan wahum na-imoona

---

7:97. Did those people then feel secure from Our punishment coming to them by night while they slept?

أَوَأَمِنَ أَهْلُ ٱلْقُرَىٰٓ أَن يَأْتِيَهُم بَأْسُنَا ضُحًى وَهُمْ يَلْعَبُونَ ٩٨

98. Awa amina ahlu alqura an ya/tiyahum ba/suna duhan wahum yalAAaboona

7:98. Or, did they feel secure from Our punishment coming to them in the morning while they played[34]?

34. Please take note that those ancient people's daytime activities were described as mere play. Obviously, they were indulging in such activities, other than those divinely ordained for earning lawful livelihood besides paying obeisance, as required, to the Creator. Such activities are just pastime in the Creator's eyes.

أَفَأَمِنُوا۟ مَكْرَ ٱللَّهِ فَلَا يَأْمَنُ مَكْرَ ٱللَّهِ إِلَّا ٱلْقَوْمُ ٱلْخَٰسِرُونَ ٩٩

99. Afaaminoo makra Allahi fala ya/manu makra Allahi illa alqawmu alkhasiroona

7:99. Did they then feel secure from Allah's plan? But none felt secure from Allah's plan except those who were doomed.

أَوَلَمْ يَهْدِ لِلَّذِينَ يَرِثُونَ ٱلْأَرْضَ مِنْ بَعْدِ أَهْلِهَآ أَن لَّوْ نَشَآءُ أَصَبْنَٰهُم بِذُنُوبِهِمْ وَنَطْبَعُ عَلَىٰ قُلُوبِهِمْ فَهُمْ لَا يَسْمَعُونَ ۝

100. Awa lam yahdi lillatheena yarithoona al-arda min baAAdi ahliha an law nashao asabnahum bithunoobihim wanatbaAAu AAala quloobihim fahum la yasmaAAoona

---

7:100. Has it not dawned on those who have inherited the earth from their earlier occupants that if We please, We would punish them for their sins and set a seal on their minds so they wouldn't hear?

تِلْكَ ٱلْقُرَىٰ نَقُصُّ عَلَيْكَ مِنْ أَنۢبَآئِهَا وَلَقَدْ جَآءَتْهُمْ رُسُلُهُم بِٱلْبَيِّنَٰتِ فَمَا كَانُوا۟ لِيُؤْمِنُوا۟ بِمَا كَذَّبُوا۟ مِن قَبْلُ كَذَٰلِكَ يَطْبَعُ ٱللَّهُ عَلَىٰ قُلُوبِ ٱلْكَٰفِرِينَ ۝

101. Tilka alqura naqussu AAalayka min anba-iha walaqad jaat-hum rusuluhum bialbayyinati fama kanoo liyu/minoo bima kaththaboo min qablu kathalika yatbaAAu Allahu AAala quloobi alkafireena

---

7:101. Those places of human habitation! We relate to you some of their stories. And their Messengers did come to them with evidences. But they could not believe because, earlier, they had denied[35]! Allah thus seals the minds of those who suppress the Truth.

---

35. Allah Almighty brings into focus a general human weakness here. It is very difficult for any human being to admit any mistake on his part. Those ancient peoples, about whom Allah speaks here, were steeped in polytheism and other wrong beliefs and deeds. When the Messengers brought proofs of their beliefs and deeds being wrong, they wouldn't even budge. This trait/weakness is responsible for many a human conflict in today's world too. It has its roots in the satanic trait of pride. Man is too proud to admit that he had been wrong.

وَمَا وَجَدْنَا لِأَكْثَرِهِم مِّنْ عَهْدٍ وَإِن وَجَدْنَا أَكْثَرَهُمْ لَفَاسِقِينَ 

102. Wama wajadna li-aktharihim min AAahdin wa-in wajadna aktharahum lafasiqeena

7:102. And We found most of them unreliable. And We did indeed find most of them to be dissolute.

ثُمَّ بَعَثْنَا مِنْ بَعْدِهِم مُّوسَىٰ بِآيَاتِنَا إِلَىٰ فِرْعَوْنَ وَمَلَإِيْهِ فَظَلَمُواْ بِهَا فَانظُرْ كَيْفَ كَانَ عَاقِبَةُ ٱلْمُفْسِدِينَ

103. Thumma baAAathna min baAAdihim moosa bi-ayatina ila firAAawna wamala-ihi fathalamoo biha faonuthur kayfa kana AAaqibatu almufsideena

7:103. We then, after them, sent Moses with Our Signs to Pharaoh and his chieftains, but they wronged those Signs! See then what end the transgressors met with.

وَقَالَ مُوسَىٰ يَا فِرْعَوْنُ إِنِّي رَسُولٌ مِّن رَّبِّ ٱلْعَالَمِينَ

104. Waqala moosa ya firAAawnu innee rasoolun min rabbi alAAalameena

7:104. And Moses said, "O Pharaoh! I am indeed a Messenger from the Lord of the worlds."

حَقِيقٌ عَلَىٰٓ أَن لَّآ أَقُولَ عَلَى ٱللَّهِ إِلَّا ٱلْحَقَّ قَدْ جِئْتُكُم بِبَيِّنَةٍ مِّن رَّبِّكُمْ فَأَرْسِلْ مَعِىَ بَنِىٓ إِسْرَٰٓءِيلَ ﴿١٠٥﴾

105. Haqeequn AAala an la aqoola AAala Allahi illa alhaqqa qad ji/tukum bibayyinatin min rabbikum faarsil maAAiya banee isra-eela

7:105. "It is just and proper for me that I say about Allah nothing but the Truth. I have come to you indeed with evidence from your Lord. So send the Children of Israel with me."

قَالَ إِن كُنتَ جِئْتَ بِـَٔايَةٍ فَأْتِ بِهَآ إِن كُنتَ مِنَ ٱلصَّٰدِقِينَ ﴿١٠٦﴾

106. Qala in kunta ji/ta bi-ayatin fa/ti biha in kunta mina alssadiqeena

7:106. He [Pharaoh] said, "If you have come with a sign, then come out with it, if you are of the truthful ones."

فَأَلْقَىٰ عَصَاهُ فَإِذَا هِىَ ثُعْبَانٌ مُّبِينٌ ﴿١٠٧﴾

107. Faalqa AAasahu fa-itha hiya thuAAbanun mubeenun

7:107. So, he [Moses] threw down his staff, when, lo and behold, it was a veritable serpent!

وَنَزَعَ يَدَهُ فَإِذَا هِىَ بَيْضَآءُ لِلنَّاظِرِينَ ۝

108. WanazaAAa yadahu fa-itha hiya baydao lilnnathireena

7:108. And he stretched his hand, when, lo and behold, it was shining white to the onlookers!

قَالَ ٱلْمَلَأُ مِن قَوْمِ فِرْعَوْنَ إِنَّ هَـٰذَا لَسَـٰحِرٌ عَلِيمٌ ۝

109. Qala almalao min qawmi firAAawna inna hatha lasahirun AAaleemun

7:109. The chieftains among Pharaoh's people said, "This one is indeed an expert magician."

يُرِيدُ أَن يُخْرِجَكُم مِّنْ أَرْضِكُمْ فَمَاذَا تَأْمُرُونَ ۝

110. Yureedu an yukhrijakum min ardikum famatha ta/muroona

7:110. "He intends to drive you out of your land. What counsel do you then give?"[36]

36. The context suggests that it was Pharaoh who said this to the Chieftains.

111. Qaloo arjih waakhahu waarsil fee almada-ini hashireena

7:111. They said, "Defer the matter concerning him and his brother, and send callers into the cities and towns, [37]

37. The Chieftains' reply continues in the next Verse.

112. Ya/tooka bikulli sahirin AAaleemin

7:112. to bring to you every expert magician."

وَجَآءَ ٱلسَّحَرَةُ فِرْعَوْنَ قَالُوٓاْ إِنَّ لَنَا لَأَجْرًا إِن كُنَّا نَحْنُ ٱلْغَـٰلِبِينَ ﴿١١٣﴾

113. Waja_a alssa_haratu firAAawna qaloo inna lana_ laajran in kunna_ na_hnu algha_libeena

---

7:113. And the magicians came to Pharaoh and said, "We should indeed have a reward if we are the victors."

قَالَ نَعَمْ وَإِنَّكُمْ لَمِنَ ٱلْمُقَرَّبِينَ ﴿١١٤﴾

114. Qa_la naAAam wa-innakum lamina almuqarrabeena

7:114. He said, "Yes, and you shall indeed be of those who are close[38]."

---

38. Close to Pharaoh that is.

قَالُواْ يَـٰمُوسَىٰٓ إِمَّآ أَن تُلْقِىَ وَإِمَّآ أَن نَّكُونَ نَحْنُ ٱلْمُلْقِينَ ﴿١١٥﴾

115. Qaloo ya_ moosa_ imma_ an tulqiya wa-imma_ an nakoona na_hnu almulqeena

---

7:115. They said, "O Moses! Either you do the throwing down, or we do it."

قَالَ أَلْقُوا فَلَمَّا أَلْقَوْا سَحَرُوٓا أَعْيُنَ ٱلنَّاسِ وَٱسْتَرْهَبُوهُمْ وَجَآءُو بِسِحْرٍ عَظِيمٍ ﴿١١٦﴾

116. Qala alqoo falamma alqaw saharoo aAAyuna alnnasi waistarhaboohum wajaoo bisihrin AAatheemin

---

7:116. He said, "You throw!" So, when they did, they hoodwinked the people's eyes and frightened them, and they displayed some great magic.

۞ وَأَوْحَيْنَآ إِلَىٰ مُوسَىٰٓ أَنْ أَلْقِ عَصَاكَ فَإِذَا هِىَ تَلْقَفُ مَا يَأْفِكُونَ ﴿١١٧﴾

117. Waawhayna ila moosa an alqi AAasaka fa-itha hiya talqafu ma ya/fikoona

---

7:117. And We revealed Our instruction to Moses, "Throw down your staff." And, lo and behold, it swallowed up what they had conjured up!

فَوَقَعَ ٱلْحَقُّ وَبَطَلَ مَا كَانُوا يَعْمَلُونَ ﴿١١٨﴾

118. FawaqaAAa alhaqqu wabatala ma kanoo yaAAmaloona

7:118. So, the truth prevailed, and what they did became null and void.

119. Faghuliboo hun_alika wa_inqalaboo <u>s</u>aghireena

7:119. They were thus defeated there, and they turned back subdued.

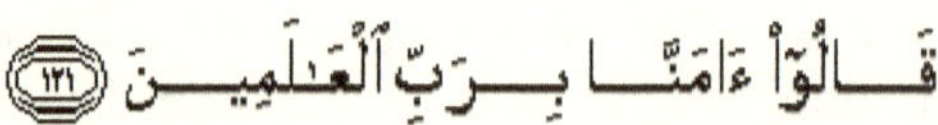

120. Waolqiya alssa<u>h</u>aratu s_ajideena

7:120. And the magicians fell prostrating.

---

121. Q_aloo _amann_a birabbi alAA_alameena

7:121. They said, "We believe in the Lord of the worlds,

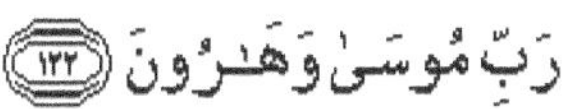

122. Rabbi moos̲a wah̲aroon**a**

7:122. the Lord of Moses and Aaron."

---

123. Q̲ala firAAawnu a̲mantum bihi qabla an ath̲ana lakum inna h̲ath̲a lamakrun makartumoohu fee almadeenati litukhrijoo minh̲a ahlah̲a fasawfa taAAamoon**a**

7:123. Pharaoh said, "Did you believe in Him before I permitted you!? This indeed is a plot which you have devised in the city to drive its people out. But you shall soon know!

124. Laoqat̲iAAanna aydiyakum waarjulakum min khil̲afin thumma laos̲allibannakum ajmaAAeen**a**

7:124. I will certainly cut off your hands and your feet on opposite sides. Then will I crucify you all!"

قَـالُوٓاْ إِنَّـآ إِلَـىٰ رَبِّنَـا مُنقَلِبُـونَ ۝

125. Qaloo inna ila rabbina munqaliboona

7:125. They said, "Surely to our Lord shall we go back.

وَمَا تَنقِمُ مِنَّآ إِلَّآ أَنْ ءَامَنَّا بِـَٔايَٰتِ رَبِّنَا لَمَّا جَآءَتْنَا رَبَّنَآ أَفْرِغْ عَلَيْنَا صَبْرًا وَتَوَفَّنَا مُسْلِمِينَ ۝

126. Wama tanqimu minna illa an amanna bi-ayati rabbina lamma jaatna rabbana afrigh AAalayna sabran watawaffana muslimeena

7:126. And you do not take revenge on us except because we have believed in the signs of our Lord when these came to us! Our Lord! Grant us patience and cause us to die as Muslims[39]."

39. I.e., those who submit to Allah's Will.

وَقَالَ ٱلۡمَلَأُ مِن قَوۡمِ فِرۡعَوۡنَ أَتَذَرُ مُوسَىٰ وَقَوۡمَهُۥ لِيُفۡسِدُواْ فِى

ٱلۡأَرۡضِ وَيَذَرَكَ وَءَالِهَتَكَ قَالَ سَنُقَتِّلُ أَبۡنَآءَهُمۡ وَنَسۡتَحۡىِۦ نِسَآءَهُمۡ وَإِنَّا

فَوۡقَهُمۡ قَٰهِرُونَ ﴿١٢٧﴾

127. Waqala almalao min qawmi firAAawna atatharu moosa waqawmahu liyufsidoo fee al-ardi wayatharaka waalihataka qala sanuqattilu abnaahum wanastahyee nisaahum wa-inna fawqahum qahiroona

---

7:127. And the chieftains among Pharaoh's people said, "Would you leave Moses and his people free to make mischief in the land and to forsake you and your gods?" He said, "We will kill their sons and spare their women. And we do indeed have absolute power over them."

قَالَ مُوسَىٰ لِقَوۡمِهِ ٱسۡتَعِينُواْ بِٱللَّهِ وَٱصۡبِرُوٓاْ إِنَّ ٱلۡأَرۡضَ لِلَّهِ يُورِثُهَا مَن

يَشَآءُ مِنۡ عِبَادِهِۦ وَٱلۡعَٰقِبَةُ لِلۡمُتَّقِينَ ﴿١٢٨﴾

128. Qala moosa liqawmihi istaAAeenoo biAllahi waisbiroo inna al-arda lillahi yoorithuha man yashao min AAibadihi waalAAaqibatu lilmuttaqeena

---

7:128. Moses said to his people, "Ask for help from Allah and be patient. The land is Allah's; He leases[40] it to such of His subjects[41] as He wills. And the good end is reserved for those who are pious[42].

---

40. The word used in the Verse is *yoorithu*. It has been translated as 'causes to inherit'. But since the land is Allah's and no one inherits from Allah, a better translation would be 'leases'.

41. All human beings have willy-nilly to obey Nature's laws. Some of them may not recognise Nature as Allah, but nevertheless they must obey those laws. They cannot exist otherwise. In that sense, all human beings – believers or non-believers – are subjects of Allah.

42. Refer study note 2:2 on <u>Verse 2:2</u> to know what the corresponding word used in the Arabic text means, in Qur'aanic terms.

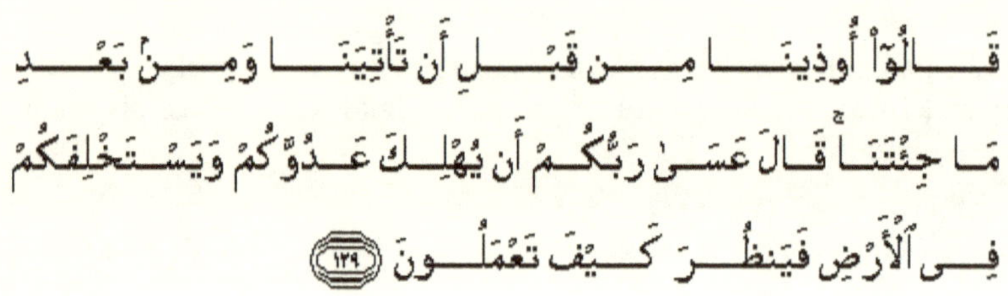

129. Qaloo oo<u>th</u>eena min qabli an ta/tiyana wamin baAAdi ma ji/tana qala AAasa rabbukum an yuhlika AAaduwwakum wayastakhlifakum fee al-ar<u>d</u>i fayan<u>th</u>ura kayfa taAAamaloona

---

7:129. They said, "We have been persecuted before you came to us and since you have come to us." He said, "It may be that your Lord will destroy your enemy and make you rulers in the land, and then He will see how you act."

130. Walaqad akha<u>th</u>na <u>a</u>la firAAawna bia<u>l</u>ssineena wanaq<u>s</u>in mina al<u>thth</u>amar<u>a</u>ti laAAallahum ya<u>ththakkaroona</u>

7:130. And We did seize Pharaoh's people with years of drought and loss in agricultural produce that they may take heed.

فَإِذَا جَآءَتْهُمُ ٱلْحَسَنَةُ قَالُوا۟ لَنَا هَٰذِهِۦ ۖ وَإِن تُصِبْهُمْ سَيِّئَةٌ يَطَّيَّرُوا۟ بِمُوسَىٰ وَمَن مَّعَهُۥٓ ۚ أَلَآ إِنَّمَا طَٰٓئِرُهُمْ عِندَ ٱللَّهِ وَلَٰكِنَّ أَكْثَرَهُمْ لَا يَعْلَمُونَ

131. Fa-itha jaat-humu alhasanatu qaloo lana hathihi wa-in tusibhum sayyi-atun yattayyaroo bimoosa waman maAAahu ala innama ta-iruhum AAinda Allahi walakinna aktharahum la yaAAlamoona

7:131. But when they got anything good, they said, "We certainly deserve this." And when any bad thing befell them, they attributed its cause to Moses and those with him. Nay! The cause for anything happening to them lay only with Allah, but most of them knew not.

وَقَالُوا۟ مَهْمَا تَأْتِنَا بِهِۦ مِنْ ءَايَةٍ لِّتَسْحَرَنَا بِهَا فَمَا نَحْنُ لَكَ بِمُؤْمِنِينَ

132. Waqaloo mahma ta/tina bihi min ayatin litasharana biha fama nahnu laka bimu/mineena

7:132. And they said, "Whatever be the sign you bring to beguile us with, we will not believe in you."

فَأَرْسَلْنَا عَلَيْهِمُ ٱلطُّوفَانَ وَٱلْجَرَادَ وَٱلْقُمَّلَ وَٱلضَّفَادِعَ وَٱلدَّمَ ءَايَـٰتٍ مُّفَصَّلَـٰتٍ فَٱسْتَكْبَرُواْ وَكَانُواْ قَوْمًا مُّجْرِمِينَ ﴿١٣٣﴾

133. Faarsal<u>na</u> AAalayhimu al<u>tt</u>oof<u>a</u>na waaljar<u>a</u>da waalqummala waal<u>dd</u>afadiAAa waal<u>dd</u>ama <u>a</u>y<u>a</u>tin mufa<u>ss</u>al<u>a</u>tin faistakbaroo wak<u>a</u>noo qawman mujrimeena

---

7:133. We then sent upon them the storm, the locusts, the lice, the frogs and the blood as distinct signs[43]; but they behaved haughtily, and they were a sinning people.

---

43. These were some of the other signs that Allah Almighty showed to Pharaoh's people, besides those mentioned in Verse 107 and 108 above. These other signs were in the form of calamities afflicting the people in general. The Qur'aan does not explain what the sign of the blood was. And it is not at all necessary for us now to know the details thereof. What is enough for us to know now is that Allah did give a long rope to the recalcitrant people to bring them round.

وَلَمَّا وَقَعَ عَلَيْهِمُ ٱلرِّجْزُ قَالُواْ يَـٰمُوسَى ٱدْعُ لَنَا رَبَّكَ بِمَا عَهِدَ عِندَكَ لَئِن كَشَفْتَ عَنَّا ٱلرِّجْزَ لَنُؤْمِنَنَّ لَكَ وَلَنُرْسِلَنَّ مَعَكَ بَنِىٓ إِسْرَٰٓءِيلَ ﴿١٣٤﴾

134. Walamm<u>a</u> waqaAAa AAalayhimu alrrijzu q<u>a</u>loo y<u>a</u> moos<u>a</u> odAAu lan<u>a</u> rabbaka bim<u>a</u> AAahida AAindaka la-in kashafta AAann<u>a</u> alrrijza lanu/minanna laka walanursilanna maAAaka banee isr<u>a</u>-eela

---

7:134. And when the calamity fell upon them, they said, "O Moses! Pray for us to your Lord as He has a covenant with you. If you remove the calamity from us, we will certainly believe in you and we will certainly send the children of Israel with you."

فَلَمَّا كَشَفْنَا عَنْهُمُ ٱلرِّجْزَ إِلَىٰ أَجَلٍ هُم بَـٰلِغُوهُ إِذَا هُم يَنكُثُونَ ﴿١٣٥﴾

135. Falamma kashafna AAanhumu alrrijza ila ajalin hum balighoohu itha hum yankuthoona

---

7:135. But when We removed the calamity from them for a term within which to fulfil their promise, they broke the promise!

فَٱنتَقَمْنَا مِنْهُمْ فَأَغْرَقْنَـٰهُمْ فِى ٱلْيَمِّ بِأَنَّهُمْ كَذَّبُواْ بِـَٔايَـٰتِنَا وَكَانُواْ عَنْهَا غَـٰفِلِينَ ﴿١٣٦﴾

136. Faintaqamna minhum faaghraqnahum fee alyammi bi-annahum kaththaboo bi-ayatina wakanoo AAanha ghafileena

---

7:136. We then took our revenge[44] from them and drowned them in the sea because they rejected Our signs and paid no heed to them.

---

44. For the removal of any misconception in this regard, let me remind readers that 'revenge' means action taken in return for an offence.

وَأَوْرَثْنَا ٱلْقَوْمَ ٱلَّذِينَ كَانُوا۟ يُسْتَضْعَفُونَ مَشَٰرِقَ ٱلْأَرْضِ وَمَغَٰرِبَهَا ٱلَّتِى بَٰرَكْنَا فِيهَا ۖ وَتَمَّتْ كَلِمَتُ رَبِّكَ ٱلْحُسْنَىٰ عَلَىٰ بَنِىٓ إِسْرَٰٓءِيلَ بِمَا صَبَرُوا۟ ۖ وَدَمَّرْنَا مَا كَانَ يَصْنَعُ فِرْعَوْنُ وَقَوْمُهُۥ وَمَا كَانُوا۟ يَعْرِشُونَ ﴿١٣٧﴾

137. Waawrathna alqawma allatheena kanoo yustadAAafoona mashariqa al-ardi wamagharibaha allatee barakna feeha watammat kalimatu rabbika alhusna AAala banee isra-eela bima sabaroo wadammarna ma kana yasnaAAu firAAawnu waqawmuhu wama kanoo yaAArishoona

---

7:137. And We leased the lands to the East and to the West of the earth, in which We have placed Our Blessings,[45] to the people deemed to be weak. And the good word of your Lord was fulfilled upon the Children of Israel because they bore up sufferings patiently. And We annihilated what Pharaoh and his people had wrought and what they had built.

---

45. The part of the earth referred to here roughly corresponds to what we now call the Middle East. The Children of Israel, during Solomon's time had suzerainty over the entire area. As we know now, the area is blessed with mineral oil.

وَجَٰوَزْنَا بِبَنِىٓ إِسْرَٰٓءِيلَ ٱلْبَحْرَ فَأَتَوْا۟ عَلَىٰ قَوْمٍ يَعْكُفُونَ عَلَىٰٓ أَصْنَامٍ لَّهُمْ ۚ قَالُوا۟ يَٰمُوسَى ٱجْعَل لَّنَآ إِلَٰهًا كَمَا لَهُمْ ءَالِهَةٌ ۚ قَالَ إِنَّكُمْ قَوْمٌ تَجْهَلُونَ  ﴿١٣٨﴾

138. Wajawazna bibanee isra-eela albahra faataw AAala qawmin yaAAkufoona AAala asnamin lahum qaloo ya moosa ijAAal lana ilahan kama lahum alihatun qala innakum qawmun tajhaloona

7:138. [46]And We enabled the Children of Israel to cross the sea. Then they came upon a people given to the worship of their idols. They said, "O Moses! Make a god for us like the ones they have." He said, "You are indeed an ignorant people!

46. The leasing of the land to the Children of Israel, that was mentioned in the preceding Verse, did not happen immediately after the Pharaoh and his people were drowned, but centuries later. Now, in this Verse, the story of the exodus of the Children of Israel, under Moses, is resumed.

إِنَّ هَـٰٓؤُلَآءِ مُتَبَّرٌ مَّا هُمْ فِيهِ وَبَـٰطِلٌ مَّا كَانُوا۟ يَعْمَلُونَ ﴿١٣٩﴾

139. Inna haola-i mutabbarun ma hum feehi wabatilun ma kanoo yaAAmaloona

7:139. What these people are engrossed in is bound to be destroyed and what they do is all in vain."

قَالَ أَغَيْرَ ٱللَّهِ أَبْغِيكُمْ إِلَـٰهًا وَهُوَ فَضَّلَكُمْ عَلَى ٱلْعَـٰلَمِينَ ﴿١٤٠﴾

140. Qala aghayra Allahi abgheekum ilahan wahuwa faddalakum AAala alAAalameena

7:140. He said, "Shall I seek for you a god other than Allah, while He has favoured you over the worlds!?"

وَإِذْ أَنجَيْنَكُم مِّنْ ءَالِ فِرْعَوْنَ يَسُومُونَكُمْ سُوَءَ ٱلْعَذَابِ يُقَتِّلُونَ أَبْنَآءَكُمْ وَيَسْتَحْيُونَ نِسَآءَكُمْ وَفِى ذَٰلِكُم بَلَآءٌ مِّن رَّبِّكُمْ عَظِيمٌ ۝

141. Wa-i<u>th</u> anjay<u>na</u>kum min <u>a</u>li firAAawna yasoomoonakum soo-a alAAa<u>tha</u>bi yuqattiloona abn<u>a</u>akum wayasta<u>h</u>yoona nis<u>a</u>akum wafee <u>tha</u>likum bal<u>a</u>on min rabbikum AAa<u>th</u>eem**un**

7:141. And when We delivered you from Pharaoh's people! They were inflicting on you a terrible torment: they were killing your sons and sparing the lives of your womenfolk. And therein was a mighty trial from your Lord! [47]

---

47. This Verse is almost verbatim a replica of <u>Verse 2:49</u>. Regarding repetitions in the Qur'aan refer study note 2:124 on <u>Verse 2:92</u>.

۞ وَوَاعَدْنَا مُوسَىٰ ثَلَٰثِينَ لَيْلَةً وَأَتْمَمْنَٰهَا بِعَشْرٍ فَتَمَّ مِيقَٰتُ رَبِّهِ أَرْبَعِينَ لَيْلَةً وَقَالَ مُوسَىٰ لِأَخِيهِ هَٰرُونَ ٱخْلُفْنِى فِى قَوْمِى وَأَصْلِحْ وَلَا تَتَّبِعْ سَبِيلَ ٱلْمُفْسِدِينَ ۝

142. Waw<u>a</u>AAad<u>na</u> moos<u>a</u> thal<u>a</u>theena laylatan waatmamn<u>a</u>ha biAAashrin fatamma meeq<u>a</u>tu rabbihi arbaAAeena laylatan waq<u>a</u>la moos<u>a</u> li-akheehi h<u>a</u>roona okhlufnee fee qawmee wa-a<u>sli</u><u>h</u> wal<u>a</u> tattabiAA sabeela almufsideena

---

7:142. And We gave an appointment to Moses for thirty nights and extended the appointment by ten to complete the appointed time of his Lord to forty nights.[48] And

Manzil II: 7: Auraf

Moses said to his brother Aaron, "Be my representative among my people, be righteous and follow not the way of the mischief-makers.

---

48. This Verse gives more details of the forty nights mentioned in <u>Verse 2:51</u>.

وَلَمَّا جَآءَ مُوسَىٰ لِمِيقَٰتِنَا وَكَلَّمَهُۥ رَبُّهُۥ قَالَ رَبِّ أَرِنِىٓ أَنظُرْ إِلَيْكَ قَالَ لَن تَرَىٰنِى وَلَٰكِنِ ٱنظُرْ إِلَى ٱلْجَبَلِ فَإِنِ ٱسْتَقَرَّ مَكَانَهُۥ فَسَوْفَ تَرَىٰنِى فَلَمَّا تَجَلَّىٰ رَبُّهُۥ لِلْجَبَلِ جَعَلَهُۥ دَكًّا وَخَرَّ مُوسَىٰ صَعِقًا فَلَمَّآ أَفَاقَ قَالَ سُبْحَٰنَكَ تُبْتُ إِلَيْكَ وَأَنَا۠ أَوَّلُ ٱلْمُؤْمِنِينَ ﴿١٤٣﴾

143. Walamma jaa moosa limeeqatina wakallamahu rabbuhu qala rabbi arinee an*th*ur ilayka qala lan taranee walakini on*th*ur ila aljabali fa-ini istaqarra makanahu fasawfa taranee falamma tajalla rabbuhu liljabali jaAAalahu dakkan wakharra moosa saAAiqan falamma afaqa qala subhanaka tubtu ilayka waana awwalu almu/mineen**a**

7:143. And when Moses came at Our appointed time and his Lord spoke to him, he said, "My Lord! Reveal yourself to me so that I may see You." He said, "You cannot see Me, but look at the mountain. If it remains firm in its place, then will you see Me." But when his Lord manifested His glory to the mountain, He made it crumble and Moses fell in a swoon. Then when he recovered, he said, "Glory to You! I turn to You in repentence, and I am the first of the believers."

195

قَالَ يَـٰمُوسَىٰٓ إِنِّى ٱصْطَفَيْتُكَ عَلَى ٱلنَّاسِ بِرِسَـٰلَـٰتِى وَبِكَلَـٰمِى فَخُذْ مَآ ءَاتَيْتُكَ وَكُن مِّنَ ٱلشَّـٰكِرِينَ ﴿١٤٤﴾

144. Qala ya moosa innee istafaytuka AAala alnnasi birisalatee wabikalamee fakhuth ma ataytuka wakun mina alshshakireena

---

7:144. He said, "O Moses! I have indeed distinguished you above the people with My Messages and with My speaking to you directly. So, hold on to what I give you and be of the grateful ones."

وَكَتَبْنَا لَهُۥ فِى ٱلْأَلْوَاحِ مِن كُلِّ شَىْءٍ مَّوْعِظَةً وَتَفْصِيلًا لِّكُلِّ شَىْءٍ فَخُذْهَا بِقُوَّةٍ وَأْمُرْ قَوْمَكَ يَأْخُذُوا۟ بِأَحْسَنِهَا سَأُو۟رِيكُمْ دَارَ ٱلْفَـٰسِقِينَ ﴿١٤٥﴾

145. Wakatabna lahu fee al-alwahi min kulli shay-in mawAAithatan watafseelan likulli shay-in fakhuthha biquwwatin wa/mur qawmaka ya/khuthoo bi-ahsaniha saoreekum dara alfasiqeena

---

7:145. And We wrote down for him in the tablets[49, 50] every kind of advice/admonition, and everything in detail. "So hold on to them firmly and enjoin your people to hold on to the excellence thereof. I will show you where the dissolute abide."

---

49. Moses was given the divine Book (the Torah) in the form of tablets. The Book was revealed to him at one go, unlike the Qur'aan, which was revealed to Prophet Muhammad (peace be on him), little by little, during the period of 23 years. In the modern-day internet terminology, the Book revealed to Moses (peace be on him) was a hard copy, while the Qur'aan was a soft copy imprinted on the mind of Muhammad. The original hard copy of the Torah is apparently lost in the annals of history, and its man-

made copies got corrupted by passage of time. Allah Almighty had not guarateed its preservtion, as in His infinite knowledge, He was yet to send His final Testament, the Qur'aan, the preservation of which He guaranteed (Verse 15:9).

50. It is noteworthy that the Torah, in its original divine form, was self-sufficient for human guidance, as divinely reiterated here in this Verse. A similar reiteration in respect of the Qur'aan itself is contained in several Verses like 6:38, 12:111, 17:89, but, it is sad to note, most Muslims themselves openly dispute this divine reiteration! They say the divine guidance in the Qur'aan is incomplete without the *ahaadeeth*.

سَأَصْرِفُ عَنْ ءَايَـٰتِـىَ ٱلَّذِينَ يَتَكَبَّرُونَ فِى ٱلْأَرْضِ بِغَيْرِ ٱلْحَقِّ وَإِن يَرَوْاْ كُلَّ ءَايَةٍ لَّا يُؤْمِنُواْ بِهَا وَإِن يَرَوْاْ سَبِيلَ ٱلرُّشْدِ لَا يَتَّخِذُوهُ سَبِيلًا وَإِن يَرَوْاْ سَبِيلَ ٱلْغَيِّ يَتَّخِذُوهُ سَبِيلًا ذَٰلِكَ بِأَنَّهُمْ كَذَّبُواْ بِـَٔايَـٰتِنَا وَكَانُواْ عَنْهَا غَـٰفِلِينَ ۝

146. Saasrifu AAan ayatiya allatheena yatakabbaroona fee al-ardi bighayri alhaqqi wa-in yaraw kulla ayatin la yu/minoo biha wa-in yaraw sabeela alrrushdi la yattakhithoohu sabeelan wa-in yaraw sabeela alghayyi yattakhithoohu sabeelan thalika bi-annahum kaththaboo bi-ayatina wakanoo AAanha ghafileena

7:146. I will turn away from My Verses/signs those who are unjustly proud on the earth. And even if they see every sign, they will not believe in it. And if they see the way of rectitude, they do not take it. And if they see the way of error, they take it! That is because they rejected Our Verses/signs and were heedless of them.

وَٱلَّذِينَ كَذَّبُواْ بِـَٔايَـٰتِنَا وَلِقَآءِ ٱلْأَخِرَةِ حَبِطَتْ أَعْمَـٰلُهُمْ هَلْ يُجْزَوْنَ إِلَّا مَا كَانُواْ يَعْمَلُونَ ۝

147. Waallatheena kaththaboo bi-ayatina waliqa-i al-akhirati habitat aAAmaluhum hal yujzawna illa ma kanoo yaAAmaloona

7:147. And as for those who reject Our Verses/signs and the meeting of the Hereafter, their deeds have gone in vain. Shall they be rewarded except for what they have done?

وَٱتَّخَذَ قَوْمُ مُوسَىٰ مِنۢ بَعْدِهِۦ مِنْ حُلِيِّهِمْ عِجْلًا جَسَدًا لَّهُۥ خُوَارٌ أَلَمْ يَرَوْاْ أَنَّهُۥ لَا يُكَلِّمُهُمْ وَلَا يَهْدِيهِمْ سَبِيلًا ٱتَّخَذُوهُ وَكَانُواْ ظَٰلِمِينَ ۝

148. Waittakhatha qawmu moosa min baAAdihi min huliyyihim AAijlan jasadan lahu khuwarun alam yaraw annahu la yukallimuhum wala yahdeehim sabeelan ittakhathoohu wakanoo thalimeena

7:148. And Moses' people, after he left, made a calf of their ornaments – just a body, which emanated a sound.[51] Could they not see that it did not speak to them nor guide them to any way? They took to it and indulged in wrong-doing.

51. Verse 20:88 informs us that the calf made of ornaments was considered as a god worthy of worship!

وَلَمَّا سُقِطَ فِىٓ أَيْدِيهِمْ وَرَأَوْاْ أَنَّهُمْ قَدْ ضَلُّواْ قَالُواْ لَئِن لَّمْ يَرْحَمْنَا رَبُّنَا وَيَغْفِرْ لَنَا لَنَكُونَنَّ مِنَ ٱلْخَٰسِرِينَ ۝

149. Walamma suqita fee aydeehim waraaw annahum qad dalloo qaloo la-in lam yarhamna rabbuna wayaghfir lana lanakoonanna mina alkhasireena

7:149. And when they repented and saw that they had gone astray, they said, "Should our Lord show no mercy on us and forgive us not, we shall certainly be of those who are doomed."

وَلَمَّا رَجَعَ مُوسَىٰ إِلَىٰ قَوْمِهِۦ غَضْبَٰنَ أَسِفًا قَالَ بِئْسَمَا خَلَفْتُمُونِى مِنۢ بَعْدِىٓ أَعَجِلْتُمْ أَمْرَ رَبِّكُمْ وَأَلْقَى ٱلْأَلْوَاحَ وَأَخَذَ بِرَأْسِ أَخِيهِ يَجُرُّهُۥٓ إِلَيْهِ قَالَ ٱبْنَ أُمَّ إِنَّ ٱلْقَوْمَ ٱسْتَضْعَفُونِى وَكَادُوا۟ يَقْتُلُونَنِى فَلَا تُشْمِتْ بِىَ ٱلْأَعْدَآءَ وَلَا تَجْعَلْنِى مَعَ ٱلْقَوْمِ ٱلظَّٰلِمِينَ ﴿١٥٠﴾

150. Walamma_ rajaAAa moosa_ ila_ qawmihi ghad_ba_na asifan qala bi/sama_ khalaftumoonee min baAAdee aAAajiltum amra rabbikum waalqa_ al-alwa_ha waakhatha bira/si akheehi yajurruhu ilayhi qa_la ibna omma inna alqawma istad_AAafoonee waka_doo yaqtuloonanee fala_ tushmit biya al-aAAdaa wala_ tajAAalnee maAAa alqawmi al_thth_alimeen**a**

7:150. And when Moses returned to his people, in anger and grief, he said, "What an evil thing you have done after I left! Were you so hasty for the command of your Lord? [52]" And he threw down the tablets and caught hold of his brother by the head, dragging him towards him. He said, "Son of my mother! Indeed, the people reckoned me weak and had almost killed me. So, make not the enemies gloat over me and do not count me among the wicked people."

52. Moses was chiding his people that they did not wait till he returned to them with Allah's commands. They were so impatient that they created their own false god in the form of the golden calf!

قَالَ رَبِّ اغْفِرْ لِى وَلِأَخِى وَأَدْخِلْنَا فِى رَحْمَتِكَ وَأَنتَ أَرْحَمُ الرَّاحِمِينَ ﴿١٥١﴾

151. Qala rabbi ighfir lee wali-akhee waadkhilna fee rahmatika waanta arhamu alrrahimeena

7:151. He said, "My Lord! Forgive me and my brother and admit us to Your Mercy, and You are the Most Merciful."

إِنَّ الَّذِينَ اتَّخَذُواْ الْعِجْلَ سَيَنَالُهُمْ غَضَبٌ مِّن رَّبِّهِمْ وَذِلَّةٌ فِى الْحَيَوٰةِ الدُّنْيَا وَكَذَالِكَ نَجْزِى الْمُفْتَرِينَ ﴿١٥٢﴾

152. Inna allatheena ittakhathoo alAAijla sayanaluhum ghadabun min rabbihim wathillatun fee alhayati alddunya wakathalika najzee almuftareena

7:152. Those indeed who took to the calf, wrath from their Lord and disgrace in this world's life shall overtake them, and thus do We recompense the fabricators of lies.

وَالَّذِينَ عَمِلُواْ السَّيِّئَاتِ ثُمَّ تَابُواْ مِنْ بَعْدِهَا وَءَامَنُوٓاْ إِنَّ رَبَّكَ مِنْ بَعْدِهَا لَغَفُورٌ رَّحِيمٌ ﴿١٥٣﴾

153. Waallatheena AAamiloo alssayyi-ati thumma taboo min baAAdiha waamanoo inna rabbaka min baAAdiha laghafoorun raheemun

7:153. And your Lord is indeed Forgiving and Merciful to those who do evil deeds, but then repent thereafter and believe.

وَلَمَّا سَكَتَ عَن مُّوسَى ٱلْغَضَبُ أَخَذَ ٱلْأَلْوَاحَ وَفِى نُسْخَتِهَا هُدًى وَرَحْمَةٌ لِّلَّذِينَ هُمْ لِرَبِّهِمْ يَرْهَبُونَ ۝

154. Walamma sakata AAan moosa alghadabu akhatha al-alwaha wafee nuskhatiha hudan warahmatun lillatheena hum lirabbihim yarhaboona

7:154. And when Moses calmed down, he took up the tablets. And in the inscription thereof, there was guidance and mercy for those who fear their Lord.

وَٱخْتَارَ مُوسَىٰ قَوْمَهُۥ سَبْعِينَ رَجُلًا لِّمِيقَٰتِنَا فَلَمَّآ أَخَذَتْهُمُ ٱلرَّجْفَةُ قَالَ رَبِّ لَوْ شِئْتَ أَهْلَكْتَهُم مِّن قَبْلُ وَإِيَّـٰىَ أَتُهْلِكُنَا بِمَا فَعَلَ ٱلسُّفَهَآءُ مِنَّآ إِنْ هِىَ إِلَّا فِتْنَتُكَ تُضِلُّ بِهَا مَن تَشَآءُ وَتَهْدِى مَن تَشَآءُ أَنتَ وَلِيُّنَا فَٱغْفِرْ لَنَا وَٱرْحَمْنَا وَأَنتَ خَيْرُ ٱلْغَٰفِرِينَ ۝

155. Waikhtara moosa qawmahu sabAAeena rajulan limeeqatina falamma akhathathumu alrrajfatu qala rabbi law shi/ta ahlaktahum min qablu wa-iyyaya atuhlikuna bima faAAala alssufahao minna in hiya illa fitnatuka tudillu biha man tashao watahdee man tashao anta waliyyuna faighfir lana wairhamna waanta khayru alghafireena

7:155. And Moses chose from his people seventy men for the appointment with Us.[53] So when the violent shaking seized them, he said, "My Lord! Had You so willed, You could have destroyed them before – and me too. Will You destroy us for what the fools among us have done? It is indeed nothing but a trial from You. You make whom You will to go astray with it and You guide whom You will. You are our *Wali*[54]. So forgive us and have mercy on us, and You are the best of the forgivers."

53. From the later context in this very Verse, it is apparent that the purpose of the appointment was to ask Allah for forgiveness of Moses' people for their folly of taking the man-made golden calf as their god.

54. For the comprehensive Qur'aanic meaning of *Wali*, refer study note 2:154 on <u>Verse 2:107</u>.

وَٱكْتُبْ لَنَا فِى هَـٰذِهِ ٱلدُّنْيَا حَسَنَةً وَفِى ٱلْأَخِرَةِ إِنَّا هُدْنَآ إِلَيْكَ قَالَ عَذَابِىٓ أُصِيبُ بِهِۦ مَنْ أَشَآءُ وَرَحْمَتِى وَسِعَتْ كُلَّ شَىْءٍ فَسَأَكْتُبُهَا لِلَّذِينَ يَتَّقُونَ وَيُؤْتُونَ ٱلزَّكَوٰةَ وَٱلَّذِينَ هُم بِـَٔايَـٰتِنَا يُؤْمِنُونَ

156. Waoktub lana fee hathihi alddunya hasanatan wafee al-akhirati inna hudna ilayka qala AAathabee oseebu bihi man ashao warahmatee wasiAAat kulla shay-in fasaaktubuha lillatheena yattaqoona wayu/toona alzzakata waallatheena hum bi-ayatina yu/minoona

7:156. "And ordain for us good in this world and in the Hereafter, for indeed we turn to You for guidance." HE said, "I inflict My punishment on whom I will. And My mercy covers all things, and I ordain it [Mercy] for those who are pious, give in charity, and believe in Our Verses/signs."

اَلَّذِينَ يَتَّبِعُونَ الرَّسُولَ النَّبِىَّ الْأُمِّىَّ الَّذِى يَجِدُونَهُۥ مَكْتُوبًا عِندَهُمْ فِى التَّوْرَىٰةِ وَالْإِنجِيلِ يَأْمُرُهُم بِالْمَعْرُوفِ وَيَنْهَىٰهُمْ عَنِ الْمُنكَرِ وَيُحِلُّ لَهُمُ الطَّيِّبَٰتِ وَيُحَرِّمُ عَلَيْهِمُ الْخَبَٰئِثَ وَيَضَعُ عَنْهُمْ إِصْرَهُمْ وَالْأَغْلَٰلَ الَّتِى كَانَتْ عَلَيْهِمْ فَالَّذِينَ ءَامَنُوا بِهِۦ وَعَزَّرُوهُ وَنَصَرُوهُ وَاتَّبَعُوا النُّورَ الَّذِىٓ أُنزِلَ مَعَهُۥٓ أُوْلَٰٓئِكَ هُمُ الْمُفْلِحُونَ ﴿١٥٧﴾

157. Allatheena yattabiAAoona alrrasoola alnnabiyya al-ommiyya allathee yajidoonahu maktooban AAindahum fee alttawrati waal-injeeli ya/muruhum bialmaAAroofi wayanhahum AAani almunkari wayuhillu lahumu alttayyibati wayuharrimu AAalayhimu alkhaba-itha wayadaAAu AAanhum israhum waal-aghlala allatee kanat AAalayhim faallatheena amanoo bihi waAAazzaroohu wanasaroohu waittabaAAoo alnnoora allathee onzila maAAahu ola-ika humu almuflihoona

7:157. Those who follow the unlettered Messenger-Prophet, whom they find mentioned with them in the Torah and the Gospel, who enjoins them to do good things and forbids them from bad things, and makes pure, wholesome things lawful to them and impure things unlawful, and removes from them their burden and the fetters which were upon them.[55] So then those who believe in him, honour him and help him, and follow the light[56] which has been sent down with him – those it is that succeed.

55. This part of the Verse is in continuation of the ending part of the preceding Verse. That means Allah bestows His mercy on those who follow the Prophet. This divine reiteration is further elaborated in the remaining part of this Verse.

56. The light mentioned here is obviously the Qur'aan.

قُل يَـٰٓأَيُّهَا ٱلنَّاسُ إِنِّى رَسُولُ ٱللَّهِ إِلَيْكُمْ جَمِيعًا ٱلَّذِى لَهُۥ مُلْكُ ٱلسَّمَـٰوَٰتِ وَٱلْأَرْضِ لَآ إِلَـٰهَ إِلَّا هُوَ يُحْىِۦ وَيُمِيتُ فَـَٔامِنُوا۟ بِٱللَّهِ وَرَسُولِهِ ٱلنَّبِىِّ ٱلْأُمِّىِّ ٱلَّذِى يُؤْمِنُ بِٱللَّهِ وَكَلِمَـٰتِهِۦ وَٱتَّبِعُوهُ لَعَلَّكُمْ تَهْتَدُونَ ۝

158. Qul y_a ayyuh_a alnn_asu innee rasoolu All_ahi ilaykum jameeAAan alla_thee lahu mulku alssam_aw_ati waal-ar_di l_a il_aha ill_a huwa yu_hyee wayumeetu fa_aminoo biAll_ahi warasoolihi alnnabiyyi al-ommiyyi alla_thee yu/minu biAll_ahi wakalim_atihi waittabiAAoohu laAAallakum tahtadoona

---

7:158. Say, "O people! I am indeed the Messenger, to you all, of Allah, Whose is the absolute suzerainty over the heavens and the earth. There is no god but Him. He gives life and causes death." So, believe in Allah and His Messenger, the unlettered Prophet, who believes in Allah and His words. And follow him so that you are on the right path.

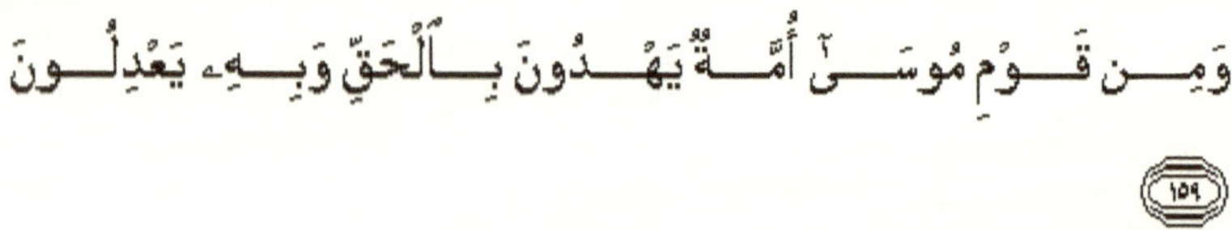

159. Wamin qawmi moos_a ommatun yahdoona bial_haqqi wabihi yaAAdiloona

---

7:159. And of Moses' people was a group, who guided with the truth, and therewih did they judge.

وَقَطَّعۡنَٰهُمُ ٱثۡنَتَیۡ عَشۡرَةَ أَسۡبَاطًا أُمَمًا وَأَوۡحَیۡنَاۤ إِلَىٰ مُوسَىٰۤ إِذِ ٱسۡتَسۡقَىٰهُ

قَوۡمُهُۥۤ أَنِ ٱضۡرِب بِّعَصَاكَ ٱلۡحَجَرَ فَٱنۢبَجَسَتۡ مِنۡهُ ٱثۡنَتَا عَشۡرَةَ عَیۡنًا قَدۡ

عَلِمَ كُلُّ أُنَاسٍ مَّشۡرَبَهُمۡ وَظَلَّلۡنَا عَلَیۡهِمُ ٱلۡغَمَٰمَ وَأَنزَلۡنَا عَلَیۡهِمُ ٱلۡمَنَّ

وَٱلسَّلۡوَىٰ كُلُواۡ مِن طَیِّبَٰتِ مَا رَزَقۡنَٰكُمۡ وَمَا ظَلَمُونَا وَلَٰكِن كَانُوۤاۡ

أَنفُسَهُمۡ یَظۡلِمُونَ ۝

160. WaqattaAAnahumu ithnatay AAashrata asba_tan omaman waaw_hayna_ ila moosa_ i_thi istasq_ahu qawmuhu ani i_drib biAAasa_ka alhajara fainbajasat minhu ithnata_ AAashrata AAaynan qad AAalima kullu ona_sin mashrabahum wa_thallalna_ AAalayhimu alghamama waanzalna_ AAalayhimu almanna wa**alssalwa**_ kuloo min _tayyiba_ti ma_ razaqna_kum wama_ _thalamoona_ wala_kin k_anoo anfusahum ya_th_limoon**a**

7:160. And We divided them into twelve tribal groups. And when his people asked Moses for water, We inspired him, "Strike the rock with your staff!" There then gushed forth twelve springs there from. Thus, did all come to know their respective sources of drinking water. And We made the clouds to provide shelter over them and We sent to them manna and quails[57]. "Eat of the good things We have provided for you." And they did not do Us any harm, but they did harm to their own souls.[58]

---

57. These were divinely provided sources of food.

58. This last sentence of the Verse is a divine reflexion on the intransigence of Moses' people, despite Allah's numerous favours on them.

وَإِذْ قِيلَ لَهُمُ ٱسْكُنُواْ هَـٰذِهِ ٱلْقَرْيَةَ وَكُلُواْ مِنْهَا حَيْثُ شِئْتُمْ وَقُولُواْ حِطَّةٌ وَٱدْخُلُواْ ٱلْبَابَ سُجَّدًا نَّغْفِرْ لَكُمْ خَطِيئَـٰتِكُمْ سَنَزِيدُ ٱلْمُحْسِنِينَ ﴿١٦١﴾

161. Wa-i<u>th</u> qeela lahumu oskunoo <u>h</u>a<u>th</u>ihi alqaryata wakuloo min<u>ha</u> <u>h</u>aythu shi/tum waqooloo <u>h</u>ittatun wa<u>o</u>dkhuloo alb<u>a</u>ba sujjadan naghfir lakum kha<u>t</u>ee-<u>a</u>tikum sanazeedu almu<u>h</u>sineena

---

7:161. And when it was said to them, "Reside in this place of habitation and eat wherever you wish there from, and say, 'hittatun[59].' And enter the gate prostrating. We will forgive you your wrong-doings. We will give more to those who do good."

---

59. In other words, the Children of Israel were asked to pray for forgiveness.

فَبَدَّلَ ٱلَّذِينَ ظَلَمُواْ مِنْهُمْ قَوْلاً غَيْرَ ٱلَّذِى قِيلَ لَهُمْ فَأَرْسَلْنَا عَلَيْهِمْ رِجْزًا مِّنَ ٱلسَّمَآءِ بِمَا كَانُواْ يَظْلِمُونَ ﴿١٦٢﴾

162. Fabaddala alla<u>th</u>eena thalamoo minhum qawlan ghayra alla<u>th</u>ee qeela lahum faarsaln<u>a</u> AAalayhim rijzan mina alssam<u>a</u>-i bim<u>a</u> k<u>a</u>noo yathlimoona

---

7:162. But then those who were wicked among them changed it for a word other than that which they had been told to utter. So We sent down upon them a calamity from the heavens because they were wicked.[60]

---

60. Please see study note 2:62 on <u>Verse 2:59</u> in this regard.

وَسْـَٔلْهُمْ عَنِ ٱلْقَرْيَةِ ٱلَّتِى كَانَتْ حَاضِرَةَ ٱلْبَحْرِ إِذْ يَعْدُونَ فِى ٱلسَّبْتِ إِذْ تَأْتِيهِمْ حِيتَانُهُمْ يَوْمَ سَبْتِهِمْ شُرَّعًا وَيَوْمَ لَا يَسْبِتُونَ لَا تَأْتِيهِمْ كَذَٰلِكَ نَبْلُوهُم بِمَا كَانُوا۟ يَفْسُقُونَ ﴿١٦٣﴾

163. Wais-alhum AAani alqaryati allatee kanat hadirata albahri ith yaAAdoona fee alssabti ith ta/teehim heetanuhum yawma sabtihim shurraAAan wayawma la yasbitoona la ta/teehim kathalika nabloohum bima kanoo yafsuqoon**a**

7:163. And ask them about the place of human habitation which stood by the sea, where they crossed the limits of the Sabbath[61]: their fish came to them, up on the surface of the water, on the day of their Sabbath, and not on other days! Thus, did We try them because they transgressed.

61. See study note 2:73.

وَإِذْ قَالَتْ أُمَّةٌ مِّنْهُمْ لِمَ تَعِظُونَ قَوْمًا ٱللَّهُ مُهْلِكُهُمْ أَوْ مُعَذِّبُهُمْ عَذَابًا شَدِيدًا قَالُوا۟ مَعْذِرَةً إِلَىٰ رَبِّكُمْ وَلَعَلَّهُمْ يَتَّقُونَ ﴿١٦٤﴾

164. Wa-ith qalat ommatun minhum lima taAAithoona qawman Allahu muhlikuhum aw muAAaththibuhum AAathaban shadeedan qaloo maAAthiratan ila rabbikum walaAAallahum yattaqoon**a**

7:164. And when a section of them[62] said, "Why do you admonish a people whom Allah would destroy or give a severe punishment?" They[63] said, "To be free of blame before your Lord! And, haply, they may fear Allah."

---

62. People to whom Allah Almighty had sent His Messengers/Prophets.

63. The Messengers/Prophets.

فَلَمَّا نَسُواْ مَا ذُكِّرُواْ بِهِۦ أَنجَيْنَا ٱلَّذِينَ يَنْهَوْنَ عَنِ ٱلسُّوٓءِ وَأَخَذْنَا ٱلَّذِينَ ظَلَمُواْ بِعَذَابٍ بَئِيسٍ بِمَا كَانُواْ يَفْسُقُونَ ﴿١٦٥﴾

165. Falamma nasoo ma thukkiroo bihi anjayna allatheena yanhawna AAani alssoo-i waakhathna allatheena thalamoo biAAathabin ba-eesin bima kanoo yafsuqoona

---

7:165. So when they forgot what they had been reminded of, We saved those who forbade evil and We severely punished those who did wrong, because they transgressed.[64]

---

64. See Verse 6:44 also in this context.

فَلَمَّا عَتَوْاْ عَن مَّا نُهُواْ عَنْهُ قُلْنَا لَهُمْ كُونُواْ قِرَدَةً خَـٰسِـِٔينَ ﴿١٦٦﴾

166. Falamma AAataw AAan ma nuhoo AAanhu qulna lahum koonoo qiradatan khasi-eena

---

7:166. And when they revoltingly persisted in what they had been forbidden, We said to them, "Be apes, despised and hated."[65]

---

65. Please see study notes 2:73 to 2:76 under Verses 2:65 & 2:66.

وَإِذْ تَأَذَّنَ رَبُّكَ لَيَبْعَثَنَّ عَلَيْهِمْ إِلَىٰ يَوْمِ الْقِيَـٰمَةِ مَن يَسُومُهُمْ سُوٓءَ الْعَذَابِ إِنَّ رَبَّكَ لَسَرِيعُ الْعِقَابِ وَإِنَّهُۥ لَغَفُورٌ رَّحِيمٌ ۝

167. Wa-i*th* taa*thth*ana rabbuka layabAAathanna AAalayhim il*a* yawmi alqiy*a*mati man yasoomuhum soo-a alAAa*th*abi inna rabbaka lasareeAAu alAAiq*a*bi wa-innahu laghafoorun ra*h*eem**un**

7:167. And when your Lord declared that He would certainly impose upon them, till the Day of Resurrection, those who would treat them badly, your Lord indeed is quick to requite and indeed He is Forgiving, Merciful![66]

---

66. This divine declaration applies to all those who 'forgot what they had been reminded of'. It's not that divine punishment was meted out only on those ancient, pre-historic peoples. It is meted out on modern, historic peoples also. And it will continue to be meted out, on this earth itself, till the Last Day. The divine punishment comes in the form of earthquakes, tsunamis, hurricanes etc. It also comes in the form of despotic rules like that of Hitler against the Jews or of Israel against the Palestinian Arabs. The victims are those who 'forgot what they had been reminded of'. And the last divine Reminder is the Qur'aan. The victims transgressed the limits of 'forgetting' what they had been reminded of. And the despots should not think that they would go scot free. Remember what happened to the Pharaoh of the ancient ages and to Hitler of the modern age.

وَقَطَّعْنَٰهُمْ فِى ٱلْأَرْضِ أُمَمًا مِّنْهُمُ ٱلصَّٰلِحُونَ وَمِنْهُمْ دُونَ ذَٰلِكَ وَبَلَوْنَٰهُم بِٱلْحَسَنَٰتِ وَٱلسَّيِّئَاتِ لَعَلَّهُمْ يَرْجِعُونَ ﴿١٦٨﴾

168. WaqattaAAnahum fee al-ardi omaman minhumu alssalihoona waminhum doona thalika wabalawnahum bialhasanati waalssayyi-ati laAAallahum yarjiAAoona

7:168. And We broke them[67], on the earth, into groups; some of them are righteous and some of them are not. And We tried them with good things and bad, so that they might turn back to the Right Path.

67. The Jews it is that are meant here, primarily, but, now, the Muslims too could be covered by this pronoun.

فَخَلَفَ مِنۢ بَعْدِهِمْ خَلْفٌ وَرِثُوا۟ ٱلْكِتَٰبَ يَأْخُذُونَ عَرَضَ هَٰذَا ٱلْأَدْنَىٰ وَيَقُولُونَ سَيُغْفَرُ لَنَا وَإِن يَأْتِهِمْ عَرَضٌ مِّثْلُهُۥ يَأْخُذُوهُ أَلَمْ يُؤْخَذْ عَلَيْهِم مِّيثَٰقُ ٱلْكِتَٰبِ أَن لَّا يَقُولُوا۟ عَلَى ٱللَّهِ إِلَّا ٱلْحَقَّ وَدَرَسُوا۟ مَا فِيهِ وَٱلدَّارُ ٱلْءَاخِرَةُ خَيْرٌ لِّلَّذِينَ يَتَّقُونَ أَفَلَا تَعْقِلُونَ ﴿١٦٩﴾

169. Fakhalafa min baAAdihim khalfun warithoo alkitaba ya/khuthoona AAarada hatha al-adna wayaqooloona sayughfaru lana wa-in ya/tihim AAaradun mithluhu ya/khuthoohu alam yu/khath AAalayhim meethaqu alkitabi an la yaqooloo AAala Allahi illa alhaqqa wadarasoo ma feehi waalddaru al-akhiratu khayrun lillatheena yattaqoona afala taAAqiloona

7:169. Then, there came after them a posterity that inherited the Book, taking what this worldly life offers and saying, "We will be forgiven!" And if a like offer came to them again, they would take it too! Was not a promise taken from them in the Book that they would not speak anything about Allah but the truth? And they have read what is there in it! And the abode of the Hereafter is better for those who fear Allah. Don't you understand?[68]

68. The reference in this Verse too is primarily to the Jews; but the reference could be stretched to the Muslims now.

170. Waalla*th*eena yumassikoona bialkit*a*bi waaq*a*moo al*ss*al*a*ta inn*a* l*a* nu*d*eeAAu ajra almu*sli*h*eena*

7:170. And as for those who hold fast to the Book and establish proper prayer, We do not indeed cause the reward of the doers of good to go waste.

171. Wa-i*th* nataqn*a* aljabala fawqahum kaannahu *th*ullatun wa*th*annoo annahu waqiAAun bihim khu*th*oo m*a* *a*tayn*a*kum biquwwatin wao*th*kuroo m*a* feehi laAAAllakum tattaqoon*a*

7:171. And when We made the mountain shake over them like a shadow – and they thought that it was certain to fall upon them – telling them, "Hold firmly what We have given you, and take heed of what there is in it, so that you become pious."[69]

---

69. Refer Verse 2:63 and study notes thereunder of these Studies.

وَإِذْ أَخَذَ رَبُّكَ مِنْ بَنِىٓ ءَادَمَ مِن ظُهُورِهِمْ ذُرِّيَّتَهُمْ وَأَشْهَدَهُمْ عَلَىٰٓ أَنفُسِهِمْ أَلَسْتُ بِرَبِّكُمْ قَالُوا۟ بَلَىٰ شَهِدْنَآ أَن تَقُولُوا۟ يَوْمَ ٱلْقِيَٰمَةِ إِنَّا كُنَّا عَنْ هَٰذَا غَٰفِلِينَ ﴿١٧٢﴾

172. Wa-i*th* akha*th*a rabbuka min banee *a*dama min *th*uhoorihim *th*urriyyatahum waashhadahum AAal*a* anfusihim alastu birabbikum q*a*loo bal*a* shahidn*a* an taqooloo yawma alqiy*a*mati inn*a* kunn*a* AAan h*a*tha ghafileena

---

7:172. And when your Lord brought forth, from Adam and his children, their offspring, and made them bear witness against their own souls, "Am I not your Lord?" they said, "Yes! We bear witness." Lest you should say on the Day of Resurrection, "Indeed, we were unaware of this."[70]

---

70. This Verse and the next one show that the fundamental beliefs, in Allah Almighty and His final Judgment on the fate of every human being, are ingrained in his/her mind at birth itself. He/she deviates from these ingrained beliefs by exercising his/her conscious freedom of choice for the short-term glitter of worldly life, at the expense of a life of piety.

أَوْ تَقُولُوٓاْ إِنَّمَآ أَشْرَكَ ءَابَآؤُنَا مِن قَبْلُ وَكُنَّا ذُرِّيَّةً مِّنْ بَعْدِهِمْ أَفَتُهْلِكُنَا بِمَا فَعَلَ ٱلْمُبْطِلُونَ ۝

173. Aw taqooloo innama ashraka abaona min qablu wakunna thurriyyatan min baAAdihim afatuhlikuna bima faAAala almubtiloona

7:173. Or you should say, "It was our fathers, before us, who worshiped others besides Allah, and we were only their offspring following them! Will You then destroy us for what those followers of falsehood did?"

وَكَذَلِكَ نُفَصِّلُ ٱلْأَيَـٰتِ وَلَعَلَّهُمْ يَرْجِعُونَ ۝

174. Wakathalika nufassilu al-ayati walaAAallahum yarjiAAoona

7:174. And thus, do We explain the Verses, in details and to facilitate their return to the Right Path.

وَٱتْلُ عَلَيْهِمْ نَبَأَ ٱلَّذِىٓ ءَاتَيْنَـٰهُ ءَايَـٰتِنَا فَٱنسَلَخَ مِنْهَا فَأَتْبَعَهُ ٱلشَّيْطَـٰنُ فَكَانَ مِنَ ٱلْغَاوِينَ ۝

175. Waotlu AAalayhim nabaa allathee ataynahu ayatina fainsalakha minha faatbaAAahu alshshaytanu fakana mina alghaweena

7:175. And recite to them the story of one to whom We gave Our Verses/signs, but he withdrew himself there from! The Satan then followed him, and he became one of those who deviate from the Right Path.

وَلَوْ شِئْنَا لَرَفَعْنَـٰهُ بِهَا وَلَـٰكِنَّهُۥٓ أَخْلَدَ إِلَى ٱلْأَرْضِ وَٱتَّبَعَ هَوَىٰهُ فَمَثَلُهُۥ كَمَثَلِ ٱلْكَلْبِ إِن تَحْمِلْ عَلَيْهِ يَلْهَثْ أَوْ تَتْرُكْهُ يَلْهَثْ ذَّٰلِكَ مَثَلُ ٱلْقَوْمِ ٱلَّذِينَ كَذَّبُوا۟ بِـَٔايَٰتِنَا فَٱقْصُصِ ٱلْقَصَصَ لَعَلَّهُمْ يَتَفَكَّرُونَ ﴿١٧٦﴾

176. Walaw shi/na larafaAAnahu biha walakinnahu akhlada ila al-ardi waittabaAAa hawahu famathaluhu kamathali alkalbi in tahmil AAalayhi yalhath aw tatruk-hu yalhath thalika mathalu alqawmi allatheena kaththaboo bi-ayatina faoqsusi alqasasa laAAallahum yatafakkaroona

7:176. And if We had so willed, We would certainly have exalted him thereby; but he remained clinging to the earth and followed his base desires. His example then is that of the dog; if you assault him he lolls out his tongue, and if you leave him alone he lolls out his tongue! [71] Similar is the example of those who reject Our Verses/signs. Relate the story then; perhaps they will reflect.[72]

71. A dog doing so is indicative of its utterly submissive behaviour towards its master. A man, who refuses to be governed by divine law, condemns himself to similar slavish behaviour towards some other human beings in pursuit of his base desires.

72. The Qur'aan does not name the person about whom this narrative is related in these two Verses 175 & 176. But it applies to a general prototype of a modern-day Muslim. To this Muslim, Allah Almighty gave the Qur'aan, but he does not follow the instructions therein – let alone follow, he does not even try to understand those instructions. The Satan then follows him, and he is led to grave-worship in pursuit of his worldly desires. Being unaware of Qur'aanic instructions, he goes to Mullahs – religious leaders – for guidance. The Mullahs generally reject the oft-repeated Qur'aanic statement that it contains instructions explained in detail on all matters concerning the Religion. And they guide the gullible prototype Muslim on matters not contained in the Qur'aan, based on man-influenced and error-prone *ahaadeeth* and other books of human authors. As a result, the Muslim *Ummah* in general is reduced to the status of the dog, mentioned in this Verse, in the comity of nations today.

سَآءَ مَثَلًا ٱلْقَوْمُ ٱلَّذِينَ كَذَّبُوا۟ بِـَٔايَـٰتِنَا وَأَنفُسَهُمْ كَانُوا۟ يَظْلِمُونَ ﴿١٧٧﴾

177. S*a*a mathalan alqawmu alla*th*eena ka*thth*aboo bi-*ay*ati*na* waanfusahum *k*anoo ya*th*limoon**a**

7:177. Evil is the example of people who reject Our Verses/signs and are unjust to their own souls.

مَن يَهْدِ ٱللَّهُ فَهُوَ ٱلْمُهْتَدِى ۖ وَمَن يُضْلِلْ فَأُو۟لَـٰٓئِكَ هُمُ ٱلْخَـٰسِرُونَ ﴿١٧٨﴾

178. Man yahdi All*a*hu fahuwa almuhtadee waman yu*d*lil faol*a*-ika humu alkh*a*siroon**a**

7:178. Whomsoever Allah guides, he is the one who follows the right way; and whomsoever He sends astray, these are the ones who are doomed.

وَلَقَدْ ذَرَأْنَا لِجَهَنَّمَ كَثِيرًا مِّنَ ٱلْجِنِّ وَٱلْإِنسِ ۖ لَهُمْ قُلُوبٌ لَّا يَفْقَهُونَ بِهَا وَلَهُمْ أَعْيُنٌ لَّا يُبْصِرُونَ بِهَا وَلَهُمْ ءَاذَانٌ لَّا يَسْمَعُونَ بِهَآ ۚ أُو۟لَـٰٓئِكَ كَٱلْأَنْعَـٰمِ بَلْ هُمْ أَضَلُّ ۚ أُو۟لَـٰٓئِكَ هُمُ ٱلْغَـٰفِلُونَ ﴿١٧٩﴾

179. Walaqad *th*ara/*na* lijahannama katheeran mina aljinni w**a**al-insi lahum quloobun *la* yafqahoona bi*ha* walahum aAAyunun *la* yubsiroona bi*ha* walahum a*tha*nun *la* yasmaAAoona bi*ha* ol*a*-ika k*a*al-anAA*a*mi bal hum a*d*allu ol*a*-ika humu algh*a*filoona

7:179. And certainly, We have grown for Hell many of the jinn and the human beings; they have minds with which they do not understand, and they have eyes with which they do not see, and they have ears with which they do not hear. They are like cattle – nay, they are worse in going astray. They are the ones grievously unaware of their destiny.

وَلِلَّهِ ٱلْأَسْمَآءُ ٱلْحُسْنَىٰ فَٱدْعُوهُ بِهَا ۖ وَذَرُوا۟ ٱلَّذِينَ يُلْحِدُونَ فِىٓ أَسْمَٰٓئِهِۦ ۚ سَيُجْزَوْنَ مَا كَانُوا۟ يَعْمَلُونَ ﴿١٨٠﴾

180. Walill*a*hi al-asm*a*o al*h*usn*a* fa*o*dAA*oo*hu bih*a* wa*th*aroo alla*th*eena yul*h*idoona fee asm*a*-ihi sayujzawna m*a* k*a*noo yaAAmaloon**a**

7:180. And Allah has the best of names, for you to call on Him wherewith. And keep away from those who violate the sanctity of His names. They shall be punished for what they did.

وَمِمَّنْ خَلَقْنَآ أُمَّةٌ يَهْدُونَ بِٱلْحَقِّ وَبِهِۦ يَعْدِلُونَ ﴿١٨١﴾

181. Wamimman khalaqn*a* ommatun yahdoona bial*h*aqqi wabihi yaAAdiloon**a**

7:181. And of those whom We have created there are people who guide with the truth and judge therewith.

وَٱلَّذِينَ كَذَّبُواْ بِـَٔايَـٰتِنَا سَنَسْتَدْرِجُهُم مِّنْ حَيْثُ لَا يَعْلَمُونَ ﴿١٨٢﴾

182. Waalla*th*eena ka*thth*aboo bi-*ay*ati*n*a sanastadrijuhum min *h*aythu l*a* yaAAamoona

---

7:182. And as to those who reject Our Verses/signs, We rein them in, by degrees, from whence they know not.

وَأُمْلِى لَهُمْ إِنَّ كَيْدِى مَتِينٌ ﴿١٨٣﴾

183. Waomlee lahum inna kaydee mateen**un**

7:183. And I (Allah) give them a long rope. Indeed, My plan is fool-proof.

أَوَلَمْ يَتَفَكَّرُواْ مَا بِصَاحِبِهِم مِّن جِنَّةٍ إِنْ هُوَ إِلَّا نَذِيرٌ مُّبِينٌ ﴿١٨٤﴾

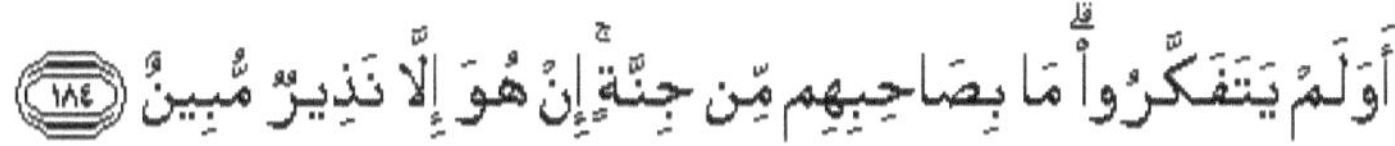

184. Awa lam yatafakkaroo m*a* bi*sah*ibihim min jinnatin in huwa ill*a* na*th*eerun mubeen**un**

7:184. Do they not reflect that their companion[73] is not unsound in mind? He is only a plain warner!

---

73. Prophet Muhammad (peace be upon him).

أَوَلَمْ يَنظُرُواْ فِى مَلَكُوتِ ٱلسَّمَـٰوَٰتِ وَٱلْأَرْضِ وَمَا خَلَقَ ٱللَّـهُ

مِن شَىْءٍ وَأَنْ عَسَىٰٓ أَن يَكُونَ قَدِ ٱقْتَرَبَ أَجَلُهُمْ فَبِأَىِّ حَدِيثٍ

بَعْدَهُۥ يُؤْمِنُونَ ﴿١٨٥﴾

185. Awalam yan*th*uroo fee malakooti alssam*a*w*a*ti waal-ar*d*i wam*a* khalaqa All*a*hu min shay-in waan AAas*a* an yakoona qadi iqtaraba ajaluhum fabi-ayyi *h*adeethin baAAdahu yu/minoona

---

7:185. Do they not ponder over the kingdom of the heavens and the earth and whatever things Allah has created, and over the likelihood of their own death being near? What *hadeeth*[74] would they then believe in after this?

---

74. This Arabic word has been used in the Qur'aan variously in the meanings of (i) story, (ii) discourse, (iii) speech, or (iv) the Qur'aan itself. In the context of the preceding sentence, in this very Verse, the word here could connote the broad statement as under:

> The orderly behaviour of the entire universe gives enough proof of the existence of a super-intelligent Being faultlessly governing it. When that Being can so control such a gigantic thing, He can obviously do the far less complex task of managing and controlling, inter alia, every human life. It is this Being – Whom we call Allah – that is guiding mankind in the proper conduct of their lives, through this Qur'aan. Every human being should grasp this Reality before it is too late. No one knows when death would come. It may be just around the corner.

But the word *hadeeth* came to acquire another meaning after the completion of the revelation of the Qur'aan, and the departure of the Prophet from this world. Centuries after the death of the Prophet, his orally reported sayings, and those of his companions, came to be recorded in writing. And these recorded sayings came to be known as *ahaadeeth* (plural of *hadeeth*). Allah Almighty knows all about the future. And at the time of the revelation of this Verse, He was aware of this future meaning of the term *hadeeth*. He (Allah), in that sense, is disapprovingly hinting here at future generations of the Muslim *Ummah* believing in such man-influenced, error-prone *ahaadeeth* in preference to the well-explained teachings in the Qur'aan, which can also be taken as referred to by the pronoun *hu* in *baAAdahu* of the Arabic text. The Verse is thus telling us categorically that the Qur'aan is the best *hadeeth*; one need not go after other *ahaadeeth*.

مَـن يُضْلِلِ ٱللَّـهُ فَلَا هَادِىَ لَـهُۥ وَيَـذَرُهُمْ فِـى طُغْيَـٰنِهِـمْ يَعْمَهُـونَ

186. Man yu*d*lili All*a*hu fal*a* h*a*diya lahu waya*th*aruhum fee *t*ughy*a*nihim yaAAmahoon*a*

7:186. Whomsoever Allah sends astray, there is no guide for him. And He leaves them alone wandering blindly in their inordinateness.

يَسْـَٔلُونَكَ عَـنِ ٱلسَّـاعَةِ أَيَّـانَ مُرْسَـٰهَا قُلْ إِنَّمَا عِلْمُهَا عِنـدَ رَبِّـى لَا يُجَلِّيهَا لِوَقْتِهَآ إِلَّا هُوَ ثَقُلَتْ فِى ٱلسَّمَـٰوَٰتِ وَٱلْأَرْضِ لَا تَأْتِيكُمْ إِلَّا بَغْتَـةً يَسْـَٔلُونَكَ كَأَنَّكَ حَـفِىٌّ عَنْهَا قُلْ إِنَّمَا عِلْمُهَا عِنـدَ ٱللَّـهِ وَلَـٰكِنَّ أَكْثَرَ ٱلنَّاسِ لَا يَعْلَمُـونَ ۝

187. Yas-aloonaka AAani alssaAAati ayy*a*na murs*a*ha qul innam*a* AAilmuh*a* AAinda rabbee l*a* yujalleeh*a* liwaqtih*a* ill*a* huwa thaqulat fee alssam*a*w*a*ti w*a*al-ar*d*i l*a* ta/teekum ill*a* baghtatan yas-aloonaka kaannaka *h*afiyyun AAanh*a* qul innam*a* AAilmuh*a* AAinda All*a*hi wal*a*kinna akthara alnn*a*si l*a* yaAAlamoon*a*

7:187. They ask you [Prophet] about the Hour (the time when the present world will end and the Hereafter begin), "When is it coming?" Say, "The knowledge of it is only with my Lord. None but He shall manifest it at its time; it will be a hard time in the heavens and the earth; it will not come on you but of a sudden." They ask you as if you were well-informed about it. Say, "Its knowledge is only with Allah, but most people know not."

قُل لَّآ أَمۡلِكُ لِنَفۡسِى نَفۡعًا وَلَا ضَرًّا إِلَّا مَا شَآءَ ٱللَّهُ وَلَوۡ كُنتُ أَعۡلَمُ ٱلۡغَيۡبَ لَٱسۡتَكۡثَرۡتُ مِنَ ٱلۡخَيۡرِ وَمَا مَسَّنِىَ ٱلسُّوٓءُ إِنۡ أَنَا۠ إِلَّا نَذِيرٌ وَبَشِيرٌ لِّقَوۡمٍ يُؤۡمِنُونَ ۝١٨٨

188. Qul la amliku linafsee nafAAan wala darran illa ma shaa Allahu walaw kuntu aAAlamu alghayba laistakthartu mina alkhayri wama massaniya alssoo-o in ana illa natheerun wabasheerun liqawmin yu/minoona

---

7:188. Say, "I cannot have any benefit or harm for my own self except as Allah pleases. And had I known the unseen I would have had much of good and no evil would have touched me. I am but a warner and the giver of good news to people who believe.

۞ هُوَ ٱلَّذِى خَلَقَكُم مِّن نَّفۡسٍ وَٰحِدَةٍ وَجَعَلَ مِنۡهَا زَوۡجَهَا لِيَسۡكُنَ إِلَيۡهَا فَلَمَّا تَغَشَّىٰهَا حَمَلَتۡ حَمۡلًا خَفِيفًا فَمَرَّتۡ بِهِۦ فَلَمَّآ أَثۡقَلَت دَّعَوَا ٱللَّهَ رَبَّهُمَا لَئِنۡ ءَاتَيۡتَنَا صَٰلِحًا لَّنَكُونَنَّ مِنَ ٱلشَّٰكِرِينَ ۝١٨٩

189. Huwa allathee khalaqakum min nafsin wahidatin wajaAAala minha zawjaha liyaskuna ilayha falamma taghashshaha hamalat hamlan khafeefan famarrat bihi falamma athqalat daAAawa Allaha rabbahuma la-in ataytana salihan lanakoonanna mina alshshakireena

---

7:189. He it is Who created you from a single being, and He made there from his mate, that he might have the pleasure of living with her. So when he mounts her she bears a light burden, and she moves about with it. And when it grows heavy, they both call upon Allah, their Lord, "If You give us a good child, we shall certainly be of those who are grateful."

فَلَمَّآ ءَاتَىٰهُمَا صَٰلِحًا جَعَلَا لَهُۥ شُرَكَآءَ فِيمَآ ءَاتَىٰهُمَا فَتَعَٰلَى ٱللَّهُ عَمَّا يُشْرِكُونَ ۝

190. Falamma atahuma salihan jaAAala lahu shurakaa feema atahuma fataAAala Allahu AAamma yushrikoona

7:190. But when He gives them a good child, they set up associates with Him in what He had given them. But high is Allah above what they associate with Him.

أَيُشْرِكُونَ مَا لَا يَخْلُقُ شَيْئًا وَهُمْ يُخْلَقُونَ ۝

191. Ayushrikoona ma la yakhluqu shay-an wahum yukhlaqoona

7:191. Do they associate with Allah those who do not create anything but are themselves created!?

وَلَا يَسْتَطِيعُونَ لَهُمْ نَصْرًا وَلَآ أَنفُسَهُمْ يَنصُرُونَ ۝

192. Wala yastateeAAoona lahum nasran wala anfusahum yansuroona

7:192. And they can muster no help, nor can they help themselves.

وَإِن تَدْعُوهُمْ إِلَى ٱلْهُدَىٰ لَا يَتَّبِعُوكُمْ سَوَآءٌ عَلَيْكُمْ أَدَعَوْتُمُوهُمْ أَمْ أَنتُمْ صَامِتُونَ ۝

193. Wa-in tadAAoohum il*a* alhud*a* l*a* yattabiAAookum saw*a*on AAalaykum adaAAawtumoohum am antum *s*amitoon*a*

7:193. And if you invite them to guidance, they follow you not. It is immaterial whether you invite them or not.

إِنَّ ٱلَّذِينَ تَدْعُونَ مِن دُونِ ٱللَّهِ عِبَادٌ أَمْثَالُكُمْ فَٱدْعُوهُمْ فَلْيَسْتَجِيبُواْ لَكُمْ إِن كُنتُمْ صَادِقِينَ ۝

194. Inna alla*th*eena tadAAoona min dooni All*a*hi AAib*a*dun amth*a*lukum faodAAoohum falyastajeeboo lakum in kuntum *s*adiqeen*a*

7:194. All those whom you pray to, besides Allah, are under Allah's absolute control just like you are. Call on them then and let them answer you if you are right.

أَلَهُمْ أَرْجُلٌ يَمْشُونَ بِهَآ أَمْ لَهُمْ أَيْدٍ يَبْطِشُونَ بِهَآ أَمْ لَهُمْ أَعْيُنٌ يُبْصِرُونَ بِهَآ أَمْ لَهُمْ ءَاذَانٌ يَسْمَعُونَ بِهَا قُلِ ٱدْعُواْ شُرَكَآءَكُمْ ثُمَّ كِيدُونِ فَلَا تُنظِرُونِ ۝

195. Alahum arjulun yamshoona bih*a* am lahum aydin yab*t*ishoona bih*a* am lahum aAAyunun yub*s*iroona bih*a* am lahum *ath*anun yasmaAAoona bih*a* quli odAAoo shurak*a*akum thumma keedooni fal*a* tun*th*irooni

7:195. Have they feet with which they walk, or have they hands with which they hold, or have they eyes with which they see, or have they ears with which they hear? Say, "Call those whom you worship besides Allah, then plot against me and give me no concession."

196. Inna waliyyiya Allahu allathee nazzala alkitaba wahuwa yatawalla alssaliheena

7:196. Allah is indeed my *Wali*[75], Who has sent down the Book. And He is close to the good, righteous people.

75. Refer <u>study note 2:154</u> **for a comprehensive Qur'aanic meaning of this Arabic term.**

197. Waallatheena tadAAoona min doonihi la yastateeAAoona nasrakum wala anfusahum yansuroona

7:197. And those, whom you pray to, besides Him, are not able to help you, nor can they help themselves!

وَإِن تَدْعُوهُمْ إِلَى ٱلْهُدَىٰ لَا يَسْمَعُواْ وَتَرَىٰهُمْ يَنظُرُونَ إِلَيْكَ وَهُمْ لَا يُبْصِرُونَ ۝

198. Wa-in tadAAoohum ila alhuda la yasmaAAoo watarahum yan*th*uroona ilayka wahum la yubsiroona

---

7:198. And if you invite them to the Guidance, they do not listen. And you see them looking towards you, yet they do not see.

خُذِ ٱلْعَفْوَ وَأْمُرْ بِٱلْعُرْفِ وَأَعْرِضْ عَنِ ٱلْجَـٰهِلِينَ ۝

199. Khu*th*i alAAafwa wa/mur bialAAurfi waaAAri*d* AAani alj*a*hileena

---

7:199. Show forgiveness and enjoin what is good and be indulgent towards the ignorant people.

وَإِمَّا يَنزَغَنَّكَ مِنَ ٱلشَّيْطَٰنِ نَزْغٌ فَٱسْتَعِذْ بِٱللَّهِ إِنَّهُ سَمِيعٌ عَلِيمٌ ۝

200. Wa-imm*a* yanzaghannaka mina alshshay*ta*ni nazghun faistaAAi*th* biAll*a*hi innahu sameeAAun AAaleem*un*

7:200. And if a mischief from the Satan affects you, seek refuge in Allah. HE does indeed hear, know.

إِنَّ ٱلَّذِينَ ٱتَّقَوْاْ إِذَا مَسَّهُمْ طَٰٓئِفٌ مِّنَ ٱلشَّيْطَٰنِ تَذَكَّرُواْ فَإِذَا هُم مُّبْصِرُونَ ﴿٢٠١﴾

201. Inna alla*thee*na ittaqaw i*tha* massahum *ta*-ifun mina alshshay*ta*ni ta*th*akkaroo fa-i*tha* hum mub*s*iroon**a**

7:201. Those indeed that fear Allah remember Him much when a visitation from the Satan affects them. Then lo! They see[76].

---

76. They see that the visitation is from the Satan trying to mislead them.

وَإِخْوَٰنُهُمْ يَمُدُّونَهُمْ فِى ٱلْغَىِّ ثُمَّ لَا يُقْصِرُونَ ﴿٢٠٢﴾

202. Wa-ikhw*a*nuhum yamuddoonahum fee alghayyi thumma l*a* yuq*s*iroon**a**

7:202. And their brethren relentlessly help them in wrong-doing!

وَإِذَا لَمْ تَأْتِهِم بِـَٔايَةٍ قَالُواْ لَوْلَا ٱجْتَبَيْتَهَا قُلْ إِنَّمَآ أَتَّبِعُ مَا يُوحَىٰ إِلَىَّ مِن رَّبِّى هَٰذَا بَصَآئِرُ مِن رَّبِّكُمْ وَهُدًى وَرَحْمَةٌ لِّقَوْمٍ يُؤْمِنُونَ ﴿٢٠٣﴾

203. Wa-i*tha* lam ta/tihim bi-*a*yatin q*a*loo lawl*a* ijtabaytah*a* qul innam*a* attabiAAu m*a* yoo*ha* ilayya min rabbee *ha*tha ba*sa*-iru min rabbikum wahudan wara*h*matun liqawmin yu/minoon**a**

7:203. And when you do not bring them a miracle/sign[77], they say, "Why have you not brought it?" Say, "I follow only that which is revealed to me from my Lord. These[78] are clear insights from your Lord and guidance and a mercy for a people who believe."

---

77. Refer study notes 2:264 to 2:268 on <u>Verse 2:164</u> **in this context.**

78. The Qur'aanic Verses.

وَإِذَا قُرِئَ ٱلْقُرْءَانُ فَٱسْتَمِعُوا۟ لَهُۥ وَأَنصِتُوا۟ لَعَلَّكُمْ تُرْحَمُونَ ۝

204. Wa-itha quri-a alqur-anu faistamiAAoo lahu waansitoo laAAallakum turhamoona

---

7:204. And when the Qur'aan is recited, then listen to it and remain silent, so that you are showered with mercy.[79]

---

79. Most Muslims today do not take care to abide by this divine directive. No wonder then that Allah Almighty has withdrawn His hand of mercy from them.

وَٱذْكُر رَّبَّكَ فِى نَفْسِكَ تَضَرُّعًا وَخِيفَةً وَدُونَ ٱلْجَهْرِ مِنَ ٱلْقَوْلِ بِٱلْغُدُوِّ وَٱلْءَاصَالِ وَلَا تَكُن مِّنَ ٱلْغَـٰفِلِينَ ۝

205. Waothkur rabbaka fee nafsika tadarruAAan wakheefatan wadoona aljahri mina alqawli bialghuduwwi waal-asali wala takun mina alghafileena

---

7:205. And remember your Lord within yourself, humbly and in fear – and in a voice that is not loud – morning and evening and be not of those who are heedless.

إِنَّ ٱلَّذِينَ عِندَ رَبِّكَ لَا يَسْتَكْبِرُونَ عَنْ عِبَادَتِهِۦ وَيُسَبِّحُونَهُۥ وَلَهُۥ يَسْجُدُونَ ۩ ٢٠٦

206. Inna alla*th*eena AAinda rabbika l*a* yastakbiroona AAan AAib*a*datihi wayusabbi*h*oonahu walahu yasjudoon*a*

7:206. Indeed, those with your Lord are not too proud to worship Him, and they declare His glory and to Him they prostrate.

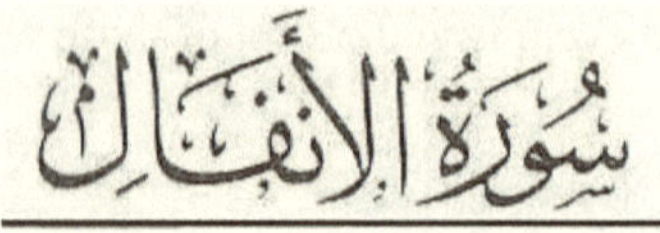

Chapter 8: Al-Anfal (The Spoils of War)

In the Name of Allah, the Gracious, the Merciful

بِسۡمِ اللهِ الرَّحۡمَٰنِ الرَّحِيمِ

يَسۡـَٔلُونَكَ عَنِ ٱلۡأَنفَالِ قُلِ ٱلۡأَنفَالُ لِلَّهِ وَٱلرَّسُولِ فَٱتَّقُواْ ٱللَّهَ وَأَصۡلِحُواْ ذَاتَ بَيۡنِكُمۡ وَأَطِيعُواْ ٱللَّهَ وَرَسُولَهُۥٓ إِن كُنتُم مُّؤۡمِنِينَ ۝

1. Yas-aloonaka AAani al-anf*a*li quli al-anf*a*lu lill*a*hi waalrrasooli fa*i*ttaqoo All*a*ha waa*s*li*h*oo *tha*ta baynikum waa*tee*AAoo All*a*ha warasoolahu in kuntum mu/mineena

---

8:1. They ask you about the spoils[1] of war. Say, "The spoils are for Allah and the Messenger.[2] So fear Allah and improve mutual relationships among yourselves. And obey Allah and His Messenger[3] if you do believe!"

---

1. Things captured from a vanquished enemy.

2. The spoils, in other words in modern terms, belong to the State whose army has gained victory. These are then utilized for common welfare measures for its people.

3. Refer study notes 3:35 to 3:37 on Verse 3:31 on what obeying the Messenger now means.

إِنَّمَا ٱلۡمُؤۡمِنُونَ ٱلَّذِينَ إِذَا ذُكِرَ ٱللَّهُ وَجِلَتۡ قُلُوبُهُمۡ وَإِذَا تُلِيَتۡ عَلَيۡهِمۡ ءَايَٰتُهُۥ زَادَتۡهُمۡ إِيمَٰنًا وَعَلَىٰ رَبِّهِمۡ يَتَوَكَّلُونَ ۝

2. Innam*a* almu/minoona alla*thee*na i*tha thu*kira All*a*hu wajilat quloobuhum wa-i*tha* tuliyat AAalayhim *a*y*a*tuhu *za*dat-hum eem*a*nan waAAal*a* rabbihim yatawakkaloona

8:2. The believers are only those whose hearts are moved with fear when Allah is mentioned. And when His Verses/signs are recited to them, it (recitation) strengthens them in faith. And in their Lord do they trust!

$$ \text{اَلَّـذِينَ يُقِيمُونَ ٱلصَّلَوٰةَ وَمِمَّا رَزَقْنَٰهُمْ يُنفِقُونَ ۝} $$

3. Alla*th*eena yuqeemoona al*s*sal*a*ta wamimm*a* razaqn*a*hum yunfiqoon**a**

8:3. Those who establish proper prayer[4] and spend[5] out of what We have given them.

4. Refer study notes 2:4 and 2:108 for the Qur'aanic meaning of the Arabic term used for 'establish proper prayer'.

5. Refer study note 2:385 on Verse 2:215 to know what is meant by 'spending' in Qur'aanic terms.

$$ \text{أُوْلَـٰٓئِكَ هُمُ ٱلْمُؤْمِنُونَ حَقًّا لَّهُمْ دَرَجَٰتٌ عِندَ رَبِّهِمْ وَمَغْفِرَةٌ} $$
$$ \text{وَرِزْقٌ كَرِيمٌ ۝} $$

4. Ol*a*-ika humu almu/minoona *h*aqqan lahum daraj*a*tun AAinda rabbihim wamaghfiratun warizqun kareem**un**

8:4. These are the real believers. For them are high grades from their Lord, and forgiveness, and good wholesome provisions.

كَمَآ أَخْرَجَكَ رَبُّكَ مِنْ بَيْتِكَ بِالْحَقِّ وَإِنَّ فَرِيقًا مِّنَ الْمُؤْمِنِينَ لَكَٰرِهُونَ ۞

5. Kama akhrajaka rabbuka min baytika bial*h*aqqi wa-inna fareeqan mina almu/mineena lak*a*rihoona

---

8:5. Likewise, in truth, did your Lord cause you to go forth from your house.[6] And indeed a section of the believers were against it.

---

6. As succeeding Verses of this Chapter would reveal, the Messenger (peace be upon him) had then set forth on a mission of armed conflict (the first one) with the non-believers.

يُجَٰدِلُونَكَ فِى الْحَقِّ بَعْدَ مَا تَبَيَّنَ كَأَنَّمَا يُسَاقُونَ إِلَى الْمَوْتِ وَهُمْ يَنظُرُونَ ۞

6. Yuj*a*diloonaka fee al*h*aqqi baAAda m*a* tabayyana kaannam*a* yus*a*qoona il*a* almawti wahum yan*th*uroona

---

8:6. They disputed[7] with you the truth after what had become clear, as if they were being driven, with their eyes wide open, to death!

---

7. When it became clear that they were going into a war, a section of the believers started questioning the advisibility of fighting an enemy that was superior in number and equipment. They were afraid they were going to meet certain death.

وَإِذْ يَعِدُكُمُ ٱللَّهُ إِحْدَى ٱلطَّآئِفَتَيْنِ أَنَّهَا لَكُمْ وَتَوَدُّونَ أَنَّ غَيْرَ ذَاتِ ٱلشَّوْكَةِ تَكُونُ لَكُمْ وَيُرِيدُ ٱللَّهُ أَن يُحِقَّ ٱلْحَقَّ بِكَلِمَٰتِهِۦ وَيَقْطَعَ دَابِرَ ٱلْكَٰفِرِينَ ۝

7. Wa-i*th* yaAAidukumu All*a*hu i*h*da al*tta*-ifatayni annah*a* lakum watawaddoona anna ghayra *tha*ti alshshawkati takoonu lakum wayureedu All*a*hu an yu*h*iqqa al*h*aqqa bikalim*a*tihi wayaq*ta*AAa d*a*bira alk*a*fireen*a*

8:7. And when Allah promised you that one of the two enemy groups shall be yours, and you preferred that the one not armed should he yours, Allah desired to make manifest the truth of His words and to cut off the root of those who suppress the Truth.[8]

---

8. Obviously, the believers could not avail of their easier option and had to face the tougher option of fighting the well-armed enemy group. Man proposes, but Allah disposes. HE wished that the well-armed group be defeated so that the vital strength of the suppressors of Truth is weakened.

لِيُحِقَّ ٱلْحَقَّ وَيُبْطِلَ ٱلْبَٰطِلَ وَلَوْ كَرِهَ ٱلْمُجْرِمُونَ ۝

8. Liyu*h*iqqa al*h*aqqa wayub*t*ila alb*at*ila walaw kariha almujrimoon*a*

8:8. That He may establish the truth and destroy the falsehood, the wrong-doers' dislike notwithstanding!

إِذْ تَسْتَغِيثُونَ رَبَّكُمْ فَٱسْتَجَابَ لَكُمْ أَنِّى مُمِدُّكُم بِأَلْفٍ مِّنَ ٱلْمَلَٰٓئِكَةِ مُرْدِفِينَ ۝

9. I*th* tastagheethoona rabbakum fa*i*staj*a*ba lakum annee mumiddukum bi-alfin mina almal*a*-ikati murdifeena

8:9. As you sought aid from your Lord, so He answered you, "I will assist you with waves after waves of a thousand of the angels."

وَمَا جَعَلَهُ ٱللَّهُ إِلَّا بُشْرَىٰ وَلِتَطْمَئِنَّ بِهِ ۦ قُلُوبُكُمْ وَمَا ٱلنَّصْرُ إِلَّا مِنْ عِندِ ٱللَّهِ إِنَّ ٱللَّهَ عَزِيزٌ حَكِيمٌ ۝

10. Wam*a* jaAAalahu All*a*hu ill*a* bushr*a* walita*t*ma-inna bihi quloobukum wam*a* a*l*na*s*ru ill*a* min AAindi All*a*hi inna All*a*ha AAazeezun *h*akeemun

8:10. And Allah did not make it[9] but as good news, so that your hearts might be at peace thereby. And there is no help except from Allah. Allah is indeed Omnipotent, Wise!

9. Helping the believers with an army of angels.

إِذْ يُغَشِّيكُمُ ٱلنُّعَاسَ أَمَنَةً مِّنْهُ وَيُنَزِّلُ عَلَيْكُم مِّنَ ٱلسَّمَآءِ مَآءً لِّيُطَهِّرَكُم بِهِ ۦ وَيُذْهِبَ عَنكُمْ رِجْزَ ٱلشَّيْطَـٰنِ وَلِيَرْبِطَ عَلَىٰ قُلُوبِكُمْ وَيُثَبِّتَ بِهِ ٱلْأَقْدَامَ ۝

11. I*th* yughashsheekumu a*l*nuAA*a*sa amanatan minhu wayunazzilu AAalaykum mina a*l*sama-i m*a*an liyu*t*ahhirakum bihi wayu*th*hiba AAankum rijza a*l*shshay*t*ani waliyarbi*t*a AAal*a* quloobikum wayuthabbita bihi al-aqd*a*ma

8:11. When[10] He caused you to be overcome with drowsiness as a means of mental peace from Him and sent down upon you water from the cloud that He might thereby purify you. And He rid you of satanic pollution that He might fortify your hearts and might steady your footsteps thereby.

10. I.e., before the battle.

إِذْ يُوحِى رَبُّكَ إِلَى ٱلْمَلَـٰٓئِكَةِ أَنِّى مَعَكُمْ فَثَبِّتُوا۟ ٱلَّذِينَ ءَامَنُوا۟ سَأُلْقِى فِى قُلُوبِ ٱلَّذِينَ كَفَرُوا۟ ٱلرُّعْبَ فَٱضْرِبُوا۟ فَوْقَ ٱلْأَعْنَاقِ وَٱضْرِبُوا۟ مِنْهُمْ كُلَّ بَنَانٍ ۝

12. I*th* yoohee rabbuka ila almala-ikati annee maAAakum fathabbitoo alla*th*eena *a*manoo saolqee fee quloobi alla*th*eena kafaroo alrruAAba faidriboo fawqa al-aAAnaqi waidriboo minhum kulla ban*a*n**in**

8:12. When your Lord revealed to the angels, "I am with you, so make the believers firm and steady. I will cast terror into the hearts of those who suppress the Truth. Then hit on their necks and cut all fingers off them[11]."

11. Cutting the fingers off effectively makes a person unfit for war.

ذَٰلِكَ بِأَنَّهُمْ شَآقُّوا۟ ٱللَّهَ وَرَسُولَهُۥ وَمَن يُشَاقِقِ ٱللَّهَ وَرَسُولَهُۥ فَإِنَّ ٱللَّهَ شَدِيدُ ٱلْعِقَابِ ۝

13. *Th*alika bi-annahum shaqqoo All*a*ha warasoolahu waman yushaqiqi All*a*ha warasoolahu fa-inna All*a*ha shadeedu alAAiq*a*b**i**

8:13. That is because they opposed Allah and His Messenger. And whoever opposes Allah and His Messenger, then, indeed, Allah is severe in punishment.

ذَٰلِكُمْ فَذُوقُوهُ وَأَنَّ لِلْكَٰفِرِينَ عَذَابَ ٱلنَّارِ ۝

14. *Tha*likum fa*th*ooqoohu waanna lilk*a*fireena AA*ath*aba alnn*a*ri

8:14. "That it is, so taste it; and punishment for the suppressors of the Truth is the Fire!"

يَٰٓأَيُّهَا ٱلَّذِينَ ءَامَنُوٓا۟ إِذَا لَقِيتُمُ ٱلَّذِينَ كَفَرُوا۟ زَحْفًا فَلَا تُوَلُّوهُمُ ٱلْأَدْبَارَ

15. Y*a* ayyuh*a* alla*th*eena *a*manoo i*th*a laqeetumu alla*th*eena kafaroo za*h*fan fal*a* tuwalloohumu al-adb*a*ra

8:15. O you who believe! When you meet the suppressors of the Truth in war, turn not your backs to them.

وَمَن يُوَلِّهِمْ يَوْمَئِذٍ دُبُرَهُ إِلَّا مُتَحَرِّفًا لِّقِتَالٍ أَوْ مُتَحَيِّزًا إِلَىٰ فِئَةٍ فَقَدْ بَآءَ بِغَضَبٍ مِّنَ ٱللَّهِ وَمَأْوَىٰهُ جَهَنَّمُ وَبِئْسَ ٱلْمَصِيرُ ۝

16. Waman yuwallihim yawma-i*th*in duburahu illa muta*h*arrifan liqit*a*lin aw muta*h*ayyizan il*a* fi-atin faqad b*a*a bigha*d*abin mina All*a*hi wama/w*a*hu jahannamu wabi/sa alma*s*eeru

8:16. And whoever turns his back to them on that day – unless it is only to turn back to fighting or to withdraw to one's own company – then he does indeed incur Allah's wrath, and his abode is Hell. And it is an evil destination!

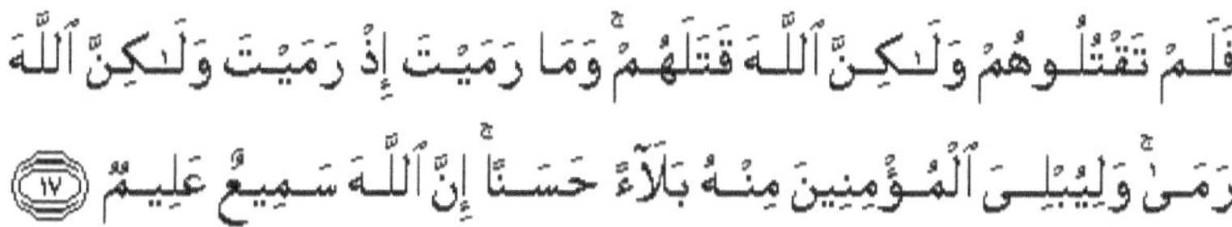

17. Falam taqtuloohum wal*a*kinna All*a*ha qatalahum wam*a* ramayta i*th* ramayta wal*a*kinna All*a*ha rama waliyubliya almu/mineena minhu bal*a*an *h*asanan inna All*a*ha sameeAAun AAaleem*u*n

8:17. Then it was not you who killed them, but it was Allah Who killed them. And it was not you who threw when you threw, but it was Allah Who threw. And He did it to test the believers with a good test from Himself.[12] Indeed, Allah listens, knows.

12. The battleground is the scenario. Apparently, it was the believers who were throwing arrows/spears at the enemy men and killing them. But the Qur'aan insists here that it was Allah Who did that. And herein lay the acid test for the believers. Did they give credit to themselves or did they give the credit to Allah Almighty and thank Him for giving them thus the upperhand? The acid test for all believers is the same. Whatever we can do, it is because Allah facilitates its doing. Without His tacit but conscious consent, nothing can happen. We should believe in this. We are not believers otherwise.

18. *Th*alikum waanna All*a*ha moohinu kaydi alk*a*fireena

8:18. Thus it is that Allah undermines the scheme of the suppressors of the Truth.

إِن تَسْتَفْتِحُواْ فَقَدْ جَآءَكُمُ ٱلْفَتْحُ وَإِن تَنتَهُواْ فَهُوَ خَيْرٌ لَّكُمْ وَإِن

تَعُودُواْ نَعُدْ وَلَن تُغْنِىَ عَنكُمْ فِئَتُكُمْ شَيْئًا وَلَوْ كَثُرَتْ وَأَنَّ ٱللَّهَ مَعَ

ٱلْمُؤْمِنِينَ ۝

19. In tastaftihoo faqad jaakumu alfathu wa-in tantahoo fahuwa khayrun lakum wa-in taAAoodoo naAAud walan tughniya AAankum fi-atukum shay-an walaw kathurat waanna Allaha maAAa almu/mineena

---

8:19. If you had sought a decisive judgment, it certainly has then come to you in the form of victory to the believers. And if you desist from waging a war against them henceforth, then that will be good for you. And if you return, We return! And your forces, though numerous, shall avail you nothing. And you should know that Allah is with the believers.[13]

---

13. Ostensibly, this is a virtual address from the angels to the defeated army of the non-believers.

يَٰٓأَيُّهَا ٱلَّذِينَ ءَامَنُوٓاْ أَطِيعُواْ ٱللَّهَ وَرَسُولَهُۥ وَلَا تَوَلَّوْاْ عَنْهُ وَأَنتُمْ

تَسْمَعُونَ ۝

20. Ya ayyuha allatheena amanoo ateeAAoo Allaha warasoolahu wala tawallaw AAanhu waantum tasmaAAoona

---

8:20. O you who believe! Obey Allah and His Messenger and turn not away while listening to him.

وَلَا تَكُونُوا۟ كَٱلَّذِينَ قَالُوا۟ سَمِعْنَا وَهُمْ لَا يَسْمَعُونَ ﴿٢١﴾

21. Wala takoonoo kaalla*th*eena *q*aloo samiAAn*a* wahum *la* yasmaAAoona

8:21. And be not like those who said, 'We hear', and they did not hear.

۞ إِنَّ شَرَّ ٱلدَّوَآبِّ عِندَ ٱللَّهِ ٱلصُّمُّ ٱلْبُكْمُ ٱلَّذِينَ لَا يَعْقِلُونَ ﴿٢٢﴾

22. Inna sharra alddaw*a*bbi AAinda All*a*hi al*ss*ummu albukmu alla*th*eena *la* yaAAqiloona

8:22. Indeed, the worst moving creatures, in Allah's sight, are the deaf and dumb that understand not.[14]

14. For its mind to understand what the sound bytes float around in the air, a creature ought to have the hearing facility. It can't understand any oral advice given to it, otherwise. People who do possess the hearing facility, and yet take no heed to what they hear, are wasting their Allah-given hearing facility. They are no better than any deaf/dumb creature. Like those heedless people during the Prophet's time, an overwhelming majority of the people living in the world now, including most Muslims, are deaf and dumb to what they hear of the divine Message of the Qur'aan. Those who do understand the Qur'aan, and yet speak not about it to others, are also deaf and dumb in Allah's sight. They fail in their Allah-given duty to pass on to others what they have learnt from the Qur'aan. They act dumb.

وَلَوْ عَلِمَ ٱللَّهُ فِيهِمْ خَيْرًا لَّأَسْمَعَهُمْ وَلَوْ أَسْمَعَهُمْ لَتَوَلَّوا۟ وَّهُم مُّعْرِضُونَ

23. Walaw AAalima All*a*hu feehim khayran laasmaAAahum walaw asmaAAahum latawallaw wahum muAAri*d*oona

---

8:23. And if Allah had known any good in them He would have made them hear, and if He makes them hear they would turn away and contradict.

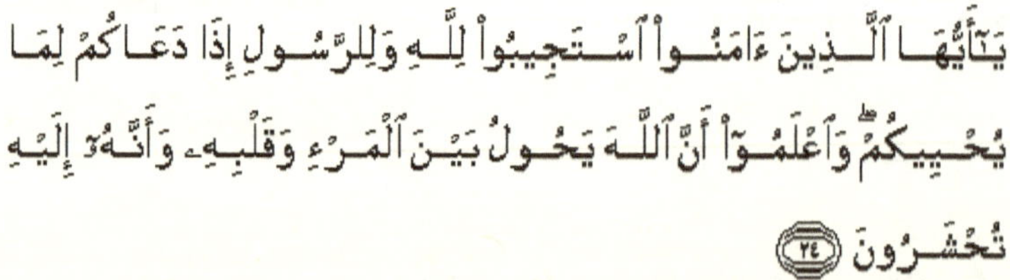

24. Y*a* ayyuh*a* alla*th*eena *a*manoo istajeeboo lill*a*hi walilrrasooli i*th*a daAA*a*kum lim*a* yu*h*yeekum waiAAlamoo anna All*a*ha ya*h*oolu bayna almar-i waqalbihi waannahu ilayhi tu*h*sharoona

---

8:24. O you who believe! Respond to Allah and His Messenger when he calls you to that for which Allah gives you life.[15] And know that Allah intervenes between man and his mind[16], and that to Him you shall be gathered.

---

15. **The Islamic outlook is that human life on earth is not the be-all and end-all of existence. This is only a testing ground for a better and higher life. Allah and His Messenger call us to the code of conduct in this life necessary for passing the test. And that code of conduct is laid down in the Qur'aan.**

16. **In other words, Allah Almighty tells us that He knows all the secrets of our minds.**

وَٱتَّقُواْ فِتْنَةً لَّا تُصِيبَنَّ ٱلَّذِينَ ظَلَمُواْ مِنكُمْ خَاصَّةً وَٱعْلَمُوٓاْ أَنَّ ٱللَّهَ شَدِيدُ ٱلْعِقَابِ ۝

25. Waittaqoo fitnatan *la* tuseebanna alla*th*eena *th*alamoo minkum kh*ass*atan waiAAlamoo anna All*a*ha shadeedu alAAiq*a*bi

---

8:25. And beware of a trial[17] which may not afflict particularly only those of you who do wrong. And know that Allah is severe in punishment.[18]

---

17. The long-drawn-out test of this earthly life is split into several trials and tribulations, and includes exemplary punishments, in this life itself, for <u>excessive</u> wrongs done. The punishments apart, trials and tribulations are, by their nature, not restricted to just the wrong-doers. It is to such a trial that this Verse refers to here.

18. This is a severe warning to those who do not respond to the call of Allah and His Messenger and neglect to follow the Qur'aan.

وَٱذْكُرُوٓاْ إِذْ أَنتُمْ قَلِيلٌ مُّسْتَضْعَفُونَ فِى ٱلْأَرْضِ تَخَافُونَ أَن يَتَخَطَّفَكُمُ ٱلنَّاسُ فَـَٔاوَىٰكُمْ وَأَيَّدَكُم بِنَصْرِهِۦ وَرَزَقَكُم مِّنَ ٱلطَّيِّبَٰتِ لَعَلَّكُمْ تَشْكُرُونَ ۝

26. Wao*th*kuroo i*th* antum qaleelun musta*dA*Aafoona fee al-ar*d*i takh*a*foona an yatakha*tt*afakumu a*lnna*su fa*a*w*a*kum waayyadakum bina*s*rihi warazaqakum mina al*tt*ayyib*a*ti laAAallakum tashkuroona

---

8:26. And remember when you were few, deemed weak in the land, fearing lest people might carry you off by force. Then He sheltered you, strengthened you with His aid and provided you with good things so that you feel grateful.

يَـٰٓأَيُّهَا ٱلَّذِينَ ءَامَنُوا۟ لَا تَخُونُوا۟ ٱللَّهَ وَٱلرَّسُولَ وَتَخُونُوٓا۟ أَمَـٰنَـٰتِكُمْ وَأَنتُمْ تَعْلَمُونَ ﴿٢٧﴾

27. Ya ayyuha alla*theena a*manoo la takhoonoo All*a*ha waalrrasoola watakhoonoo am*a*n*a*tikum waantum taAAlamoona

---

8:27. O you who believe! Betray not Allah and the Messenger, nor betray your trusts, knowingly.

وَٱعْلَمُوٓا۟ أَنَّمَآ أَمْوَٰلُكُمْ وَأَوْلَـٰدُكُمْ فِتْنَةٌ وَأَنَّ ٱللَّهَ عِندَهُۥٓ أَجْرٌ عَظِيمٌ ﴿٢٨﴾

28. WalAAlamoo annam*a* amw*a*lukum waawl*a*dukum fitnatun waanna All*a*ha AAindahu ajrun AAa*theemun*

8:28. And know that your property and your children are a trial, and that, with Allah, there is a magnificent reward! [19]

---

19. The reward is for those who deal with their property and children, and conduct all their other affairs, in accordance with the code laid down in the Qur'aan.

يَـٰٓأَيُّهَا ٱلَّذِينَ ءَامَنُوٓا۟ إِن تَتَّقُوا۟ ٱللَّهَ يَجْعَل لَّكُمْ فُرْقَانًا وَيُكَفِّرْ عَنكُمْ سَيِّـَٔاتِكُمْ وَيَغْفِرْ لَكُمْ وَٱللَّهُ ذُو ٱلْفَضْلِ ٱلْعَظِيمِ ﴿٢٩﴾

29. Ya ayyuha alla*theena a*manoo in tattaqoo All*a*ha yajAAal lakum furq*a*nan wayukaffir AAankum sayyi-*a*tikum wayaghfir lakum waAll*a*hu *thoo* alfa*d*li alAAa*theemi*

8:29. O you who believe! If you fear Allah, He will create in you an ability to distinguish between right and wrong and do away with your evil tendencies and forgive you. And Allah possesses great Grace.

وَإِذْ يَمْكُرُ بِكَ ٱلَّذِينَ كَفَرُوا لِيُثْبِتُوكَ أَوْ يَقْتُلُوكَ أَوْ يُخْرِجُوكَ وَيَمْكُرُونَ وَيَمْكُرُ ٱللَّهُ وَٱللَّهُ خَيْرُ ٱلْمَـٰكِرِينَ ﴿٣٠﴾

30. Wa-ith yamkuru bika allatheena kafaroo liyuthbitooka aw yaqtulooka aw yukhrijooka wayamkuroona wayamkuru Allahu waAllahu khayru almakireena

8:30. And those who suppressed the Truth plotted to confine you, kill you or drive you away. They plotted, and Allah plotted. And Allah is the best of plotters.

وَإِذَا تُتْلَىٰ عَلَيْهِمْ ءَايَـٰتُنَا قَالُوا قَدْ سَمِعْنَا لَوْ نَشَآءُ لَقُلْنَا مِثْلَ هَـٰذَآ إِنْ هَـٰذَآ إِلَّا أَسَـٰطِيرُ ٱلْأَوَّلِينَ ﴿٣١﴾

31. Wa-itha tutla AAalayhim ayatuna qaloo qad samiAAna law nashao laqulna mithla hatha in hatha illa asateeru al-awwaleena

8:31. And when Our Verses/signs are recited to them, they say, "We have heard. We certainly could, if we pleased, say things like that. These are nothing but fables of the ancients."

وَإِذْ قَالُواْ ٱللَّهُمَّ إِن كَانَ هَـٰذَا هُوَ ٱلْحَقَّ مِنْ عِندِكَ فَأَمْطِرْ عَلَيْنَا حِجَارَةً مِّنَ ٱلسَّمَاءِ أَوِ ٱئْتِنَا بِعَذَابٍ أَلِيمٍ ۝

32. Wa-ith qaloo allahumma in kana hatha huwa alhaqqa min AAindika faamtir AAalayna hijaratan mina alssama-i awi i/tina biAAathabin aleemin

---

8:32. And they said, "O Allah! If this is the Truth from You, then rain upon us stones from the sky or bring on us a painful punishment."

وَمَا كَانَ ٱللَّهُ لِيُعَذِّبَهُمْ وَأَنتَ فِيهِمْ وَمَا كَانَ ٱللَّهُ مُعَذِّبَهُمْ وَهُمْ يَسْتَغْفِرُونَ ۝

33. Wama kana Allahu liyuAAaththibahum waanta feehim wama kana Allahu muAAaththibahum wahum yastaghfiroona

---

8:33. But Allah was not going to punish them while you dwelt among them, nor was Allah going to punish them while they may yet ask for forgiveness.

وَمَا لَهُمْ أَلَّا يُعَذِّبَهُمُ ٱللَّهُ وَهُمْ يَصُدُّونَ عَنِ ٱلْمَسْجِدِ ٱلْحَرَامِ وَمَا كَانُواْ أَوْلِيَاءَهُ إِنْ أَوْلِيَاؤُهُ إِلَّا ٱلْمُتَّقُونَ وَلَـٰكِنَّ أَكْثَرَهُمْ لَا يَعْلَمُونَ ۝

34. Wama lahum alla yuAAaththibahumu Allahu wahum yasuddoona AAani almasjidi alharami wama kanoo awliyaahu in awliyaohu illa almuttaqoona walakinna aktharahum la yaAAlamoona

242

8:34. And why should Allah not punish them when they hinder people from the Sacred Place of Worship and when they cannot be its custodians. Its custodians can only be those who fear Allah, but most of them know not.

وَمَا كَانَ صَلَاتُهُمْ عِندَ ٱلْبَيْتِ إِلَّا مُكَآءً وَتَصْدِيَةً فَذُوقُواْ ٱلْعَذَابَ بِمَا كُنتُمْ تَكْفُرُونَ ﴿٣٥﴾

35. Wama kana salatuhum AAinda albayti illa mukaan watasdiyatan fathooqoo alAAathaba bima kuntum takfuroona

8:35. And their prayer before the House is nothing but whistling and clapping. Taste then the punishment; for, you have been suppressing the Truth.

إِنَّ ٱلَّذِينَ كَفَرُواْ يُنفِقُونَ أَمْوَٰلَهُمْ لِيَصُدُّواْ عَن سَبِيلِ ٱللَّهِ فَسَيُنفِقُونَهَا ثُمَّ تَكُونُ عَلَيْهِمْ حَسْرَةً ثُمَّ يُغْلَبُونَ وَٱلَّذِينَ كَفَرُوٓاْ إِلَىٰ جَهَنَّمَ يُحْشَرُونَ ﴿٣٦﴾

36. Inna allatheena kafaroo yunfiqoona amwalahum liyasuddoo AAan sabeeli Allahi fasayunfiqoonaha thumma takoonu AAalayhim hasratan thumma yughlaboona waallatheena kafaroo ila jahannama yuhsharoona

8:36. Indeed, those who suppress the Truth spend their wealth to hinder people from the Path of Allah. And they shall continue to spend it so, till they are overcome with intense regret thereupon. And those, who suppress the Truth, shall be driven together to Hell!

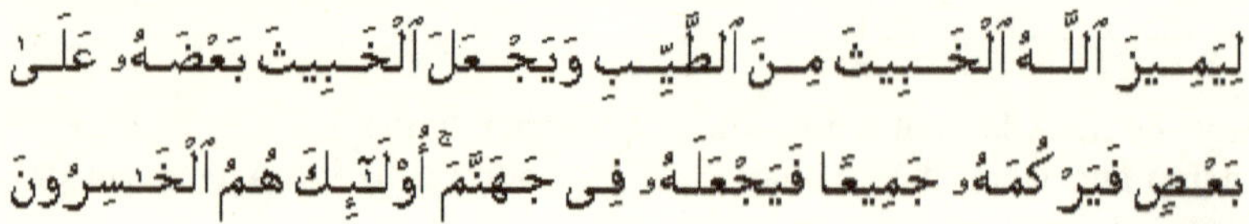

37. Liyameeza Allahu alkhabeetha mina alttayyibi wayajAAala alkhabeetha baAAdahu AAala baAAdin fayarkumahu jameeAAan fayajAAalahu fee jahannama ola-ika humu alkhasiroona

---

8:37. That Allah might separate the bad from the good, and pile up the bad, one upon another, and then cast them together into Hell. These are the ones that are doomed.

---

38. Qul lillatheena kafaroo in yantahoo yughfar lahum ma qad salafa wa-in yaAAoodoo faqad madat sunnatu al-awwaleena

---

8:38. Tell those who suppress the Truth that if they desist, that which is past shall be forgiven to them. And if they persist, what happened to the ancients is already on record.[20]

---

20. The Qur'aan is the record of what happened to recalcitrant people like those of Prophets Noah, Lot etc., Pharaoh's army, the _AAad_, the _Thamood_ et al of the ancient ages.

244

وَقَٰتِلُوهُمْ حَتَّىٰ لَا تَكُونَ فِتْنَةٌ وَيَكُونَ ٱلدِّينُ كُلُّهُۥ لِلَّهِ فَإِنِ ٱنتَهَوْا۟

فَإِنَّ ٱللَّهَ بِمَا يَعْمَلُونَ بَصِيرٌ ﴿٣٩﴾

39. Waqatiloohum *hatta la* takoona fitnatun wayakoona alddeenu kulluhu lill*a*hi fa-ini intahaw fa-inna All*a*ha bim*a* yaAAmaloona ba*s*eer**un**

8:39. And fight with them until revolt/insurrection stops, and the way of life is restored in its entirety to Allah. Then if they desist, Allah does indeed see what they do.[21]

21. In other words, it is for Allah to see whether an individual human being believes in Islam or not. Such personal beliefs are outside the domain of any human authority. The fighting, urged in this Verse, is not related, per se, to such beliefs. If it were so, the very purpose of Allah's creation of human beings would be defeated. Allah has created human beings to test them individually whether they come to believe in Him, in this earthly life, without seeing Him and willingly follow His directives. No coercion is applied. The human beings are expected to be just and peaceful in their relations with one another. That, broadly, is the divine scheme of things in this world. Anyone or any group of individuals, acting against this divine scheme, is raising the banner of revolt/insurrection. It is this revolt/insurrection that believers are urged to fight against, in this Verse.

وَإِن تَوَلَّوْا۟ فَٱعْلَمُوٓا۟ أَنَّ ٱللَّهَ مَوْلَىٰكُمْ نِعْمَ ٱلْمَوْلَىٰ وَنِعْمَ

ٱلنَّصِيرُ ﴿٤٠﴾

40. Wa-in tawallaw faiAAlamoo anna All*a*ha mawl*a*kum niAAma almawl*a* waniAAma alnna*s*eer**u**

8:40. And if they turn back, then know that Allah is your Patron – the best Patron and the best One to help.

وَٱعْلَمُوٓاْ أَنَّمَا غَنِمْتُم مِّن شَىْءٍ فَأَنَّ لِلَّهِ خُمُسَهُۥ وَلِلرَّسُولِ وَلِذِى ٱلْقُرْبَىٰ وَٱلْيَتَـٰمَىٰ وَٱلْمَسَـٰكِينِ وَٱبْنِ ٱلسَّبِيلِ إِن كُنتُمْ ءَامَنتُم بِٱللَّهِ وَمَآ أَنزَلْنَا عَلَىٰ عَبْدِنَا يَوْمَ ٱلْفُرْقَانِ يَوْمَ ٱلْتَقَى ٱلْجَمْعَانِ ۗ وَٱللَّهُ عَلَىٰ كُلِّ شَىْءٍ قَدِيرٌ

41. WalAAlamoo annama ghanimtum min shay-in faanna lillahi khumusahu walilrrasooli walithee alqurba waalyatama waalmasakeeni waibni alssabeeli in kuntum amantum biAllahi wama anzalna AAala AAabdina yawma alfurqani yawma iltaqa aljamAAani waAllahu AAala kulli shay-in qadeerun

---

8:41. And know that whatever booty you get, a fifth of it is for Allah and for the Messenger and for those near and dear, the orphans, the needy and the wayfarer, if you do believe in Allah and in that which We bestowed upon Our Slave on the day right was distinguished from wrong, the day on which the two armies met.[22] And Allah has power over all things.

---

22. This refers to the war with the non-believers described in Verses 5 to 19 of this Qur'aanic Chapter. While in Verse 1, the general rule for the disposal of the spoils of war is laid down, in this Verse, 4/5th of the spoils is apparently distributed among those believers, who actively faught in the battle, as reward for their bravery. 'Our Slave' here obviously refers to the Prophet (peace be upon him). He is referred to here, as in many other places in the Qur'aan, as a Slave because he obeyed every divine order. It is the duty of every slave to obey every order of his master. In that sense, the Prophet was the most obedient slave of the Almighty Creator. Believers must aspire to attain his level of absolute obedience to Allah. Human life in this world is nothing but a divine test to see whether this is done or not.

إِذْ أَنتُم بِٱلْعُدْوَةِ ٱلدُّنْيَا وَهُم بِٱلْعُدْوَةِ ٱلْقُصْوَىٰ وَٱلرَّكْبُ أَسْفَلَ مِنكُمْ وَلَوْ

تَوَاعَدتُّمْ لَٱخْتَلَفْتُمْ فِى ٱلْمِيعَادِ وَلَـٰكِن لِّيَقْضِىَ ٱللَّهُ أَمْرًا كَانَ مَفْعُولًا

لِّيَهْلِكَ مَنْ هَلَكَ عَنۢ بَيِّنَةٍ وَيَحْيَىٰ مَنْ حَىَّ عَنۢ بَيِّنَةٍ وَإِنَّ ٱللَّهَ لَسَمِيعٌ عَلِيمٌ

42. I*th* antum bialAAudwati aldduny*a* wahum bialAAudwati alqu*s*w*a* wa**a**lrrakbu asfala minkum walaw taw*a*AAadtum laikhtalaftum fee almeeAA*a*di wal*a*kin liyaq*d*iya All*a*hu amran k*a*na mafAAoolan liyahlika man halaka AAan bayyinatin waya*h*ya man *h*ayya AAan bayyinatin wa-inna All*a*ha lasameeAAun AAaleem**un**

8:42. The scenario was that you were on the nearer side, and they on the farther side, and the caravan was in the valley down below you. And even if you had planned to attack the caravan, you would certainly have missed the target, so that Allah might accomplish a matter which was to be accomplished – that he would manifestly perish that He wished to perish, and he would manifestly keep alive that He wished to keep alive.[23] And indeed Allah listens, knows.

---

23. Please see Verse 8:7 **and the study note 8 thereunder.**

إِذْ يُرِيكَهُمُ ٱللَّهُ فِى مَنَامِكَ قَلِيلًا وَلَوْ أَرَىٰكَهُمْ كَثِيرًا لَّفَشِلْتُمْ

وَلَتَنَٰزَعْتُمْ فِى ٱلْأَمْرِ وَلَـٰكِنَّ ٱللَّهَ سَلَّمَ إِنَّهُۥ عَلِيمٌۢ بِذَاتِ ٱلصُّدُورِ ٤٣

43. I*th* yureekahumu All*a*hu fee man*a*mika qaleelan walaw ar*a*kahum katheeran lafashiltum walatan*a*zaAAtum fee al-amri wal*a*kinna All*a*ha sallama innahu AAaleemun bi*th*ati al*ss*udoor**i**

8:43. Then Allah showed them to you in your dream as few. And if He had shown them to you as many, you would certainly have lost courage and you would have quarrelled over the matter. But Allah acted to set things right. He is indeed aware of what goes on in your minds.

وَإِذْ يُرِيكُمُوهُمْ إِذِ ٱلْتَقَيْتُمْ فِىٓ أَعْيُنِكُمْ قَلِيلًا وَيُقَلِّلُكُمْ فِىٓ أَعْيُنِهِمْ لِيَقْضِىَ ٱللَّهُ أَمْرًا كَانَ مَفْعُولًا وَإِلَى ٱللَّهِ تُرْجَعُ ٱلْأُمُورُ ﴿٤٤﴾

44. Wa-ith yureekumoohum ithi iltaqaytum fee aAAyunikum qaleelan wayuqallilukum fee aAAyunihim liyaqdiya Allahu amran kana mafAAoolan wa-ila Allahi turjaAAu al-omooru

8:44. And then He showed them to you, when you met, as few in your eyes and He made you to appear few in their eyes, in order that Allah brought a matter, which was to be done, to fruition. And to Allah are all matters returned.

يَٰٓأَيُّهَا ٱلَّذِينَ ءَامَنُوٓاْ إِذَا لَقِيتُمْ فِئَةً فَٱثْبُتُواْ وَٱذْكُرُواْ ٱللَّهَ كَثِيرًا لَّعَلَّكُمْ تُفْلِحُونَ ﴿٤٥﴾

45. Ya ayyuha allatheena amanoo itha laqeetum fi-atan faothbutoo waothkuroo Allaha katheeran laAAallakum tuflihoona

8:45. O you who believe! When you face an enemy in battle, be firm, and remember Allah a great deal, so that you may be successful.

وَأَطِيعُوا۟ ٱللَّهَ وَرَسُولَهُۥ وَلَا تَنَٰزَعُوا۟ فَتَفْشَلُوا۟ وَتَذْهَبَ رِيحُكُمْ ۖ وَٱصْبِرُوٓا۟ ۚ إِنَّ ٱللَّهَ مَعَ ٱلصَّٰبِرِينَ ﴿٤٦﴾

46. WaateeAAoo Allaha warasoolahu wala tanazaAAoo fatafshaloo watathhaba reehukum waisbiroo inna Allaha maAAa alssabireena

8:46. And obey Allah and His Messenger and do not quarrel; for, then, you will lose courage and your power will go away. And be patient! Indeed, Allah is with those who are patient.

وَلَا تَكُونُوا۟ كَٱلَّذِينَ خَرَجُوا۟ مِن دِيَٰرِهِم بَطَرًا وَرِئَآءَ ٱلنَّاسِ وَيَصُدُّونَ عَن سَبِيلِ ٱللَّهِ ۚ وَٱللَّهُ بِمَا يَعْمَلُونَ مُحِيطٌ ﴿٤٧﴾

47. Wala takoonoo kaallatheena kharajoo min diyarihim bataran wari-aa alnnasi wayasuddoona AAan sabeeli Allahi waAllahu bima yaAAmaloona muheetun

8:47. And be not like those who came out of their homes boasting and showing off, and who turned people away from the Path of Allah. And Allah surrounded all that they did.

وَإِذْ زَيَّنَ لَهُمُ ٱلشَّيْطَٰنُ أَعْمَٰلَهُمْ وَقَالَ لَا غَالِبَ لَكُمُ ٱلْيَوْمَ مِنَ ٱلنَّاسِ وَإِنِّى جَارٌ لَّكُمْ ۖ فَلَمَّا تَرَآءَتِ ٱلْفِئَتَانِ نَكَصَ عَلَىٰ عَقِبَيْهِ وَقَالَ إِنِّى بَرِىٓءٌ مِّنكُمْ إِنِّىٓ أَرَىٰ مَا لَا تَرَوْنَ إِنِّىٓ أَخَافُ ٱللَّهَ ۚ وَٱللَّهُ شَدِيدُ ٱلْعِقَابِ ﴿٤٨﴾

48. Wa-ith zayyana lahumu alshshaytanu aAAmalahum waqala la ghaliba lakumu alyawma mina alnnasi wa-innee jarun lakum falamma taraati alfi-atani nakasa AAala AAaqibayhi waqala innee baree-on minkum innee ara ma la tarawna innee akhafu Allaha waAllahu shadeedu alAAiqabi

8:48. And then the Satan made their deeds fair seeming to them, and said, "No man can overcome you this day, and indeed I am your supporter." But when the two armies confronted each other, he turned his back and said, "I do indeed bear no responsibility for you. I do indeed see what you do not see[24]. I do indeed fear Allah. And Allah is severe in giving punishment!"

24. Angels.

إِذْ يَقُولُ ٱلْمُنَٰفِقُونَ وَٱلَّذِينَ فِى قُلُوبِهِم مَّرَضٌ غَرَّ هَٰٓؤُلَآءِ دِينُهُمْ ۚ وَمَن يَتَوَكَّلْ عَلَى ٱللَّهِ فَإِنَّ ٱللَّهَ عَزِيزٌ حَكِيمٌ ۝

49. I*th* yaqoolu almun*a*fiqoona waalla*th*eena fee quloobihim mara*d*un gharra h*a*ola-i deenuhum waman yatawakkal AAal*a* All*a*hi fa-inna All*a*ha AAazeezun *h*akeem**un**

8:49. The hypocrites and those in whose hearts was a disease said, "Their religion has deceived them." And when anyone places his trust on Allah, then indeed Allah is Omnipotent, Wise.

وَلَوْ تَرَىٰٓ إِذْ يَتَوَفَّى ٱلَّذِينَ كَفَرُوٓاْ ٱلْمَلَٰٓئِكَةُ يَضْرِبُونَ وُجُوهَهُمْ وَأَدْبَٰرَهُمْ وَذُوقُواْ عَذَابَ ٱلْحَرِيقِ ۝

50. Walaw tar*a* i*th* yatawaff*a* alla*th*eena kafaroo almal*a*-ikatu ya*d*riboona wujoohahum waadb*a*rahum wa*th*ooqoo AAa*th*aba al*h*areeqi

8:50. And if you could see the angels causing those who suppress the Truth to die, you would see them (angels) smiting their faces and their backs, and saying, "Taste the torment of the Fire!"

ذَٰلِكَ بِمَا قَدَّمَتْ أَيْدِيكُمْ وَأَنَّ ٱللَّهَ لَيْسَ بِظَلَّٰمٍ لِّلْعَبِيدِ ﴿٥١﴾

51. *Tha*lika bim*a* qaddamat aydeekum waanna All*a*ha laysa bi*tha*ll*a*min lilAAabeed**i**

8:51. That is because of what your own hands have sent in before. And Allah is not in the least unjust to those whom He created and who ought therefore to obey Him.

كَدَأْبِ ءَالِ فِرْعَوْنَ وَٱلَّذِينَ مِن قَبْلِهِمْ كَفَرُواْ بِـَٔايَٰتِ ٱللَّهِ فَأَخَذَهُمُ ٱللَّهُ بِذُنُوبِهِمْ إِنَّ ٱللَّهَ قَوِيٌّ شَدِيدُ ٱلْعِقَابِ ﴿٥٢﴾

52. Kada/bi *a*li firAAawna waalla*the*ena min qablihim kafaroo bi-*aya*ti All*a*hi faakha*tha*humu Allahu bi*th*unoobihim inna All*a*ha qawiyyun shadeedu alAAiq*a*b**i**

8:52. Like Pharaoh's people and those before them: they suppressed the Truth in Allah's Verses/signs, and then Allah seized them for their sins. Allah is indeed strong, severe in punishment.

ذَٰلِكَ بِأَنَّ ٱللَّهَ لَمْ يَكُ مُغَيِّرًا نِّعْمَةً أَنْعَمَهَا عَلَىٰ قَوْمٍ حَتَّىٰ يُغَيِّرُواْ مَا بِأَنفُسِهِمْ وَأَنَّ ٱللَّهَ سَمِيعٌ عَلِيمٌ ﴿٥٣﴾

53. *Thalika* bi-anna All*a*ha lam yaku mughayyiran niAAmatan anAAamah*a* AAal*a* qawmin *hatta* yughayyiroo m*a* bi-anfusihim waanna All*a*ha sameeAAun AAaleemun

8:53. That was because Allah has never changed a favour which He has conferred upon a people until they themselves become responsible for any change in it. And because Allah listens, knows.[25]

25. We are witness today to the Truth contained in this Verse. Soon after the revelation of the Qur'aan, the Muslims had climbed to the pinnacle of glory because they then, by and large, adhered to the Qur'aanic tenets. But, now, they are the lowest of the low among the comity of nations because they now, by and large, treat the Qur'aan as a thing of no real importance!

كَدَأْبِ ءَالِ فِرْعَوْنَ وَٱلَّذِينَ مِن قَبْلِهِمْ كَذَّبُواْ بِـَٔايَـٰتِ رَبِّهِمْ فَأَهْلَكْنَـٰهُم بِذُنُوبِهِمْ وَأَغْرَقْنَآ ءَالَ فِرْعَوْنَ وَكُلٌّ كَانُواْ ظَـٰلِمِينَ ﴿٥٤﴾

54. Kada/bi *a*li firAAawna waalla*theena* min qablihim ka*ththaboo* bi-*aya*ti rabbihim faahlaknahum bi*thunoobihim* waaghraqn*a* ala firAAawna wakullun k*a*noo *thalimeena*

8:54. Like Pharaoh's people and those before them: they rejected the Verses/signs of their Lord, so We destroyed them because of their sins and We drowned Pharaoh's people, and they were all unjust.

إِنَّ شَرَّ ٱلدَّوَآبِّ عِندَ ٱللَّهِ ٱلَّذِينَ كَفَرُواْ فَهُمْ لَا يُؤْمِنُونَ ﴿٥٥﴾

55. Inna sharra alddaw*a*bbi AAinda All*a*hi alla*theena* kafaroo fahum l*a* yu/minoona

8:55. Indeed, the worst of the moving creatures, in Allah's sight, are those who suppress the Truth. And then they would not believe.

ٱلَّذِينَ عَٰهَدتَّ مِنْهُمْ ثُمَّ يَنقُضُونَ عَهْدَهُمْ فِى كُلِّ مَرَّةٍ وَهُمْ لَا يَتَّقُونَ ۝

56. Alla*th*eena AA*a*hadta minhum thumma yanqu*d*oona AA*a*hdahum fee kulli marratin wahum l*a* yattaqoon*a*

8:56. Those with whom you had a covenant, and they broke it every time and they did not fear Allah.

فَإِمَّا تَثْقَفَنَّهُمْ فِى ٱلْحَرْبِ فَشَرِّدْ بِهِم مَّنْ خَلْفَهُمْ لَعَلَّهُمْ يَذَّكَّرُونَ ۝

57. Fa-imm*a* tathqafannahum fee al*h*arbi fasharrid bihim man khalfahum laAA*a*llahum ya*thth*akkaroon*a*

8:57. And if you face them in war, make a deterrent example of them for those who would follow them.

وَإِمَّا تَخَافَنَّ مِن قَوْمٍ خِيَانَةً فَٱنۢبِذْ إِلَيْهِمْ عَلَىٰ سَوَآءٍ إِنَّ ٱللَّهَ لَا يُحِبُّ ٱلْخَآئِنِينَ ۝

58. Wa-imm*a* takh*a*fanna min qawmin khiy*a*natan fainbi*th* ilayhim AAal*a* sawa-in inna All*a*ha l*a* yu*h*ibbu alkh*a*-ineen*a*

8:58. And if you fear treachery on the part of a people, then throw back the covenant to them in an equitable manner. Indeed, Allah does not like the treacherous people.

وَلَا يَحْسَبَنَّ ٱلَّذِينَ كَفَرُوا۟ سَبَقُوٓا۟ إِنَّهُمْ لَا يُعْجِزُونَ ۝

59. Wala yahsabanna allatheena kafaroo sabaqoo innahum la yuAAjizoona

8:59. And let not those who suppress the Truth think that they will get away. They will certainly not escape.

وَأَعِدُّوا۟ لَهُم مَّا ٱسْتَطَعْتُم مِّن قُوَّةٍ وَمِن رِّبَاطِ ٱلْخَيْلِ تُرْهِبُونَ بِهِۦ عَدُوَّ ٱللَّهِ وَعَدُوَّكُمْ وَءَاخَرِينَ مِن دُونِهِمْ لَا تَعْلَمُونَهُمُ ٱللَّهُ يَعْلَمُهُمْ وَمَا تُنفِقُوا۟ مِن شَىْءٍ فِى سَبِيلِ ٱللَّهِ يُوَفَّ إِلَيْكُمْ وَأَنتُمْ لَا تُظْلَمُونَ ۝

60. WaaAAiddoo lahum ma istaraAAtum min quwwatin wamin ribati alkhayli turhiboona bihi AAaduwwa Allahi waAAaduwwakum waakhareena min doonihim la taAAlamoonahumu Allahu yaAAlamuhum wama tunfiqoo min shay-in fee sabeeli Allahi yuwaffa ilaykum waantum la tuthlamoona

8:60. And prepare against them what force and means of transport you can muster, to deter thereby the enemy of Allah and your enemy and others besides them, whom you do not know but Allah knows. And whatever thing you spend in Allah's path, it will be paid back to you in full and you shall not be wronged.

وَإِن جَنَحُواْ لِلسَّلْمِ فَٱجْنَحْ لَهَا وَتَوَكَّلْ عَلَى ٱللَّهِ إِنَّهُۥ هُوَ ٱلسَّمِيعُ ٱلْعَلِيمُ ۝

61. Wa-in jana*h*oo lilssalmi fa*i*jna*h* lah*a* watawakkal AAal*a* All*a*hi innahu huwa alssameeAAu alAAaleemu

8:61. And if they incline towards peace, then incline towards it and trust in Allah. HE does indeed listen, know.

وَإِن يُرِيدُوٓاْ أَن يَخْدَعُوكَ فَإِنَّ حَسْبَكَ ٱللَّهُ هُوَ ٱلَّذِىٓ أَيَّدَكَ بِنَصْرِهِۦ وَبِٱلْمُؤْمِنِينَ ۝

62. Wa-in yureedoo an yakhdaAAooka fa-inna *h*asbaka All*a*hu huwa alla*th*ee ayyadaka binasrihi wabialmu/mineen*a*

8:62. And if they intend to deceive you[26], then Allah is indeed enough for you. He it is Who strengthened you with His help and with the believers.

26. Since, in the Arabic text, the personal pronoun used is in the singular, the addressee is the Prophet, obviously.

وَأَلَّفَ بَيْنَ قُلُوبِهِمْ لَوْ أَنفَقْتَ مَا فِى ٱلْأَرْضِ جَمِيعًا مَّآ أَلَّفْتَ بَيْنَ قُلُوبِهِمْ وَلَٰكِنَّ ٱللَّهَ أَلَّفَ بَيْنَهُمْ إِنَّهُۥ عَزِيزٌ حَكِيمٌ ۝

63. Waallafa bayna quloobihim law anfaqta m*a* fee al-ar*d*i jameeAAan m*a* allafta bayna quloobihim wal*a*kinna All*a*ha allafa baynahum innahu AAazeezun *h*akeem**un**

8:63. And He united their hearts. Had you (singular) spent all that is in the earth, you could not have united their hearts, but Allah united them. He is indeed Omnipotent, Wise.

يَـٰٓأَيُّهَا ٱلنَّبِىُّ حَسْبُكَ ٱللَّـهُ وَمَنِ ٱتَّبَعَكَ مِنَ ٱلْمُؤْمِنِينَ ۝

64. Y*a* ayyuh*a* alnnabiyyu *h*asbuka All*a*hu wamani ittabaAA*a*ka mina almu/mineen**a**

8:64. O Prophet! Allah is enough for you and for such of the believers that follow you[27].

---

27. Refer study notes 3:35 to 3:37 on <u>Verse 3:31</u> **in this context. To follow the Qur'aan is to follow the Prophet now.**

يَـٰٓأَيُّهَا ٱلنَّبِىُّ حَرِّضِ ٱلْمُؤْمِنِينَ عَلَى ٱلْقِتَالِ إِن يَكُن مِّنكُمْ عِشْرُونَ صَـٰبِرُونَ يَغْلِبُوٓاْ مِائَتَيْنِ وَإِن يَكُن مِّنكُم مِّائَةٌ يَغْلِبُوٓاْ أَلْفًا مِّنَ ٱلَّذِينَ كَفَرُواْ بِأَنَّهُمْ قَوْمٌ لَّا يَفْقَهُونَ ۝

65. Y*a* ayyuh*a* alnnabiyyu *h*arri*d*i almu/mineena AAal*a* alqit*a*li in yakun minkum AAishroona *s*abiroona yaghliboo mi-atayni wa-in yakun minkum mi-atun yaghliboo alfan mina alla*th*eena kafaroo bi-annahum qawmun l*a* yafqahoon**a**

8:65. O Prophet! Exhort the believers to fight. If there be twenty of you exercising patience, they shall overcome two hundred; and if there be a hundred of you, they shall overcome a thousand of those who suppress the Truth, because they (the latter) are a people who do not understand.

ٱلَّـٰنَ خَفَّفَ ٱللَّهُ عَنكُمْ وَعَلِمَ أَنَّ فِيكُمْ ضَعْفًا فَإِن يَكُن مِّنكُم مِّائَةٌ صَابِرَةٌ يَغْلِبُوا۟ مِائَتَيْنِ وَإِن يَكُن مِّنكُمْ أَلْفٌ يَغْلِبُوٓا۟ أَلْفَيْنِ بِإِذْنِ ٱللَّهِ وَٱللَّهُ مَعَ ٱلصَّـٰبِرِينَ ﴿٦٦﴾

66. Al-*a*na khaffafa All*a*hu AAankum waAAalima anna feekum *d*aAAfan fa-in yakun minkum mi-atun *s*abiratun yaghliboo mi-atayni wa-in yakun minkum alfun yaghliboo alfayni bi-i*th*ni All*a*hi waAll*a*hu maAAa al*ss*abireen**a**

8:66 For now, Allah has made your burden light, and He knows that there is weakness in you. So if there be a hundred of you exercising patience, they shall overcome two hundred; and if there be a thousand, they shall overcome two thousand by Allah's permission. And Allah is with those who are patient.

مَا كَانَ لِنَبِيٍّ أَن يَكُونَ لَهُۥٓ أَسْرَىٰ حَتَّىٰ يُثْخِنَ فِى ٱلْأَرْضِ تُرِيدُونَ عَرَضَ ٱلدُّنْيَا وَٱللَّهُ يُرِيدُ ٱلْءَاخِرَةَ وَٱللَّهُ عَزِيزٌ حَكِيمٌ ﴿٦٧﴾

67. M*a* k*a*na linabiyyin an yakoona lahu asr*a hatta* yuthkhina fee al-ar*di* tureedoona AAara*d*a aldduny*a* waAll*a*hu yureedu al-*a*khirata waAll*a*hu AAazeezun *h*akeem**un**

8:67. It is not fit for a prophet that he should have captives unless he is firmly established on the earth.[28] You desire to avail goods of this world, while Allah desires for you the Hereafter. And Allah is Omnipotent, Wise.

28. The war that is described in this Qur'aanic Chapter had obviously taken place at the beginning of the Islamic rule, which had yet to take roots. Allah here strongly disapproves of the Prophet allowing his army to take prisoners of war at this stage. The Muslim army took the prisoners probably in the hope of getting ransom money later for their release. Allah Almighty hence chides them, further in this Verse, for being desirous of worldly goods.

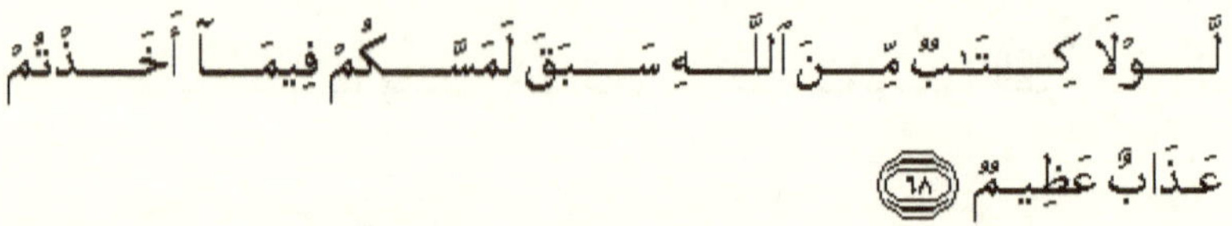

68. Lawl*a* kit*a*bun mina All*a*hi sabaqa lamassakum *f*eem*a* akha*th*tum AAa*th*abun AAa*th*eem**un**

8:68. Had it not been for an ordinance from Allah already gone forth, surely there would have befallen you a great calamity[29] in what you had taken.

29. The calamity is not specified, but it could be that the prisoners themselves would prove to be potentially dangerous. The nascent Mulim state did not have the necessary infrastructure for taking care of the prisoners. They roamed about in the Muslim society probably as slaves of individual Muslims. They were thus potentially capable of inflicting harm on the Prophet and his companions by way of reprisals. But Allah, in His mercy for the believers, prevented the prisoners from getting any such ideas.

69. Fakuloo mimm*a* ghanimtum *h*al*a*lan *t*ayyiban wa*i*ttaqoo All*a*ha inna All*a*ha ghafoorun ra*h*eem**un**

8:69. Eat then of the lawful and good things which you get as windfall or spoils of war. And fear Allah. Indeed, Allah is Forgiving, Merciful.

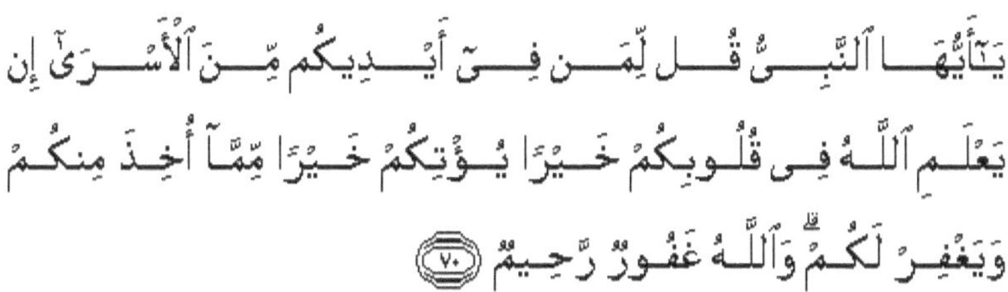

70. Y*a* ayyuh*a* alnnabiyyu qul liman fee aydeekum mina al-asr*a* in yaAAlami All*a*hu fee quloobikum khayran yu/tikum khayran mimm*a* okhi*th*a minkum wayaghfir lakum waAll*a*hu ghafoorun ra*h*eem**un**

8:70. O Prophet! Say to those of the captives who are in your hands, "If Allah knows there is anything good in your hearts, He will give you better than that which has been taken away from you and He will forgive you. And Allah is Forgiving, Merciful."

وَإِن يُرِيدُواْ خِيَانَتَكَ فَقَدْ خَانُواْ ٱللَّهَ مِن قَبْلُ فَأَمْكَنَ مِنْهُمْ وَٱللَّهُ عَلِيمٌ حَكِيمٌ ۝

71. Wa-in yureedoo khiy*a*nataka faqad kh*a*noo All*a*ha min qablu faamkana minhum waAll*a*hu AAaleemun *h*akeem**un**

8:71. And if they intend to be unfaithful to you, they were indeed unfaithful towards Allah before, so He gave you power over them. And Allah is Aware, Wise.

إِنَّ ٱلَّذِينَ ءَامَنُواْ وَهَاجَرُواْ وَجَٰهَدُواْ بِأَمْوَٰلِهِمْ وَأَنفُسِهِمْ فِى سَبِيلِ ٱللَّهِ وَٱلَّذِينَ ءَاوَواْ وَّنَصَرُوٓاْ أُوْلَٰٓئِكَ بَعْضُهُمْ أَوْلِيَآءُ بَعْضٍ وَٱلَّذِينَ ءَامَنُواْ وَلَمْ يُهَاجِرُواْ مَا لَكُم مِّن وَلَٰيَتِهِم مِّن شَىْءٍ حَتَّىٰ يُهَاجِرُواْ وَإِنِ ٱسْتَنصَرُوكُمْ فِى ٱلدِّينِ فَعَلَيْكُمُ ٱلنَّصْرُ إِلَّا عَلَىٰ قَوْمٍ بَيْنَكُمْ وَبَيْنَهُم مِّيثَٰقٌ وَٱللَّهُ بِمَا تَعْمَلُونَ بَصِيرٌ ﴿٧٢﴾

72. Inna alla*theena a*manoo wahajaroo waja*hadoo bi-amwa*lihim waanfusihim fee sabeeli Alla*hi waalla*theena a*waw wanasaroo ola-ika baAA*d*uhum awliya*o baAA*d*in waalla*theena a*manoo walam yuhajiroo ma* lakum min wala*yatihim min shay-in *hatta* yuhajiroo wa-ini istansarookum fee alddeeni faAAalaykumu alnnasru illa* AAala* qawmin baynakum wabaynahum meetha*qun waAlla*hu bima* taAAamaloona ba*seerun

---

8:72. Those indeed who believed and migrated and struggled hard in Allah's path with their property and their lives, and those who gave shelter and help – these are *awliya*[30] of one another. And as for those who believed but did not migrate, you have no responsibility of being their *wali* until they migrate. And if they seek aid from you in matters of religion, aid is obligatory on you except against a people between whom and you there is a treaty. And Allah sees what you do.

---

30. This Arabic term is the plural form of *wali*. Refer study note 2:154 **for its comprehensive Qur'aanic meaning.**

وَٱلَّذِينَ كَفَرُواْ بَعْضُهُمْ أَوْلِيَآءُ بَعْضٍ إِلَّا تَفْعَلُوهُ تَكُن فِتْنَةٌ فِى ٱلْأَرْضِ وَفَسَادٌ كَبِيرٌ ﴿٧٣﴾

73. Waalla*theena kafaroo baAA*d*uhum awliya*o baAA*d*in illa* tafAAaloohu takun fitnatun fee al-ar*d*i wafasa*dun kabeerun

---

8:73. And as for those who suppress the Truth, they are the *awliya* of one another. If you do it not[31], there will be disorder on earth and great discord.

---

31. In other words, 'if the believers fail to be *awliya* of one another ...' In this Verse, there is a clear divine warning that if the believers of the world do not unite, there will be disorder and discord on this earth, as presently is the case.

وَٱلَّذِينَ ءَامَنُواْ وَهَاجَرُواْ وَجَـٰهَدُواْ فِى سَبِيلِ ٱللَّهِ وَٱلَّذِينَ ءَاوَواْ وَّنَصَرُوٓاْ أُوْلَـٰٓئِكَ هُمُ ٱلْمُؤْمِنُونَ حَقًّا لَّهُم مَّغْفِرَةٌ وَرِزْقٌ كَرِيمٌ ﴿٧٤﴾

74. Waalla*th*eena *a*manoo wah*a*jaroo waj*a*hadoo fee sabeeli All*a*hi waalla*th*eena *a*waw wanasaroo ol*a*-ika humu almu/minoona *h*aqqan lahum maghfiratun warizqun kareem**un**

8:74. And as for those who believed and migrated and struggled hard in Allah's path, and those who gave shelter and help, those are the true believers. They shall have forgiveness and honourable provision.

وَٱلَّذِينَ ءَامَنُواْ مِنۢ بَعْدُ وَهَاجَرُواْ وَجَـٰهَدُواْ مَعَكُمْ فَأُوْلَـٰٓئِكَ مِنكُمْ وَأُوْلُواْ ٱلْأَرْحَامِ بَعْضُهُمْ أَوْلَىٰ بِبَعْضٍ فِى كِتَـٰبِ ٱللَّهِ إِنَّ ٱللَّهَ بِكُلِّ شَىْءٍ عَلِيمٌ ﴿٧٥﴾

75. Waalla*th*eena *a*manoo min baAAdu wah*a*jaroo waj*a*hadoo maAAakum faol*a*-ika minkum waloo al-ar*h*ami baAA*d*uhum awl*a* bibaAA*d*in fee kit*a*bi All*a*hi inna All*a*ha bikulli shay-in AAaleem**un**

8:75. And as for those who believed afterwards and migrated and struggled hard along with you, they are of you. And blood relatives are nearer to one another in Allah's Record. Allah does indeed know all things.

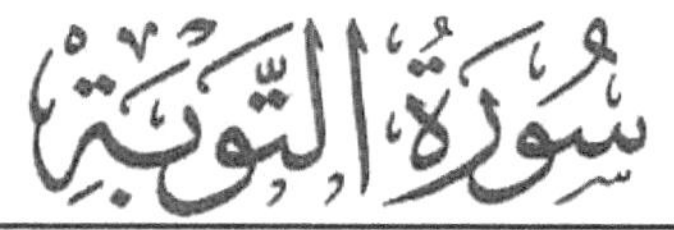

Chapter 9: At-Taubah (The Repentance)[1]

1. It is one of the mysteries of the Qur'aan that, unlike all other Chapters, this one does not begin with the customary invocation in the Name of Allah. And in terms of Verse 3.7, the believers must accept it, without questioning, as from Allah.

بَرَآءَةٌ مِّنَ ٱللَّـهِ وَرَسُولِهِۦٓ إِلَى ٱلَّـذِينَ عَـٰهَدتُّم مِّنَ ٱلْمُشْرِكِينَ ۞

1. Baraatun mina Allahi warasoolihi ila allatheena AAahadtum mina almushrikeena

9:1. Abrogation of any obligation, by Allah and His Messenger, under any treaty you made with any polytheists.[2]

2. In Verse 8:58, the believers were instructed to throw back to the polytheists the covenant made with them in an equitable manner in case of treachery on the latters' part. The abrogation here ought to have therefore been a sequel to treacherous acts on the part of the non-believers.

فَسِيحُوا۟ فِى ٱلْأَرْضِ أَرْبَعَةَ أَشْهُرٍ وَٱعْلَمُوٓا۟ أَنَّكُمْ غَيْرُ مُعْجِزِى ٱللَّهِ وَأَنَّ ٱللَّهَ مُخْزِى ٱلْكَـٰفِرِينَ ۞

2. Faseehoo fee al-ardi arbaAAata ashhurin waiAAlamoo annakum ghayru muAAjizee Allahi waanna Allaha mukhzee alkafireena

9:2. So travel freely on earth for four months and know that you cannot frustrate Allah and that Allah will bring disgrace to those who suppress the Truth.

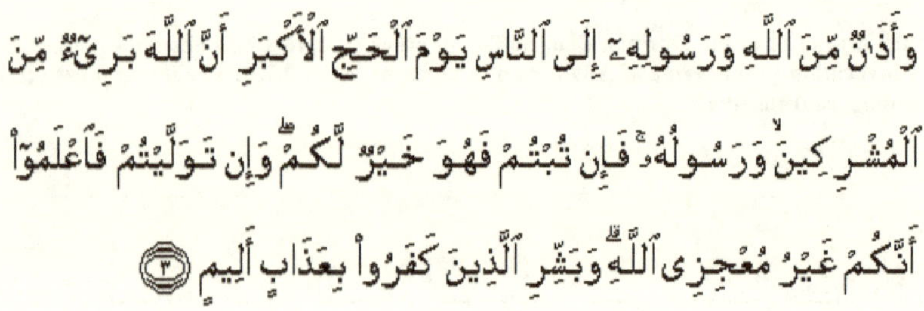

3. Waa*th*anun mina All*a*hi warasoolihi il*a* alnn*a*si yawma al*h*ajji al-akbari anna All*a*ha baree-on mina almushrikeena warasooluhu fa-in tubtum fahuwa khayrun lakum wa-in tawallaytum faiAAalamoo annakum ghayru muAAjizee All*a*hi wabashshiri alla*th*eena kafaroo biAAa*th*abin aleem**in**

9:3. And a proclamation from Allah and His Messenger to the people on the day of the great pilgrimage[3] that Allah and His Messenger are free from any contractual obligations to the idolaters. If you then repent, it will be better for you, and if you turn away, then know that you cannot frustrate Allah. And pronounce painful punishment to those who suppress the Truth!

3. The Hajj rites are performed for several days starting from 8th of *Dhul-Hijja*, the 10th of the lunar month being considered the main day. It is this 10th day that may have been referred to here as the day of the great pilgrimage. But there is a controversy on this point. The controversy, however, is of no significance for the Muslims now. It is immaterial for us now to know the exact day when the proclamation was made over 1400 years back.

4. Ill*a* alla*th*eena AA*a*hadtum mina almushrikeena thumma lam yanqu*s*ookum shay-an walam yu*th*ahiroo AAalaykum a*h*adan faatimmoo ilayhim AA*a*hdahum il*a* muddatihim inna All*a*ha yu*h*ibbu almuttaqeen**a**

9:4. But as for those of the polytheists with whom you have a treaty, then they have not failed you in anything and have not backed up any one against you, fulfill their treaty to the end of its term. Indeed, Allah loves those who fear Him and do righteous things.

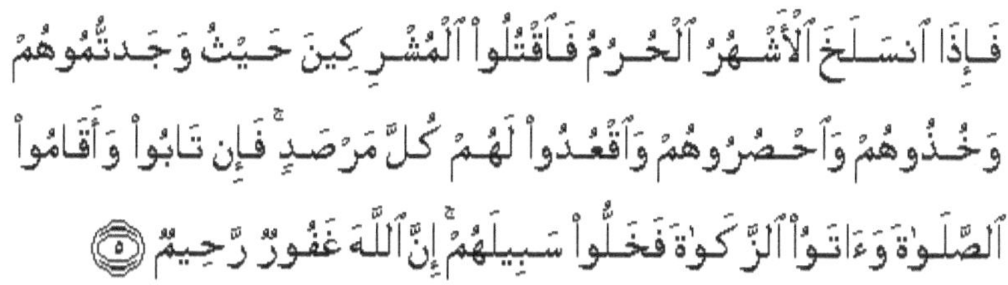

5. Fa-i*th*a insalakha al-ashhuru al*h*urumu faoqtuloo almushrikeena *h*aythu wajadtumoohum wakhu*th*oohum wao*h*suroohum waoqAAudoo lahum kulla marsadin fa-in t*a*boo waaq*a*moo al*s*sal*a*ta wa*a*tawoo al*zz*akata fakhalloo sabeelahum inna All*a*ha ghafoorun ra*h*eem**un**

9:5. Then when the prohibited months[4] pass away, kill the idolaters wherever you find them, seize and besiege them and lie in wait for them at every place for ambush.[5] Then if they repent, establish proper prayer and give charity, leave their way free to them. Indeed, Allah is Forgiving, Merciful.

4. The 4 months mentioned in Verse 2 above.

5. This should not be misconstrued as an open divine order for perpetrating a pogrom of ethnic cleansing. This order should be read in its proper context. And the context is that the believers at Medina had entered into a series of no-war treaties with non-believers around them. When these treaties were repeatedly broken by the non-believers, they were given a 4-month notice before declaration of a state of war with them. The divine order here was given in that state of war. This order must be read with the order in Verse 6 below. For the background scenario, see Verses 8:58 & 9:1 to 9:4 above.

وَإِنْ أَحَدٌ مِّنَ ٱلْمُشْرِكِينَ ٱسْتَجَارَكَ فَأَجِرْهُ حَتَّىٰ يَسْمَعَ كَلَـٰمَ ٱللَّهِ ثُمَّ أَبْلِغْهُ مَأْمَنَهُۥ ذَٰلِكَ بِأَنَّهُمْ قَوْمٌ لَّا يَعْلَمُونَ ۝

6. Wa-in a*h*adun mina almushrikeena istaj*a*raka faajirhu *h*att*a* yasmaAAa kal*a*ma All*a*hi thumma ablighhu ma/manahu *th*alika bi-annahum qawmun l*a* yaAAlamoon*a*

9:6. And if any of the idolaters seeks protection from you, grant him protection till he hears Allah's Word, then take him to his place of safety. It is so ordained because they are a people who do not know.

كَيْفَ يَكُونُ لِلْمُشْرِكِينَ عَهْدٌ عِندَ ٱللَّهِ وَعِندَ رَسُولِهِۦٓ إِلَّا ٱلَّذِينَ عَـٰهَدتُّمْ عِندَ ٱلْمَسْجِدِ ٱلْحَرَامِ فَمَا ٱسْتَقَـٰمُوا۟ لَكُمْ فَٱسْتَقِيمُوا۟ لَهُمْ إِنَّ ٱللَّهَ يُحِبُّ ٱلْمُتَّقِينَ ۝

7. Kayfa yakoonu lilmushrikeena AAahdun AAinda All*a*hi waAAinda rasoolihi ill*a* alla*th*eena AAahadtum AAinda almasjidi al*h*ar*a*mi fam*a* istaq*a*moo lakum faistaqeemoo lahum inna All*a*ha yu*h*ibbu almuttaqeena

---

9:7. How can there be a treaty for the polytheists with Allah and with His Messenger except for those with whom you made a treaty at the Sacred Place of Worship?[6] Then, if they are true to you, be true to them. Allah does indeed love those who fear Him and do righteous deeds.

---

6. From what follows in this Verse, it becomes clear that, except for a few, the idolators generally did not deserve a treaty of peace being made with them, because of their history of repeated breach of trust on their part. Verse 8 and several subsequent Verses below further explain this point and give the raison d'etre in details for the declaration of war with the idolators.

كَيْفَ وَإِن يَظْهَرُواْ عَلَيْكُمْ لَا يَرْقُبُواْ فِيكُمْ إِلَّا وَلَا ذِمَّةً يُرْضُونَكُم
بِأَفْوَاهِهِمْ وَتَأْبَىٰ قُلُوبُهُمْ وَأَكْثَرُهُمْ فَـٰسِقُونَ ۝

8. Kayfa wa-in ya*th*haroo AAalaykum l*a* yarquboo feekum illan wal*a* *th*immatan yur*d*oonakum bi-afw*a*hihim wata/b*a* quloobuhum waaktharuhum f*a*siqoon**a**

9:8. And how can there be a treaty when, if they prevail against you they would not heed ties of relationship with you, or those of a covenant. They please you with their mouths while their hearts are averse. And most of them are corrupt.

أَشْتَرَوْاْ بِـَٔايَٰتِ ٱللَّهِ ثَمَنًا قَلِيلًا فَصَدُّواْ عَن سَبِيلِهِۦٓ
إِنَّهُمْ سَآءَ مَا كَانُواْ يَعْمَلُونَ ۝

9. Ishtaraw bi-*a*y*a*ti All*a*hi thamanan qaleelan fa*s*addoo AAan sabeelihi innahum s*a*a m*a* k*a*noo yaAAmaloon**a**

9:9. They have traded Allah's Verses/signs for a small price and then they turn people away from His Path. What they do is certainly bad.

لَا يَرْقُبُونَ فِى مُؤْمِنٍ إِلَّا وَلَا ذِمَّةً وَأُوْلَـٰٓئِكَ هُمُ ٱلْمُعْتَدُونَ ۝

10. L*a* yarquboona fee mu/minin illan wal*a* *th*immatan waol*a*-ika humu almuAAtadoon**a**

9:10. They do not heed ties of relationship with a believer, or those of a covenant. And these are the hostile ones.

فَإِن تَابُواْ وَأَقَامُواْ ٱلصَّلَوٰةَ وَءَاتَوُاْ ٱلزَّكَوٰةَ فَإِخُوَٰنُكُمْ فِى ٱلدِّينِ وَنُفَصِّلُ ٱلْأَيَٰتِ لِقَوْمٍ يَعْلَمُونَ ﴿١١﴾

11. Fa-in *ta*boo waaq*a*moo al*s*sal*a*ta wa*a*tawoo alzzak*a*ta fa-ikhw*a*nukum fee alddeeni wanufa*ss*ilu al-*aya*ti liqawmin yaAAlamoona

9:11. Then if they repent, establish proper prayer and give charity, they are your brethren in faith. And We make the Verses/signs clear for people that are knowledgeable.

وَإِن نَّكَثُوٓاْ أَيْمَٰنَهُم مِّنۢ بَعْدِ عَهْدِهِمْ وَطَعَنُواْ فِى دِينِكُمْ فَقَٰتِلُوٓاْ أَئِمَّةَ ٱلْكُفْرِ إِنَّهُمْ لَآ أَيْمَٰنَ لَهُمْ لَعَلَّهُمْ يَنتَهُونَ ﴿١٢﴾

12. Wa-in nakathoo aym*a*nahum min baAAdi AAahdihim wa*r*aAAanoo fee deenikum faq*a*tiloo a-immata alkufri innahum l*a* aym*a*na lahum laAAallahum yantahoona

9:12. And if they break their terms after their covenant and taunt your religion, then fight the leading lights of the suppression of Truth – the terms are nothing to them, indeed – so that they may desist.

أَلَا تُقَـٰتِلُونَ قَوْمًا نَّكَثُوٓاْ أَيْمَـٰنَهُمْ وَهَمُّوا۟ بِـإِخْرَاجِ ٱلرَّسُولِ وَهُم بَدَءُوكُمْ أَوَّلَ مَرَّةٍ أَتَخْشَوْنَهُمْ فَٱللَّهُ أَحَقُّ أَن تَخْشَوْهُ إِن كُنتُم مُّؤْمِنِينَ

13. Ala tuqatiloona qawman nakathoo aymanahum wahammoo bi-ikhraji alrrasooli wahum badaookum awwala marratin atakhshawnahum faAllahu ahaqqu an takhshawhu in kuntum mu/mineena

---

9:13. Will you not fight a people, who broke their terms of agreement and tried hard for expulsion of the Messenger and attacked you first!? Are you afraid of them? But Allah it is Who has the right to be afraid of, if you do believe!

قَـٰتِلُوهُمْ يُعَذِّبْهُمُ ٱللَّهُ بِـأَيْدِيكُمْ وَيُخْزِهِمْ وَيَنصُرْكُمْ عَلَيْهِمْ وَيَشْفِ صُدُورَ قَوْمٍ مُّؤْمِنِينَ ١٤

14. Qatiloohum yuAAaththibhumu Allahu bi-aydeekum wayukhzihim wayansurkum AAalayhim wayashfi sudoora qawmin mu/mineena

---

9:14. Fight them! Allah will punish them by your hands, bring them to disgrace and assist you against them. And He will heal the hearts of a believing people.

وَيُذْهِبْ غَيْظَ قُلُوبِهِمْ وَيَتُوبُ ٱللَّهُ عَلَىٰ مَن يَشَآءُ وَٱللَّهُ عَلِيمٌ حَكِيمٌ

15. Wayu*th*hib ghay*th*a quloobihim wayatoobu All*a*hu AAal*a* man yash*a*o waAll*a*hu AAaleemun *h*akeem**un**

9:15. And remove the anguish of their hearts. And Allah grants pardon to whom He wills. And Allah is Knowledgeable, Wise.

أَمْ حَسِبْتُمْ أَن تُتْرَكُواْ وَلَمَّا يَعْلَمِ ٱللَّهُ ٱلَّذِينَ جَـٰهَدُواْ مِنكُمْ وَلَمْ يَتَّخِذُواْ مِن دُونِ ٱللَّهِ وَلَا رَسُولِهِۦ وَلَا ٱلْمُؤْمِنِينَ وَلِيجَةً وَٱللَّهُ خَبِيرٌ بِمَا تَعْمَلُونَ 

16. Am *h*asibtum an tutrakoo walamm*a* yaAAlami All*a*hu alla*th*eena j*a*hadoo minkum walam yattakhi*th*oo min dooni All*a*hi wal*a* rasoolihi wal*a* almu/mineena waleejatan waAll*a*hu khabeerun bim*a* taAAamaloon**a**

9:16. Do you think that you will be spared before Allah has known those of you who have struggled hard in Allah's Path and have not taken any sanctuary besides Allah, His Messenger and the believers? And Allah is aware of what you do.

مَا كَانَ لِلْمُشْرِكِينَ أَن يَعْمُرُواْ مَسَـٰجِدَ ٱللَّهِ شَـٰهِدِينَ عَلَىٰٓ أَنفُسِهِم بِٱلْكُفْرِ أُوْلَـٰٓئِكَ حَبِطَتْ أَعْمَـٰلُهُمْ وَفِى ٱلنَّارِ هُمْ خَـٰلِدُونَ

17. Ma k*a*na lilmushrikeena an yaAAmuroo mas*a*jida All*a*hi sh*a*hideena AAal*a* anfusihim bialkufri ol*a*-ika *h*abi*t*at aAAm*a*luhum wafee alnn*a*ri hum kh*a*lidoon**a**

9:17. The idolaters cannot be maintainers of the places for worshipping Allah while bearing witness against themselves to suppression of the Truth. These it is who have nullified their deeds, and in the Fire shall they abide.

إِنَّمَا يَعْمُرُ مَسَـٰجِدَ ٱللَّهِ مَنْ ءَامَنَ بِٱللَّهِ وَٱلْيَوْمِ ٱلْأَخِرِ وَأَقَامَ ٱلصَّلَوٰةَ وَءَاتَى ٱلزَّكَوٰةَ وَلَمْ يَخْشَ إِلَّا ٱللَّهَ فَعَسَىٰ أُوْلَـٰئِكَ أَن يَكُونُواْ مِنَ ٱلْمُهْتَدِينَ ﴿١٨﴾

18. Innama yaAAmuru masajida Allahi man amana biAllahi waalyawmi al-akhiri waaqama alssalata waata alzzakata walam yakhsha illa Allaha faAAasa ola-ika an yakoonoo mina almuhtadeena

9:18. Only he shall visit and maintain the places for worshipping Allah who believes in Allah and the Last Day, establishes proper prayer, gives charity and fears none but Allah. These it is who are among those on right guidance.

۞ أَجَعَلْتُمْ سِقَايَةَ ٱلْحَاجِّ وَعِمَارَةَ ٱلْمَسْجِدِ ٱلْحَرَامِ كَمَنْ ءَامَنَ بِٱللَّهِ وَٱلْيَوْمِ ٱلْأَخِرِ وَجَـٰهَدَ فِى سَبِيلِ ٱللَّهِ لَا يَسْتَوُۥنَ عِندَ ٱللَّهِ وَٱللَّهُ لَا يَهْدِى ٱلْقَوْمَ ٱلظَّـٰلِمِينَ ﴿١٩﴾

19. AjaAAaltum siqayata alhajji waAAimarata almasjidi alharami kaman amana biAllahi waalyawmi al-akhiri wajahada fee sabeeli Allahi la yastawoona AAinda Allahi waAllahu la yahdee alqawma alththalimeena

9:19. Do you consider serving drinks to the pilgrims and maintaining the Sacred Place of Worship like the deed of one who believes in Allah and the Last Day and strives hard in Allah's Path? They are not equal in Allah's sight. And Allah does not guide the people who do wrong.

ٱلَّذِينَ ءَامَنُواْ وَهَاجَرُواْ وَجَـٰهَدُواْ فِى سَبِيلِ ٱللَّهِ بِأَمْوَٰلِهِمْ وَأَنفُسِهِمْ أَعْظَمُ دَرَجَةً عِندَ ٱللَّهِ ۚ وَأُو۟لَـٰٓئِكَ هُمُ ٱلْفَآئِزُونَ ﴿٢٠﴾

20. Alla*th*eena *a*manoo wah*a*jaroo waj*a*hadoo fee sabeeli All*a*hi bi-amw*a*lihim waanfusihim aAA*th*amu darajatan AAinda All*a*hi waol*a*-ika humu alf*a*-izoona

---

9:20. Those that believed and migrated and strove hard in Allah's Path with their wealth and their lives, are higher in rank in Allah's sight. And those are the achievers.

يُبَشِّرُهُمْ رَبُّهُم بِرَحْمَةٍ مِّنْهُ وَرِضْوَٰنٍ وَجَنَّـٰتٍ لَّهُمْ فِيهَا نَعِيمٌ مُّقِيمٌ ﴿٢١﴾

21. Yubashshiruhum rabbuhum bira*h*matin minhu wari*d*w*a*nin wajann*a*tin lahum feeh*a* naAAeemun muqeem*un*

9:21. Their Lord gives them good news of His mercy and pleasure and of gardens wherein there shall be everlasting blessings for them.

خَـٰلِدِينَ فِيهَآ أَبَدًا ۚ إِنَّ ٱللَّهَ عِندَهُۥٓ أَجْرٌ عَظِيمٌ ﴿٢٢﴾

22. Kh*a*lideena feeh*a* abadan inna All*a*ha AAindahu ajrun AAa*th*eem*un*

9:22. They shall live therein for ever. Indeed, Allah has a great reward with Him.

يَـٰٓأَيُّهَا ٱلَّذِينَ ءَامَنُوا۟ لَا تَتَّخِذُوٓا۟ ءَابَآءَكُمْ وَإِخْوَٰنَكُمْ أَوْلِيَآءَ إِنِ ٱسْتَحَبُّوا۟ ٱلْكُفْرَ عَلَى ٱلْإِيمَٰنِ ۚ وَمَن يَتَوَلَّهُم مِّنكُمْ فَأُو۟لَـٰٓئِكَ هُمُ ٱلظَّـٰلِمُونَ ﴿٢٣﴾

23. Y*a* ayyuh*a* alla*theena a*manoo la tattakhi*th*oo *a*baakum wa-ikhwanakum awliyaa ini ista*h*abboo alkufra AAal*a* al-eem*a*ni waman yatawallahum minkum faol*a*-ika humu al*ththa*limoon*a*

9:23. O you who believe! Do not take your fathers and your brothers as *awliya*[7] if they love suppression of the Truth more than faith in the Truth. And those of you who take them as *awliya*, those it is that do wrong.

7. Refer study note 2:154 **for a comprehensive Qur'aanic meaning of the Arabic term.**

قُل إِن كَانَ ءَابَآؤُكُمْ وَأَبْنَآؤُكُمْ وَإِخْوَٰنُكُمْ وَأَزْوَٰجُكُمْ وَعَشِيرَتُكُمْ وَأَمْوَٰلٌ ٱقْتَرَفْتُمُوهَا وَتِجَـٰرَةٌ تَخْشَوْنَ كَسَادَهَا وَمَسَـٰكِنُ تَرْضَوْنَهَآ أَحَبَّ إِلَيْكُم مِّنَ ٱللَّهِ وَرَسُولِهِۦ وَجِهَادٍ فِى سَبِيلِهِۦ فَتَرَبَّصُوا۟ حَتَّىٰ يَأْتِىَ ٱللَّهُ بِأَمْرِهِۦ ۗ وَٱللَّهُ لَا يَهْدِى ٱلْقَوْمَ ٱلْفَـٰسِقِينَ ﴿٢٤﴾

24. Qul in k*a*na *a*baokum waabnaokum wa-ikhw*a*nukum waazwajukum waAAasheeratukum waamwalun iqtaraftumooha watij*a*ratun takhshawna kas*a*daha wamas*a*kinu tar*d*awnaha a*h*abba ilaykum mina All*a*hi warasoolihi wajih*a*din fee sabeelihi fatarabba*s*oo *h*atta ya/tiya All*a*hu bi-amrihi waAll*a*hu l*a* yahdee alqawma alf*a*siqeena

9:24. Say, "If your fathers and your sons and your brethren and your mates and your kinsfolk and property which you have acquired, and the trade – slackness of which you fear – and dwellings which you like, are dearer to you than Allah and His Messenger and striving in His Path, then wait till Allah manifests His command. And Allah does not guide the corrupt people."

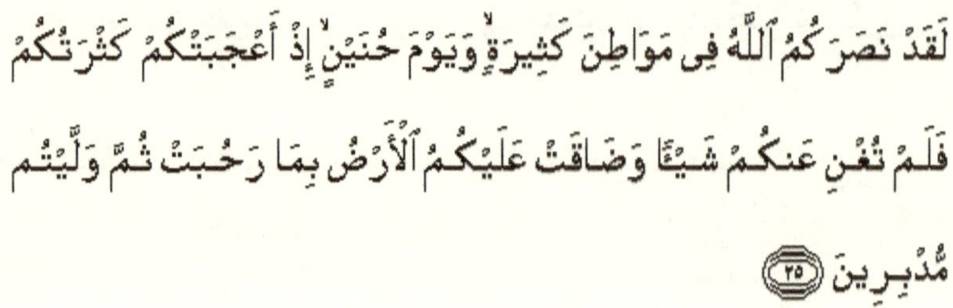

25. Laqad nasarakumu Allahu fee mawatina katheeratin wayawma hunaynin ith aAAjabatkum kathratukum falam tughni AAankum shay-an wadaqat AAalaykumu al-ardu bima rahubat thumma wallaytum mudbireena

9:25. Certainly Allah helped you in many battlefields and on the day of Hunain[8], when your being in great numbers pleased you, but they availed you nothing and the earth, vast as it is, narrowed upon you. Then you turned back retreating.

8. The battle of Hunain was faught after the conquest of Makkah.

26. Thumma anzala Allahu sakeenatahu AAala rasoolihi waAAala almu/mineena waanzala junoodan lam tarawha waAAaththaba allatheena kafaroo wathalika jazao alkafireena

9:26. Then Allah caused His Messenger and the believers to be calm and He sent down forces you did not see, and He punished those who suppressed the Truth. And that is the recompense for the suppressors of the Truth!

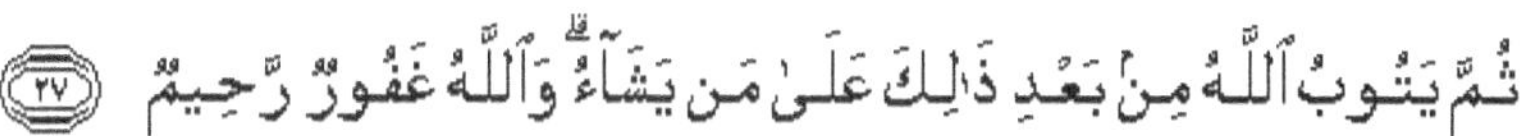

27. Thumma yatoobu All*a*hu min baAAdi *tha*lika AAal*a* man yash*a*o waAll*a*hu ghafoorun ra*h*eem**un**

9:27. Then, after that, Allah pardons whom He wills. And Allah is Forgiving, Merciful.

28. Y*a* ayyuh*a* alla*thee*na *a*manoo innam*a* almushrikoona najasun fal*a* yaqraboo almasjida al*h*ar*a*ma baAAda AAamihim *h*atha wa-in khiftum AAaylatan fasawfa yughneekumu All*a*hu min fa*d*lihi in sh*a*a inna All*a*ha AAaleemun *h*akeem**un**

9:28. O you who believe! The polytheists are nothing but pollution[9]. So, they shall not approach the Sacred Place of Worship[10] after this year. And if you fear poverty then Allah will enrich you out of His grace if He wills.[11] Indeed, Allah is Knowledgeable, Wise.

9. This is a strong but appropriate divine condemnation of all those who worship anyone other than Allah (or any other appropriate name He is called by), the Sole Creator of the entire universe and everything therein. Everything in the universe points to a Single Authority administering the entire show. This Single Authority, and no one else, deserves to be worshipped; for, if someone else is worshipped, then that someone else could only be a created being, and it would be preposterous to

worship a created being as one would worship the Creator! Such a worship of anyone other than the Creator would not only be an act of utter injustice, but it would be tantamount to perpetration of falsehood. It would be an anachronism in the True Creator's creation. It would be nothing but pollution. It could not but pollute the human society created by that Sole Creator.

10. The Kaabah at Makkah.

11. The Kaabah was held in veneration by the Arab people even before Islam. In fact, it was a source of pecuniary benefits to Makkans from visitors from all over the Arabian Peninsula. Now if non-believers, who still constituted a great number among the Arab people, were to be banned entry to the Kaabah, it would be a financial loss to the Makkans. It is this fear that is alluded to here. And Allah promises the Makkans to enrich them by His grace. We are all witnesses now to the fulfillment of this divine promise and prophecy. The Arab country is not only flush with petro-money, but the Kaabah is visited now, all the year round, by millions of people from all over the world.

قَـٰتِلُواْ ٱلَّذِينَ لَا يُؤْمِنُونَ بِٱللَّهِ وَلَا بِٱلْيَوْمِ ٱلْأَخِرِ وَلَا يُحَرِّمُونَ مَا حَرَّمَ ٱللَّهُ

وَرَسُولُهُۥ وَلَا يَدِينُونَ دِينَ ٱلْحَقِّ مِنَ ٱلَّذِينَ أُوتُواْ ٱلْكِتَـٰبَ حَتَّىٰ يُعْطُواْ

ٱلْجِزْيَةَ عَن يَدٍ وَهُمْ صَـٰغِرُونَ ﴿٢٩﴾

29. Qatiloo alla*theena la* yu/minoona biAll*a*hi wal*a* bialyawmi al-*a*khiri wal*a* yu*h*arrimoona m*a h*arrama All*a*hu warasooluhu wal*a* yadeenoona deena al*h*aqqi mina alla*theena* ootoo alkit*a*ba *h*atta yuAA*t*oo aljizyata AAan yadin wahum *sa*ghiroona

9:29. Fight those who do not believe in Allah, nor in the Last Day, nor prohibit what Allah and His Messenger have prohibited, and fight those people of the Book, who do not follow the Religion of the Truth, until they willingly pay tax as subjects.

وَقَالَتِ ٱلْيَهُودُ عُزَيْرٌ ٱبْنُ ٱللَّهِ وَقَالَتِ ٱلنَّصَـٰرَى ٱلْمَسِيحُ ٱبْنُ ٱللَّهِ ذَٰلِكَ

قَوْلُهُم بِأَفْوَٰهِهِمْ يُضَـٰهِـُٔونَ قَوْلَ ٱلَّذِينَ كَفَرُواْ مِن قَبْلُ قَـٰتَلَهُمُ ٱللَّهُ

أَنَّىٰ يُؤْفَكُونَ ﴿٣٠﴾

30. Waq*a*lati alyahoodu AAuzayrun ibnu All*a*hi waq*a*lati a*l*nna*sara* almasee*h*u ibnu All*a*hi *tha*lika qawluhum bi-afw*a*hihim yu*da*hi-oona qawla alla*th*eena kafaroo min qablu q*a*talahumu All*a*hu ann*a* yu/fakoon**a**

9:30. And the Jews say, "Uzayr[12] is the son of Allah." And the Christians say, "The Messiah is the son of Allah." Those are their oral sayings. They imitate the saying of those who suppressed the Truth before. May Allah destroy them; how deluded are they!

---

12. This Arabic name is ascribed to Ezra, who had led some Jews back to Jerusalem from their Babylonian exile. But since there is no Jewish scripture available now, which mentions Ezra as 'son of God', Uzayr may be someone whom only the Jews living in Arabia during the time of revelation of the Qur'aan called 'son of God'. Ezra too is held by the Jews in such a high veneration that everything he said was considered sacrosanct, and, in that sense, he was elevated to the status of a lord besides Allah, and such elevation is condemned in the next Verse.

ٱتَّخَذُوٓاْ أَحْبَارَهُمْ وَرُهْبَٰنَهُمْ أَرْبَابًا مِّن دُونِ ٱللَّهِ وَٱلْمَسِيحَ ٱبْنَ مَرْيَمَ

وَمَآ أُمِرُوٓاْ إِلَّا لِيَعْبُدُوٓاْ إِلَٰهًا وَٰحِدًا لَّآ إِلَٰهَ إِلَّا هُوَ سُبْحَٰنَهُۥ عَمَّا يُشْرِكُونَ

31. Ittakha*th*oo a*h*barahum waruhb*a*nahum arb*a*ban min dooni All*a*hi wa*a*lmasee*h*a ibna maryama wam*a* omiroo ill*a* liyaAAbudoo il*a*han w*a*hidan l*a* il*a*ha ill*a* huwa sub*h*anahu AAamm*a* yushrikoon**a**

9:31. They have taken their rabbis and their priests and the Messiah, son of Mary, for lords besides Allah. And they were not enjoined but that they have none but One Allah to worship. There is no god but He. HE is too high in glory, above what they worship besides Him.

يُرِيدُونَ أَن يُطْفِئُوا نُورَ ٱللَّهِ بِأَفْوَٰهِهِمْ وَيَأْبَى ٱللَّهُ إِلَّا أَن يُتِمَّ نُورَهُۥ وَلَوْ
كَرِهَ ٱلْكَٰفِرُونَ ﴿٣٢﴾

32. Yureedoona an yu*tf*i-oo noora Alla*h*i bi-afwa*h*ihim waya/b*a* Alla*h*u ill*a* an yutimma noorahu walaw kariha alk*a*firoon*a*

9:32. They wish to put out Allah's light with their mouths, and Allah refuses to consent to anything but to perfect His light[13], even though the suppressors of the Truth are averse.

---

13. This Verse is another divine reiteration that Allah's light is perfected. HIS will cannot but be fulfilled. And what is Allah's light? A light is something with which we can see our way in doing various things. And in the context here, Allah's light is His guidance for man to lead his life correctly to attain salvation. This divine guidance, as this Verse reiterates, is bound to be <u>perfected</u>. The Qur'aan, no doubt, is the divine guidance and it is perfected, in view of <u>Verse 5:3</u>. Now, despite Allah Almighty giving us this perfect Qur'aan, Muslims in this age insist that it is not perfect. They say the *ahaadeeth* are needed to make it perfect. And the sad part is that even renowned Islamic scholars believe in this. I have heard Dr Zakir Naik say that the Muslims offer their Zuhr and Asr prayers silently in pursuance of instructions in the *ahaadeeth*, even though the divine instruction in Qur'aanic Verse 17:110 is expressly against such silently offered prayers. It is sad indeed that even with the scholars, the man-influenced and error-prone *ahaadeeth* supersede the divinely perfected and preserved Qur'aan!!

هُوَ ٱلَّذِى أَرْسَلَ رَسُولَهُۥ بِٱلْهُدَىٰ وَدِينِ ٱلْحَقِّ لِيُظْهِرَهُۥ
عَلَى ٱلدِّينِ كُلِّهِۦ وَلَوْ كَرِهَ ٱلْمُشْرِكُونَ ﴿٣٣﴾

33. Huwa alla*t*hee arsala rasoolahu bialhud*a* wadeeni al*h*aqqi liyu*t*hhirahu AAal*a* alddeeni kullihi walaw kariha almushrikoon*a*

9:33. HE it is Who sent His Messenger with guidance and the Religion (Way of Life) of the Truth, that He might cause it to prevail over all religions, even though the polytheists are averse.[14]

14. In view of this Verse, Islam supersedes all other religions for the entire mankind.

﴿ يَـٰٓأَيُّهَا ٱلَّذِينَ ءَامَنُوٓاْ إِنَّ كَثِيرًا مِّنَ ٱلْأَحْبَارِ وَٱلرُّهْبَانِ لَيَأْكُلُونَ أَمْوَٰلَ ٱلنَّاسِ بِٱلْبَـٰطِلِ وَيَصُدُّونَ عَن سَبِيلِ ٱللَّهِ ۗ وَٱلَّذِينَ يَكْنِزُونَ ٱلذَّهَبَ وَٱلْفِضَّةَ وَلَا يُنفِقُونَهَا فِى سَبِيلِ ٱللَّهِ فَبَشِّرْهُم بِعَذَابٍ أَلِيمٍ ﴾ ٣٤

34. Ya ayyuha alla*th*eena *a*manoo inna katheeran mina al-a*h*bari waalrruhbani laya/kuloona amwala alnnasi bialba*t*ili wayasuddoona AAan sabeeli Allahi waalla*th*eena yaknizoona al*thth*ahaba waalfi*dd*ata wala yunfiqoonaha fee sabeeli Allahi fabashshirhum biAAa*th*abin aleem*in*

9:34. O you who believe! Indeed, many of the rabbis and the priests eat away people's property falsely and turn them away from Allah's Path.[15] And to those, who hoard up gold and silver and do not spend it in Allah's Path, announce a painful punishment,

15. At the time of the revelation of the Qur'aan, the religious leaders of the Jews and the Christians did this, but now, Muslim religious leaders too do it.

﴿ يَوْمَ يُحْمَىٰ عَلَيْهَا فِى نَارِ جَهَنَّمَ فَتُكْوَىٰ بِهَا جِبَاهُهُمْ وَجُنُوبُهُمْ وَظُهُورُهُمْ ۖ هَـٰذَا مَا كَنَزْتُمْ لِأَنفُسِكُمْ فَذُوقُواْ مَا كُنتُمْ تَكْنِزُونَ ﴾ ٣٥

35. Yawma yu*h*ma AAalayha fee nari jahannama fatukwa biha jibahuhum wajunoobuhum wa*th*uhooruhum ha*th*a ma kanaztum li-anfusikum fa*th*ooqoo ma kuntum taknizoona

9:35. On the day (when the said hoarders will be punished) it[16] shall be subjected to the intense heat in the fire of hell, and then their (hoarders') foreheads and their sides and their backs shall be branded with it. (They will then be told,) 'This is what you hoarded up for yourselves; have a taste, then, of what you hoarded!'

---

16. I.e., what is hoarded, as this Verse itself explains later.

إِنَّ عِدَّةَ ٱلشُّهُورِ عِندَ ٱللَّهِ ٱثْنَا عَشَرَ شَهْرًا فِى كِتَـٰبِ ٱللَّهِ يَوْمَ خَلَقَ ٱلسَّمَـٰوَٰتِ وَٱلْأَرْضَ مِنْهَآ أَرْبَعَةٌ حُرُمٌ ذَٰلِكَ ٱلدِّينُ ٱلْقَيِّمُ فَلَا تَظْلِمُواْ فِيهِنَّ أَنفُسَكُمْ وَقَـٰتِلُواْ ٱلْمُشْرِكِينَ كَآفَّةً كَمَا يُقَـٰتِلُونَكُمْ كَآفَّةً وَٱعْلَمُوٓاْ أَنَّ ٱللَّهَ مَعَ ٱلْمُتَّقِينَ ﴿٣٦﴾

36. Inna AAiddata alshshuhoori AAinda Allahi ithna AAashara shahran fee kitabi Allahi yawma khalaqa alssamawati waal-arda minha arbaAAatun hurumun thalika alddeenu alqayyimu fala tathlimoo feehinna anfusakum waqatiloo almushrikeena kaffatan kama yuqatiloonakum kaffatan waiAAlamoo anna Allaha maAAa almuttaqeena

---

9:36. Indeed, since the day when Allah created the heavens and the earth, the number of months recorded with Allah is twelve, of which four are sacred.[17] That is the established way. So, commit no wrong in this regard[18] and fight the polytheists in the same total way as they fight you. And know that Allah is with those who fear Him and do righteous things.

---

17. Refer study note 328 on <u>Verse 2:194</u> **in this regard.**

18. The Hindus have the system of having additional (13th) month every few years to make their lunar year synchronise with the solar year. The Arabs too were observing, before the advent of Islam, a similar system primarily in the interest of their trading activities. And they adjusted their sacred months too to suit their worldly purpose, as the next Verse indicates. Allah here prohibits such practices. Had these practices been allowed to continue the fasting and the Hajj months would have remained in the same season and not rotating through different seasons. In this rotation lies Allah's Mercy in that we wouldn't always have to face the same climatic extremities during fasting and Hajj pilgrimage.

إِنَّمَا ٱلنَّسِىٓءُ زِيَادَةٌ فِى ٱلْكُفْرِ يُضَلُّ بِهِ ٱلَّذِينَ كَفَرُوا۟ يُحِلُّونَهُۥ عَامًا وَيُحَرِّمُونَهُۥ عَامًا لِّيُوَاطِـُٔوا۟ عِدَّةَ مَا حَرَّمَ ٱللَّهُ فَيُحِلُّوا۟ مَا حَرَّمَ ٱللَّهُ زُيِّنَ لَهُمْ سُوٓءُ أَعْمَٰلِهِمْ وَٱللَّهُ لَا يَهْدِى ٱلْقَوْمَ ٱلْكَٰفِرِينَ ﴿٣٧﴾

37. Innam*a* alnnasee-o ziy*a*datun fee alkufri yu*d*allu bihi alla*th*eena kafaroo yu*h*illoonahu AA*a*man wayu*h*arrimoonahu AA*a*man liyuwa*t*i-oo AAiddata m*a* *h*arrama All*a*hu fayu*h*illoo m*a* *h*arrama All*a*hu zuyyina lahum soo-o aAAm*a*lihim waAll*a*hu l*a* yahdee alqawma alk*a*fireen**a**

9:37. The intercalation in a calendar is only an addition to the suppression of the Truth, wherewith the suppressors are led astray. They treat a month as non-sacred for one year and make it sacred in another to make up the number of months that Allah has made sacred. Thus, do they then violate the sanctity of what Allah has made sacred! The evil of their deeds is made to seem fair to them. And Allah does not guide the people who suppress the Truth.

يَٰٓأَيُّهَا ٱلَّذِينَ ءَامَنُوا۟ مَا لَكُمْ إِذَا قِيلَ لَكُمُ ٱنفِرُوا۟ فِى سَبِيلِ ٱللَّهِ ٱثَّاقَلْتُمْ إِلَى ٱلْأَرْضِ أَرَضِيتُم بِٱلْحَيَوٰةِ ٱلدُّنْيَا مِنَ ٱلْءَاخِرَةِ فَمَا مَتَٰعُ ٱلْحَيَوٰةِ ٱلدُّنْيَا فِى ٱلْءَاخِرَةِ إِلَّا قَلِيلٌ ﴿٣٨﴾

38. Y*a* ayyuh*a* alla*th*eena *a*manoo m*a* lakum i*th*a qeela lakumu infiroo fee sabeeli All*a*hi iththaqaltum ila al-ar*d*i ara*d*eetum bial*h*ayati alddunya mina al-*a*khirati fam*a* mat*a*AAu al*h*ay*a*ti alddunya fee al-akhirati ill*a* qaleel**un**

9:38. O you who believe! What is the matter with you that when you are asked to set out in Allah's Path, you cling heavily to the earth? Do you prefer this life to the Hereafter when the provisions of this life count for nothing but little in the Hereafter? [19]

---

19. The Verse itself depicts the circumstances in which it – as also the Verses that follow – was revealed. The Prophet (peace be upon him) was to embark on a difficult military expedition. And several men were reluctant to go with him.

إِلَّا تَنفِرُواْ يُعَذِّبْكُمْ عَذَابًا أَلِيمًا وَيَسْتَبْدِلْ قَوْمًا غَيْرَكُمْ وَلَا تَضُرُّوهُ شَيْئًا وَٱللَّهُ عَلَىٰ كُلِّ شَىْءٍ قَدِيرٌ ﴿٣٩﴾

39. Illa tanfiroo yuAAaththibkum AAathaban aleeman wayastabdil qawman ghayrakum wala tadurroohu shay-an waAllahu AAala kulli shay-in qadeerun

---

9:39. If set you out not, He will punish you with a painful punishment and replace you with another people, and you can do Him no harm! And Allah has power over all things.

إِلَّا تَنصُرُوهُ فَقَدْ نَصَرَهُ ٱللَّهُ إِذْ أَخْرَجَهُ ٱلَّذِينَ كَفَرُواْ ثَانِىَ ٱثْنَيْنِ إِذْ هُمَا فِى ٱلْغَارِ إِذْ يَقُولُ لِصَحِبِهِ لَا تَحْزَنْ إِنَّ ٱللَّهَ مَعَنَا فَأَنزَلَ ٱللَّهُ سَكِينَتَهُ عَلَيْهِ وَأَيَّدَهُ بِجُنُودٍ لَّمْ تَرَوْهَا وَجَعَلَ كَلِمَةَ ٱلَّذِينَ كَفَرُواْ ٱلسُّفْلَىٰ وَكَلِمَةُ ٱللَّهِ هِىَ ٱلْعُلْيَا وَٱللَّهُ عَزِيزٌ حَكِيمٌ ﴿٤٠﴾

40. Illa tansuroohu faqad nasarahu Allahu ith akhrajahu allatheena kafaroo thaniya ithnayni ith huma fee alghari ith yaqoolu lisahibihi la tahzan inna Allaha maAAana faanzala Allahu sakeenatahu AAalayhi waayyadahu bijunoodin lam tarawha wajaAAala kalimata allatheena kafaroo alssufla wakalimatu Allahi hiya alAAulya waAllahu AAazeezun hakeemun

---

9:40. If you help him not, Allah did certainly help him when those who suppressed the Truth expelled him. He was one of the two in the cave when he said to his companion, "Grieve not, Allah is indeed with us." Then Allah caused him to be calm and peaceful[20]

and strengthened him with armies you couldn't see[21]. And He lowered the word of those who suppressed the Truth and raised the word of Allah high[22]. And Allah is Omnipotent, Wise.

20. This refers to the episode when the Prophet and his companion Abu Bakr were hiding in a cave with the murderous Makkans in hot poursuit of him. After reaching Medina safely, the Prophet laid down the foundation of a fledgling Islamic State there.

21. Then, in the first war against the polytheist Makkans at Badr, Allah Almighty had helped the believers with a contingent of angels (<u>Verses 8:9 and 8:10</u>).

22. And, ultimately, polytheistic Makkah was conquered by the believers in a bloodless war. Islam became the dominant force in the entire Arabian Peninsula.

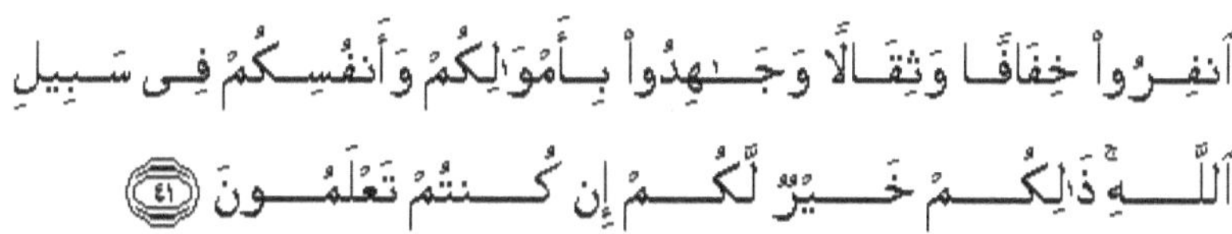

41. Infiroo khi*f*a*f*an wathiq*a*lan waj*a*hidoo bi-amw*a*likum waanfusikum fee sabeeli All*a*hi *tha*likum khayrun lakum in kuntum taAAlamoon*a*

9:41. Set out light and heavy[23] and strive hard in Allah's Path with your property and your persons! This is better for you, if you would know.

23. I.e., with whatever arms are available.

لَـوۡ كَـانَ عَرَضًا قَرِيبًا وَسَـفَرًا قَـاصِدًا لَّاتَّبَعُـوكَ وَلَـٰكِـنۢ
بَعُـدَتۡ عَلَيۡهِـمُ ٱلشُّقَّةُ وَسَـيَحۡلِفُونَ بِٱللَّـهِ لَـوِ ٱسۡـتَطَعۡنَا لَخَرَجۡنَـا
مَعَكُـمۡ يُهۡلِكُـونَ أَنفُسَـهُمۡ وَٱللَّـهُ يَعۡلَـمُ إِنَّهُـمۡ لَكَـٰذِبُـونَ ۝

42. Law kana AAaradan qareeban wasafaran qasidan laittabaAAooka walakin baAAudat AAalayhimu alshshuqqatu wasayahlifoona biAllahi lawi istaAAna lakharajna maAAakum yuhlikoona anfusahum waAllahu yaAAlamu innahum lakathiboona

---

9:42. Had it been a near expedition and a short journey, they would certainly have followed you, but the long journey was too much for them. And they swear by Allah, "If only we could, we would certainly have set out with you." They are killing their own souls, and Allah knows for certain that they are lying!

عَفَا ٱللَّـهُ عَنكَ لِمَ أَذِنتَ لَهُمۡ حَتَّىٰ يَتَبَيَّنَ لَكَ ٱلَّذِينَ صَدَقُواْ وَتَعۡلَمَ
ٱلۡكَـٰذِبِينَ ۝

43. AAafa Allahu AAanka lima athinta lahum hatta yatabayyana laka allatheena sadaqoo wataAAlama alkathibeena

---

9:43. May Allah pardon you (the Prophet)! Why did you exempt them before it became clear to you as to who were speaking the truth and you knew who the liars were?

لَا يَسۡتَـٔۡذِنُكَ ٱلَّـذِينَ يُؤۡمِنُونَ بِٱللَّهِ وَٱلۡيَوۡمِ ٱلۡأَخِرِ أَن يُجَـٰهِدُواْ بِأَمۡوَٰلِهِمۡ
وَأَنفُسِـهِمۡ وَٱللَّـهُ عَلِيمٌۢ بِـٱلۡمُتَّقِينَ ۝

44. *La* yasta/*th*inuka alla*th*eena yu/minoona biAll*a*hi wa*a*lyawmi al-*a*khiri an yuj*a*hidoo bi-amw*a*lihim waanfusihim waAll*a*hu AAaleemun bialmuttaqeena

---

9:44. Those who believe in Allah and the Last Day do not ask you to exempt them from exerting themselves in Allah's Path with their wealth and their persons. And Allah knows those who guard against evil.

إِنَّمَا يَسْتَئْذِنُكَ الَّذِينَ لَا يُؤْمِنُونَ بِاللَّهِ وَالْيَوْمِ الْآخِرِ وَارْتَابَتْ قُلُوبُهُمْ فَهُمْ فِى رَيْبِهِمْ يَتَرَدَّدُونَ ﴿٤٥﴾

45. Innam*a* yasta/*th*inuka alla*th*eena *la* yu/minoona biAll*a*hi wa*a*lyawmi al-*a*khiri wa*l*rt*a*bat quloobuhum fahum fee raybihim yataraddadoon*a*

9:45. Only those, who do not believe in Allah and the Last Day, ask you for exemption and their hearts are in doubt. And they waver in their doubts.

۞ وَلَوْ أَرَادُواْ الْخُرُوجَ لَأَعَدُّواْ لَهُ عُدَّةً وَلَكِن كَرِهَ اللَّهُ انْبِعَاثَهُمْ فَثَبَّطَهُمْ وَقِيلَ اقْعُدُواْ مَعَ الْقَاعِدِينَ ﴿٤٦﴾

46. Walaw ar*a*doo alkhurooja laaAAaddoo lahu AAuddatan wal*a*kin kariha All*a*hu inbiAA*a*thahum fathabba*ra*hum waqeela oqAAudoo maAA*a* alq*a*AAideen*a*

9:46. And if they had really intended to set out, they would certainly have prepared for it. But Allah did not like them proceeding, so He held them back. And they were told to sit back with those who sit back.

لَوْ خَرَجُواْ فِيكُم مَّا زَادُوكُمْ إِلَّا خَبَالًا وَلَأَوْضَعُواْ خِلَلَكُمْ يَبْغُونَكُمُ الْفِتْنَةَ وَفِيكُمْ سَمَّعُونَ لَهُمْ وَاللَّهُ عَلِيمٌ بِالظَّـٰلِمِينَ ﴿٤٧﴾

47. Law kharajoo feekum ma zadookum illa khabalan walaawdaAAoo khilalakum yabghoonakumu alfitnata wafeekum sammaAAoona lahum waAllahu AAaleemun bialththalimeena

---

9:47. Had they been out in your midst, they would have added nothing but corruption in your ranks, and they would certainly have been active seeking dissension amongst you. And among you there are those who would listen to them. And Allah is aware of the wrong-doers.

لَقَدِ ابْتَغَوُاْ الْفِتْنَةَ مِن قَبْلُ وَقَلَّبُواْ لَكَ الْأُمُورَ حَتَّىٰ جَآءَ الْحَقُّ وَظَهَرَ أَمْرُ اللَّهِ وَهُمْ كَٰرِهُونَ ﴿٤٨﴾

48. Laqadi ibtaghawoo alfitnata min qablu waqallaboo laka al-omoora hatta jaa alhaqqu wathahara amru Allahi wahum karihoona

---

9:48. They certainly sought dissension before, and upset matters for you, until the truth came, and Allah's commandment prevailed, despite their dislike.

وَمِنْهُم مَّن يَقُولُ ائْذَن لِّى وَلَا تَفْتِنِّىٓ أَلَا فِى الْفِتْنَةِ سَقَطُواْ وَإِنَّ جَهَنَّمَ لَمُحِيطَةٌ بِالْكَٰفِرِينَ ﴿٤٩﴾

49. Waminhum man yaqoolu i/than lee wala taftinnee ala fee alfitnati saqatoo wa-inna jahannama lamuheetatun bialkafireena

9:49. And among them, there is one who says, "Allow me and try me not." Have they not already failed in the trial? And Hell does indeed encompass those who suppress the Truth!

إِن تُصِبْكَ حَسَنَةٌ تَسُؤْهُمْ وَإِن تُصِبْكَ مُصِيبَةٌ يَقُولُواْ قَدْ أَخَذْنَآ أَمْرَنَا مِن قَبْلُ وَيَتَوَلَّواْ وَّهُمْ فَرِحُونَ ۞

50. In tusibka *h*asanatun tasu/hum wa-in tusibka mu*s*eebatun yaqooloo qad akha*th*na amran*a* min qablu wayatawallaw wahum fari*h*oon**a**

9:50. If anything good comes your way, it grieves them. And if hardship afflicts you, they say, "Certainly, it was to our good that we had taken our affairs into our own hands beforehand." And they turn back happy!

قُل لَّن يُصِيبَنَآ إِلَّا مَا كَتَبَ ٱللَّهُ لَنَا هُوَ مَوْلَنَا وَعَلَى ٱللَّهِ فَلْيَتَوَكَّلِ ٱلْمُؤْمِنُونَ ۞

51. Qul lan yu*s*eeban*a* ill*a* m*a* kataba All*a*hu lan*a* huwa mawl*a*na waAAal*a* All*a*hi falyatawakkali almu/minoon**a**

9:51. Say, "Nothing afflicts us save what Allah has ordained for us. He is our Patron." And on Allah then let the believers put their trust.

قُـلْ هَـلْ تَرَبَّصُـونَ بِنَا إِلَّا إِحْـدَى ٱلْحُسْنَيَيْنِ وَنَحْنُ نَتَرَبَّصُ بِـكُم أَن يُصِيبَكُـمُ ٱللَّـهُ بِعَـذَابٍ مِّـنْ عِنـدِهِ أَوْ بِأَيْدِينَا فَتَرَبَّصُوٓاْ إِنَّا مَعَكُـم مُّتَرَبِّصُونَ ۝

52. Qul hal tarabbasoona bina illa ihda alhusnayayni wanahnu natarabbasu bikum an yuseebakumu Allahu biAAathabin min AAindihi aw bi-aydeena fatarabbasoo inna maAAakum mutarabbisoona

---

9:52. Say, "Do you expect anything but either of two good things[24] happening to us? And for you we expect punishment from Allah Himself or by our hands. So, wait; we too will wait with you!"

---

24. Victory or martyrdom.

قُلْ أَنفِقُواْ طَوْعًا أَوْ كَرْهًا لَّن يُتَقَبَّلَ مِنكُمْ إِنَّكُمْ كُنتُمْ قَوْمًا فَـٰسِقِينَ ۝

53. Qul anfiqoo tawAAan aw karhan lan yutaqabbala minkum innakum kuntum qawman fasiqeena

---

9:53. Say, "Whether you make the contribution willingly or unwillingly, it shall not be accepted from you. Indeed, you are a people working against Allah's commandments."[25]

---

25. Allah's commandment was to obey the Prophet and willingly follow him in the expedition he was undertaking. The rigours of the expedition were a test for the belief of the people. And some of them failed in that test when they sought exemptions under one pretext or the other (refer Verses above). Such people would come forth with some material contribution, in lieu of personal participation. It was such contribution which was rejected in this Verse.

وَمَا مَنَعَهُمْ أَن تُقْبَلَ مِنْهُمْ نَفَقَتُهُمْ إِلَّا أَنَّهُمْ كَفَرُواْ بِاللَّهِ وَبِرَسُولِهِۦ وَلَا

يَأْتُونَ ٱلصَّلَوٰةَ إِلَّا وَهُمْ كُسَالَىٰ وَلَا يُنفِقُونَ إِلَّا وَهُمْ كَٰرِهُونَ ۞

54. Wama manaAAahum an tuqbala minhum nafaqatuhum illa annahum kafaroo biAllahi wabirasoolihi wala ya/toona alssalata illa wahum kusala wala yunfiqoona illa wahum karihoona

9:54. And nothing prevents their contributions being accepted from them, except that they disbelieve in Allah and in His Messenger. And they do not come to prayer but sluggishly, and they do not contribute but unwillingly.[26]

26. The people described here were, of course, those living during the lifetime of the Prophet. But aren't exactly the same types of persons living now, in this age, as Muslims? There indeed are! They are there in very great numbers, and, perhaps, they constitute the majority, unfortunately, among the Muslims in the world today. Allah Almighty is aware of this, and He has relegated them to a humiliating position in the affairs of this world. They count for nothing. Even a small state like Israel can oppress them with impunity. This is a divine warning to them (Muslims) to mend their ways and revert to complete submission to Allah's commands as given in the Qur'aan. But are the Muslims taking the warning seriously?

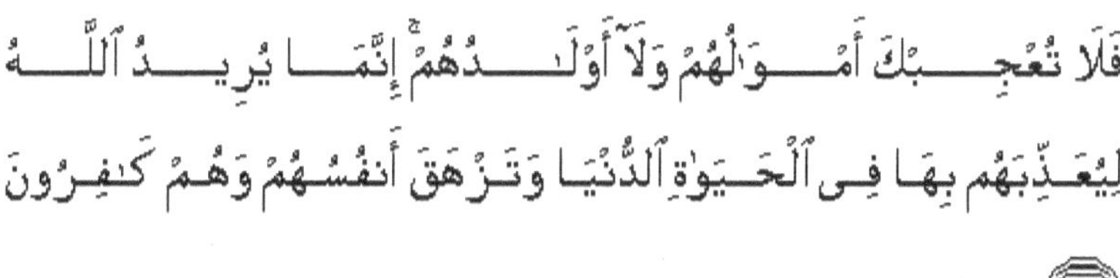

فَلَا تُعْجِبْكَ أَمْوَٰلُهُمْ وَلَآ أَوْلَٰدُهُمْ إِنَّمَا يُرِيدُ ٱللَّهُ

لِيُعَذِّبَهُم بِهَا فِى ٱلْحَيَوٰةِ ٱلدُّنْيَا وَتَزْهَقَ أَنفُسُهُمْ وَهُمْ كَٰفِرُونَ ۞

55. Fala tuAAjibka amwaluhum wala awladuhum innama yureedu Allahu liyuAAaththibahum biha fee alhayati alddunya watazhaqa anfusuhum wahum kafiroona

9:55. Let not their wealth and their children then impress you. Allah wishes only to punish them with these, in this life, and to cause their souls to depart while they suppress the Truth.

وَيَحْلِفُونَ بِاللَّهِ إِنَّهُمْ لَمِنكُمْ وَمَا هُم مِّنكُمْ وَلَـٰكِنَّهُمْ قَوْمٌ يَفْرَقُونَ ۝

56. Wayahlifoona biAllahi innahum laminkum wama hum minkum walakinnahum qawmun yafraqoona

9:56. And they swear by Allah that they are indeed with you. And they are not with you, but they are a people who are scared[27].

27. The hypocrites' fear is born of their uncertainty. They do not have a staunch belief in Allah and His Messenger but are afraid to say so openly.

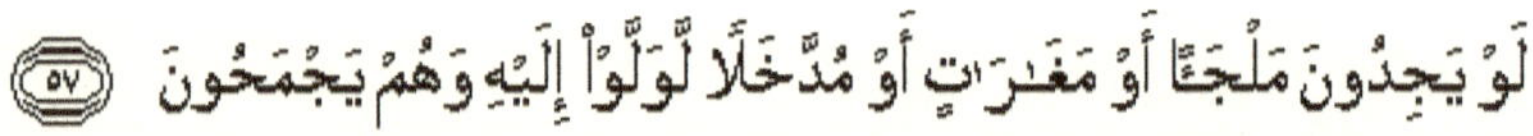

لَوْ يَجِدُونَ مَلْجَأً أَوْ مَغَـٰرَاتٍ أَوْ مُدَّخَلًا لَّوَلَّوْاْ إِلَيْهِ وَهُمْ يَجْمَحُونَ ۝

57. Law yajidoona maljaan aw magharatin aw muddakhalan lawallaw ilayhi wahum yajmahoona

9:57. If they could find a refuge or caves or a place to go to, they would certainly have rushed thereto.

وَمِنْهُم مَّن يَلْمِزُكَ فِى ٱلصَّدَقَٰتِ فَإِنْ أُعْطُواْ مِنْهَا رَضُواْ وَإِن لَّمْ يُعْطَوْاْ مِنْهَآ إِذَا هُمْ يَسْخَطُونَ ۝

58. Waminhum man yalmizuka fee alssadaqati fa-in oAAroo minha radoo wa-in lam yuAAraw minha itha hum yaskharoona

---

9:58. And among them are those who blame you for misuse of the welfare funds[28]. If they are given anything from it they are pleased. And if they are not given anything from it, they are indignant.

---

28. The Arabic word used is *sadaqaat*. Translators have rendered its meaning to be the same as of *zakaat*, viz, alms or charities. *Zakaat* has been defined in Verse 30.39 as something given away seeking only the pleasure of Allah. *Zakaat* therefore constitutes a voluntary deed. *Sadaqah* [singular form of *Sadaqaat*], on the other hand, is a Fund collected through mandatory cuts from individual persons' incomes. It is collected, in the manner of a tax levied by modern governments, for welfare measures to be undertaken by the State. This is apparent from Verse 9.60 below. 'Welfare Funds' would therefore be a better translation for *sadaqaat*.

وَلَوْ أَنَّهُمْ رَضُواْ مَآ ءَاتَىٰهُمُ ٱللَّهُ وَرَسُولُهُۥ وَقَالُواْ حَسْبُنَا ٱللَّهُ سَيُؤْتِينَا ٱللَّهُ مِن فَضْلِهِۦ وَرَسُولُهُۥٓ إِنَّآ إِلَى ٱللَّهِ رَٰغِبُونَ ۝

59. Walaw annahum radoo ma atahumu Allahu warasooluhu waqaloo hasbuna Allahu sayu/teena Allahu min fadlihi warasooluhu inna ila Allahi raghiboona

---

9:59. And if only they were content with what Allah and His Messenger gave them! And had they only said, "Allah is sufficient for us. Allah and His Messenger will give us out of His grace. To Allah indeed we do turn in hope and humility!"

إِنَّمَا ٱلصَّدَقَٰتُ لِلْفُقَرَآءِ وَٱلْمَسَٰكِينِ وَٱلْعَٰمِلِينَ عَلَيْهَا وَٱلْمُؤَلَّفَةِ قُلُوبُهُمْ وَفِى ٱلرِّقَابِ وَٱلْغَٰرِمِينَ وَفِى سَبِيلِ ٱللَّهِ وَٱبْنِ ٱلسَّبِيلِ فَرِيضَةً مِّنَ ٱللَّهِ وَٱللَّهُ عَلِيمٌ حَكِيمٌ ۝

60. Innama alssadaqatu lilfuqara-i waalmasakeeni waalAAamileena AAalayha waalmu-allafati quloobuhum wafee alrriqabi waalgharimeena wafee sabeeli Allahi waibni alssabeeli fareedatan mina Allahi waAllahu AAaleemun hakeemun

---

9:60. The *Sadaqaat*[29] are to be spent only for the poor, the needy, the administrators over those (*Sadaqaat*), the bringing together of their minds in mutual affection[30], the captives, those in debts, in the path of Allah, and those who tread that path. It's a mandatory ordinance from Allah. And Allah is Knowledgeable, Wise.

---

29. See study note 28 above.

30. The poor, the needy, and the administrators need to be properly trained in Islamic values, to generate mutual affection amongst them, and to prevent any misuse of the welfare fund.

وَمِنْهُمُ ٱلَّذِينَ يُؤْذُونَ ٱلنَّبِىَّ وَيَقُولُونَ هُوَ أُذُنٌ قُلْ أُذُنُ خَيْرٍ لَّكُمْ يُؤْمِنُ بِٱللَّهِ وَيُؤْمِنُ لِلْمُؤْمِنِينَ وَرَحْمَةٌ لِّلَّذِينَ ءَامَنُواْ مِنكُمْ وَٱلَّذِينَ يُؤْذُونَ رَسُولَ ٱللَّهِ لَهُمْ عَذَابٌ أَلِيمٌ

61. Waminhumu allatheena yu/thoona alnnabiyya wayaqooloona huwa othunun qul othunu khayrin lakum yu/minu biAllahi wayu/minu lilmu/mineena warahmatun lillatheena amanoo minkum waallatheena yu/thoona rasoola Allahi lahum AAathabun aleemun

---

9:61. And among them are those who hurt the Prophet and say, "He is all ear[31]." Say, "His ear is for what is good for you. He believes in Allah and believes those who believe and is a mercy for those of you who believe." And for those who hurt the Messenger of Allah, a painful punishment.

---

31. I.e., the Prophet lends his ear to all and sundry.

يَحْلِفُونَ بِٱللَّهِ لَكُمْ لِيُرْضُوكُمْ وَٱللَّهُ وَرَسُولُهُۥٓ أَحَقُّ أَن يُرْضُوهُ إِن كَانُواْ مُؤْمِنِينَ ﴿٦٢﴾

62. Yahlifoona biAllahi lakum liyurdookum waAllahu warasooluhu ahaqqu an yurdoohu in kanoo mu/mineena

---

9:62. They swear to you by Allah, so that they might thereby please you! Allah – and His Messenger – has a greater right that they should please Him, if they do believe.

أَلَمْ يَعْلَمُوٓاْ أَنَّهُۥ مَن يُحَادِدِ ٱللَّهَ وَرَسُولَهُۥ فَأَنَّ لَهُۥ نَارَ جَهَنَّمَ خَـٰلِدًا فِيهَا ذَٰلِكَ ٱلْخِـزْىُ ٱلْعَظِيـمُ ﴿٦٣﴾

63. Alam yaAAlamoo annahu man yuhadidi Allaha warasoolahu faanna lahu nara jahannama khalidan feeha thalika alkhizyu alAAatheemu

---

9:63. Do they not know that he, who opposes Allah and His Messenger, shall surely have the fire of Hell to abide in? That is the great disgrace!

يَحْــذَرُ ٱلْمُنَـٰفِقُــونَ أَن تُــنَزَّلَ عَلَيْهِــمْ سُــورَةٌ تُنَبِّئُــهُم بِمَا فِــى
قُلُوبِهِمْ قُلِ ٱسْتَهْزِءُوٓاْ إِنَّ ٱللَّهَ مُخْرِجٌ مَّا تَحْذَرُونَ ﴿٦٤﴾

64. Ya*hth*aru almun*a*fiqoona an tunazzala AAalayhim sooratun tunabbi-ohum bim*a* fee quloobihim quli istahzi-oo inna All*a*ha mukhrijun m*a* ta*hth*aroon**a**

9:64. The hypocrites fear lest a chapter of the Qur'aan should be sent down to them telling them plainly of what is in their hearts. Say, "Mock you may[32]! Allah will indeed bring out what you fear."

---

32. One may wonder how the hypocrites could be mocking when they were seized by fear. Yes, indeed, the hypocrites were in an ambivalent state of mind. They indeed mocked at the believers when they swore by Allah about their belief in Allah and His Messenger being genuine (Verse 62 above). At the same time, they were afraid that their hypocricy might be brought out in the Qur'aan. See also the next Verse 65.

وَلَئِــن سَــأَلْتَهُمْ لَيَقُــولُنَّ إِنَّمَــا كُنَّــا نَخُــوضُ وَنَلْعَــبُ قُــلْ
أَبِٱللَّـهِ وَءَايَـٰتِـهِۦ وَرَسُــولِهِۦ كُــنتُمْ تَسْــتَهْزِءُونَ ﴿٦٥﴾

65. Wala-in saaltahum layaqoolunna innam*a* kunn*a* nakhoo*d*u wanalAAabu qul abiAll*a*hi wa*a*yatihi warasoolihi kuntum tastahzi-oon**a**

9:65. And if you should question them, they would certainly say, "We were just passing our time with idle talk." Say, "Was it at Allah and His Verses and His Messenger that you mocked!?"

لَا تَعْتَذِرُواْ قَدْ كَفَرْتُم بَعْدَ إِيمَٰنِكُمْ إِن نَّعْفُ عَن طَآئِفَةٍ مِّنكُمْ نُعَذِّبْ طَآئِفَةَۢ بِأَنَّهُمْ كَانُواْ مُجْرِمِينَ ۝

66. La taAAatathiroo qad kafartum baAAda eemanikum in naAAfu AAan ta-ifatin minkum nuAAaththib ta-ifatan bi-annahum kanoo mujrimeena

---

9:66. Make no excuses. You have resorted to suppression of the Truth indeed after you had registered your belief. If We do pardon a section of you, We do punish another because they are sinners.

ٱلْمُنَٰفِقُونَ وَٱلْمُنَٰفِقَٰتُ بَعْضُهُم مِّنۢ بَعْضٍ يَأْمُرُونَ بِٱلْمُنكَرِ وَيَنْهَوْنَ عَنِ ٱلْمَعْرُوفِ وَيَقْبِضُونَ أَيْدِيَهُمْ نَسُواْ ٱللَّهَ فَنَسِيَهُمْ إِنَّ ٱلْمُنَٰفِقِينَ هُمُ ٱلْفَٰسِقُونَ ۝

67. Almunafiqoona waalmunafiqatu baAAduhum min baAAdin ya/muroona bialmunkari wayanhawna AAani almaAAroofi wayaqbidoona aydiyahum nasoo Allaha fanasiyahum inna almunafiqeena humu alfasiqoona

---

9:67. The hypocritical men and the hypocritical women are all one from another. They enjoin evil and forbid good and withhold their hands from doing good. They have forgotten Allah, so He has forgotten them. Indeed these – the hypocrites – are the rebels[33].

---

33. against Allah's commandments.

وَعَـدَ ٱللَّـهُ ٱلْمُنَـٰفِقِيـنَ وَٱلْمُنَـٰفِقَـٰتِ وَٱلْكُفَّارَ نَارَ جَهَنَّمَ خَـٰلِدِينَ فِيهَا هِىَ حَسْبُهُمْ وَلَعَنَهُمُ ٱللَّـهُ وَلَهُمْ عَذَابٌ مُّقِيمٌ ۝

68. WaAAada Allahu almunafiqeena waalmunafiqati waalkuffara nara jahannama khalideena feeha hiya hasbuhum walaAAanahumu Allahu walahum AAathabun muqeemun

9:68. Allah has promised to the hypocritical men, the hypocritical women and the suppressors of the Truth, the fire of Hell to abide therein. It is enough for them. And Allah has cursed them. And they shall have lasting punishment.

كَٱلَّذِينَ مِـن قَبْلِكُـمْ كَانُوٓاْ أَشَدَّ مِنكُمْ قُوَّةً وَأَكْثَرَ أَمْوَٰلًا وَأَوْلَـٰدًا فَٱسْتَمْتَعُوٓاْ بِخَـٰلَـٰقِهِمْ فَٱسْتَمْتَعْتُم بِخَـٰلَـٰقِكُمْ كَمَا ٱسْتَمْتَعَ ٱلَّذِينَ مِـن قَبْلِكُـم بِخَـٰلَـٰقِهِمْ وَخُـضْتُمْ كَٱلَّذِى خَاضُوٓاْ أُوْلَـٰئِكَ حَـبِطَتْ أَعْمَـٰلُهُمْ فِى ٱلدُّنْيَا وَٱلْأَخِـرَةِ وَأُوْلَـٰئِكَ هُمُ ٱلْخَـٰسِرُونَ ۝

69. Kaallatheena min qablikum kanoo ashadda minkum quwwatan waakthara amwalan waawladan faistamtaAAoo bikhalaqihim faistamtaAAtum bikhalaqikum kama istamtaAAa allatheena min qablikum bikhalaqihim wakhudtum kaallathee khadoo ola-ika habitat aAAmaluhum fee alddunya waal-akhirati waola-ika humu alkhasiroona

9:69. Like those[34] before you; they were stronger than you in power and more abundant in wealth and children, and they enjoyed their lot. And you have enjoyed your lot as those before you enjoyed their lot. And you indulged in vain talk like they did. Those it is that lost their deeds in this world and in the other. And those are the ones that are doomed!

34. Hypocrites and suppressors of the Truth.

أَلَمْ يَأْتِهِمْ نَبَأُ ٱلَّذِينَ مِن قَبْلِهِمْ قَوْمِ نُوحٍ وَعَادٍ وَثَمُودَ وَقَوْمِ إِبْرَٰهِيمَ وَأَصْحَٰبِ مَدْيَنَ وَٱلْمُؤْتَفِكَٰتِ أَتَتْهُمْ رُسُلُهُم بِٱلْبَيِّنَٰتِ فَمَا كَانَ ٱللَّهُ لِيَظْلِمَهُمْ وَلَٰكِن كَانُوٓاْ أَنفُسَهُمْ يَظْلِمُونَ ۝

70. Alam ya/tihim nabao alla*theena* min qablihim qawmi noo*h*in waAAadin wathamooda waqawmi ibraheema waas-*h*abi madyana waalmu/tafikati atat-hum rusuluhum bialbayyinati fama kana Allahu liyathlimahum walakin kanoo anfusahum yathlimoona

9:70. Has not the information about those before them come to them – of the people of Noah, AA<u>a</u>d and Thamood, the people of Abraham, the dwellers of Midian and the overturned cities [of the people of Lot]? Their Messengers came to them with clear Messages. And it was not Allah Who wronged them, but they wronged themselves.

وَٱلْمُؤْمِنُونَ وَٱلْمُؤْمِنَٰتُ بَعْضُهُمْ أَوْلِيَآءُ بَعْضٍ يَأْمُرُونَ بِٱلْمَعْرُوفِ وَيَنْهَوْنَ عَنِ ٱلْمُنكَرِ وَيُقِيمُونَ ٱلصَّلَوٰةَ وَيُؤْتُونَ ٱلزَّكَوٰةَ وَيُطِيعُونَ ٱللَّهَ وَرَسُولَهُۥٓ أُوْلَٰٓئِكَ سَيَرْحَمُهُمُ ٱللَّهُ إِنَّ ٱللَّهَ عَزِيزٌ حَكِيمٌ ۝

71. Waalmu/minoona waalmu/minatu baAAduhum awliyao baAAdin ya/muroona bialmaAAroofi wayanhawna AAani almunkari wayuqeemoona alssalata wayu/toona alzzakata wayuteeAAoona Allaha warasoolahu ola-ika sayarhamuhumu Allahu inna Allaha AAazeezun hakeemun

9:71. And the believing men and the believing women have close friendly relations with one another. They enjoin good and forbid evil, establish proper prayers, give charity and obey Allah and His Messenger. Allah will be merciful to them. Allah is indeed Omnipotent, Wise.

وَعَدَ ٱللَّهُ ٱلْمُؤْمِنِينَ وَٱلْمُؤْمِنَٰتِ جَنَّٰتٍ تَجْرِى مِن تَحْتِهَا ٱلْأَنْهَٰرُ خَٰلِدِينَ فِيهَا وَمَسَٰكِنَ طَيِّبَةً فِى جَنَّٰتِ عَدْنٍ وَرِضْوَٰنٌ مِّنَ ٱللَّهِ أَكْبَرُ ذَٰلِكَ هُوَ ٱلْفَوْزُ ٱلْعَظِيمُ ﴿٧٢﴾

72. WaAAada All*a*hu almu/mineena wa*a*lmu/min*a*ti jann*a*tin tajree min ta*h*tih*a* al-anh*a*ru kh*a*lideena feeh*a* wamas*a*kina *t*ayyibatan fee jann*a*ti AAadnin wari*d*w*a*nun mina All*a*hi akbaru *th*alika huwa alfawzu alAAa*th*eem**u**

9:72. Allah has promised to the believing men and the believing women gardens, beneath which rivers flow. They will live therein in well-furnished houses built within gardens of perpetual abode. And the best thing there will be Allah being well-pleased with them. That then is the highest success.

يَٰٓأَيُّهَا ٱلنَّبِىُّ جَٰهِدِ ٱلْكُفَّارَ وَٱلْمُنَٰفِقِينَ وَٱغْلُظْ عَلَيْهِمْ وَمَأْوَٰهُمْ جَهَنَّمُ وَبِئْسَ ٱلْمَصِيرُ ﴿٧٣﴾

73. Y*a* ayyuh*a* alnnabiyyu j*a*hidi alkuff*a*ra wa*a*lmun*a*fiqeena waoghlu*th* AAalayhim wama/*wa*hum jahannamu wabi/sa alma*s*ee**ru**

9:73. O Prophet! Wage a struggle[35] against the suppressors of the Truth and the hypocrites and be severe on them. And their abode is Hell, and it is the worst destination.

---

35. The Arabic three-letter root word *jahada*, with all its grammatical variations, is generally misunderstood to mean killing in the interest of religion. An incident of a bomb exploding in a busy place killing many innocent persons has acquired the misnomer of a *jihadi* act. Nothing is farther from the truth. The literal meaning of the word is to struggle. There is no struggle involved in the cowardly act of killing innocent unsuspecting persons. Struggle is involved when one resists anyone doing anything wrong. Struggle is involved when one resists the temptation of doing anything wrong for one's own benefit. Here, Allah Almighty is advising the Prophet – and through him the believers – to resist any attempt by non-believers and hypocrites at doing anything wrong. It should be clearly understood that no action was warranted against non-believers just because of their non-belief. This is clear from Verse

2:256 which categorically states that there is no compulsion in religion. The Prophet here was asked to resist them and the hypocrites only because of their overt and covert acts against the believers.

يَحْلِفُونَ بِاللَّهِ مَا قَالُوا وَلَقَدْ قَالُوا كَلِمَةَ الْكُفْرِ وَكَفَرُوا بَعْدَ إِسْلَٰمِهِمْ وَهَمُّوا بِمَا لَمْ يَنَالُوا وَمَا نَقَمُوا إِلَّا أَنْ أَغْنَىٰهُمُ اللَّهُ وَرَسُولُهُ مِن فَضْلِهِۦ فَإِن يَتُوبُوا يَكُ خَيْرًا لَّهُمْ وَإِن يَتَوَلَّوْا يُعَذِّبْهُمُ اللَّهُ عَذَابًا أَلِيمًا فِى الدُّنْيَا وَالْأَخِرَةِ وَمَا لَهُمْ فِى الْأَرْضِ مِن وَلِيٍّ وَلَا نَصِيرٍ ۝

74. Ya*h*lifoona biAll*a*hi m*a* q*a*loo walaqad q*a*loo kalimata alkufri wakafaroo baAAda isl*a*mihim wahammoo bim*a* lam yan*a*loo wam*a* naqamoo ill*a* an aghn*a*humu All*a*hu warasooluhu min fa*d*lihi fa-in yatooboo yaku khayran lahum wa-in yatawallaw yuAAa*ththi*bhumu All*a*hu AAa*tha*ban aleeman fee aldduny*a* w*a*al-*a*khirati wam*a* lahum fee al-ar*d*i min waliyyin wal*a* na*s*eer*i*n

9:74. They swear by Allah that they did not utter, and certainly they did utter, the word signifying suppression of the Truth. And they suppressed the Truth after they had declared their faith in Islam. And they intended to do what they could not. And they avenged not except for this that Allah and His Messenger enriched them out of His grace.[36] Now if they repent, it will be good for them. And if they turn back to their evil ways, Allah will punish them with a painful punishment in this world and in the Hereafter. And they shall have none to be close to or to help them on earth.

36. In Verse 58 above, we are informed that the hypocrites accused the Prophet of misuse of the Welfare Fund. And in Verse 61, we see them accusing him of lending his ear to everyone. These accusations are nothing but words of *kufr* uttered by them. Their intention in doing so was obviously to turn the other believers against the Prophet and thus to undermine Islam while it was still in its infancy. They were thus trying to cut the very proverbial branch on which they were sitting. Allah Almighty, however, nipped their nefarious intentions in the bud.

❀ وَمِنْهُم مَّنْ عَٰهَدَ ٱللَّهَ لَئِنْ ءَاتَىٰنَا مِن فَضْلِهِۦ لَنَصَّدَّقَنَّ وَلَنَكُونَنَّ مِنَ ٱلصَّٰلِحِينَ ۝٧٥

75. Waminhum man AAahada Allaha la-in atana min fadlihi lanassaddaqanna walanakoonanna mina alssaliheena

---

9:75. And there are those of them who sought a covenant with Allah, "If He gives us out of His grace, we will certainly subscribe to the Welfare Fund, and we will certainly be of those who do good deeds."

فَلَمَّآ ءَاتَىٰهُم مِّن فَضْلِهِۦ بَخِلُوا۟ بِهِۦ وَتَوَلَّوا۟ وَّهُم مُّعْرِضُونَ ۝٧٦

76. Falamma atahum min fadlihi bakhiloo bihi watawallaw wahum muAAridoona

---

9:76. But when He gave them out of His grace, they became miserly with it and they turned back and withdrew.

فَأَعْقَبَهُمْ نِفَاقًا فِى قُلُوبِهِمْ إِلَىٰ يَوْمِ يَلْقَوْنَهُۥ بِمَآ أَخْلَفُوا۟ ٱللَّهَ مَا وَعَدُوهُ وَبِمَا كَانُوا۟ يَكْذِبُونَ ۝٧٧

77. FaaAAqabahum nifaqan fee quloobihim ila yawmi yalqawnahu bima akhlafoo Allaha ma waAAadoohu wabima kanoo yakthiboona

---

9:77. So He made hypocrisy to follow them in their hearts till the Day when they shall meet Him because they broke their covenant with Allah and because they lied.

أَلَمۡ يَعۡلَمُوٓاْ أَنَّ ٱللَّهَ يَعۡلَمُ سِرَّهُمۡ وَنَجۡوَىٰهُمۡ وَأَنَّ ٱللَّهَ عَلَّـٰمُ ٱلۡغُيُوبِ ﴿٧٨﴾

78. Alam yaAAlamoo anna Allaha yaAAlamu sirrahum wanajwahum waanna Allaha AAallamu alghuyoobi

9:78. Do they not know that Allah knows their hidden thoughts and their secret counsels, and that Allah is the great Knower of the unseen things?

ٱلَّذِينَ يَلۡمِزُونَ ٱلۡمُطَّوِّعِينَ مِنَ ٱلۡمُؤۡمِنِينَ فِى ٱلصَّدَقَٰتِ وَٱلَّذِينَ لَا يَجِدُونَ إِلَّا جُهۡدَهُمۡ فَيَسۡخَرُونَ مِنۡهُمۡ سَخِرَ ٱللَّهُ مِنۡهُمۡ وَلَهُمۡ عَذَابٌ أَلِيمٌ ﴿٧٩﴾

79. Alla*th*eena yalmizoona almu*tt*awwiAAeena mina almu/mineena fee al*s*sadaq*a*ti waalla*th*eena l*a* yajidoona ill*a* juhdahum fayaskharoona minhum sakhira All*a*hu minhum walahum AAa*th*abun aleem**un**

9:79. As for those who criticise and scoff at the believers who obediently contribute to the Welfare Fund, and at the believers who find nothing to give but their earnings, Allah scoffs at such scoffers, and they shall have a painful punishment.

اَسْتَغْفِرْ لَهُمْ أَوْ لَا تَسْتَغْفِرْ لَهُمْ إِن تَسْتَغْفِرْ لَهُمْ سَبْعِينَ مَرَّةً فَلَن يَغْفِرَ ٱللَّهُ لَهُمْ ذَٰلِكَ بِأَنَّهُمْ كَفَرُواْ بِٱللَّهِ وَرَسُولِهِ وَٱللَّهُ لَا يَهْدِى ٱلْقَوْمَ ٱلْفَٰسِقِينَ ۝

80. Istaghfir lahum aw *la* tastaghfir lahum in tastaghfir lahum sabAAeena marratan falan yaghfira All*a*hu lahum *tha*lika bi-annahum kafaroo biAll*a*hi warasoolihi waAll*a*hu *la* yahdee alqawma alf*a*siqeen*a*

9:80. Whether you ask forgiveness for them or not – and even if you ask forgiveness seventy times for them – Allah will forgive them not! That is because they suppress the Reality of Allah and His Messenger. And Allah does not guide the people who rebel against Allah's commandments.

فَرِحَ ٱلْمُخَلَّفُونَ بِمَقْعَدِهِمْ خِلَٰفَ رَسُولِ ٱللَّهِ وَكَرِهُوٓاْ أَن يُجَٰهِدُواْ بِأَمْوَٰلِهِمْ وَأَنفُسِهِمْ فِى سَبِيلِ ٱللَّهِ وَقَالُواْ لَا تَنفِرُواْ فِى ٱلْحَرِّ قُلْ نَارُ جَهَنَّمَ أَشَدُّ حَرًّا لَّوْ كَانُواْ يَفْقَهُونَ ۝

81. Fari*h*a almukhallafoona bimaqAAadihim khil*a*fa rasooli All*a*hi wakarihoo an yuj*a*hidoo bi-amw*a*lihim waanfusihim fee sabeeli All*a*hi waq*a*loo *la* tanfiroo fee al*h*arri qul n*a*ru jahannama ashaddu *h*arran law k*a*noo yafqahoon*a*

9:81. Those that remained back were pleased with their sitting back against Allah's Messenger and they were averse to striving in Allah's Path with their wealth and their lives. And they said, "Do not travel in the heat." Say, "The Hell fire is the most severe in heat, if only they could understand."

302

فَلْيَضْحَكُواْ قَلِيلًا وَلْيَبْكُواْ كَثِيرًا جَزَآءً بِمَا كَانُواْ يَكْسِبُونَ ﴿٨٢﴾

82. Falyadhakoo qaleelan walyabkoo katheeran jazaan bima kanoo yaksiboona

9:82. They shall laugh little then and weep more because of what they earned.

فَإِن رَّجَعَكَ ٱللَّهُ إِلَىٰ طَآئِفَةٍ مِّنْهُمْ فَٱسْتَـٔذَنُوكَ لِلْخُرُوجِ فَقُل لَّن تَخْرُجُواْ مَعِىَ أَبَدًا وَلَن تُقَـٰتِلُواْ مَعِىَ عَدُوًّا إِنَّكُمْ رَضِيتُم بِٱلْقُعُودِ أَوَّلَ مَرَّةٍ فَٱقْعُدُواْ مَعَ ٱلْخَـٰلِفِينَ ﴿٨٣﴾

83. Fa-in rajaAAaka Allahu ila ta-ifatin minhum faista/thanooka lilkhurooji faqul lan takhrujoo maAAiya abadan walan tuqatiloo maAAiya AAaduwwan innakum radeetum bialquAAoodi awwala marratin faoqAAudoo maAAa alkhalifeena

9:83. Then if Allah brings you back to any section of them and they ask your permission to go out on an expedition, say, "Never shall you go out with me and never shall you fight an enemy with me. You were indeed content to stay put the first time, stay put now too with those who stay behind."

وَلَا تُصَلِّ عَلَىٰ أَحَدٍ مِّنْهُم مَّاتَ أَبَدًا وَلَا تَقُمْ عَلَىٰ قَبْرِهِ إِنَّهُمْ كَفَرُواْ بِٱللَّهِ وَرَسُولِهِ وَمَاتُواْ وَهُمْ فَٰسِقُونَ ﴿٨٤﴾

84. Wala tusalli AAala ahadin minhum mata abadan wala taqum AAala qabrihi innahum kafaroo biAllahi warasoolihi wamatoo wahum fasiqoona

9:84. And never offer prayer for any one of them who dies, and never stand by his grave. They did indeed suppress the Reality of Allah and His Messenger. And they shall die in a state of rebellion against Allah's commandments.

وَلَا تُعْجِبْكَ أَمْوَالُهُمْ وَأَوْلَـٰدُهُمْ إِنَّمَا يُرِيدُ ٱللَّهُ أَن يُعَذِّبَهُم بِهَا فِى ٱلدُّنْيَا وَتَزْهَقَ أَنفُسُهُمْ وَهُمْ كَـٰفِرُونَ ﴿٨٥﴾

85. Wala tuAAjibka amwaluhum waawladuhum innama yureedu Allahu an yuAAaththibahum biha fee alddunya watazhaqa anfusuhum wahum kafiroona

9:85. And let not their wealth and their children impress you. Allah only wishes to punish them with these in this world and to cause their souls to depart while they indulge in suppression of the Truth.

وَإِذَآ أُنزِلَتْ سُورَةٌ أَنْ ءَامِنُواْ بِٱللَّهِ وَجَـٰهِدُواْ مَعَ رَسُولِهِ ٱسْتَـْٔذَنَكَ أُوْلُواْ ٱلطَّوْلِ مِنْهُمْ وَقَالُواْ ذَرْنَا نَكُن مَّعَ ٱلْقَـٰعِدِينَ ﴿٨٦﴾

86. Wa-itha onzilat sooratun an aminoo biAllahi wajahidoo maAAa rasoolihi ista/thanaka oloo alttawli minhum waqaloo tharna nakun maAAa alqaAAideena

9:86. And when a Qur'aanic Chapter is revealed, exhorting people to believe in Allah and engage themselves in righteous struggle along with His Messenger, those with means plead with you and say, "Grant us leave to be with those who stay back."

رَضُواْ بِأَن يَكُونُواْ مَعَ ٱلْخَوَالِفِ وَطُبِعَ عَلَىٰ قُلُوبِهِمْ فَهُمْ لَا يَفْقَهُونَ ۞

87. Ra*d*oo bi-an yakoonoo maAAa alkhaw*a*lifi wa*t*ubiAAa AAal*a* quloobihim fahum l*a* yafqahoon**a**

9:87. They chose to be with those back home, and a seal is set on their hearts, so they do not understand.

لَٰكِنِ ٱلرَّسُولُ وَٱلَّذِينَ ءَامَنُواْ مَعَهُۥ جَٰهَدُواْ بِأَمْوَٰلِهِمْ وَأَنفُسِهِمْ وَأُوْلَٰٓئِكَ لَهُمُ ٱلْخَيْرَٰتُ وَأُوْلَٰٓئِكَ هُمُ ٱلْمُفْلِحُونَ ۞

88. L*a*kini alrrasoolu waalla*th*eena *a*manoo maAAahu j*a*hadoo bi-amw*a*lihim waanfusihim waol*a*-ika lahumu alkhayr*a*tu waol*a*-ika humu almufli*h*oon**a**

9:88. But the Messenger and those who believe with him engage themselves in righteous struggle with their wealth and their lives. And for those certainly, are the good things. And those it is that succeed.

أَعَدَّ ٱللَّهُ لَهُمْ جَنَّٰتٍ تَجْرِى مِن تَحْتِهَا ٱلْأَنْهَٰرُ خَٰلِدِينَ فِيهَا ذَٰلِكَ ٱلْفَوْزُ ٱلْعَظِيمُ ۞

89. aAAadda All*a*hu lahum jann*a*tin tajree min ta*h*tih*a* al-anh*a*ru kh*a*lideena feeh*a* *th*alika alfawzu alAAa*th*eem**u**

9:89. Allah has prepared for them gardens, beneath which rivers flow, wherein to live. That is the highest success.

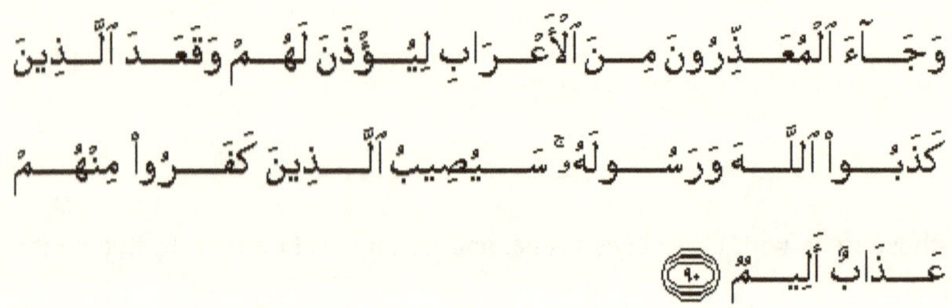

90. Waj*aa* almuAA*ath*thiroona mina al-aAA*rabi* liyu/*th*ana lahum waqaAA*ada* alla*theena ka*thaboo Alla*ha* warasoolahu sayu*seebu* alla*theena* kafaroo minhum AA*athabun* aleem**un**

9:90. And there came to you those from among the Bedouins who had excuses to offer for exempting them from joining the expedition. And those who denied Allah and His Messenger, sat at home. A painful punishment shall afflict those of them who suppressed the Truth.[37]

37. The Verse indicates that the Bedouin Arabs (those not settled in towns like Makkah and Medina and leading a nomadic life), at the time of this revelation, were of 3 categories: one, those who had staunch belief in Islam; two, those whose belief was not strong enough; and, three, those who had no belief in Islam. Bedouins of the third category did not at all bother to come to the Prophet at his call of conscription and remained at home. Bedouins of the first and second category either joined the expedition or came with excuses for claiming exemption. The divine warning of painful punishment applied to the third category and to those of the second category who had come with lame excuses to avoid joining the expedition.

لَّيْسَ عَلَى ٱلضُّعَفَآءِ وَلَا عَلَى ٱلْمَرْضَىٰ وَلَا عَلَى ٱلَّذِينَ لَا يَجِدُونَ مَا

يُنفِقُونَ حَرَجٌ إِذَا نَصَحُواْ لِلَّهِ وَرَسُولِهِۦ مَا عَلَى ٱلْمُحْسِنِينَ مِن سَبِيلٍ

وَٱللَّهُ غَفُورٌ رَّحِيمٌ ﴿٩١﴾

91. Laysa AAala aldduAAafa-i wala AAala almarda wala AAala allatheena la yajidoona ma yunfiqoona harajun itha nasahoo lillahi warasoolihi ma AAala almuhsineena min sabeelin waAllahu ghafoorun raheemun

---

9:91. There is no blame on the weak, the sick, or on those who do not find the means to spend for the expedition, so long as they are sincere to Allah and His Messenger. No ground to blame the righteous people. And Allah is Forgiving, Merciful.

وَلَا عَلَى ٱلَّذِينَ إِذَا مَآ أَتَوْكَ لِتَحْمِلَهُمْ قُلْتَ لَا

أَجِدُ مَآ أَحْمِلُكُمْ عَلَيْهِ تَوَلَّواْ وَّأَعْيُنُهُمْ تَفِيضُ مِنَ ٱلدَّمْعِ حَزَنًا أَلَّا

يَجِدُواْ مَا يُنفِقُونَ ﴿٩٢﴾

92. Wala AAala allatheena itha ma atawka litahmilahum qulta la ajidu ma ahmilukum AAalayhi tawallaw waaAAyunuhum tafeedu mina alddamAAi hazanan alla yajidoo ma yunfiqoona

---

9:92. And there is no blame on those who when they came to you to equip them for the expedition, you said, "I find no means to equip you." They went back, and their eyes welled up with tears for grief at not finding the means to bear the expenses for the expedition.

۞ إِنَّمَا ٱلسَّبِيلُ عَلَى ٱلَّذِينَ يَسْتَـْٔذِنُونَكَ وَهُمْ أَغْنِيَآءُ رَضُوا۟ بِأَن يَكُونُوا۟ مَعَ ٱلْخَوَالِفِ وَطَبَعَ ٱللَّهُ عَلَىٰ قُلُوبِهِمْ فَهُمْ لَا يَعْلَمُونَ ﴿٩٣﴾

93. Innam*a* alssabeelu AAal*a* alla*th*eena yasta/*th*inoonaka wahum aghniy*a*o ra*d*oo bi-an yakoonoo maAAa alkhaw*a*lifi wa*t*abaAAa All*a*hu AAal*a* quloobihim fahum l*a* yaAAlamoon*a*

9:93. The blame lies only on those who ask you to grant them leave despite being rich. They chose to be with those staying back home. And Allah has set a seal upon their hearts, so they do not know.

يَعْتَذِرُونَ إِلَيْكُمْ إِذَا رَجَعْتُمْ إِلَيْهِمْ قُل لَّا تَعْتَذِرُوا۟ لَن نُّؤْمِنَ لَكُمْ قَدْ نَبَّأَنَا ٱللَّهُ مِنْ أَخْبَارِكُمْ وَسَيَرَى ٱللَّهُ عَمَلَكُمْ وَرَسُولُهُۥ ثُمَّ تُرَدُّونَ إِلَىٰ عَـٰلِمِ ٱلْغَيْبِ وَٱلشَّهَـٰدَةِ فَيُنَبِّئُكُم بِمَا كُنتُمْ تَعْمَلُونَ ﴿٩٤﴾

94. YaAAta*th*iroona ilaykum i*th*a rajaAAtum ilayhim qul l*a* taAAta*th*iroo lan nu/mina lakum qad nabbaan*a* All*a*hu min akhb*a*rikum wasayar*a* All*a*hu AAamalakum warasooluhu thumma turaddoona il*a* AAal*i*mi alghaybi wa*a*lshshah*a*dati fayunabbi-okum bim*a* kuntum taAAmaloon*a*

9:94. They[38] will come up to you with excuses when you go back to them. Say, "Give no excuses, we won't believe you! Allah has already informed us about you. And Allah and His Messenger will watch your deeds. Then you shall be returned to the Knower of the unseen and the seen. Then He will inform you of what you had been doing."

---

38. I.e., those mentioned in the preceding Verse who, despite being rich, did not join the expedition and remained back home with women and children.

سَيَحْلِفُونَ بِٱللَّهِ لَكُمْ إِذَا ٱنقَلَبْتُمْ إِلَيْهِمْ لِتُعْرِضُوا۟ عَنْهُمْ ۖ فَأَعْرِضُوا۟ عَنْهُمْ ۖ إِنَّهُمْ رِجْسٌ ۖ وَمَأْوَىٰهُمْ جَهَنَّمُ جَزَآءًۢ بِمَا كَانُوا۟ يَكْسِبُونَ ﴿٩٥﴾

95. Sayahlifoona biAllahi lakum itha inqalabtum ilayhim lituAAridoo AAanhum faaAAridoo AAanhum innahum rijsun wama/wahum jahannamu jazaan bima kanoo yaksiboona

9:95. They will swear to you by Allah when you return to them, in order that you take no action against them. Do leave them alone! They are indeed pollution. And their abode is Hell – a retribution for what they earned.

يَحْلِفُونَ لَكُمْ لِتَرْضَوْا۟ عَنْهُمْ ۖ فَإِن تَرْضَوْا۟ عَنْهُمْ فَإِنَّ ٱللَّهَ لَا يَرْضَىٰ عَنِ ٱلْقَوْمِ ٱلْفَـٰسِقِينَ ﴿٩٦﴾

96. Yahlifoona lakum litardaw AAanhum fa-in tardaw AAanhum fa-inna Allaha la yarda AAani alqawmi alfasiqeena

9:96. They will swear to you in order that you may be pleased with them. And even if you are pleased with them, Allah is indeed not pleased with the people who rebel against Allah's commandments.

ٱلْأَعْرَابُ أَشَدُّ كُفْرًا وَنِفَاقًا وَأَجْدَرُ أَلَّا يَعْلَمُوا۟ حُدُودَ مَآ أَنزَلَ ٱللَّهُ عَلَىٰ رَسُولِهِۦ ۗ وَٱللَّهُ عَلِيمٌ حَكِيمٌ ﴿٩٧﴾

97. Al-aAAr*a*bu ashaddu kufran wanif*a*qan waajdaru all*a* yaAAlamoo *h*udooda m*a* anzala All*a*hu AAal*a* rasoolihi waAll*a*hu AAaleemun *h*akeem**un**

9:97. The Bedouin Arabs are more involved in suppression of the Truth and in hypocrisy, and more disposed not to know the laws that Allah has revealed to His Messenger. And Allah is Knowledgeable, Wise.

وَمِنَ ٱلْأَعْرَابِ مَن يَتَّخِذُ مَا يُنفِقُ مَغْرَمًا وَيَتَرَبَّصُ بِكُمُ ٱلدَّوَآئِرَ

عَلَيْهِمْ دَآئِرَةُ ٱلسَّوْءِ وَٱللَّهُ سَمِيعٌ عَلِيمٌ ۝

98. Wamina al-aAAr*a*bi man yattakhi*th*u m*a* yunfiqu maghraman wayatarabba*s*u bikumu alddaw*a*-ira AAalayhim d*a*-iratu alssaw-i waAll*a*hu sameeAAun AAaleem**un**

9:98. And among the Bedouin Arabs there are those who take what they spend [in Allah's way] as an imposition, and they wait for turns in fortune for you. But it is upon them that the evil turn shall befall. And Allah listens, knows.[39]

---

39. Interestingly, immediately after the Prophet's death, the Bedouins rose in revolt against payment of *sadaqah* **as enjoined in** <u>Verse 9:60</u>**. Caliph AbuBakr (Allah be pleased with him) waged wars against them and vanquished them. This divine Verse foretells that future event.**

وَمِنَ ٱلْأَعْرَابِ مَن يُؤْمِنُ بِٱللَّهِ وَٱلْيَوْمِ ٱلْأَخِرِ وَيَتَّخِذُ مَا

يُنفِقُ قُرُبَتٍ عِندَ ٱللَّهِ وَصَلَوَاتِ ٱلرَّسُولِ أَلَا إِنَّهَا قُرْبَةٌ لَّهُمْ سَيُدْخِلُهُمُ

ٱللَّهُ فِى رَحْمَتِهِ إِنَّ ٱللَّهَ غَفُورٌ رَّحِيمٌ ۝

99. Wamina al-aAAr*a*bi man yu/minu biAll*a*hi waalyawmi al-*a*khiri wayattakhi*th*u m*a* yunfiqu qurub*a*tin AAinda All*a*hi wa*s*alaw*a*ti alrrasooli ala innah*a* qurbatun lahum sayudkhiluhumu All*a*hu fee ra*h*matihi inna All*a*ha ghafoorun ra*h*eemun

9:99. And among the Bedouin Arabs there are those who believe in Allah and the Hereafter and take what they spend as means of nearness with Allah and blessings of the Messenger. Surely it shall be the means of nearness for them. Allah will admit them to His Mercy. Indeed, Allah is Forgiving, Merciful.

وَٱلسَّٰبِقُونَ ٱلْأَوَّلُونَ مِنَ ٱلْمُهَٰجِرِينَ وَٱلْأَنصَارِ وَٱلَّذِينَ ٱتَّبَعُوهُم بِإِحْسَٰنٍ رَّضِىَ ٱللَّهُ عَنْهُمْ وَرَضُوا۟ عَنْهُ وَأَعَدَّ لَهُمْ جَنَّٰتٍ تَجْرِى تَحْتَهَا ٱلْأَنْهَٰرُ خَٰلِدِينَ فِيهَآ أَبَدًا ذَٰلِكَ ٱلْفَوْزُ ٱلْعَظِيمُ ﴿١٠٠﴾

100. Waalssabiqoona al-awwaloona mina almuhajireena waal-ansari waallatheena ittabaAAoohum bi-ihsanin radiya Allahu AAanhum waradoo AAanhu waaAAadda lahum jannatin tajree tahtaha al-anharu khalideena feeha abadan thalika alfawzu alAAatheemu

9:100. And Allah is pleased with the first and the foremost of those who migrated and with those who gave shelter, [40] and with those who followed them in goodness. And they are pleased with Him. And He has prepared for them gardens beneath which rivers flow, wherein to live for ever. That is the highest success.

40. Reference here is drawn to the migration of the Prophet (peace be upon him) and his followers from Makkah to Medina and to the shelter given to them by the inhabitants of Medina. But the reference could be extended to all those who shed their non-Islamic mindsets and to those who help them do so.

وَمِمَّنْ حَوْلَكُم مِّنَ ٱلْأَعْرَابِ مُنَٰفِقُونَ وَمِنْ أَهْلِ ٱلْمَدِينَةِ مَرَدُوا۟ عَلَى ٱلنِّفَاقِ لَا تَعْلَمُهُمْ نَحْنُ نَعْلَمُهُمْ سَنُعَذِّبُهُم مَّرَّتَيْنِ ثُمَّ يُرَدُّونَ إِلَىٰ عَذَابٍ عَظِيمٍ ﴿١٠١﴾

101. Wamimman *h*awlakum mina al-aAAr*a*bi mun*a*fiqoona wamin ahli almadeenati maradoo AAal*a* alnnifaqi l*a* taAAlamuhum na*h*nu naAAlamuhum sanuAAa*thth*ibuhum marratayni thumma yuraddoona il*a* AAa*th*abin AAa*th*eem*i*n

---

9:101. And some of the Bedouins around you are hypocrites, and so are some residents of Medina. They are insolent in hypocrisy. You do not know them; We know them. Twice shall We punish them. And then will they be brought back for the highest punishment.[41]

---

41. When the Prophet and the believers returned from the apparently successful expedition, the hypocrites' game was up. They had hoped for a humiliating defeat for the believers at the hands of the mighty forces against whom the expedition was undertaken. But they found that the expedition had enhanced the prestige and power of the nascent Islamic State! This chagrin by itself was punishment number one. And punishment number two was the harsh treatment they got, thereafter, at the hands of the believers. These were the two punishments they got here in this world. And the Hell was waiting for them, in the Hereafter.

وَءَاخَرُونَ ٱعۡتَرَفُواْ بِذُنُوبِهِمۡ خَلَطُواْ عَمَلٗا صَٰلِحٗا وَءَاخَرَ سَيِّئًا عَسَى ٱللَّهُ أَن يَتُوبَ عَلَيۡهِمۡۚ إِنَّ ٱللَّهَ غَفُورٞ رَّحِيمٞ ۝

102. Wa*a*kharoona iAAtarafoo bi*th*unoobihim khala*t*oo AAamalan *sali*han wa*a*khara sayyi-an AAas*a* All*a*hu an yatooba AAalayhim inna All*a*ha ghafoorun ra*h*eem*u*n

---

9:102. And there are others who have confessed that they were at fault. They have mingled a good deed with a bad one. Allah may pardon them. Indeed, Allah is Forgiving, Merciful.

خُذۡ مِنۡ أَمۡوَٰلِهِمۡ صَدَقَةٗ تُطَهِّرُهُمۡ وَتُزَكِّيهِم بِهَا وَصَلِّ عَلَيۡهِمۡۖ إِنَّ صَلَوٰتَكَ سَكَنٞ لَّهُمۡۗ وَٱللَّهُ سَمِيعٌ عَلِيمٌ ۝

103. Khu*th* min amw*a*lihim *s*adaqatan tu*t*ahhiruhum watuzakkeehim bih*a* wa*s*alli AAalayhim inna *s*al*a*taka sakanun lahum waAll*a*hu samee AAun AAaleem*u*n

9:103. Take a fine as *sadaqah*[42] from them to cleanse and purify them thereby and pray for them! Your prayer does indeed give them peace of mind. And Allah listens, knows.

42. *Sadaqah* is the singular form of *sadaqaat* (see <u>Verses 58 and 60</u> of this Chapter and study notes thereon). In its singular form, the Arabic word would mean the mandatory tax or a fine imposed on individuals, which would go to the State Welfare Fund.

104. Alam yaAAlamoo anna All*a*ha huwa yaqbalu alttawbata AAan AAib*a*dihi waya/khu*th*u al*s*sadaq*a*ti waanna All*a*ha huwa alttaww*a*bu alrra*h*eem*u*

9:104. Do they not know that it is Allah Who accepts repentance from His subjects[43] and takes the *sadaqaat*, and that Allah is the Acceptor of repentance, the Merciful?

43. See <u>study note 41</u> on Verse 7.128.

313

105. Waquli iAAmaloo fasayara Allahu AAamalakum warasooluhu waalmu/minoona wasaturaddoona ila AAalimi alghaybi waalshshahadati fayunabbi-okum bima kuntum taAAmaloona

---

9:105. And say, "Go on, do your deeds! Allah, His Messenger and the believers will watch your deeds. And you shall be brought back to the Knower of the unseen and the seen. Then He will inform you of what you did."

$$\text{وَءَاخَـرُونَ مُرْجَـوْنَ لِأَمْـرِ ٱللَّـهِ إِمَّـا يُعَـذِّبُهُمْ وَإِمَّـا يَتُـوبُ عَلَيْهِـمْ}$$

$$\text{وَٱللَّـهُ عَلِيـمٌ حَـكِيمٌ ﴿١٠٦﴾}$$

106. Waakharoona murjawna li-amri Allahi imma yuAAaththibuhum wa-imma yatoobu AAalayhim waAllahu AAaleemun hakeemun

---

9:106. And there are others whose cases are deferred for Allah's decree. He may punish them, or He may pardon them. And Allah is Knowledgeable, Wise.

$$\text{وَٱلَّذِينَ ٱتَّخَذُواْ مَسْجِدًا ضِرَارًا وَكُفْرًا وَتَفْرِيقًا بَيْنَ ٱلْمُؤْمِنِينَ وَإِرْصَادًا}$$

$$\text{لِّمَنْ حَارَبَ ٱللَّهَ وَرَسُولَهُ مِن قَبْلُ وَلَيَحْلِفُنَّ إِنْ أَرَدْنَآ إِلَّا ٱلْحُسْنَىٰ وَٱللَّهُ}$$

$$\text{يَشْهَدُ إِنَّهُمْ لَكَـذِبُونَ ﴿١٠٧﴾}$$

107. Waallatheena ittakhathoo masjidan diraran wakufran watafreeqan bayna almu/mineena wa-irsadan liman haraba Allaha warasoolahu min qablu walayahlifunna in aradna illa alhusna waAllahu yashhadu innahum lakathiboona

---

9:107. And those who established a masjid to cause harm and for suppression of Truth and to cause disunion among the believers and to serve as a base for him who made war against Allah and His Messenger before. And they will certainly swear, "Our intentions were nothing but good." And Allah bears witness that they are most surely liars.[44]

44. The masjid (place of worship) that this Verse speaks about was built by the hypocrites ostensibly for the convenience of people in Medina who stayed away from Masjid-e-Nabvi. But the masjid was in fact used by the hypocrites for hatching plots against the Prophet. Upon the revelation of these Verses (107 to 110), the Prophet ordered the demolition of the Masjid even before he reached Medina from the expedition to Tabuk.

لَا تَقُمْ فِيهِ أَبَدًا لَّمَسْجِدٌ أُسِّسَ عَلَى ٱلتَّقْوَىٰ مِنْ أَوَّلِ يَوْمٍ أَحَقُّ أَن تَقُومَ فِيهِ فِيهِ رِجَالٌ يُحِبُّونَ أَن يَتَطَهَّرُواْ وَٱللَّهُ يُحِبُّ ٱلْمُطَّهِّرِينَ ۝١٠٨

108. La taqum feehi abadan lamasjidun ossisa AAala alttaqwa min awwali yawmin ahaqqu an taqooma feehi feehi rijalun yuhibboona an yatatahharoo waAllahu yuhibbu almuttahhireena

9:108. Never should you stand in it! Certainly, the masjid founded on piety from the very first day is more deserving that you stand therein. In it are men who love to be pure and clean. And Allah loves those who get themselves purified and cleaned.

أَفَمَنْ أَسَّسَ بُنْيَٰنَهُۥ عَلَىٰ تَقْوَىٰ مِنَ ٱللَّهِ وَرِضْوَٰنٍ خَيْرٌ أَم مَّنْ أَسَّسَ بُنْيَٰنَهُۥ عَلَىٰ شَفَا جُرُفٍ هَارٍ فَٱنْهَارَ بِهِۦ فِى نَارِ جَهَنَّمَ وَٱللَّهُ لَا يَهْدِى ٱلْقَوْمَ ٱلظَّٰلِمِينَ ۝١٠٩

109. Afaman assasa bunyanahu AAala taqwa mina Allahi waridwanin khayrun am man assasa bunyanahu AAala shafa jurufin harin fainhara bihi fee nari jahannama waAllahu la yahdee alqawma alththalimeena

9:109. Who is better then: the one who lays his foundation on fear of Allah and His good pleasure, or the one who lays his foundation on the brink of a crumbling hollowed bank, and which crumbles down with him into the fire of Hell[45]? And Allah does not guide the people who deliberately do wrong, unjust things.

---

45. The simile used here portrays the fate of a person who conducts his/her life without belief in Allah and therefore does not bide by His commands. He/she is bound to go to Hell! The foundation of the edifice he/she builds in this worldly life is hollow. This is a divine warning also to those who call themselves Muslims today. Most of them do not bother even to know what Allah's commands in His Message of the Qur'aan are, leave alone abide by them!

لَا يَزَالُ بُنْيَـٰنُهُمُ ٱلَّذِى بَنَوْاْ رِيبَةً فِى قُلُوبِهِمْ إِلَّآ أَن تَقَطَّعَ قُلُوبُهُمْ وَٱللَّهُ عَلِيمٌ حَكِيمٌ ﴿١١٠﴾

110. La yazalu bunyanuhumu alla*th*ee banaw reebatan fee quloobihim ill*a* an taqa*tt*aAAa quloobuhum waAll*a*hu AAaleemun *h*akeemun

---

9:110. This structure which they have built will not diminish the doubt in their hearts, unless their hearts get cut into pieces.[46] And Allah is Knowledgeable, Wise.

---

46. Masjids serve the interest of Islam by bringing people praying therein closer to Allah. But the structure which the hypocrites had built would never cause the hypocricy in their hearts to diminish.

۞ إِنَّ ٱللَّهَ ٱشْتَرَىٰ مِنَ ٱلْمُؤْمِنِينَ أَنفُسَهُمْ وَأَمْوَٰلَهُم بِأَنَّ لَهُمُ ٱلْجَنَّةَ

يُقَٰتِلُونَ فِى سَبِيلِ ٱللَّهِ فَيَقْتُلُونَ وَيُقْتَلُونَ وَعْدًا عَلَيْهِ حَقًّا فِى ٱلتَّوْرَىٰةِ

وَٱلْإِنجِيلِ وَٱلْقُرْءَانِ وَمَنْ أَوْفَىٰ بِعَهْدِهِۦ مِنَ ٱللَّهِ فَٱسْتَبْشِرُوا۟ بِبَيْعِكُمُ

ٱلَّذِى بَايَعْتُم بِهِۦ وَذَٰلِكَ هُوَ ٱلْفَوْزُ ٱلْعَظِيمُ ۝

111. Inna All*a*ha ishtar*a* mina almu/mineena anfusahum waamw*a*lahum bi-anna lahumu aljannata yuq*a*tiloona fee sabeeli All*a*hi fayaqtuloona wayuqtaloona waAAdan AAalayhi *h*aqqan fee alttawr*a*ti waal-injeeli waalqur-*a*ni waman awf*a* biAAahdihi mina All*a*hi faistabshiroo bibayAAikumu alla*th*ee b*a*yaAAtum bihi wa*th*alika huwa alfawzu alAAa*th*eemu

---

9:111. Indeed, Allah has bought from the believers their lives and their property for this, that they shall have the Paradise. They fight in Allah's Path, so they kill and get killed. It is a promise which He has bound Himself to, in the Torah, the Gospel and the Qur'aan. And who can be more faithful to one's promise than Allah? So, rejoice at the bargain you have struck; for, **that** is the highest success.

ٱلتَّٰٓئِبُونَ ٱلْعَٰبِدُونَ ٱلْحَٰمِدُونَ ٱلسَّٰٓئِحُونَ ٱلرَّٰكِعُونَ ٱلسَّٰجِدُونَ

ٱلْءَامِرُونَ بِٱلْمَعْرُوفِ وَٱلنَّاهُونَ عَنِ ٱلْمُنكَرِ وَٱلْحَٰفِظُونَ لِحُدُودِ ٱللَّهِ

وَبَشِّرِ ٱلْمُؤْمِنِينَ ۝

112. Altt*a*-iboona alAA*a*bidoona al*h*amidoona alss*a*-ihoona alrrakiAAoona alss*a*jidoona al-*a*miroona bialmaAAroofi waalnn*a*hoona AAani almunkari waal*h*afi*th*oona li*h*udoodi All*a*hi wabashshiri almu/mineena

---

9:112. And give this good news to those who repent, obey, praise Allah, fast, bow down and prostrate to Him, enjoin what is good and forbid what is evil, and, abide by Allah's laws.

مَا كَانَ لِلنَّبِيِّ وَالَّذِينَ ءَامَنُوٓاْ أَن يَسْتَغْفِرُواْ لِلْمُشْرِكِينَ وَلَوْ كَانُوٓاْ أُوْلِى قُرْبَىٰ مِنۢ بَعْدِ مَا تَبَيَّنَ لَهُمْ أَنَّهُمْ أَصْحَٰبُ ٱلْجَحِيمِ ۝١١٣

113. Ma kana lilnnabiyyi waalla*th*eena *a*manoo an yastaghfiroo lilmushrikeena walaw k*a*noo olee qurb*a* min baAAdi m*a* tabayyana lahum annahum a*s*-*h*abu alja*h*eemi

---

9:113. It does not behove the Prophet and those who believe that they should ask forgiveness for the polytheists, even if they are near relatives, after it has become clear to them that they would be inmates of the flaming Fire.

وَمَا كَانَ ٱسْتِغْفَارُ إِبْرَٰهِيمَ لِأَبِيهِ إِلَّا عَن مَّوْعِدَةٍ وَعَدَهَآ إِيَّاهُ فَلَمَّا تَبَيَّنَ لَهُۥٓ أَنَّهُۥ عَدُوٌّ لِّلَّهِ تَبَرَّأَ مِنْهُ إِنَّ إِبْرَٰهِيمَ لَأَوَّٰهٌ حَلِيمٌ ۝١١٤

114. Wam*a* k*a*na istighf*a*ru ibr*a*heema li-abeehi ill*a* AAan mawAAidatin waAAadah*a* iyy*a*hu falamm*a* tabayyana lahu annahu AAaduwwun lill*a*hi tabarraa minhu inna ibr*a*heema laaww*a*hun *h*aleem**un**

9:114. And Abraham asking forgiveness for his father was only because of a promise which the former had made to the latter. But when it became clear to him (Abraham) that he (father) was an enemy of Allah, he disassociated from his father. Abraham was indeed very tender-hearted, kind.

وَمَا كَانَ ٱللَّهُ لِيُضِلَّ قَوْمًۢا بَعْدَ إِذْ هَدَىٰهُمْ حَتَّىٰ يُبَيِّنَ لَهُم مَّا يَتَّقُونَ إِنَّ ٱللَّهَ بِكُلِّ شَىْءٍ عَلِيمٌ ۝١١٥

115. Wam*a* k*a*na All*a*hu liyu*d*illa qawman baAAda i*th* had*a*hum *h*att*a* yubayyina lahum m*a* yattaqoona inna All*a*ha bikulli shay-in AAaleem**un**

9:115. Allah would never lead a people astray after guiding them to His Straight Path until He makes clear to them what they should guard against. Allah does indeed know all things.

إِنَّ ٱللَّهَ لَهُۥ مُلْكُ ٱلسَّمَـٰوَٰتِ وَٱلْأَرْضِ يُحْىِۦ وَيُمِيتُ وَمَا لَكُم مِّن دُونِ ٱللَّهِ مِن وَلِىٍّ وَلَا نَصِيرٍ ﴿١١٦﴾

116. Inna Allaha lahu mulku alssamawati waal-ardi yuhyee wayumeetu wama lakum min dooni Allahi min waliyyin wala naseerin

9:116. Allah does indeed hold the absolute sovereignty over the heavens and the earth. He gives life and causes death. And there is none, other than Allah, to patronise and help you.

لَّقَد تَّابَ ٱللَّهُ عَلَى ٱلنَّبِىِّ وَٱلْمُهَـٰجِرِينَ وَٱلْأَنصَارِ ٱلَّذِينَ ٱتَّبَعُوهُ فِى سَاعَةِ ٱلْعُسْرَةِ مِنۢ بَعْدِ مَا كَادَ يَزِيغُ قُلُوبُ فَرِيقٍ مِّنْهُمْ ثُمَّ تَابَ عَلَيْهِمْ إِنَّهُۥ بِهِمْ رَءُوفٌ رَّحِيمٌ ﴿١١٧﴾

117. Laqad taba Allahu AAala alnnabiyyi waalmuhajireena waal-ansari allatheena ittabaAAoohu fee saAAati alAAusrati min baAAdi ma kada yazeeghu quloobu fareeqin minhum thumma taba AAalayhim innahu bihim raoofun raheemun

9:117. Certainly, has Allah pardoned the Prophet, the refugees and the helpers – those who followed him in the hour of need, after the hearts of a section of them were about to deviate and He pardoned them.[47] He is indeed Kind, Merciful to them.

47. Even the Prophet was reprimanded for his leniency in accepting the lame excuses of hypocrites in not joining the expedition (see <u>Verse 43</u> of this Chapter). And some of the believers [both from among the refugees (Mohajirs) who had migrated from Makkah and from among the inhabitants of Medina (Ansars) who helped the refugees in settling down at Medina] were initially reluctant to go for the expedition (see <u>Verses 38 to 41</u> of this Chapter). Then they agreed to go. Allah pardoned the Prophet and the believers their inadvertent lapses.

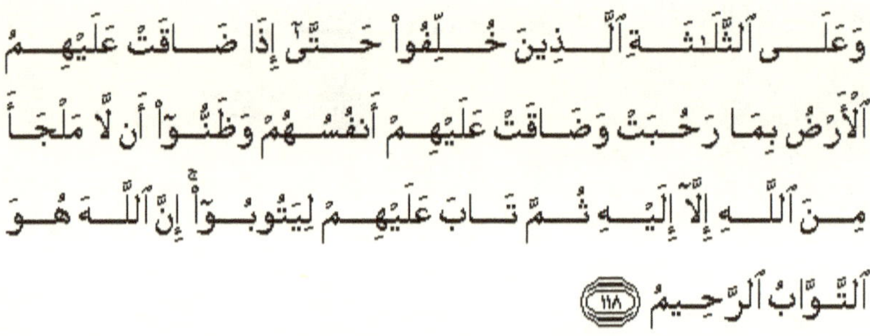

118. WaAAal*a* alththal*a*thati alla*theena* khullifoo *hatta itha* da*q*at AAalayhimu al-ar*d*u bim*a* ra*h*ubat wa*d*aqat AAalayhim anfusuhum wa*th*annoo an l*a* maljaa mina All*a*hi ill*a* ilayhi thumma *t*aba AAalayhim liyatooboo inna All*a*ha huwa alttaww*a*bu alrra*h*eemu

---

9:118. And He pardoned the three[48] who were left behind, whose cases were deferred until the earth, vast though it is, became straitened unto them and their own selves became straitened to them. And they knew it for certain that there was no refuge from Allah but unto Him.[49] Then He pardoned them that they might repent. Indeed, Allah is the One Who forgives, the One Who is Merciful.

---

48. These were those referred to in <u>Verse 102</u> above.

49. Those three were good believers, essentially. They had taken active part in earlier campaigns undertaken by the believers. But Satan seduced them from joining the long and strenuous Tabuk expedition, just as he had seduced Adam and Eve in disobeying Allah's order against going to the borbidden tree. All the three confessed their guilt to the Prophet on his return from Tabuk. Pending a clear decree from Allah Almighty, the Prophet ordered the believers to boycott them. Even their wives had to go to their Parents' places. The boycott was ended when these two Verses 117 and 118 were revealed.

يَٰٓأَيُّهَا ٱلَّذِينَ ءَامَنُواْ ٱتَّقُواْ ٱللَّهَ وَكُونُواْ مَعَ ٱلصَّٰدِقِينَ ﴿١١٩﴾

119. Ya ayyuha allatheena amanoo ittaqoo Allaha wakoonoo maAAa alssadiqeena

9:119. O you who believe! Fear Allah and be on the side of the righteous ones.

مَا كَانَ لِأَهْلِ ٱلْمَدِينَةِ وَمَنْ حَوْلَهُم مِّنَ ٱلْأَعْرَابِ أَن يَتَخَلَّفُواْ عَن رَّسُولِ ٱللَّهِ وَلَا يَرْغَبُواْ بِأَنفُسِهِمْ عَن نَّفْسِهِ ذَٰلِكَ بِأَنَّهُمْ لَا يُصِيبُهُمْ ظَمَأٌ وَلَا نَصَبٌ وَلَا مَخْمَصَةٌ فِى سَبِيلِ ٱللَّهِ وَلَا يَطَئُونَ مَوْطِئًا يَغِيظُ ٱلْكُفَّارَ وَلَا يَنَالُونَ مِنْ عَدُوٍّ نَّيْلًا إِلَّا كُتِبَ لَهُم بِهِۦ عَمَلٌ صَٰلِحٌ إِنَّ ٱللَّهَ لَا يُضِيعُ أَجْرَ ٱلْمُحْسِنِينَ ﴿١٢٠﴾

120. Ma kana li-ahli almadeenati waman hawlahum mina al-aAArabi an yatakhallafoo AAan rasooli Allahi wala yarghaboo bi-anfusihim AAan nafsihi thalika bi-annahum la yuseebuhum thamaon wala nasabun wala makhmasatun fee sabeeli Allahi wala yataoona mawti-an yagheethu alkuffara wala yanaloona min AAaduwwin naylan illa kutiba lahum bihi AAamalun salihun inna Allaha la yudeeAAu ajra almuhsineena

9:120. It did not behove the inhabitants of Medina, and those around them of the Bedouins, to stay behind from Allah's Messenger, nor to prefer their own selves over his. Because, no thirst, fatigue or hunger in Allah's way afflicts them, nor do they tread a path that enrages the suppressors of the Truth, nor do they attain from the enemy an attainment, but a good work is credited to their account therefor. Allah does indeed not allow the reward of good people to go waste.

وَلَا يُنفِقُونَ نَفَقَةً صَغِيرَةً وَلَا كَبِيرَةً وَلَا يَقْطَعُونَ وَادِيًا إِلَّا كُتِبَ لَهُمْ لِيَجْزِيَهُمُ ٱللَّهُ أَحْسَنَ مَا كَانُوا يَعْمَلُونَ ۝

121. Wala yunfiqoona nafaqatan sagheeratan wala kabeeratan wala yaqtaAAoona wadiyan illa kutiba lahum liyajziyahumu Allahu ahsana ma kanoo yaAAmaloona

---

9:121. And they spend not a spending, small or big, and they traverse not a valley, but it is credited to their account for Allah to reward them with the best of what they have done.

۞ وَمَا كَانَ ٱلْمُؤْمِنُونَ لِيَنفِرُوا كَآفَّةً فَلَوْلَا نَفَرَ مِن كُلِّ فِرْقَةٍ مِّنْهُمْ طَآئِفَةٌ لِّيَتَفَقَّهُوا فِى ٱلدِّينِ وَلِيُنذِرُوا قَوْمَهُمْ إِذَا رَجَعُوا إِلَيْهِمْ لَعَلَّهُمْ يَحْذَرُونَ ۝

122. Wama kana almu/minoona liyanfiroo kaffatan falawla nafara min kulli firqatin minhum ta-ifatun liyatafaqqahoo fee alddeeni waliyunthiroo qawmahum itha rajaAAoo ilayhim laAAallahum yahtharoona

---

9:122 And the believers cannot move out, all of them, at one time. Then why should not a group from among every section move out to get deeper understanding of the Religion, so that they may warn their people when they come back to them to be pious?[50]

---

50. After the conquest of Makkah and the battle of Hunain, people living in every part of the Arabian Peninsula had accepted Islam. It was an enmasse conversion. So, most of the people, so converting, did not have the necessary deeper knowledge of the Religion. They had converted because others had done so. The situation was a breeding ground for hypocricy. The Bedouins living in the desert area were more prone to it. Refer Verse 97 above in this context. Allah Ta'ala therefore advised in this Verse that the believers staying away from Medina should send groups from among themselves to get deeper understanding of Islam. The groups should then go back to their own people and in turn impart the knowledge to them. That way the dangers inherent in the enmasse conversion could be minimised. It should be clearly understood here that the deputed groups were not to learn just the rituals, like how to

offer prayers etc., but also, more importantly, to acquire the intellectual understanding of Islam. But, nowadays, in the Islamic Madrasas, emphasis is laid on ritualistic Islam only. The students coming out of such Madrasas are therefore devoid of the intellectual knowledge that the Qur'aan tries to impart. The result is there for us all to see. The *Ummah* generally today is Muslim only in name. Their faith is hollow. Allah has therefore withdrawn His hand of Mercy from them.

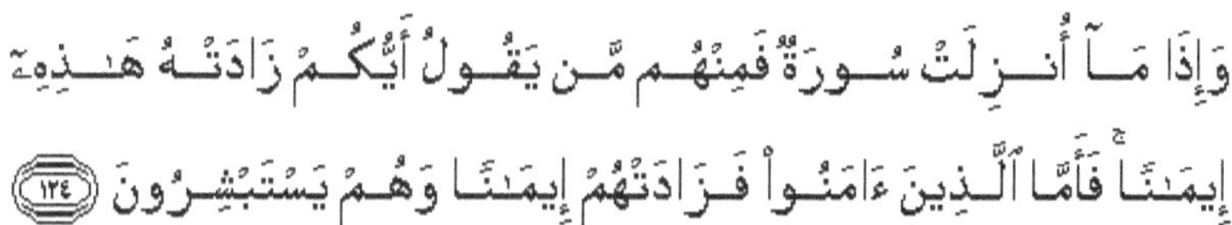

123. Y*a* ayyuh*a* alla*th*eena *a*manoo q*a*tiloo alla*th*eena yaloonakum mina alkuff*a*ri walyajidoo feekum ghil*th*atan wa*i*AAlamoo anna All*a*ha maAA*a* almuttaqeen*a*

9:123. O you who believe! Fight those of the suppressors of Truth who are near to you and they should find you stern and firm. And know that Allah is with those who fear Him.[51]

51. Please see study notes on <u>Verse 5</u> of this Chapter. The 'fight' mentioned here (Verse 123) is with reference to the war declared under that Verse.

124. Wa-i*tha* m*a* onzilat sooratun faminhum man yaqoolu ayyukum z*a*dat-hu h*ath*ihi eem*a*nan faamm*a* alla*th*eena *a*manoo fazadat-hum eem*a*nan wahum yastabshiroon*a*

9:124. And whenever a Chapter[52] is revealed, there are some of them who say, "Has it strengthened the faith of anyone amongst you?" It has indeed strengthened the faith of those who believe, and they rejoice.

52. I.e., a chapter of the Qur'aan.

وَأَمَّا ٱلَّذِينَ فِى قُلُوبِهِم مَّرَضٌ فَزَادَتْهُمْ رِجْسًا إِلَىٰ رِجْسِهِمْ وَمَاتُوا۟ وَهُم كَٰفِرُونَ ﴿١٢٥﴾

125. Waamma alla*th*eena fee quloobihim mara*d*un faza*d*at-hum rijsan ila rijsihim wam*a*too wahum k*a*firoona

9:125. And as for those in whose hearts is a disease, it adds dirt to their dirt. And they die as suppressors of the Truth.

أَوَلَا يَرَوْنَ أَنَّهُمْ يُفْتَنُونَ فِى كُلِّ عَامٍ مَّرَّةً أَوْ مَرَّتَيْنِ ثُمَّ لَا يَتُوبُونَ وَلَا هُمْ يَذَّكَّرُونَ ﴿١٢٦﴾

126. Awa l*a* yarawna annahum yuftanoona fee kulli AA*a*min marratan aw marratayni thumma l*a* yatooboona wal*a* hum ya*thth*akkaroona

9:126. Do they not see that they are tried once or twice every year? Yet they repent not, nor do they take heed.[53]

53. Allah Almighty tries modern-day Muslims too. Earthquakes have struck Turkey, Iran, Pakistan and Kashmir. But the Muslims dimiss them as natural phenomena, and they laugh at the idea that the Creator is causing them as warnings against their lifestyles. They are at the receiving end of ignominious treatments at places like Bosnia, Chechnia, Palestine, Afghanistan, Iraq et al, but they fail to realize that the Almighty is punishing them for their lifestyles contrary to the divine commands in the Qur'aan. As the Qur'aan says here, 'Yet they repent not, nor do they take heed."

وَإِذَا مَآ أُنزِلَتْ سُورَةٌ نَّظَرَ بَعْضُهُمْ إِلَىٰ بَعْضٍ هَلْ يَرَىٰكُم مِّنْ أَحَدٍ ثُمَّ انصَرَفُواْ صَرَفَ اللَّهُ قُلُوبَهُم بِأَنَّهُمْ قَوْمٌ لَّا يَفْقَهُونَ ﴿١٢٧﴾

127. Wa-*itha* m*a* onzilat sooratun na*th*ara baAA*d*uhum il*a* baAA*d*in hal yar*a*kum min a*h*adin thumma in*s*arafoo *s*arafa All*a*hu quloobahum bi-annahum qawmun l*a* yafqahoon*a*

9:127. And whenever a Chapter is revealed, they cast glances at one another, "Is any one looking at you?" Then they leave. It is Allah Who has left their hearts because they are a people who do not understand.[54]

54. This Verse and Verse 124 above indicate that the Prophet used to call a gathering of believers to announce fresh divine revelations to him. In these gatherings, there used to be some hypocrites too. The hypocrites' behaviour in such gatherings is described in these two Verses.

لَقَدْ جَآءَكُمْ رَسُولٌ مِّنْ أَنفُسِكُمْ عَزِيزٌ عَلَيْهِ مَا عَنِتُّمْ حَرِيصٌ عَلَيْكُم بِالْمُؤْمِنِينَ رَءُوفٌ رَّحِيمٌ ﴿١٢٨﴾

128. Laqad j*a*akum rasoolun min anfusikum AAazeezun AAalayhi m*a* AAanittum *h*aree*s*un AAalaykum bialmu/mineena raoofun ra*h*eem*u*n

9:128. Certainly, a Messenger has come to you from among yourselves. Solicitous of you, your distress is disturbing to him. To the believers he is compassionate, merciful.

فَإِن تَوَلَّوْاْ فَقُلْ حَسْبِىَ ٱللَّهُ لَآ إِلَـٰهَ إِلَّا هُوَ عَلَيْهِ تَوَكَّلْتُ وَهُوَ رَبُّ ٱلْعَرْشِ ٱلْعَظِيمِ ﴿١٣٩﴾

129. Fa-in tawallaw faqul *h*asbiya All*a*hu l*a* il*a*ha ill*a* huwa AAalayhi tawakkaltu wahuwa rabbu alAAarshi alAAa*th*eem

---

9:129. Yet, if they turn away, say, "Allah is enough for me; there is no god but Him. On Him I do place my trust. And He is Lord of the Mighty Throne[55].

---

55. It is not possible for the limited human intelligence to understand what this Mighty Throne of the Lord could be like. Chapter 112 of the Qur'aan informs us that there is none comparable to Allah. So He cannot be compared to a human king sitting on his throne. A human king is a limited being, and so is his throne. We can see the throne because it is limited. We cannot see Allah, because He is not limited. The Throne of an unlimited Being ought to be unlimited by itself. So, we cannot comprehend the Mighty Throne. Words like these in the Qur'aan are *mutashaabihaat* in terms of Verse 3:7. So, they are beyond human understanding to comprehend. We must accept them as they are, without trying to visualise their meanings. Suffice it for us to know that the Lord has Mighty, Unlimited Power.